User Guide

Adobe Illustrator®   version 9.0

© 2000 Adobe Systems Incorporated. All rights reserved.

Adobe® Illustrator® 9.0 User Guide for Windows® and Macintosh

This manual, as well as the software described in it, is furnished under license and may be used or copied only in accordance with the terms of such license. The content of this manual is furnished for informational use only, is subject to change without notice, and should not be construed as a commitment by Adobe Systems Incorporated. Adobe Systems Incorporated assumes no responsibility or liability for any errors or inaccuracies that may appear in this book.

Except as permitted by such license, no part of this publication may be reproduced, stored in a retrieval system, or transmitted, in any form or by any means, electronic, mechanical, recording, or otherwise, without the prior written permission of Adobe Systems Incorporated.

Please remember that existing artwork or images that you may want to include in your project may be protected under copyright law. The unauthorized incorporation of such material into your new work could be a violation of the rights of the copyright owner. Please be sure to obtain any permission required from the copyright owner.

Any references to company names in sample templates are for demonstration purposes only and are not intended to refer to any actual organization.

Adobe, the Adobe logo, Acrobat, Acrobat Reader, Adobe Dimensions, Adobe Premiere, Adobe Gamma, Adobe Type Manager, ATM, After Effects, Classroom in a Book, Gallery Effects, GoLive, Illustrator, InDesign, LiveMotion, Minion, PageMaker, Photoshop, PostScript, PressReady, PSPrinter, and Streamline are trademarks of Adobe Systems Incorporated. Microsoft, OpenType, Windows, and Windows NT are registered trademarks of Microsoft Corporation in the U.S and/or other countries. Apple, Macintosh, Power Macintosh, QuickTime, and TrueType are trademarks of Apple Computer, Inc. registered in the U.S. and other countries. QuickTime and the QuickTime logo are trademarks used under license. Helvetica and Times are trademarks of Linotype-Hell AG and/or its subsidiaries. IBM and OS/2 are registered trademarks of International Business Machines Corporation. Kodak is a registered trademark and Photo CD is a trademark of Eastman Kodak Company. UNIX is a registered trademark in the United States and other countries, licensed exclusively through X/Open Company, Ltd. Pentium is a registered trademark of Intel Corporation. Flash is a trademark of Macromedia, Inc. Sun is a trademark or registered trademark of Sun Microsystems, Inc. in the United States and other countries. All other trademarks are the property of their respective owners.

PANTONE®, PANTONE MATCHING SYSTEM®, and PANTONE Process Color System® are trademarks of Pantone, Inc.

PANTONE® Computer Video simulations displayed may not match PANTONE-identified solid color standards. Use current PANTONE Color Reference Manuals for accurate color.

"PANTONE Open Color Environment™ (POCE™) © Pantone, Inc., 1994, 1996

Pantone, Inc. is the copyright owner of "PANTONE Open Color Environment™ (POCE™)" and Software, which are licensed to Adobe Systems Incorporated to distribute for use only in combination with Adobe Illustrator. "PANTONE Open Color Environment™ (POCE™)" and Software shall not be copied onto another diskette or into memory unless as part of the execution of Adobe Illustrator software.

ImageStream Graphics and Presentation Filters copyright 1991–1996 Inso Corporation. All rights reserved. International Correct Spell Concise Correction software, version 8.1, licensed from Inso Corporation. Copyright 1986–1994, Inso Corporation, Microlytics, Inc., Xerox Corp. All rights reserved worldwide.

Portions copyright © Eastman Kodak Company, 2000 and used under license. All rights reserved.

Protected by U.S. Patents U.S. 4,837,613; 5,831,632; 5,870,091; and 5,943,063; patents pending

Contains an implementation of the LZW algorithm licensed under U.S. Patent 4,558,302.

Adobe Systems Incorporated, 345 Park Avenue, San Jose, California 95110, USA

Notice to U.S. government end users. The software and documentation are "commercial items," as that term is defined at 48 C.F.R. §2.101, consisting of "commercial computer software" and "commercial computer software documentation," as such terms are used in 48 C.F.R. §12.212 or 48 C.F.R. §227.7202, as applicable. Consistent with 48 C.F.R. §12.212 or 48 C.F.R. §§227.7202-1 through 227.7202-4, as applicable, the commercial computer software and commercial computer software documentation are being licensed to U.S. government end users (A) only as commercial items and (B) with only those rights as are granted to all other end users pursuant to the terms and conditions set forth in the Adobe standard commercial agreement for this software. Unpublished rights reserved under the copyright laws of the United States.

Part number: 90020039 (M/W)

Contents

Introduction

Registration 1
Installing Adobe Illustrator 1
Learning Adobe Illustrator 1
Using Web resources 3
Other learning resources 5
Customer support 6

An Overview of Adobe Illustrator

Using tools and palettes 10
Looking at the artwork window 11
Drawing basic paths and shapes 15
Using the pen tool 17
Selecting objects for editing 19
Applying changes to objects 20
Grouping objects 22
Painting stylized strokes 24
Applying fills and strokes 25
Applying advanced fills and strokes 27

What's New in Illustrator 9.0

Enhanced Web workflow 34
Optimized Web bitmap export 37
Flexible Web vector export 38
Versatile transparency 40
Blending modes 41
Masks 42
Layers palette enhancements 44
Effects 45
Graphic styles 45
Integration with Photoshop 47
Integration with other Adobe programs 48
Integration with Web-design programs 49
Other new and enhanced features 49

Looking at the Work Area

Chapter 1
Using the tools 55
Using palettes 55
Using context menus 57
Viewing artwork 57
Using the Navigator palette 60
Using the status bar 61
Previewing placed EPS images 61
Using plug-in modules 61
Customizing shortcuts 62
Setting preferences 63

Setting Up Artwork in Illustrator

Chapter 2
About vector graphics and bitmap images 67
About resolution in bitmap images 68
About the work area 70
Setting up the work area 70
Tiling artwork and adjusting page boundaries 72
About imported artwork 72
Opening and placing artwork 73
Managing linked and embedded images 76

Drawing

Chapter 3
About paths 83
Changing a tool pointer 84
Drawing and editing freeform paths 84
Drawing with the pen tool 87
Adjusting path segments 92
Drawing shapes 97
Drawing graphs 100
Drawing and editing brushed paths 101
Managing brushes 103
Creating brushes 104
Using the brush libraries 110
Tips for using brushes 111
Tracing artwork 111

Working with Objects

Chapter 4

- Correcting mistakes 115
- Using rulers 115
- Using the measure tool 117
- Using guides and grids 118
- Using Smart Guides 120
- Selecting objects 121
- Moving, copying, and deleting objects 125
- Rotating the *x* and *y* axes 130
- Stacking objects 131
- Grouping and ungrouping objects 133
- Locking and hiding objects 134

Transforming and Distorting Shapes

Chapter 5

- Transforming selected objects 139
- Using the Transform palette 147
- Modifying shapes with filters and effects 148
- Creating line effects 153
- Blending shapes 155
- Using the Pen and Ink filters 160
- Using the Pathfinder palette and Effect menu to modify shapes 163
- Converting strokes to filled objects 165
- Cutting objects 166
- Working with compound paths 166
- Working with clipping masks 167

Applying Color

Chapter 6

- Color modes and models 173
- About spot and process color types 176
- Working with swatches and unnamed colors 178
- Applying color 178
- Applying color using the toolbox 179
- Using the Color palette 180
- Applying color by dragging and dropping 180
- Using the Stroke palette 181
- Using the Swatches palette 182

Creating global colors and tints 185
Using the Swatch Libraries command 188
Using the Color Picker 191
Modifying colors 192
Using filters to modify colors 195

Producing Consistent Color

Chapter 7

Why colors sometimes don't match 199
About color management 199
Creating a viewing environment for color management 200
Setting up color management 201
Customizing color management settings 205
Customizing advanced color management settings 208
Saving and loading custom color management settings 210
Soft-proofing colors 210
Changing the color profile of a document 211
Embedding profiles in saved documents 212
Obtaining, installing, and updating color profiles 212
Creating an ICC monitor profile 214

Using Transparency, Gradients, and Patterns

Chapter 8

About transparency 219
Using grouped objects with the Transparency palette 220
Using the Transparency palette 220
Displaying the Transparency Grid 220
Setting transparency preferences 221
Specifying transparency 221
Creating opacity masks 222
Selecting blending modes 223
About gradients, gradient meshes, and blends 227
Creating and working with gradient fills 228
Creating multicolored objects with the gradient mesh tool 230
Creating and working with patterns 233
Changing gradients, blends, and patterns into filled objects 237

Using Layers

Chapter 9
- About layers 241
- Using the Layers palette 242
- Viewing layers, groups, and objects 243
- Creating layered artwork 246
- Targeting layers, groups, and objects to apply appearance attributes 252
- Creating clipping masks 253
- Creating template layers 254
- Importing and exporting Adobe Photoshop layers 255

Using Appearance Attributes, Styles, and Effects

Chapter 10
- About appearance attributes, styles, and effects 259
- Using appearance attributes 260
- Using styles 265
- Using effects 271

Working with Bitmap Images

Chapter 11
- Using bitmap images 275
- Changing vector graphics into bitmap images 275
- Colorizing 1-bit images 276
- Using filters and filter effects on bitmap images 277
- Improving performance with filters and filter effects 279
- Choosing a filter or filter effect 280
- Using the Color Halftone command 280
- Using the Object Mosaic filter 281
- Using the Photo Crosshatch filter 282

Using Type

Chapter 12
- About using type in Illustrator 287
- Creating type 287
- Setting type attributes 293
- Painting type 300
- Copying type attributes between objects 300
- Transforming type 301
- Changing text orientation 302
- Changing the shape of letterforms 303

	Working with columns of text 304
	Formatting columns and paragraphs 309
	Editing text 318
Preparing Graphics for the Web	**Chapter 13**
	Preparing Web graphics in Illustrator 325
	Viewing artwork as pixels 326
	Linking objects to URLs for Internet Web pages 326
	Optimizing in Illustrator 327
	Viewing images during optimization 328
	Choosing a file format for optimization 329
	Optimizing files and choosing options 331
	Working with the color table 336
	Making transparent and matted images 339
	Saving optimized images 342
Saving and Exporting Artwork	**Chapter 14**
	Saving files 345
	Saving files as PDF 347
	About exporting artwork 349
	About graphic file formats 356
Printing	**Chapter 15**
	About printing 363
	Printing artwork and composites 364
	Using color management when printing 365
	Printing with Adobe PressReady 366
	Setting crop marks and trim marks 367
	Changing resolution and rasterization settings for complex or transparent artwork 368
	Printing gradients, gradient mesh objects, color blends, and transparencies 370
	Improving printer performance 374
	About the EPSF Riders file 376
	File data and annotating objects 378

Producing Color Separations

Chapter 16

About separations	381
Step 1: Calibrate your monitor and check colors in your artwork	382
Step 2: Select overprint options for overlapping colors	383
Step 3: Create a trap to compensate for misregistration on press	385
Step 4: Set the printing bounding box and place crop marks around the image to be separated	388
Step 5: Set separation options	390
Step 6: Print and save separations	396

Automating Tasks

Chapter 17

About actions	401
Using the Actions palette	401
Creating and recording actions	402
Playing actions	405
Batch processing	406
Editing actions	407
Organizing sets of actions	409

Index 411

Introduction

Welcome to Adobe® Illustrator® 9.0, the industry-standard illustration program for print, multimedia, and online graphics. Whether you're a novice or an illustration expert, Adobe Illustrator offers you the tools you need to get professional-quality results.

You'll find that Adobe Illustrator excels as an art production tool, whether you are a designer or technical illustrator producing artwork for print publishing, an artist producing multimedia graphics, or a creator of Web pages or online content. Illustrator gives you an unmatched level of precision and control over your artwork and the flexibility to produce anything from small designs to large, complex projects. It also provides a consistent work environment with other Adobe applications including Adobe Photoshop®, Adobe GoLive™, Adobe InDesign™, and Adobe LiveMotion™.

Registration

Adobe is confident you will find that its software greatly increases your productivity. So that Adobe can continue to provide you with the highest quality software, offer technical support, and inform you about new Illustrator software developments, please register your application.

When you first start the application, you're prompted to register online. You can choose to submit the form directly or fax a printed copy. You can also register by filling out and returning the warranty registration card included with your software package.

Installing Adobe Illustrator

You must install Illustrator from the Adobe Illustrator CD onto your hard drive; you cannot run the program from the CD.

Follow the on-screen installation instructions. For more detailed information, see the *InstallReadMe* file on the CD.

Learning Adobe Illustrator

Adobe provides a variety of options for you to learn Illustrator, including printed guides, online Help, and tool tips. Using the Adobe Online feature, you can easily access a host of continually updated Web resources for learning Illustrator, from tips and tutorials to tech support information.

Adobe Acrobat® Reader™ software, included on the Illustrator CD, lets you view PDF files. Acrobat Reader or Adobe Acrobat is required to view many documents included on this CD.

Using the printed documentation

Two printed documents are included with Adobe Illustrator 9.0.

Adobe Illustrator 9.0 User Guide Contains information on using all Adobe Illustrator commands and features. The user guide also indicates when further information on a topic is available in online Help.

The guide assumes you have a working knowledge of your computer and its operating conventions, including how to use a mouse and standard menus and commands. It also assumes you know how to open, save, and close files. For help with any of these techniques, please see your Microsoft® Windows® or Mac OS documentation.

Adobe Illustrator Quick Reference Card Contains basic information about the Adobe Illustrator tools and palettes, and shortcuts for using them. Shortcuts are also included in the online Help.

Using online Help

Adobe Illustrator also includes complete documentation in an HTML-based help system. The Illustrator help system includes all of the information in the *Adobe Illustrator 9.0 User Guide* plus keyboard shortcuts, full-color illustrations, and more detailed information about some procedures.

Online Help provides three ways of locating information. The Contents and Index tabs let you find general information, and the Search tab lets you look up specific words or phrases.

For more detailed information about using online Help, click the Help on Help button next to the Content, Index, and Search tabs.

To properly view online Help topics, you need Netscape Communicator 4.0 (or later) or Microsoft® Internet Explorer 4.0 (or later). You must also have Javascript active.

To start online Help:

Choose Help > Illustrator Help, or press F1 (Windows).

Using tool tips

The tool tips feature lets you display the name of tools, or buttons and controls in palettes.

To identify a tool or control:

Position the pointer over a tool or control and pause. A tool tip appears showing the name and keyboard shortcut (if any) for the item.

If tool tips don't appear, the preference for displaying them may be turned off.

To display tool tips:

1 Choose Edit > Preferences > General.

2 Select Show Tool Tips, and click OK.

Note: Tool tips are not available in most dialog boxes.

Using Web resources

If you have an Internet connection and a Web browser installed on your system, you can use the Adobe Online feature to access additional resources for learning Illustrator located on the Adobe Systems home page on the World Wide Web. These resources are continually updated and include the following:

How Tos and Backgrounders Provide access to procedures for performing tasks in Illustrator and to detailed reference information on a variety of topics. This information provides help on everything from common processes to the complex inter-application tasks necessary to prepare graphics for the Web.

Tutorials and Techniques Provide step-by-step instructions on using Illustrator's features or help on performing advanced techniques. These tutorials can help you go beyond the reference information contained in the user guide and show you how to use Illustrator with other applications.

Quicktips Provide short, time-saving procedures to help you use Illustrator more effectively. Tips can be shortcuts for using new features, or instructions on using existing features more effectively.

Troubleshooting Provides access to solutions to problems you may encounter using Illustrator. You should check out troubleshooting information available through Adobe Online and the Adobe Web site before you call customer support.

To access Adobe's home page for your region:

1 Open Adobe's U.S. home page at www.adobe.com.

2 From the Adobe Sites menu, choose your geographical region. Adobe's home page is customized for 20 different geographical regions.

About Adobe Online

Adobe Online provides access to the latest tutorials, quicktips, and other Web content for Illustrator and other Adobe products. Using Adobe Online, you can also download and view the current version of the Illustrator Top Issues document containing the latest Illustrator technical support solutions. Bookmarks are also included to take you quickly to noteworthy Adobe- and Illustrator-related sites.

Using Adobe Online

Adobe Online is constantly changing, so you should refresh before you use it. Refreshing through Adobe Online updates bookmarks and buttons so you can quickly access the most current content available. You can use preferences to automatically refresh Adobe Online daily, weekly, or monthly.

When you set up Adobe Online to connect to your Web browser, Adobe can either notify you whenever new information is available through the Downloadables feature or automatically download that information to your hard disk. If you choose not to use Adobe's automatic download feature, you can still view and download new files whenever they are available using the Downloadables command in the Help menu.

To use Adobe Online:

1 In Illustrator, choose Help > Adobe Online, or click the icon at the top of the toolbox.

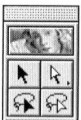

Note: You must have an Internet connection and an Internet browser installed. Adobe Online will launch your browser using your default Internet configuration.

2 Do any of the following:

• Click Refresh to make sure you have the latest version of the Adobe Online window and its buttons, as well as the latest bookmarks. It is important to refresh the screen so that the current options are available for you to choose from.

• Click Preferences to specify connection options. General preferences affect how Adobe Online interacts with all Adobe products installed on your system, and Application preferences affect how Adobe Online interacts with Illustrator. To see an explanation of each preference option, click Setup and follow the prompts. You also can set up an automatic refresh using the Update Options.

Note: You can also set Adobe Online preferences by choosing Edit > Preferences > Online Settings.

• Click any button in the Adobe Online window to open the Web page to which the button is linked.

• Click the bookmark button( ) to view Adobe-suggested Web sites related to Illustrator and Adobe. These bookmarks are automatically updated as new Web sites become available.

• Click Close to return to Illustrator.

Accessing Adobe Online through the Help menu

The Help menu includes options to view and download information from Adobe's Web site.

To view updated articles or documents:

Click Help and choose the topic you want to view.

To view and download information from Adobe's Web site using the Help menu:

1 In Illustrator, choose Help > Downloadables.

2 Select a View Option:

• Select Show Only New Files to view only the files that are new since the last time you viewed downloadable files or were notified of them.

• Select Show All Files to view all the files on Adobe's Web site that are currently available for download.

3 Select Download Options:

• Select Auto Install Downloaded Components if you want Adobe to start the component's installer (if available) as soon as the download is complete. You can then follow the prompts to install the files.

• Select Download in Background if you want to continue working in Illustrator and other applications while the file downloads.

• Select Notify When Download Complete if you want Adobe to display a message when the files have been transferred to your computer.

4 To view a list of files, open the Downloadables folder and any other folder listed.

5 To see a description of a file, position the mouse cursor over a filename and view its description in the Item Description section.

6 To see the location where a file will be installed if downloaded, select a file and view its location in the Download Directory section. To change the location, click the Folder button (▢).

7 To download a file, select it and click Download.

8 To close the Downloadables dialog box, click Done.

Other learning resources

Other learning resources are available but are not included with your application.

Classroom in a Book Is the official training series for Adobe graphics and publishing software. This book is developed by experts at Adobe and published by Adobe Press. The *Adobe Illustrator Classroom in a Book* includes lessons about using Illustrator. For information on purchasing *Adobe Illustrator Classroom in a Book*, visit the Adobe Web site at www.adobe.com, or contact your local book distributor.

Official Adobe Print Publishing Guide Provides in-depth information on successful print production, including topics such as color management, commercial printing, constructing a publication, imaging and proofing, and project management guidelines. For information on purchasing the *Official Adobe Print Publishing Guide*, visit the Adobe Web site at www.adobe.com.

Official Adobe Electronic Publishing Guide Tackles the fundamental issues essential to ensuring quality online publications in HTML and PDF. Using simple, expertly illustrated explanations, design and publishing professionals tell you how to design electronic publications for maximum speed, legibility, and effectiveness. For information on purchasing the *Official Adobe Electronic Publishing Guide*, visit the Adobe Web site at www.adobe.com.

The Adobe Certification program Offers users, instructors, and training centers the opportunity to demonstrate their product proficiency and promote their software skills as Adobe Certified Experts, Adobe Certified Instructors, or Adobe Authorized Learning Providers. Certification is available for several different geographical regions. Visit the Partnering with Adobe Web site at www.partners.adobe.com to learn how you can become certified.

Customer support

When you register your product, you may be entitled to technical support for up to 90 days from the date of your first call. Terms may vary depending on the country of residence. For more information, refer to the technical support card provided with the Illustrator documentation.

Customer support on Adobe Online

Adobe Online provides access to FAQs (Frequently Asked Questions) and troubleshooting information that provides solutions to common problems.

Additional customer support resources

Adobe Systems provides several forms of automated technical support:

• See the ReadMe and ReadMe First! files installed with the program for information that became available after this guide went to press.

• Explore the extensive customer support information on Adobe's World Wide Web site (www.adobe.com). To access Adobe's Web site from Illustrator, choose Help > Adobe Online or click the icon at the top of the toolbox. See "Using Web resources" on page 3.

• Read the Top Issues PDF that is available from the Help menu.

An Overview of Adobe Illustrator

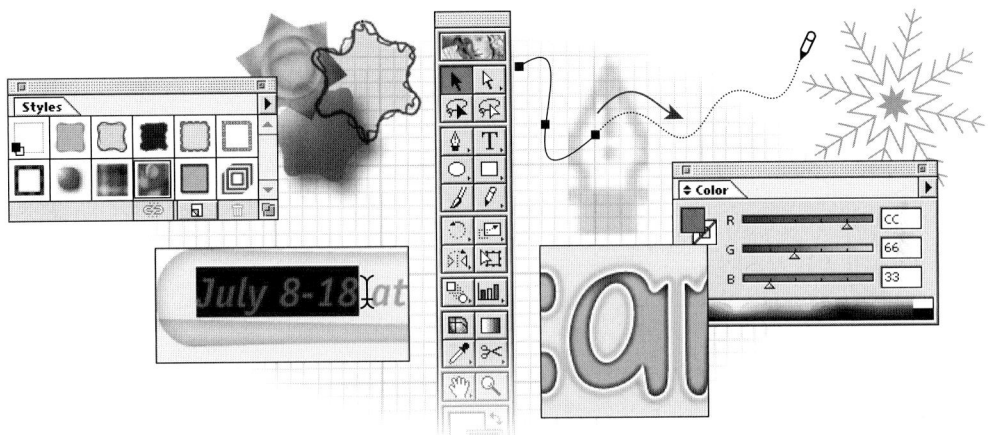

This interactive overview of Adobe Illustrator contains a number of brief lesson modules designed to introduce key features of the program. These modules are independent, so you can complete the modules in sequence, or you can choose specific modules to tailor your program introduction. Once you learn the basics of using the program, you'll be ready to explore the extensive drawing, painting, and editing features of Illustrator.

Getting to know the work area

Using tools and palettes

If you've worked with other Adobe applications, the Illustrator work area will look familiar, with its command menus, artwork window, toolbox, and floating palettes. The toolbox contains tools for selecting, drawing, painting, and editing your artwork. The floating palettes contain additional features that help you monitor, modify, and enhance your artwork. You can hide and rearrange the toolbox and palettes to organize your work area as needed.

Select a tool To select a tool, simply click its icon in the toolbox. Some tools in the toolbox have additional hidden tools. To select a hidden tool, hold down the mouse button on the current tool in the toolbox and drag to your desired tool.

For easier access to a group of hidden tools, you can tear off the hidden tools. To separate a group of hidden tools from the toolbox, select the small triangle that appears on the right end of the group.

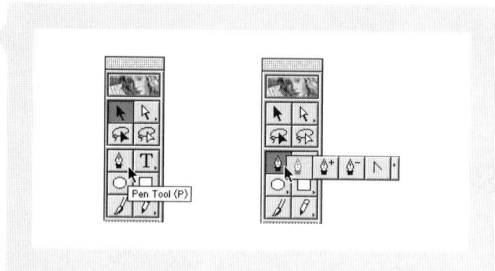

Tool tip showing tool's name and shortcut; hidden tools

Display the palettes When you first start Adobe Illustrator, the floating palettes appear stacked in default groups. Use the following techniques to show and hide palettes:

- To bring a palette to the front of its group, click the palette's tab.

- To show or hide a palette as you work, choose the appropriate Window > Show or Window > Hide command.

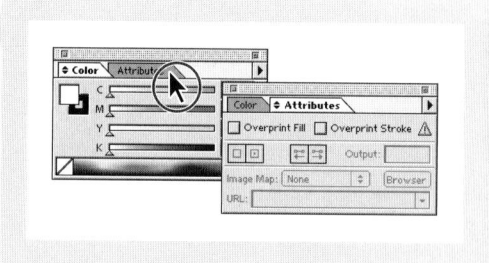

Click a palette tab to bring the palette to the front.

- To cycle through the minimized, compact, and expanded views of a palette, click the small triangle pair that appears in the palette tab.

- To hide or display all open palettes and the toolbox, press Tab. To hide or display palettes only, press Shift+Tab.

Arrange the palettes Depending on your available screen area and work preferences, you may want to reposition and regroup the palettes more efficiently. You can move an entire palette group by dragging the group's title bar. You can rearrange or separate a palette group by dragging a palette's tab. You can drag a palette to another group or to its own separate group.

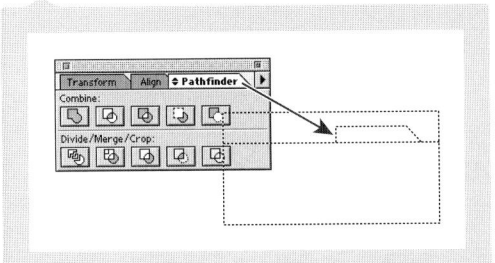 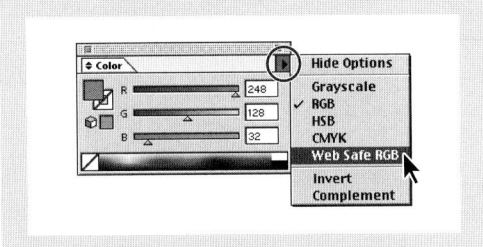

Drag a palette tab to separate the palette from the group.

Display a palette menu Most palettes have pop-up menus containing commands and options that add to the palette functionality. To display a palette menu, position the pointer over the black triangle at the top right of the palette, and hold down the mouse button.

Looking at the artwork window

You view, create, and edit your artwork inside the artwork window. The artwork window contains boundary lines that help you lay out your artwork in relation to the printable and nonprintable areas of your page.

Open or create an artwork window To open an existing artwork file, choose File > Open, and locate and open the file. To create a new artwork window, choose File > New. The New Document dialog box lets you specify the following options:

- Color Mode. Determines the color model that will be used to define colors added to the artwork. You can choose between CMYK Color (the color model based on four-color process printing inks) and RGB Color (the color model used by computer monitors).

- Artboard Size. Determines the dimensions of the printable area of the artwork window. You may often set the artboard size to match your printed page. The maximum artboard dimensions that you can specify are 227 inches by 227 inches.

Look at the artwork window Notice the solid and dotted rectangular boundaries inside the window.

- The solid lines represent the boundaries of the artboard, or the maximum imageable area. The artboard often, but not necessarily always, matches your printed page size.

- The dotted lines enclose the imageable area, which represents the portion of the page on which the selected printer can print. Because many printers cannot print to the edge of the page, the imageable area is often slightly smaller than the page.

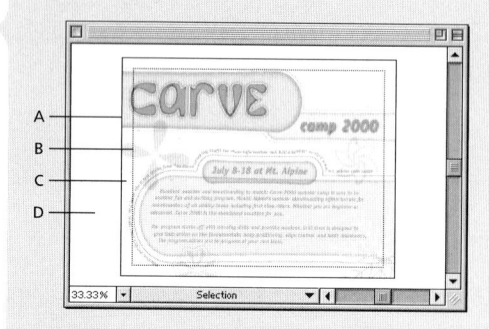

A. Artboard B. Imageable area C. Nonimageable area
D. Scratch area

- The area outside the artboard represents the scratch area. You can create, work with, and store artwork elements in the scratch area before moving them onto the artboard. Objects in the scratch area remain visible on-screen, but they do not print with the artwork.

Adjust the artboard If you have opened an existing artwork file, you can customize the size of the artboard by choosing File > Document Setup. In addition to choosing from a menu of standard artboard sizes, you can specify the following:

- Custom width and height values.

- Measurement units. When you choose a unit of measurement, the width and height values you enter are automatically converted to the chosen units. For example, if you choose Points and enter "5 inches," that value automatically changes to 360 pt. Along with traditional measurement units such as picas and inches, Illustrator 9.0 offers the new option of pixels, useful for defining the dimensions of Web graphics.

- Orientation. You can choose between portrait and landscape orientations.

- Use Print Setup (Windows) or Use Page Setup (Mac OS) option. When you select this option, the artboard size automatically matches the page size defined in the Print Setup (Windows) or Page Setup (Mac OS) dialog box.

Set rulers, grids, and guides To help place, align, and measure objects accurately on the artboard, use rulers, grids, and guides:

- To display rulers along the top and left side of the artwork window, choose View > Show Rulers. (You change the ruler units by choosing Edit > Preferences > Units & Undo.)

- To display grid lines throughout the artwork window, choose View > Show Grid. (You control the style and spacing of the grid by choosing Edit > Preferences > Guides & Grid.)

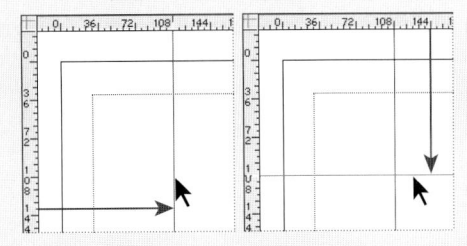

Drag vertical guide from left ruler.   *Drag horizontal guide from top ruler.*

- To create a horizontal or vertical guide, drag from either the top or left ruler. You can also convert objects in your artwork (such as rectangles or paths) to guides.

View your artwork Illustrator provides several convenient tools for viewing your artwork. For example, you can drag in the artwork with the hand tool ( ) to move a different area into view.

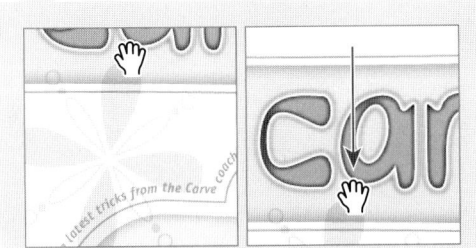

Drag with hand tool to move area into view.

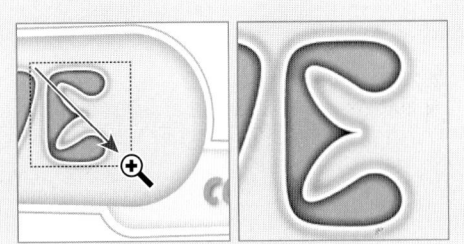

Drag with zoom tool to magnify the view.

You can also use the zoom tool ( ) to magnify the display of your artwork. You can click to select the zoom tool, and then click or drag in your artwork to increase the magnification. Hold down the Alt (Windows) or Option (Mac OS) key to change the zoom tool to the zoom-out tool ( ) and reduce the view magnification.

Monitor your work status As you experiment with different tools in the toolbox, look at the status bar along the bottom left edge of your artwork window. This area displays useful information about your work status, such as the name of the currently selected tool and the current magnification percentage of your artwork.

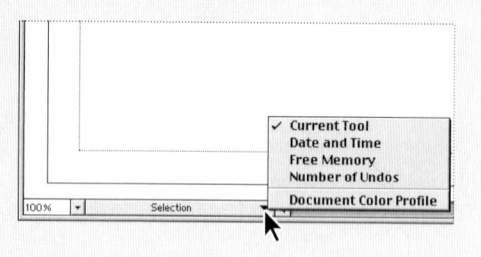

Drawing

Drawing basic paths and shapes

Creating a path in Illustrator can be as simple as selecting the pencil tool and drawing a freeform path in the artwork window. You can also create round and sharp-cornered rectangles, ellipses, polygons, spirals, and stars using preset shape tools. You can build many types of graphic objects by starting with basic shapes and paths and then modifying or combining them.

Draw with the pencil tool To draw a freeform path, use the pencil tool ( ) to drag inside the artwork window. (If you can't see the pencil stroke in your artwork, you may need to specify a stroke color first. See "Applying fills and strokes" on page 25 for more information.)

Notice that Illustrator places anchor points periodically along the path you've drawn. Anchor points help to define the shape and smoothness of the path.

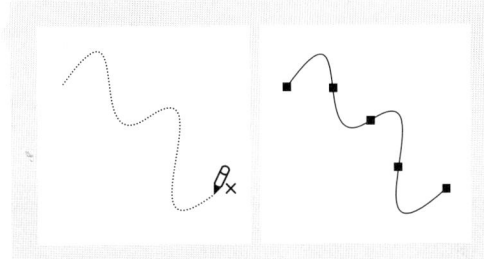

Drag with pencil tool to draw.

You can control the sensitivity and smoothness of the pencil by double-clicking its icon in the toolbox and adjusting the preference settings. In general, you can double-click most tools in the toolbox to display their preference settings.

Edit the pencil path as you draw A major benefit of the pencil tool is the ease it allows you in editing paths:

- To continue an existing path, drag from an anchor endpoint with the pencil tool.
- To modify a path, position the pencil on or near the path, and drag to reshape.

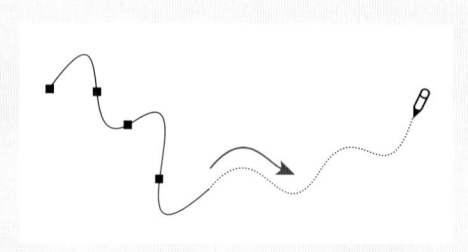
Drag from an endpoint to continue the path.

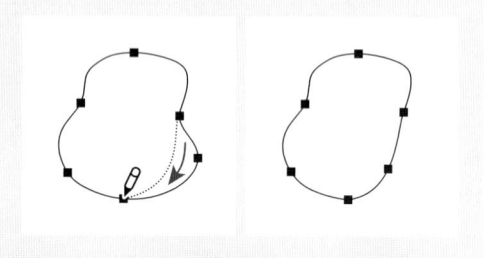
Use the pencil tool to edit a closed shape.

- To draw a closed path, start dragging with the pencil, press Alt (Windows) or Option (Mac OS), and continue dragging. Release the mouse and then release Alt/Option to close the path.

Draw a preset shape You draw preset shapes by selecting a shape tool (○, ○, ☆, ◎, □, ○) and then dragging in the artwork window. Drag to define the desired size of your shape from edge to edge, and then release the mouse to draw the shape. You can also use these alternate techniques for drawing shapes.

- To draw a rectangle or ellipse starting from its center, hold down Alt (Windows) or Option (Mac OS) as you drag.
- To constrain a rectangle or ellipse to a square or circle, hold down Shift as you drag.
- To draw a shape by entering numeric values for its dimensions, click with the shape tool in the artwork. In the dialog box that appears, enter the desired dimensions for the shape.

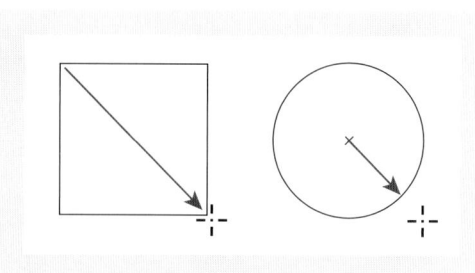
Drawing from edge and center

Using the pen tool

The pen tool (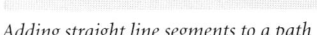) lets you draw straight lines and flowing curves. Although it is less intuitive to use than the pencil tool, the pen tool offers you the advantage of creating streamlined paths that can be controlled and reshaped with great precision. With a little practice, you'll be able to draw combinations of straight and curved segments to create flexible, smoothly shaped illustrations.

Draw straight lines You draw straight line paths with the pen tool by clicking in the artwork to set down anchor points. Your first click creates the starting anchor point; click again to set the ending anchor point for the line. You can continue clicking to add more connected line segments. To constrain the pen to horizontal, vertical, or 45° diagonal lines, hold down Shift as you click.

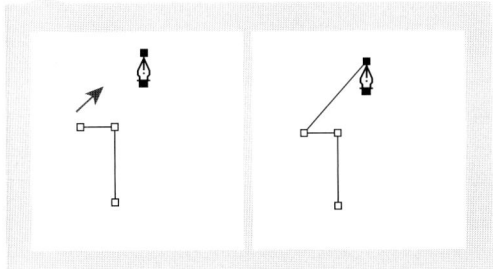

Adding straight line segments to a path

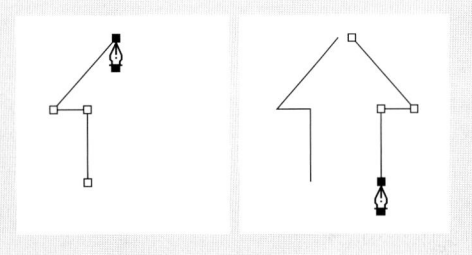

Drawing a new, unconnected open path

End your path To draw a new, unconnected path, do one of the following to end your existing path:

- To end a path by closing its shape, click the starting anchor point of the path with the pen tool.
- To end an open path (a path with distinct starting and ending anchor points), click the pen tool in the toolbox.

Begin a new curved path To draw curves with the pen tool, set down anchor points and drag to define the shape and direction of the curve. To begin a curve, press with the pen and drag in the direction that you want the curve to flow. Then position the pen where you want the curve to end, and drag in the opposite direction.

When you drag with the pen tool, Illustrator sets down a pair of direction lines that emanate from the anchor point. By varying the angle and length of your drag, you can control the shape and depth of the curve.

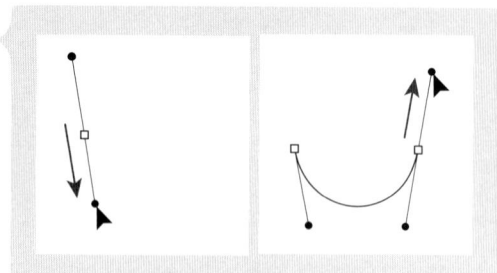

Drag in the direction of the curve to set the first anchor point. Then drag in the opposite direction to complete the curve.

Continue drawing the curve Continue adding anchor points and dragging direction lines to add more segments to your curve. For smooth results, alternate the direction of your drag for each segment.

To turn your curve sharply, you can split a pair of direction lines to create a corner anchor point. Hold down Alt (Windows) or Option (Mac OS), and drag from the anchor point in the direction that you want the curve to turn. Then release Alt/Option, and drag in the opposite direction to finish the segment.

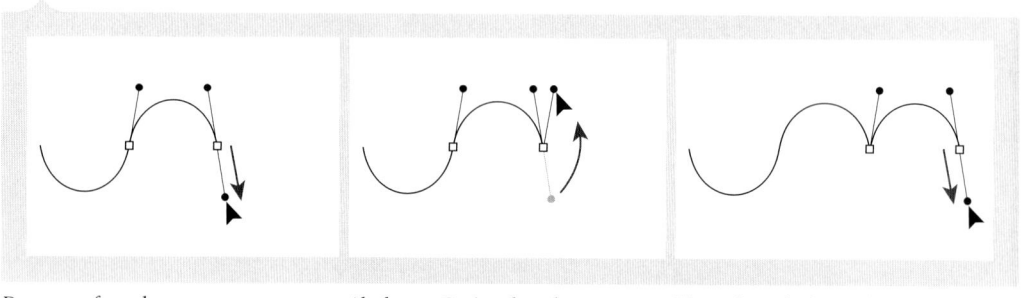

Drag away from the curve to create the next segment.

Alt-drag or Option-drag the direction of the curve.

Then release the key and drag in the opposite direction.

End the curved path Remember to end the existing curve before you begin drawing a new, unconnected path. You can click the pen tool in the toolbox, or you can hold down Ctrl (Windows) or Command (Mac OS), and click anywhere away from the path.

Editing objects

Selecting objects for editing

Before you can edit an object, you must first select it. Any edits you make affect only the objects that are currently selected. Illustrator provides several tools for selecting objects or parts of objects.

Select an entire object To select an entire object, use the selection tool ( ) to click the border of the object.

When you select an entire object, it appears surrounded by a rectangular bounding box.

Deselect your selection To deselect a selection, click in an empty area of the artwork.

Select a portion of an object To select part of an object (such as a segment or anchor point of a path), use the direct-selection tool ( ) to click or drag over the desired part. By selecting part of an object, you can precisely modify the shape of that part. (See "Applying changes to objects" on page 20.)

Switch between selection tools In addition to the selection and direct-selection tools, Illustrator provides a group-selection tool for working with grouped objects. (See "Grouping objects" on page 22.) You may switch between selection tools frequently during the course of a work session to select different areas of your artwork. As a shortcut, you can always activate the last-used selection tool by pressing Ctrl (Windows) or Command (Mac OS).

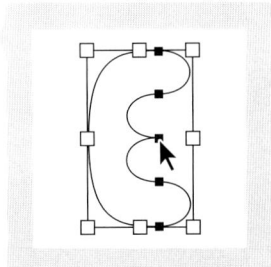

Select an object.

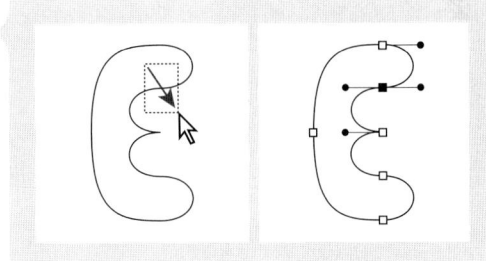

Drag the direct-selection tool to select the segment and display the direction lines.

Use the lasso tools to make selections Illustrator 9.0 provides two new selection tools, the lasso tool (🔾) and the direct-lasso tool (🔾). The lasso tool lets you select entire objects by dragging around any part of the object. The direct-lasso tool lets you select an individual segment or anchor point on an object by dragging around that part of the object.

Use additional selection techniques Use the following techniques to select objects:

Drag around objects with the lasso tool to make selections.

- To add to a selection, hold down Shift as you select additional objects.
- To select multiple objects at once, drag to create either a rectangular marquee (if you are using the selection tool) or a lasso selection around the desired objects.

Applying changes to objects

Once you have selected an object or set of objects, you can begin editing. Edits can range from simple moving and duplicating of objects to more intricate modifications of shapes. Because Illustrator defines objects mathematically as vector graphics, you can edit your artwork repeatedly without losing any quality of detail. Vector objects always retain their smooth, crisp outlines, regardless of how they are scaled or modified.

Reposition a selected object When you select an entire object, the object is surrounded by a rectangular bounding box. You use the selection tool (▶) to move, duplicate, and resize entire objects:

To move an object, drag the object's border to the new location.

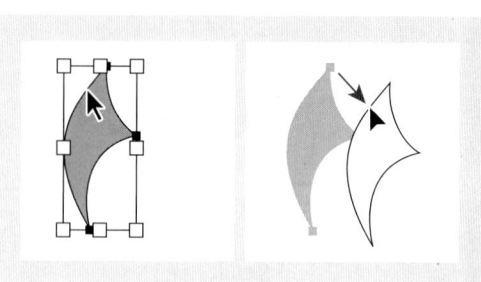

Select an object, and drag to reposition it.

Duplicate the object To duplicate an object, Alt-drag (Windows) or Option-drag (Mac OS) the object's border. A copy of the original object appears where you release the mouse.

Resize the copied object To resize an object, drag one of the handles (hollow squares) on the selection bounding box. You can constrain the proportions of the scaling by Shift-dragging a corner handle.

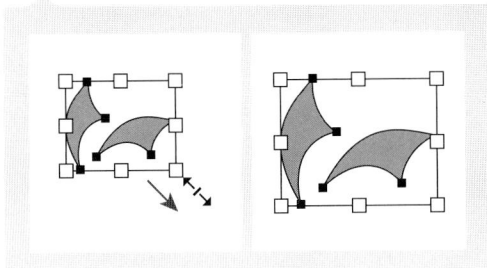

Selected objects before and after scaling using the bounding box

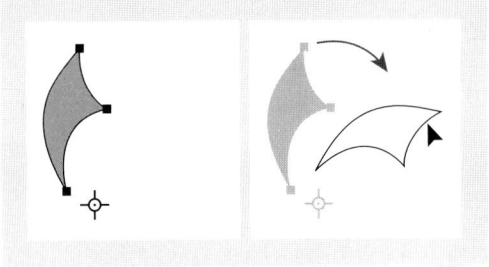

Click to set point of origin. Then drag to rotate.

Transform the object The Illustrator transformation tools (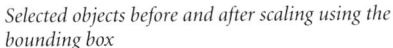) let you apply geometric edits, such as rotations, reflections, and shears, to object shapes. For example, you can select the rotate tool ( ), and drag to rotate the object around its center point, the default point of origin for most transformation tools.

Try the following variations on basic transformations:

- To transform around a point of origin other than the object's center point, first click with the transformation tool to set the desired point before using the tool.
- To duplicate the object as it is transformed, hold down Alt (Windows) or Option (Mac OS) as you use the transformation tool.

Repeat the transformation Sometimes you may find it useful to repeat the same transformation multiple times by choosing Object > Transform > Transform Again. This command cuts down on time spent duplicating edits manually and can even lead to unexpected creative results.

Choosing Object > Transform > Transform Again repeatedly

Edit a path segment In addition to modifying shapes and paths as whole objects, you can reshape individual path segments. First select the desired segment with the direct-selection tool ( ) and then drag the segment, an anchor point, or a direction line to change the shape.

The pen tool ( ) has a number of special tools that are useful for editing paths precisely.

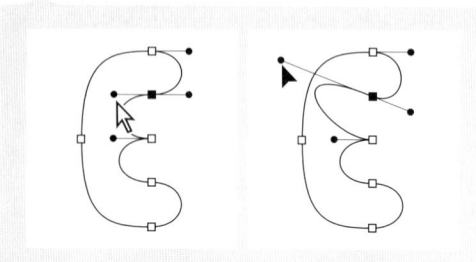

Click the direction line. Then drag to adjust.

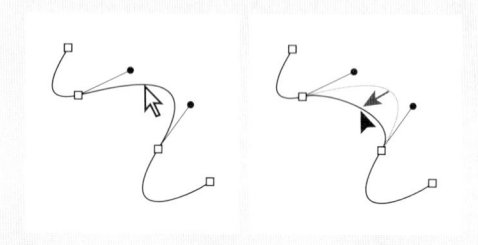

Click the curve. Then drag the segment.

Grouping objects

By associating several objects in a group, you can apply simultaneous edits to all the objects in the group. For example, you can group the individual elements of a flower illustration so that you can move and scale the flower as a single unit. You can also nest smaller groups inside larger groups to organize different levels of your artwork.

Create the group To group multiple objects, start by Shift-clicking with the selection tool ( ) to select all of the objects. Then choose Object > Group to create the group.

Select and edit the entire group If you deselect the group and then click one of its objects with the selection tool, you'll notice that the entire group is automatically selected. Try moving the group and experimenting with different transformation tools to see how changes affect the entire group.

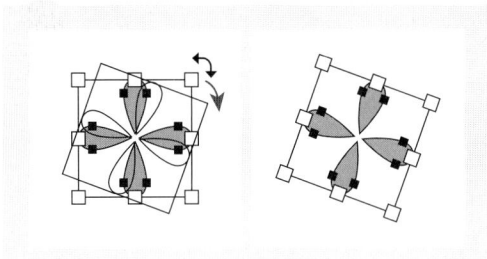 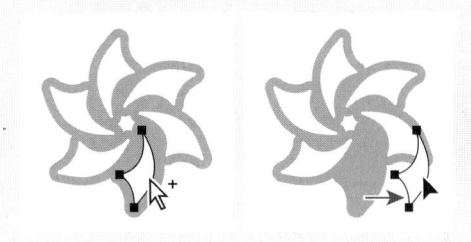

Selecting and rotating a grouped object   *Selecting an object within a group*

Select and edit an object in the group At times you may want to edit an individual object in a group without turning off the grouping behavior. To select an object within a group, you click it with the group-selection tool ( ).

Adding color to your artwork

Painting stylized strokes

The paintbrush tool lets you paint colored strokes using a variety of artistic brush styles. Paintbrush strokes can be edited in the same manner as paths and other artwork objects. In addition to drawing new strokes with the paintbrush tool, you can decorate existing paths with a desired brush style.

Select a brush from the Brushes palette Before drawing with the paintbrush, you must first select a brush by clicking a thumbnail preview in the Brushes palette. You can scroll through the palette to preview the various brushes, grouped by styles from top to bottom:

- Calligraphic brushes mimic the angled strokes created by a calligraphic pen.
- Scatter brushes spread copies of a simple graphic object along the stroke.
- Art brushes stretch a graphic object across the length of the stroke.
- Pattern brushes paint tiled patterns along the stroke.

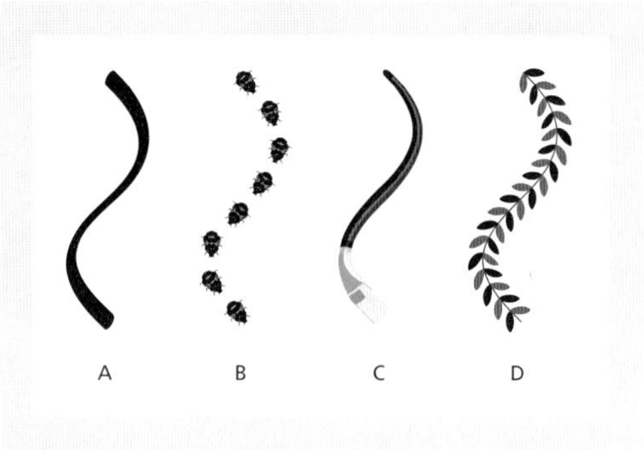

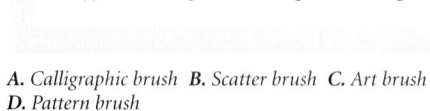

A. *Calligraphic brush* **B.** *Scatter brush* **C.** *Art brush* **D.** *Pattern brush*

Paint with the paintbrush tool Once you have selected a brush, you can use the paintbrush tool (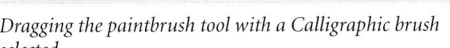) to drag freehand strokes in the artwork.

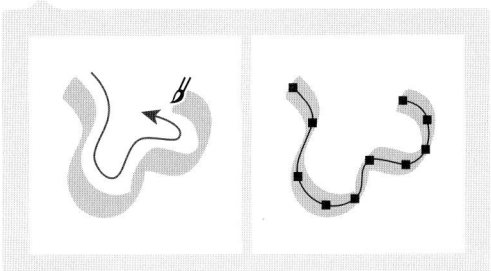

Dragging the paintbrush tool with a Calligraphic brush selected

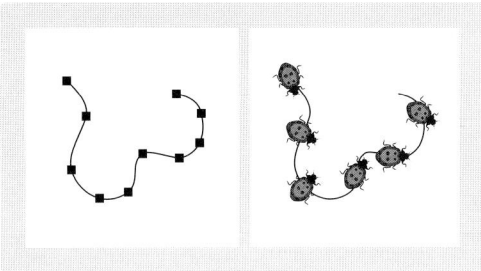

Adding a brush stroke to an existing path

Add brush strokes to an existing object In addition to drawing new brush strokes with the paintbrush tool, you can decorate existing objects with a brush style. You simply select the desired path or shape and then select a brush from the Brushes palette.

Applying fills and strokes

Painting an object is a two-step process. First you apply a fill color to the object's interior, and then you apply a stroke color to its border. You choose and edit the fill and stroke colors independently.

Activate the Fill or Stroke box Illustrator lets you assign different colors to the fill and stroke of an object. The Fill and Stroke boxes in the toolbox determine whether the colors you choose are used as the fill or stroke of an object. Before you fill or stroke a selected object, make sure that the corresponding Fill or Stroke box appears in the frontmost position. If it does not, click once to activate the desired box.

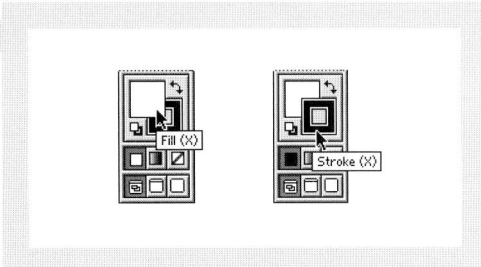

Select a fill or stroke color from the Swatches palette Next, you choose the color to use as the fill or stroke. A simple way to choose a color is to click a swatch in the Swatches palette. The Swatches palette contains a default set of colors, gradients, and patterns. You can also load additional libraries of presaved swatches into the palette.

As you experiment with choosing different colors in the Swatches palette, the object is updated with the new fill or stroke. Notice also that the Fill or Stroke box in the toolbox reflects the current color choice.

Mix a fill or stroke color in the Color palette
Another way to choose colors is by mixing your own in the Color palette. Click in the color bar at the bottom of the palette to pick a starting color. Then drag the sliders to create your own custom color for the fill or stroke.

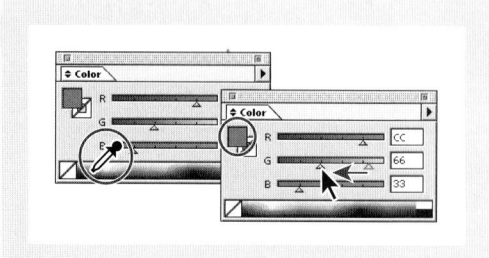

You can also try these alternate techniques for choosing a color:

- In either the toolbox or the Color palette, double-click the Fill or Stroke box to display the Color Picker. Click in the color spectrum, or enter numeric values to specify a color.

- To change the color of an object to a sampled color, first select the object. Then use the eyedropper tool to click an area of the artwork containing the color you want to sample.

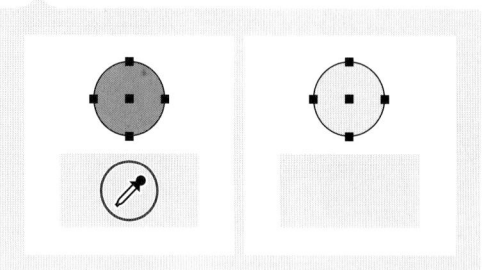 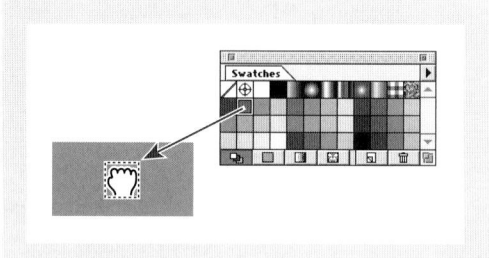

- Drag the desired color from either the Fill or Stroke box in the toolbox, the Color palette, or the Swatches palette to the object that you want to paint.

Specify custom stroke options You can use the options in the Stroke palette to change the stroke's weight (thickness), style, and corner shape.

Applying advanced fills and strokes

Illustrator gives you more advanced fill and stroke options such as patterns, gradients, and the ability to add multiple fills and strokes to a single object. In addition, you can apply versatile levels of transparency to the colors of objects.

Adjust the transparency of an object To apply partial transparency to an object, select the object, and then drag the Opacity slider in the Transparency palette until you achieve the desired appearance. For more information on the versatile features available in the Transparency palette, see "Enhanced creativity" on page 40.

Paint with a pattern To paint a selected object with a pattern, first click the Show Pattern Swatches button at the bottom of the Swatches palette to display the default pattern swatches. Then click a swatch to paint the object with that pattern.

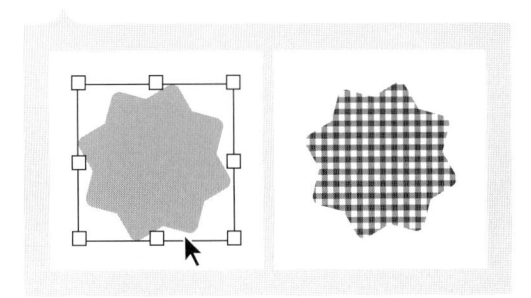

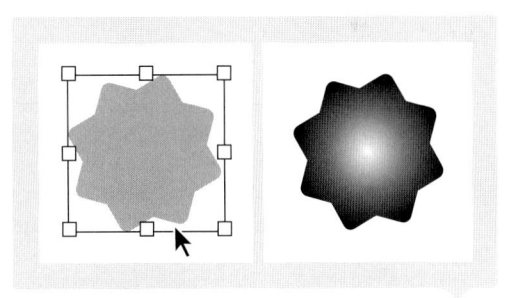

Filling object with pattern   *Painting with gradient*

Paint with a gradient To paint a selected object with a gradient, first click the Show Gradient Swatches button at the bottom of the Swatches palette. Then click the desired swatch to paint with the gradient.

You can also use a more sophisticated type of gradient fill, called a gradient mesh, to simulate multicolored contours and highlights on an object. For more information, see "Creating multicolored objects with the gradient mesh tool" on page 230.

Customize a gradient In addition to using the default gradients available in the Swatches palette, you can create your own custom gradients or modify the colors of existing gradients. To customize a gradient, first click the Gradient button in the toolbox to display the Gradient palette, and then choose Show Options from the palette menu. The options at the top of the palette let you specify either a linear or radial type of gradient. To customize the gradient colors, do any of the following:

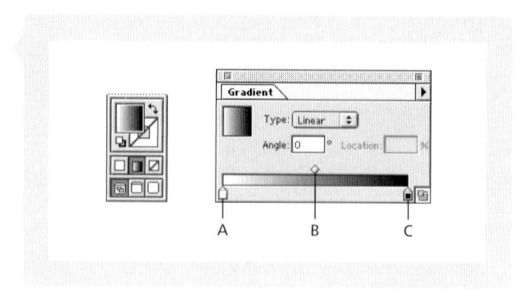

A. Starting color stop B. Midpoint between blended colors C. Ending color stop

- To specify the starting or ending color of the gradient, click the left or right color stop, respectively, below the gradient bar. Then use the Color palette to define the desired color.

- To adjust the gradient's midpoint (where the blend of starting and ending colors meet midway), drag the diamond slider to the left or right above the gradient bar.

- To save your custom gradient, drag it from the Gradient palette to the Swatches palette.

Apply and edit multiple fills and strokes to an object
The new Appearance palette lets you layer multiple fills and strokes on a single object. First select the desired object to display its fill and stroke attributes in the Appearance palette. Then customize the fill and stroke attributes:

- To add a new fill or stroke to the object, select Add New Fill or Add New Stroke from the Appearance palette menu.

- To edit the color of a fill or stroke, select the fill or stroke item in the Appearance palette, and specify the new color. For information on specifying colors, see "Applying fills and strokes" on page 25.

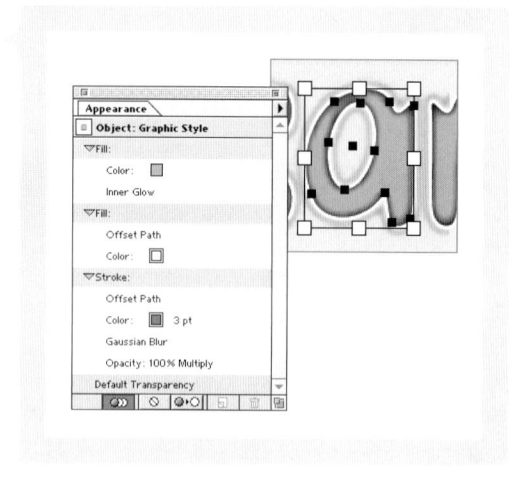

- To apply attributes such as transparency or effects to a fill or stroke, select the fill or stroke item in the Appearance palette, and specify the desired attributes. The attributes appear nested under the selected fill or stroke item in the Appearance palette, and apply only to that fill or stroke. For more information on effects, see "Increased productivity" on page 44.

Creating type

Illustrator provides a number of powerful and flexible features for creating and modifying type. You can easily control the font and layout attributes of type, refine the flow and boundaries of body text, and apply color, transformations, and other graphical enhancements to type objects.

Add type To create type, select a type tool, and set an insertion point for the type in your artwork. Then enter the desired type using the keyboard.

The toolbox offers a variety of tools for creating horizontal and vertical type:

- The type tools (T, |T) let you enter type at a point beginning where you click in the artwork. You can also drag with a type tool to define a text rectangle that encloses the type.

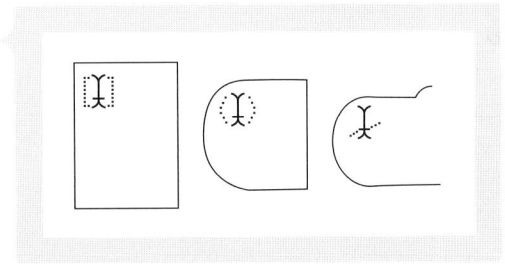

Type tool, area-type tool, and path-type tool

- The area-type tools (T, |T) let you enter type inside an object. Click the border of the object to set an insertion point.

- The path-type tools (,) let you enter type along a path. Click the path to set an insertion point.

Edit type attributes To edit type attributes, first use a type tool to highlight the type you want to change. Then choose Type > Character, and use the Character palette controls to specify traditional typesetting properties such as font, size, kerning, leading, and tracking.

Apply graphic edits to type You can use the Illustrator editing tools to move, copy, rotate, and graphically modify type in many of the same ways as other objects. (See "Applying changes to objects" on page 20 for more information.)

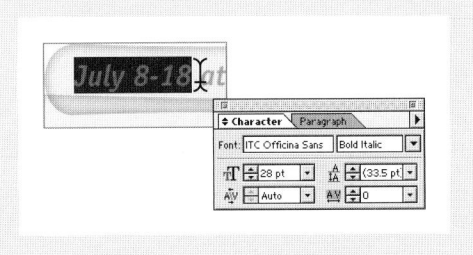

Enhancing your productivity

Illustrator provides a number of versatile features that can help you organize and save the components of your artwork for final output and future projects.

Layers palette The Layers palette lets you organize objects in your artwork on separate layers, which can be repositioned, restacked, and edited individually.

Swatches palette The Swatches palette lets you add and edit new color and pattern swatches to create a custom swatch set that is stored with your artwork file when you save it. Whenever you copy an object from one document to another, any swatches associated with the object are added to the destination document's Swatches palette. This ensures that you'll be able to access the swatches required to edit the full range of the artwork.

Actions palette The Actions palette lets you record and save sets of program tasks that can be applied automatically to your artwork as batch processes.

Styles palette The Styles palette lets you apply sets of appearance attributes, called graphic styles, to graphic and type objects in your artwork. Because styles are linked nondestructively to their objects, you can continue to reshape, resize, transform, and retype the objects with the assurance that the styles will update with your edits.

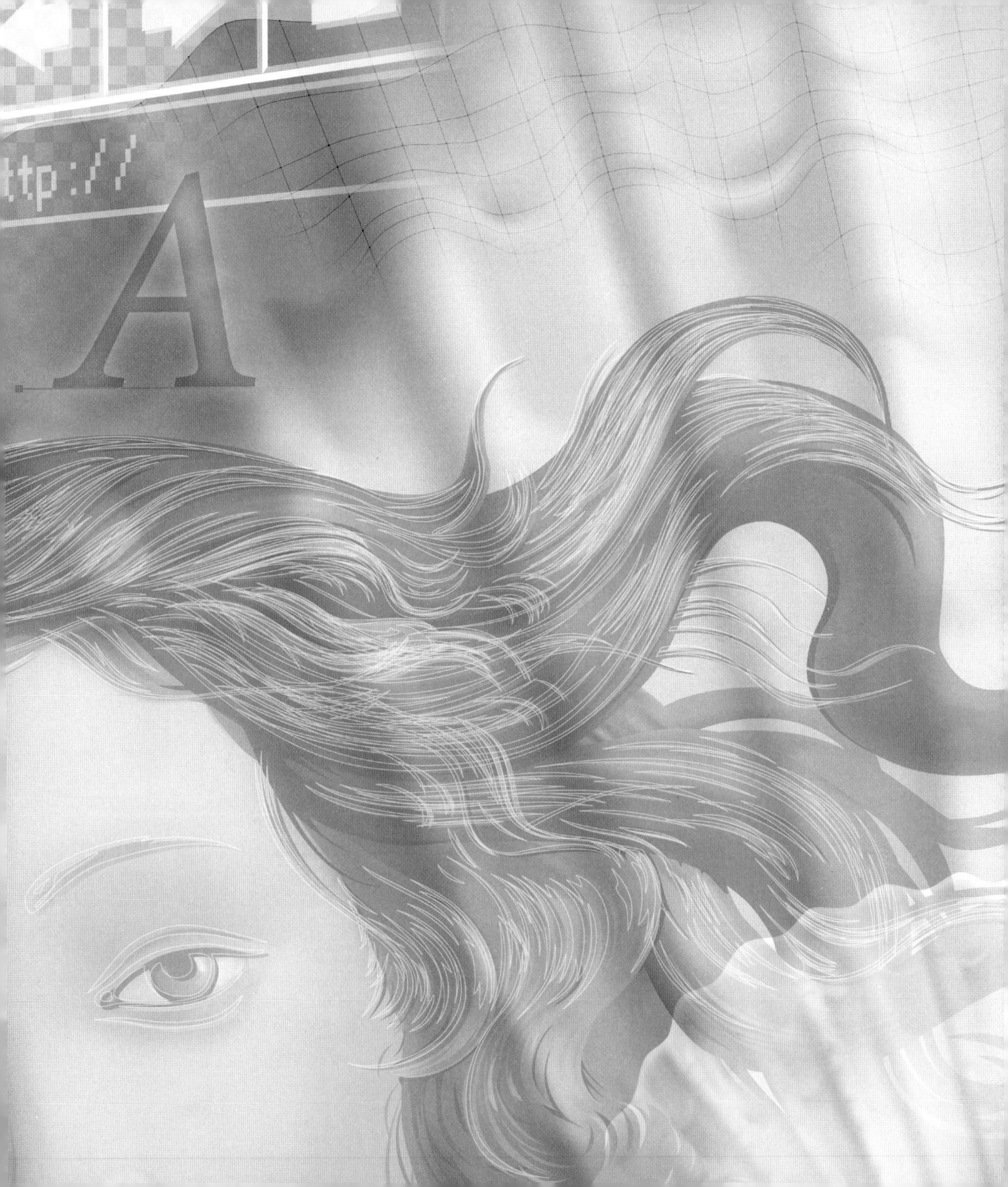
ttp://
A

What's New in Illustrator 9.0

With the release of version 9.0, Adobe Illustrator continues to set the industry software standard for print, multimedia, and online illustration. It introduces powerful new tools for preparing bitmap and vector Web graphics, applying versatile transparency and blending mode to artwork, organizing multi-layered documents, and adding a rich variety of editable and reusable graphics styles and effects. In addition, Illustrator 9.0 integrates seamlessly with the Adobe family of graphics programs for print, Web, and dynamic media, including Adobe Photoshop, Adobe InDesign, Adobe GoLive, Adobe LiveMotion, and others.

Web preparation

Enhanced Web workflow

Illustrator 9.0 offers a number of new and enhanced features to aid in the creation of graphics for the World Wide Web. The program provides extensive support for creating, laying out, and previewing artwork using the real pixel dimensions in which the artwork will appear in Web browsers. Enhanced color options let you work with documents in RGB mode and specify Web-safe colors for painting. The commands under the new Effect menu make it easy to embellish your artwork and type with drop shadows and glows to create flexible, editable buttons and banners. The Release to Layers command lets you quickly organize objects on separate layers, a feature particularly useful for preparing files for Web animation. And the Attributes palette offers the capability to create polygon-shaped image maps.

Pixel-based units and preview Because much of the vector artwork that you create in Illustrator will be rasterized for use on the Web, it's useful to monitor your work in terms of pixels. The Units & Undo preferences panel lets you specify pixels as a global measurement unit for sizing, editing, and laying out your artwork. You can also choose View > Pixel Preview to preview your vector objects as they will appear in a Web browser. When you work in Pixel Preview mode, objects will snap by default to the nearest pixel edge in the document.

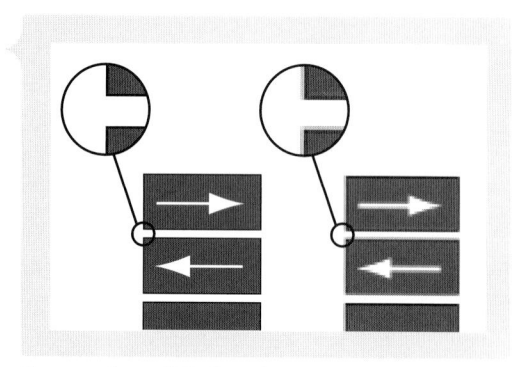

Vector preview and Pixel Preview

RGB and Web-safe color support When you create a new document, you have the option of setting the color mode to RGB; you can also convert documents to RGB mode by choosing File > Document Color Mode > RGB. New options also make it easy for you to paint with the subset of RGB colors that appear in the standard 216-color Web-safe palette. You can set the Color palette to display Web-safe RGB sliders that let you mix Web colors by dragging or by entering hexadecimal values. The Color Picker contains an Only Web Colors option that automatically selects the nearest Web-safe equivalent of the color you pick. You can also set the Info palette to display the RGB or hexadecimal values of colors in your artwork.

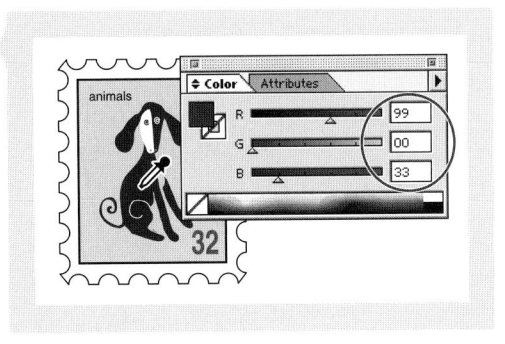

Sample a color, and use the Web-safe RGB sliders to mix its Web-safe equivalent.

Path simplification By selecting an existing path and choosing Object > Path > Simplify, you can simplify and smooth the path shape by reducing the number of its anchor points. Simplifying paths in a document helps to reduce the document's file size.

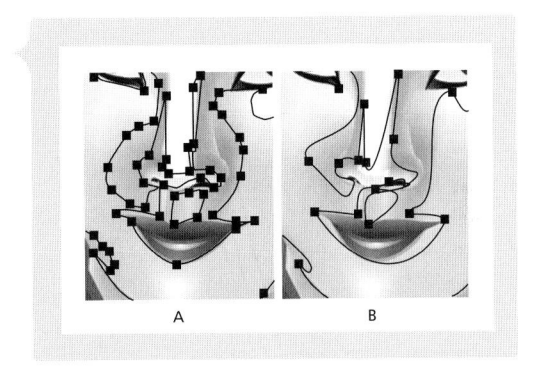

Original and simplified path

Instant drop shadows, glows, and editable shapes
The commands under the Effect menu let you convert type and graphic objects to editable rectangular or elliptical shapes, which is especially useful for creating Web buttons. These shapes can contain fully editable type objects and appearances; when you modify or transform a shape, its contents update automatically. The Stylize commands under the Effect menu let you apply appearances, such as drop shadows and glows, directly to type and graphic objects. Again, full vector editability of the objects is retained.

Type object converted to editable shape; shape automatically updates with type edits.

Instant layer generation The Release to Layers command instantly redistributes all of the objects on a layer into separate, individual layers. You can use this feature to prepare files for further Web animation work in other applications that support layers. For example, you can prepare different frames of an animation by first applying blend options to objects or by using the scatter brush to paint repeated copies of an object along a path. You can then release each object in the blend or scattered path to a separate layer and export the file as a Flash (SWF) file or to Adobe Photoshop 5.5 to set up the animation.

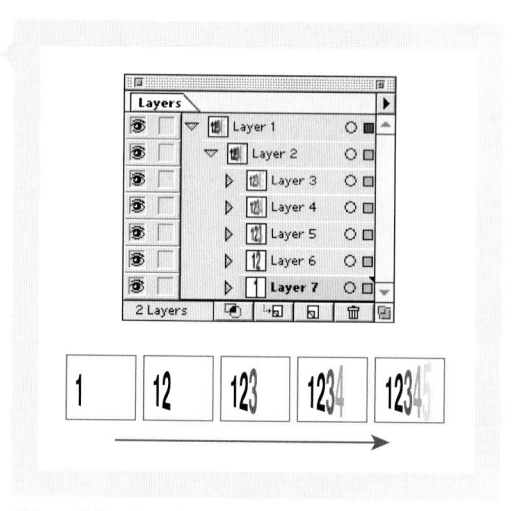

By pressing Shift as you choose the Release to Layers command, you can distribute objects onto separate layers in a cumulative sequence. For

Objects Shift-released to separate layers.

example, you can create a layer containing the first object, a layer containing the first and second objects, a layer containing the first, second, and third objects, and so on. This behavior is especially useful for building animation sequences.

Polygonal image maps A new option in the Image Map menu in the Attributes palette lets you create an image map with a polygon enclosing the selected object. By entering a URL, you can have Illustrator automatically generate a linked polygonal image map when exporting the file to a Web file format.

Creating a polygonal image map

Optimized Web bitmap export

The new Save for Web command provides comprehensive yet easy-to-use controls for previewing and exporting your artwork files in one of the standard Web bitmap formats: JPEG, GIF, PNG-8, or PNG-24. You can customize the optimization of your files to produce the best-looking Web graphics possible, while maintaining efficient downloading and display times. In addition, you can preview how your image will appear under the effects of browser dither, or under the different gamma (brightness) conditions of Windows or Mac OS monitors.

Live optimization preview The best way to balance image quality and file size is by comparing the original version of the artwork file with the optimized version on-screen, and then fine-tuning the compression settings applied. Illustrator displays paired previews side-by-side in the Save for Web dialog box, along with details such as projected file size and download speed. The optimized preview updates interactively as you adjust optimization controls. In 4-up mode, Illustrator generates two additional optimized versions for your comparison.

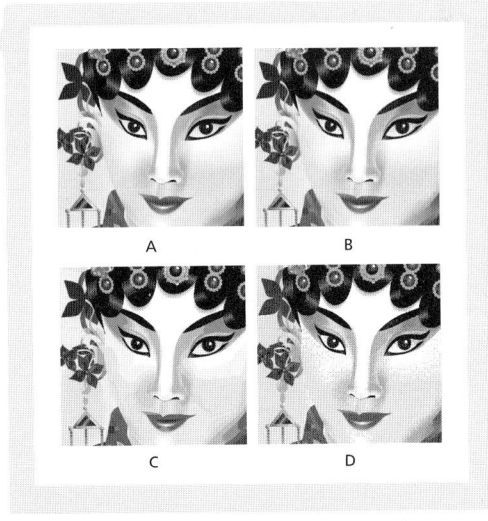

A. Original B. JPEG, 10% quality C. GIF, 32 colors, no dither D. GIF, 10 colors, with dither

Sophisticated color controls An effective way to reduce a GIF or PNG-8 file size is to minimize the number of colors saved with the file. The Color Table tab in the Save for Web dialog box displays the 8-bit color table associated with your optimized image and lets you modify the table in a variety of ways. You can edit, eliminate, or shift colors to their nearest Web-safe equivalent; you can also lock a color to prevent it from being eliminated during your edits.

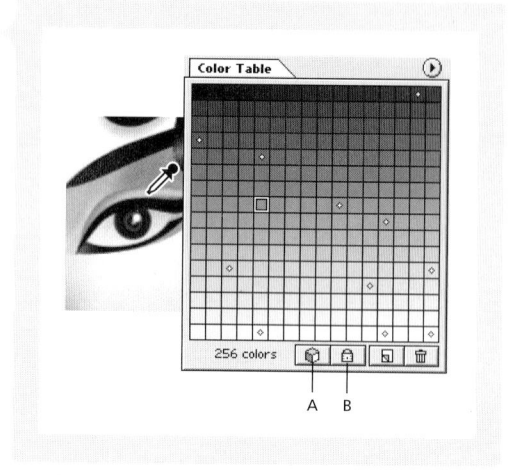

A. Web-shift button B. Lock button

Flexible Web vector export

Illustrator 9.0 provides excellent support for exporting files to Flash (SWF) format, as well as to the new SVG Web vector standard. Both Web vector formats maintain high-quality artwork and fonts, while producing smaller file sizes and faster download times than bitmap formats. Flash is widely used to design vector-based Web pages and Web animations.

SVG is an emerging, open standard that was developed by the World Wide Web Consortium (W3C) and numerous industry players, including Adobe Systems, IBM, Netscape, Sun, Corel, Hewlett-Packard, and others. The SVG standard provides all the benefits of the Flash format, plus support for the following features: Type 1 and TrueType fonts, extensible markup language (XML), cascading style sheets (CSS), interactive actions, and dynamic HTML animation. When preparing SVG output, you can assign scripted events to objects using the SVG Interactivity palette and then export that information with the file. Illustrator also ships with the SVG Viewer plug-in, which works with different browsers to play back SVG graphics and Web pages.

Flash (SWF) format To export your Illustrator file to Flash format, specify the Flash (SWF) format in the Export dialog box. In the Flash options dialog box, you can choose whether to export the entire graphic to a single SWF file; export each layer to a separate frame in a single SWF file; or export each layer to a separate SWF file.

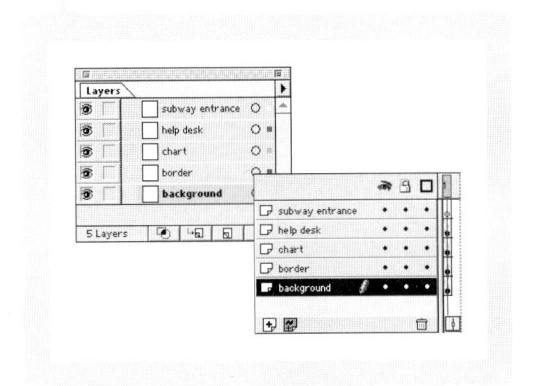

Illustrator layers exported to SWF

Object with normal appearance and with glow activated by mouse rollover

SVG format You can use the SVG Interactivity palette to enhance your SVG output with interactive behavior prompted by user-activated events, such as moving the mouse into a particular area. For example, you can write a JavaScript command that causes an object to display with a glow effect when the mouse pointer moves inside the object boundaries.

Enhanced creativity

Versatile transparency

The new Transparency palette lets you apply transparency to any graphic object, bitmap image, or type character in your artwork to partially or fully reveal underlying objects. Transparent objects and type remain fully editable. You also have the option of limiting transparency to a layer, a group of objects, a knockout shape, or an object's stroke or fill to achieve different creative results. By displaying the checkerboard transparency grid, you can monitor the opaque and transparent areas of your artwork as you work.

Transparency palette The Transparency palette provides a number of controls for specifying the transparency of objects. Simply select an object, and drag the Opacity slider or enter an opacity percentage to assign the desired level of transparency. The Transparency palette displays a thumbnail preview of the selected object.

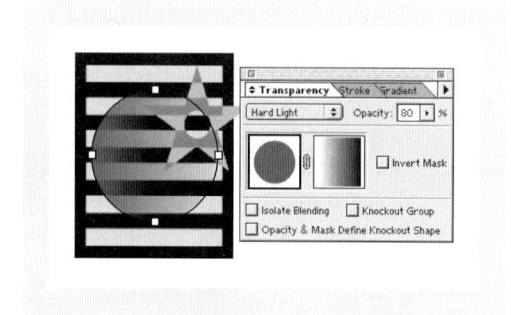

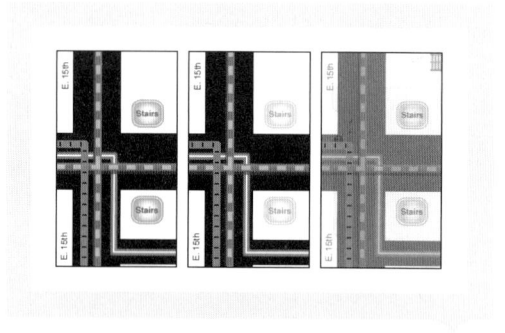

Original; transparent objects; transparent layer

Flexible transparency targets To apply transparency to a group of objects or to a layer, first target the group or layer in the Layers palette, and then specify an Opacity value. When you apply transparency to a layer as a whole, the transparencies of the individual objects on the layer are not affected.

Blending modes

Blending modes let you blend the colors of graphic objects, type, and bitmap images with underlying artwork. By experimenting with different blending modes from the Transparency palette, you can create striking effects in the overlapping areas of stacked objects. Illustrator 9.0 provides you with many of the same blending modes offered by Photoshop.

Isolate Blending option Use the Isolate Blending option in the Transparency palette to confine the action of blending modes to a group of objects. That is, the blending mode of any object in the group interacts only with the colors of the other objects in the group; colors outside the group remain untouched.

To isolate blending modes to a group, apply the desired blending modes to the individual objects. Group the objects, target the group, and select Isolate Blending in the Transparency palette.

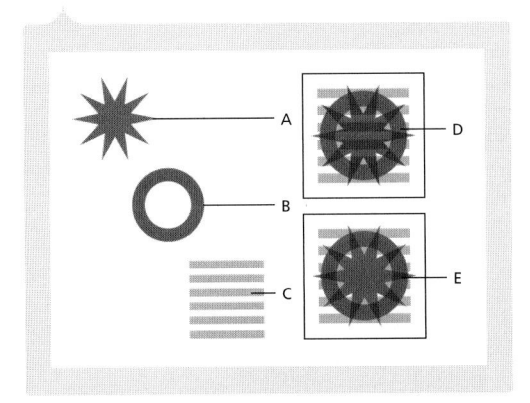

A Multiply mode B. Normal mode C. Background D. Isolate Blending off E. Isolate Blending on

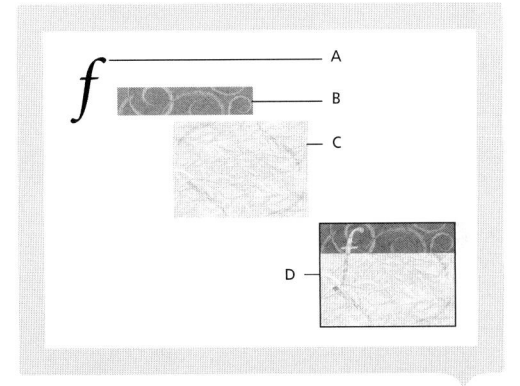

A. Knockout letterform with blending mode applied B. Texture grouped with letterform C. Ungrouped texture D. Knockout Group applied

Knockout Group option Use the Knockout Group option in the Transparency palette to use each object in the group as a knockout shape for the objects below in the group. Transparent objects knock out the underlying parts of the group to reveal artwork below the group. The transparency and blending mode of the knockout shapes interact only with objects that lie below the group.

To create a knockout group, apply the desired transparency and blending mode options to the individual objects. Group the objects, target the group, and select Knockout Group in the Transparency palette.

Masks

Two new masking features—opacity masks and layer clipping masks—let you selectively hide and reveal areas of your artwork through custom shapes. Use the Transparency palette to define any object as an opacity mask, so that artwork attached to the mask takes on modified transparency. The grayscale equivalents of the colors in the mask correspond to different levels of mask transparency. By editing the shape, placement, and fill of the mask, you can achieve sophisticated effects, such as variable transparency across an object. Clipping masks, which are defined through the Layers palette, let you reveal a set of underlying objects through a clipping shape.

Layer clipping masks To create a clipping mask, first create a layer containing the object you want to use as the masking shape and the objects you want to mask, with the masking shape at the top of the stack. Then select the objects and the masking shape, and click the Make/Release Clipping Mask button at the bottom of the Layers palette. Anything that falls within the boundaries of the clipping shape shows through; everything else on the layer is hidden.

A. Masking shape B. Underlying artwork C. Result of mask

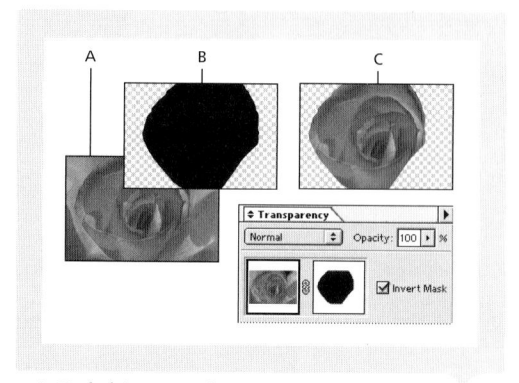

*A. Underlying artwork B. Masking shape
C. Artwork masked by shape with Invert Mask option selected*

Opacity masks To create an opacity mask, begin by placing the object you want to use as the masking shape on top of the artwork you want to mask. Then select the masking shape along with the artwork to be masked, and choose Make Opacity Mask from the Transparency palette's menu.

By editing the grayscale equivalents of the colors in the mask, you can vary the levels of opacity that allow the artwork lying underneath the masked art to show; 100% gray (black) causes underlying areas to appear fully transparent, while 0% gray (white) causes underlying areas to appear fully opaque. The Invert Mask option in the Transparency palette lets you reverse the actions of the black and white areas of the mask, so that previously transparent areas become opaque, and vice versa.

Feathering effect The Feather command under the Effect > Stylize menu softens the transition between foreground and background objects. As with other effects, the underlying vector objects remain editable.

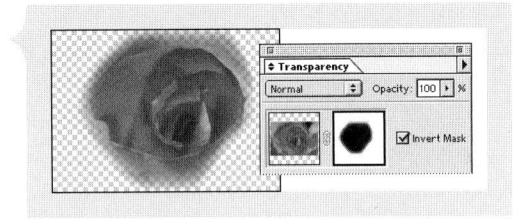

Feathering effect applied to opacity mask shape

Increased productivity

Layers palette enhancements

The Layers palette provides a number of display and ordering enhancements that help you organize, rearrange, and monitor your artwork elements with improved precision and efficiency. Now you can display an expanded hierarchy of elements directly in the Layers palette, with thumbnail previews that start with top-level layers, then groups nested inside the layers, and finally objects nested inside the groups. Other options include the Release to Layers command for automatically generating separate layers, clipping masks for shaping the display of artwork, and the ability to target elements in the Layers palette as recipients of style and appearance attributes.

Expanded nesting hierarchy The expanded Layers palette lets you organize your artwork in nested levels, from top-level layers to individual objects. By nesting layers inside other layers, you can better monitor and organize documents that contain many layer elements. You can collapse and expand the display of contents in a layer or group, and you can rename, duplicate, or reorder any layer, group, or object.

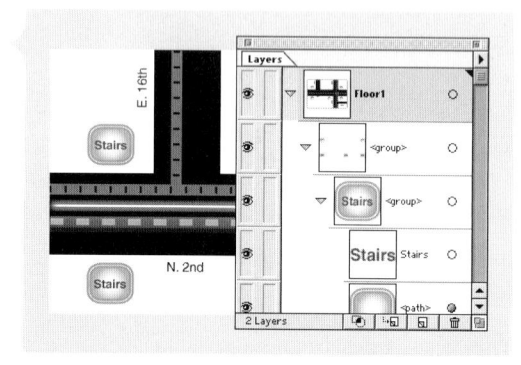

Layers palette with expanded display

Palette display options To help manage the screen space required to display the expanded Layers palette, you can choose from a variety of alternate compact views. For example, you can reduce thumbnail and row size, or you can temporarily disable the display of objects and groups under the layer level.

Effects

You can use the many commands under the new Effect menu to apply nondestructive visual effects to graphic objects, bitmap images, and type in your artwork. These effects preserve the full editability of objects to which they are applied; you can continue to reshape, resize, transform, and retype objects with the assurance that the effects will update with your edits. You can even remove an effect from an object without having to recreate the object from scratch.

Editability of objects When you apply an effect to an object, the object changes in appearance only; all editable characteristics of the original object are preserved. Although many of the commands under the Effect menu appear also under the Filter menu, only the Effect commands preserve the editable behavior of the original objects.

Editability of effects You can use the new Appearance palette to edit the specific options for an effect, even after you have applied it to an object. You simply double-click the name of the desired effect in the Appearance palette to open the options dialog box for the effect.

Editing object with effect applied

Graphic styles

The new Styles palette lets you create and save a set of appearance attributes, called a style, so that the style can be applied instantly to any number of graphic objects and type. Because styles are linked nondestructively to their objects, you can continue to reshape, resize, transform, and retype the objects with the assurance that the styles will update with your edits. A style can consist of a combination of attributes, including multiple fill and stroke colors, gradients, patterns, effects, filters, transparency, blending modes, and transformations.

Default styles The Styles palette contains a number of default graphic styles that can be applied to objects instantly. To apply a graphic style, select the target object in your artwork, and then click the style swatch in the Styles palette.

Customizable styles Use the Appearance palette to display and edit the specific attributes that make up a premade or customized graphic style. Many styles consist of multiple fill and stroke colors with transparency attributes and effects, each of which can be targeted in the Appearance palette for editing. To save a customized graphic style, drag it from the Appearance palette to the Styles palette.

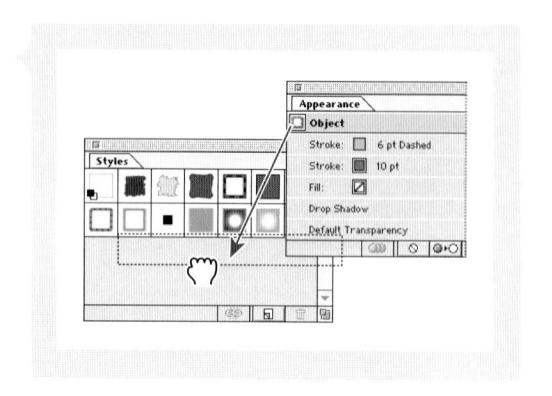

Cross-product integration

Integration with Photoshop

Illustrator 9.0 offers improved integration with Photoshop. When opening a Photoshop file in Illustrator, you can preserve masks, blending modes, and transparency, and convert layers to separate Illustrator objects. When exporting an Illustrator file to Photoshop format, you can preserve layers, opacity masks, transparency, blending modes, and editable type.

Transparency integration When you share files between Illustrator 9.0 and Photoshop, transparency is preserved. Opacity masks in Illustrator convert to layers masks in Photoshop, and vice versa.

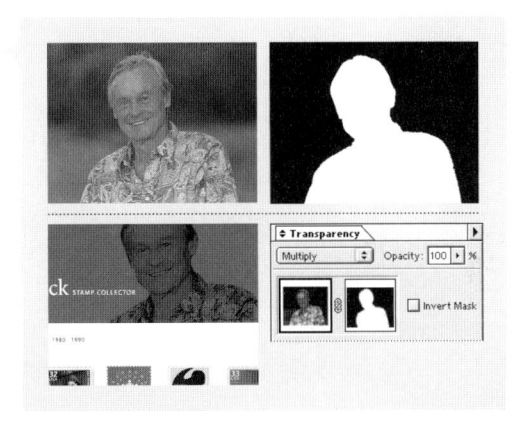

Layer mask in Photoshop converts to opacity mask in Illustrator

Editable type integration If you place type on its own layer in Illustrator, you can preserve the full editability of the type when it is exported to Photoshop.

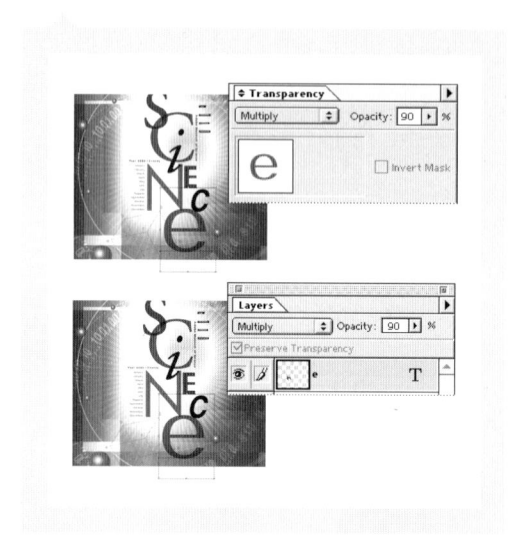

Illustrator type layer with blending mode converts to editable type layer in Photoshop

Integration with other Adobe programs

The many new and enhanced features of Illustrator 9.0 make it an even more useful tool in the desktop print-publishing workflow. The look and feel of the command menus, toolbox, palettes, and keyboard shortcuts closely mirror the standard user interface common to many Adobe programs. Illustrator 9.0 also provides superior support for a number of exportable features, such as layers, transparency, blending modes, editable text, and filters.

The native Illustrator 9.0 format is based on PDF (Portable Document Format) at its core. As a result, when you export artwork to a PDF file, you can choose to preserve the editability of the file when it is opened in Illustrator. That is, you can reopen an Illustrator-created PDF file in Illustrator and make edits without losing file features such as fonts, patterns, and vertical text.

Integration with Web-design programs

The Web workflow of Illustrator 9.0 makes it easier than ever to export files to other Adobe Web-design programs such as GoLive 5 and LiveMotion. You can place native Illustrator graphics directly in GoLive 5 files for efficient one-step optimization to Web formats such as GIF, JPEG, PNG, SWF, and SVG. You can also bring Illustrator artwork into LiveMotion for further animation, interactivity, and sound enhancements.

Other new and enhanced features

Improved color management The Color Settings command offers improved, easy-to-use controls for color-managing documents with ICC color profiles. You can now choose from a number of preset color management configurations optimized for commonly used color workflows.

Soft-proofing You can use the soft-proofing commands under the View menu to display an on-screen preview of how your document's colors will look when reproduced on a specific output device.

Overprint Preview You can use the Overprint Preview to preview how colors in your artwork will overprint and blend.

RGB printing You can send RGB color values in your artwork directly to RGB printers.

Lasso tools You can use the lasso tool to select an entire object by dragging around or across the object. You can use the direct-lasso tool to select individual anchor points or path segments by dragging around them.

Batch-processing actions You can use the Batch command in the Actions palette menu to play an action on a folder of files and subfolders.

Free Distort command You can use the Free Distort command to change the shape of a selection by dragging any of four corners. You can apply this command as a filter or as an editable effect.

New selection commands You can use new commands under the Edit > Select menu to select all objects with the same appearance, blending mode, or opacity as the current selection.

Enhanced window title bars Artwork title bars display the view modes and color modes of artwork.

Enhanced status bar You can view the name of the document's ICC color profile in the status bar.

Enhanced artboard options You can specify artboard dimensions when creating a new artwork window. You can use the Show/Hide Artboard command to show or hide the artboard.

Enhanced bounding box edits You can rotate an object using its selection bounding box.

Enhanced Info palette New options in the Info palette let you view fill and stroke color values of selected objects (in hexadecimal values for RGB or Web-safe colors) and the names of any patterns, gradients, or tints applied to selected objects.

Enhanced Rasterize command You can specify a transparent or white background when converting vector graphics to bitmap images.

Enhanced pencil and smooth tools The Edit Selected Paths option for the pencil and smooth tools lets you edit a path only when you are within a certain distance from it.

Link updating preferences A new menu in the Files & Clipboard preference panel lets you set preferences for updating links.

Enhanced file format support The Open, Place, and Save commands provide enhanced support for various file formats, including DWG/DXF, CGM, Flash (SWF), and SVG.

Changed commands and tools File > Recent Files is now File > Open Recent Files. View > Artwork is now View > Outline. The Paste Remembers Layers preference option is now a command in the Layers palette menu. The Preferences command is now under the Edit menu. The convert-direction-point tool is now the convert-anchor-point tool. The File > Selection Info command has been replaced with the Selection Only option of the Document Info command.

Custom keyboard shortcuts In addition to the standard set of keyboard shortcuts for commands and tools, you can use alternative sets of shortcuts. You can switch between shortcut sets, change individual shortcuts, and define your own shortcuts.

1

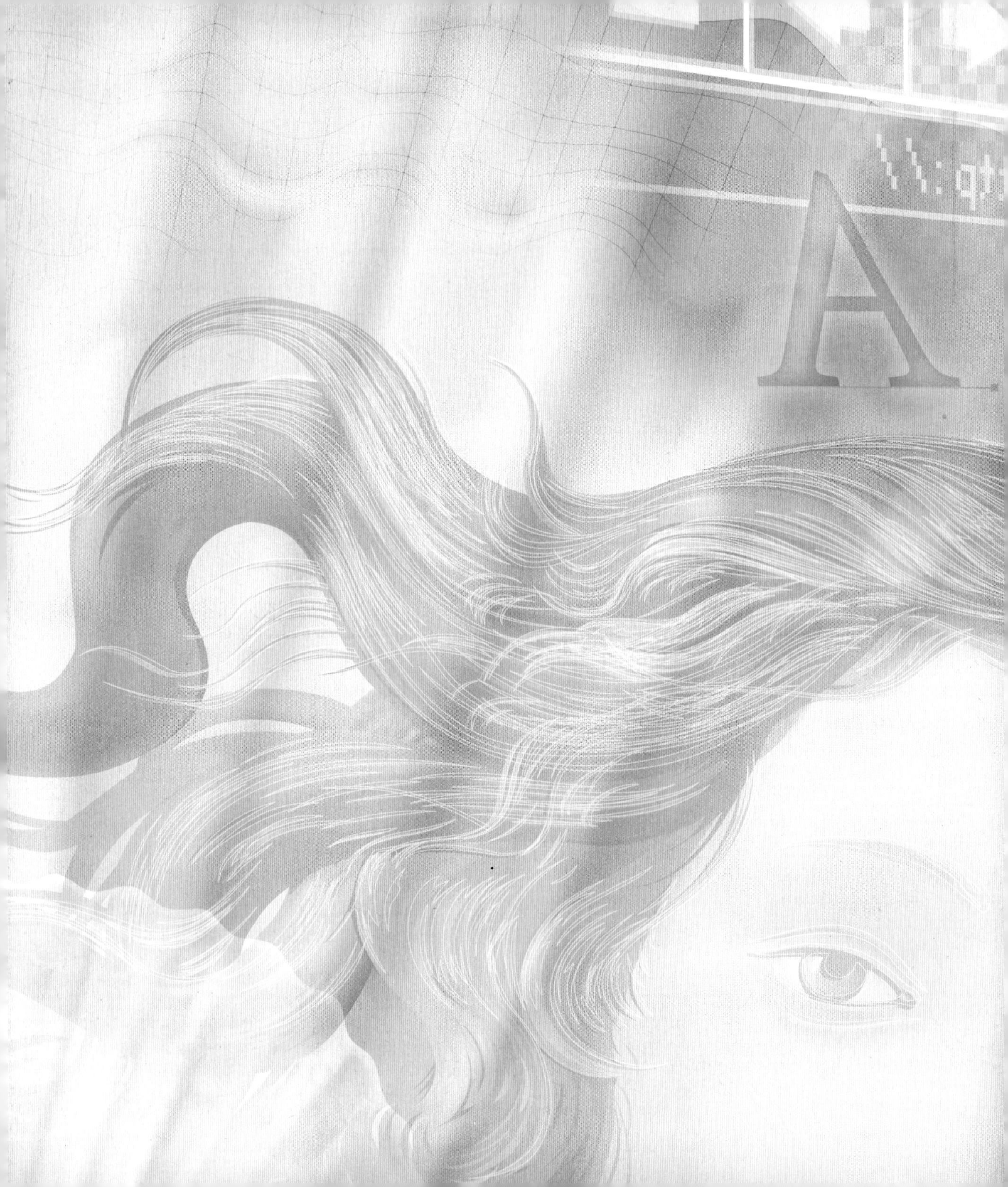

Chapter 1: Looking at the Work Area

The Adobe Illustrator work area includes the command menus at the top of your screen, the illustration window, and a variety of tools and palettes for editing and adding elements such as masks and layers. You can also add commands and filters to the menus by installing software programs called plug-in modules.

Using the tools

The first time you start Illustrator, the toolbox appears on the left side of the screen. The tools in the toolbox let you create, select, and manipulate objects in Illustrator.

When you select most tools, the mouse pointer matches the tool's icon. For example, choosing the paintbrush tool changes the pointer to a paintbrush. You can also change a tool pointer to a precision pointer, such as a cross hair ( ), for greater precision when aligning or working with detailed artwork.

To move the toolbox:

Drag the toolbox by the top bar.

To show or hide the toolbox:

To show the toolbox, choose Window > Show Tools; to hide the toolbox, choose Window > Hide Tools.

To display hidden tools on-screen:

1 Press a tool in the toolbox that has hidden tools underneath it. (Tools that have hidden tools are identified by a triangle in the lower right corner.)

2 When the toolbar of hidden tools appears, hold down the mouse button and drag to the arrow at the end of the toolbar. The toolbar detaches from the toolbox.

To close a detached toolbar:

Click the close box.

To change the pointer to a precision pointer:

Do one of the following:

• While the tool is selected, press Caps Lock on the keyboard.

• Choose Edit > Preferences > General, select Use Precise Cursors, and click OK.

For a gallery demonstrating the use of the Illustrator tools, see "Toolbox overview" in online Help.

Using palettes

Adobe Illustrator includes a number of palettes to help you monitor and modify your work. By default, these palettes appear stacked together in several groups. You can display and hide these palettes as you work. You can also dock palettes so that you can move them together.

To show or hide a palette:

Do one of the following:

• Choose Window > Show or Window > Hide. Show displays the selected palette at the front of its group; Hide conceals the entire group.

- Press Tab to hide or show all palettes and the toolbox.
- Press Shift+Tab to hide all palettes except for the toolbox.

Changing the palette display

You can rearrange your palettes to make better use of your work area by using the following techniques:

- To make a palette appear at the front of its group, click the palette's tab.
- To move an entire palette group, drag its title bar.
- To rearrange or separate a palette group, drag a palette's tab. Dragging a palette outside of an existing group creates a new palette window.
- To move a palette to another group, drag the palette's tab to that group.
- To dock palettes so that you can move them together, drag a palette's tab to the bottom of another palette.
- To move an entire docked palette group, drag its title bar.
- To display a palette menu, position the pointer on the triangle (▶) in the upper right corner of the palette and hold down the mouse button.
- To change the size of a resizable palette, drag the lower right corner of the palette (Windows) or drag the size box at the lower right corner of the palette (Mac OS).

Note: A few palettes, such as the Color palette, cannot be resized by dragging.

- To collapse a group to the palette titles only, click the minimize/maximize box (Windows) or click the zoom box (Mac OS). You can still open the palette menu from a collapsed palette.
- To cycle through the available sizes for a palette—the default size, size with hidden options showing, size as resized by dragging, and palette titles only—double-click the palette's tab.

Using the Info palette

The Info palette provides information on the area beneath the pointer and on selected objects. Depending on the tool you're using, you can use the Info palette to measure size, distance, and angle of rotation. In most cases when a tool is in use, the Info palette displays the x and y coordinates of the pointer's position in the artwork by using the units of measurement you specify.

The Info palette also displays color information for the fill and stroke of selected objects, and the names of patterns, gradients, or tints applied to the objects.

To display the Info palette:

Choose Window > Show Info. The Info palette displays the following information, depending on the tool or command you select:

- When using a selection tool, the x and y coordinates of the pointer are displayed. If an object is selected, the width (W) and height (H) of the object are also displayed.
- When using a zoom tool, the magnification factor and the x and y coordinates are displayed after you release the mouse button.

- When using a pen tool or gradient tool, or when you move a selection, the change in x (W), the change in y (H), the distance (D), and the angle (△) as you drag are displayed.

- When using the scale tool, the percentage change in width (W) and height (H) and the new width (W) and height (H) are displayed after the scale is finished.

- When using the rotate or reflect tools, the coordinates of the object's center and the angle of rotation (△) or reflection (△) are displayed.

- When using the shear tool, the coordinates of the object's center, the angle of shear axis (△), and the amount of shear (◇) are displayed.

- When using the paintbrush tool, the x and y coordinates and the name of the current brush are displayed.

To show or hide options in the Info palette:

Choose Show Options or Hide Options from the Info palette menu. When you show options, the following information appears:

- Values for the fill and stroke colors of the selected object.

- Hexadecimal values for the fill and stroke colors of the selected object, if the color mode is RGB or Web safe.

- The name of any pattern, gradient, or tint applied to the selected object.

Note: If you select multiple objects, the Info palette displays only the information that is the same for all selected objects.

Using context menus

In addition to the menus that appear at the top of your screen, Adobe Illustrator contains a number of context-sensitive menus that relate to the document or the selection. You can use context menus as a quick way to choose commonly used commands.

To display context menus:

1 Position the pointer over the document or an object in the document.

2 Do one of the following:

- In Windows, click with the right mouse button.

- In Mac OS, press Control and hold down the mouse button.

Viewing artwork

Adobe Illustrator gives you great flexibility in viewing your artwork. You can view different areas of the artwork at different magnifications, use simplified views for tasks such as editing paths, and preview how your artwork will appear in a Web browser or in print.

If you are using Illustrator's color management features, you can also display an online preview of how your document's colors will appear on a particular type of monitor or output device. (See "Soft-proofing colors" on page 210.)

Setting up windows and views

You can open additional windows to display several views at once, so that you can quickly switch between view modes or magnifications. For example, you can set one view highly magnified for doing close-up work on some objects and create another view less magnified for laying out those objects on the page.

To change the screen mode for illustration windows:

Click a screen mode button in the toolbox:

• The left button (▣) displays artwork in a standard window, with a menu bar at the top and scroll bars on the sides.

• The center button (▢) displays artwork in a full-screen window with a menu bar but with no title bar or scroll bars.

• The right button (▢) displays artwork in a full-screen window, but with no title bar, menu bar, or scroll bars.

To open a new window:

Choose Window > New Window.

A new window of the same size appears on top of the previously active window. The two windows are identical except for their window numbers. The new window is now the active window.

To close windows:

Do one of the following:

• Choose File > Close to close the active window.

• Press Alt (Windows) or Option (Mac OS) and choose File > Close to close all document windows.

To arrange multiple windows (Windows only):

Do one of the following:

• Choose Window > Cascade to display windows stacked and cascading from the top left to the bottom right of the screen.

• Choose Window > Tile to display windows edge to edge.

• Choose Window > Arrange Icons to arrange minimized windows within the program window.

To create a view:

1 Set up the view that you want.

2 Choose View > New View.

3 Enter a name for the new view, and click OK.

The view names, along with keyboard shortcuts for choosing them, appear at the bottom of the View menu. To retrieve a view, select the name of the view you want to use. It is possible to create and store up to 25 views for each document.

To rename or delete a view:

1 Choose View > Edit Views.

2 Select the view you want to edit, and rename it or click Delete.

To scroll the view with the hand tool:

1 Select the hand tool (✋).

2 Move the pointer onto the artwork, and drag in the direction in which you want the artwork to move.

To switch to the hand tool when using another tool, hold down the spacebar.

Viewing artwork as paths

Adobe Illustrator sets the view so that all artwork is previewed in color. You can also set the view so that your artwork is displayed only as paths with all paint attributes hidden. Viewing artwork without paint attributes speeds up the time it takes to redraw the screen when working with complex artwork.

To view the artwork in color or as path outlines:

Choose a viewing option:

• Choose View > Preview to display the artwork as close as possible to how it will be printed, drawn with as much color, shading, and detail as your monitor is capable of displaying.

• Choose View > Outline to display the artwork as paths, hiding each object's paint attributes. Working in this view speeds up the redraw time when working with complex artwork.

Use the New Window command to preview in one window while editing in Outline view in another.

Viewing artwork as pixels

In Pixel Preview mode, you can preview how your artwork will appear when it is rasterized and viewed in a Web browser. (For more information, see "Viewing artwork as pixels" on page 326.)

Viewing how colors will overprint

Overprint Preview mode provides an "ink preview" that approximates how blending, transparency, and overprinting will appear in color-separated output. (For more information on overprinting, see "Step 2: Select overprint options for overlapping colors" on page 383.)

To preview how colors will overprint and blend:

Choose View > Overprint Preview.

Magnifying and reducing the view

The zoom-in and zoom-out tools and commands let you magnify or reduce the display of any area in the file up to 64 times actual size. Zooming in and out does not change the actual size of the file, only the magnification at which you see it. See "Scaling" on page 142.

You see the current magnification level at the top and the bottom left of the window.

To zoom in:

Do one of the following:

• Select the zoom tool ( ). The pointer becomes a magnifying glass with a plus sign in its center. Click at the center of the area you want to magnify. Each click magnifies the view to the next preset percentage. When the file has reached its maximum magnification level of 6400%, the magnifying glass appears blank.

• Choose View > Zoom In. Each click magnifies the view to the next preset percentage. When the file has reached its maximum magnification level of 6400%, the command is dimmed.

- When no objects are selected, click the right mouse button (Windows) or Ctrl-click (Mac OS) and select the Zoom In command from the context menu.

- Enter a magnification level in the Zoom text box at the lower left of the window.

- Select a magnification level from the Zoom pop-up menu at the lower left of the window.

To zoom out:

Do one of the following:

- Select the zoom tool while holding down Alt (Windows) or Option (Mac OS). The pointer becomes a magnifying glass with a minus sign in its center. Click the center of the area you want to reduce. Each click reduces the view to the previous preset percentage. When the file has reached its maximum reduction level of 3.13%, the magnifying glass appears blank.

- Choose View > Zoom Out. Each click reduces the view to the previous preset percentage. When the file reaches its maximum reduction level of 3.13%, the command is dimmed.

- When no objects are selected, click the right mouse button (Windows) or Ctrl-click (Mac OS) and select the Zoom Out command from the context menu.

- Enter a reduction level in the Zoom text box at the lower left of the window.

- Select a magnification level from the Zoom pop-up menu at the lower left of the window.

To choose the zoom-in tool while using another tool, press Ctrl+spacebar (Windows) or Command+spacebar (Mac OS). To choose the zoom-out tool while using another tool, press Ctrl+Alt+spacebar (Windows) or Command+Option+spacebar (Mac OS).

To magnify by dragging:

1 Select the zoom-in tool ( ).

2 Drag a dotted rectangle, called a *marquee*, around the area you want to magnify. To move the marquee around the artwork, begin dragging a marquee and then hold down the spacebar while dragging the marquee to a new location.

To display a file at 100%:

Choose View > Actual Size, or double-click the zoom tool.

To change the view to fit the screen:

Choose View > Fit In Window, or double-click the hand tool.

Using the Navigator palette

The Navigator palette lets you quickly change the view of your artwork using a thumbnail display.

For more information, see "Using the Navigator palette" in online Help.

Using the status bar

At the bottom left edge of the Illustrator window is the status bar. The status bar contains the Zoom pop-up menu and the Status pop-up menu. The Status menu can display information about any of the following topics:

- The current tool in use.
- The date and time.
- The amount of virtual memory (Windows) or free RAM memory (Mac OS) available for your open file.
- The number of undos and redos available.
- The document color profile. For information on color profiles, see "About color management" on page 199.

To specify the type of information to display in the Status pop-up menu:

Select the type of information from the pop-up menu.

Previewing placed EPS images

Placed images from other applications can slow performance when previewing and printing artwork.

You can turn off previewing of placed images when you need to work quickly. You can then turn previewing back on when you want to view the finished art.

To determine how placed EPS images appear:

1 Choose File > Document Setup. Choose Artboard from the pop-up menu at the top left of the Document Setup dialog box.

2 Select Show Images in Outline to specify that placed images should display a preview image when seen in Outline view and click OK. (See "Opening and placing artwork" on page 73.)

Using plug-in modules

Plug-in modules are software programs developed by Adobe Systems, and by other software developers in conjunction with Adobe Systems, to add features to Adobe Illustrator. A number of special effects plug-ins come with your program and are automatically installed in the Plug-ins folder.

If you change the location of the Plug-ins folder, or if you want to use a different folder as your plug-ins folder, you must use the Plug-ins Preferences command to tell Illustrator about the new location of the plug-ins.

You can also use plug-ins from Adobe Photoshop version 3.0 or later. In addition, you can use any commercial plug-in designed for use with Photoshop or Illustrator.

To avoid duplicating your plug-in filters between the two programs, make a shortcut (Windows) or an alias (Mac OS) to your Photoshop plug-in filters in your Illustrator Plug-ins folder.

To specify the location of plug-in modules:

1 Choose Edit > Preferences > Plug-ins & Scratch Disks.

2 Click Choose and select the folder containing the plug-in modules, then click OK.

3 Quit Illustrator, and then start it again for the plug-in modules to take effect.

To install an Adobe Systems plug-in module:

If an installer is provided, use it to install the plug-in module. Otherwise, drag a copy of the module to the Plug-ins folder inside the Adobe Illustrator folder.

To install a third-party plug-in module:

Follow the installation instructions that came with the plug-in module.

Developing plug-in modules for Adobe Illustrator

The open architecture of the Adobe Illustrator program allows third-party developers to create features that are accessible from within Adobe Illustrator. If you are interested in creating plug-in modules compatible with Adobe Illustrator, see the Adobe Systems U.S. Web site at http://www.adobe.com. In addition, you can reach the ADA by e-mail at ada@adobe.com.

Customizing shortcuts

Illustrator provides a set of standard keyboard shortcuts for commands and tools. Illustrator also ships with alternative sets of keyboard shortcuts, including shortcuts for previous versions and for other programs.

You can switch between sets of shortcuts, change individual shortcuts within a set, and define your own sets of shortcuts.

To view, manage, or print sets of keyboard shortcuts:

1 Choose Edit > Keyboard Shortcuts.

2 Choose a set of shortcuts from the Set menu at the top of the Keyboard Shortcuts dialog box.

3 Choose a shortcut type (Menu Commands or Tools) from the menu above the shortcut display.

4 Do any of the following:

• To apply the displayed set of shortcuts, click OK.

• To delete the displayed set of shortcuts, click Delete. You can't delete the set named Illustrator Factory Defaults.

• To export the displayed set of shortcuts into a text file, click Export Text. In the Save Keyset File dialog box, enter a file name for the current keyset that you are saving, and click Save. You can use this text file to print out a copy of your keyboard shortcuts.

To define new shortcuts or sets of shortcuts:

1 Choose Edit > Keyboard Shortcuts.

2 Choose a set of shortcuts from the Set menu at the top of the Keyboard Shortcuts dialog box.

3 Choose a shortcut type (Menu Commands or Tools) from the menu above the shortcut display.

4 In the Shortcut column of the scroll list, select the shortcut you want to modify (palette shortcuts are at the end of the scroll list).

5 Enter a new shortcut. When you begin entering changes, the name in the Set menu changes to *[Custom]*.

If the shortcut is already assigned to another command or tool in the set, an alert informs you that another command or tool has the shortcut. Click away from the selection to assign the shortcut to the new command or tool, and to erase the previously assigned shortcut. Once you have reassigned a shortcut, you can click Undo to undo the change, or click Go To to go to the other command or tool and assign it a new shortcut.

6 In the Symbol column, enter the symbol that will appear on the menu or tool tip for the command or tool. You can use any of the characters that are allowed in the Shortcut column.

7 When you have finished changing shortcuts and symbols, do one of the following:

• To create a new set that includes the modifications, click OK or Save, and then save the shortcuts as a file. Enter a name for the new set in the Name text box, and click OK. The new file set will appear in the pop-up menu under the new name.

• To discard all changes and exit the dialog box, click Cancel.

• To discard the last saved change without closing the dialog box, click Undo.

To clear shortcuts and symbols from a command or tool:

1 In the Keyboard Shortcuts dialog box, select the command or tool name whose shortcut and symbol you want to delete.

2 Click Clear.

To delete an entire set of shortcuts:

1 Choose Edit > Keyboard Shortcuts.

2 In the Set pop-up menu, choose the shortcut set that you want to delete.

3 Click Delete and then OK to exit the dialog box.

Setting preferences

Numerous program settings are stored in the Adobe Illustrator preference file:

• In Windows, this file is called AIPrefs. It is located in the Windows\Application Data\Adobe\Adobe Illustrator 9 folder (Windows 98) or the WinNT\Profiles*user name*\Application Data\Adobe Illustrator 9 folder (Windows NT).

- In Mac OS, the preferences file is called Adobe Illustrator 9.0 Prefs. It is located in the Adobe Illustrator 9.0 folder within the Preferences folder in your System Folder.

The settings stored in the preference file include display options, separation setup information, tool options, ruler units, and options for exporting information. Most of these options are set in panels of the Preferences dialog box.

To find an explanation of a particular preference option or set of options, refer to the index.

To open the Preferences dialog box:

Choose the desired preference panel from the Edit > Preferences submenu.

To switch to a different preference panel:

Choose an option from the menu at the top left of the Preferences dialog box. You can also click Next to display the next panel, or click Prev to display the previous panel.

2

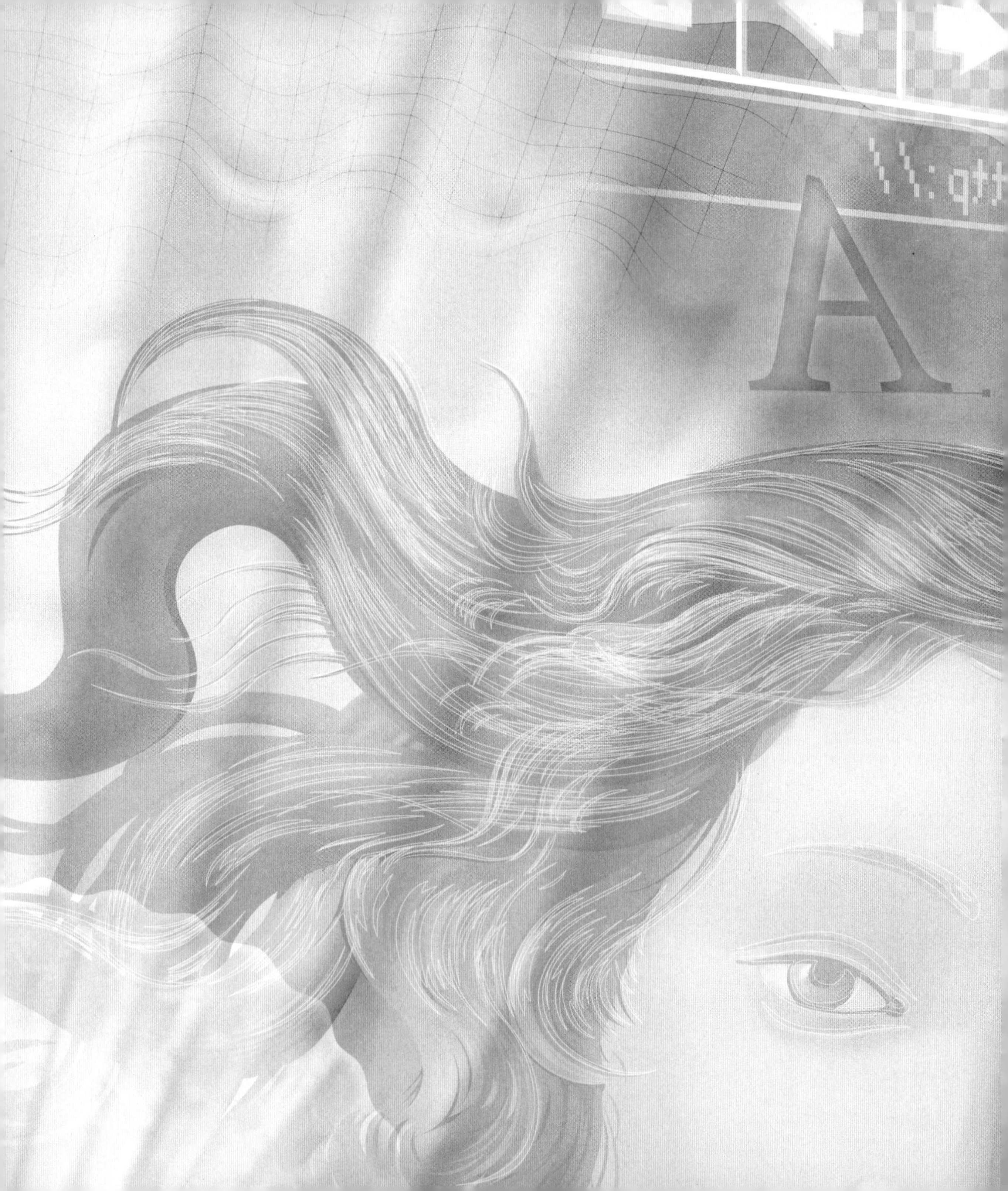
A

Chapter 2: Setting Up Artwork in Illustrator

In the Adobe Illustrator program, you can create artwork or import artwork created from other applications. To create effective artwork, you need to understand some basic concepts about vector graphics versus bitmap images, resolution, and color.

About vector graphics and bitmap images

Computer graphics fall into two main categories—vector graphics and bitmap images. Understanding the difference between the two helps as you create, edit, and import artwork.

In Illustrator the type of graphic image can have important effects on your workflow. For example, some file formats only support bitmap images and others only vector graphics. Graphic image types are particularly important when importing or exporting graphic images to and from Illustrator. Linked bitmap images cannot be edited in Illustrator. Graphic formats also affect how commands and filters can be applied to images; some filters in Illustrator will only work with bitmap images.

Vector graphics

Drawing programs such as Adobe Illustrator create vector graphics, made of lines and curves defined by mathematical objects called *vectors*. Vectors describe graphics according to their geometric characteristics. For example, a bicycle tire in a vector graphic is made up of a mathematical definition of a circle drawn with a certain radius, set at a specific location, and filled with a specific color. You can move, resize, or change the color of the tire without losing the quality of the graphic.

A vector graphic is resolution-independent—that is, it can be scaled to any size and printed on any output device at any resolution without losing its detail or clarity. As a result, vector graphics are the best choice for type (especially small type) and bold graphics that must retain crisp lines when scaled to various sizes—for example, logos.

Because computer monitors represent images by displaying them on a grid, both vector and bitmap images are displayed as pixels on-screen.

Bitmap images

Paint and image-editing software, such as Adobe Photoshop, generate bitmap images, also called *raster images*. The images use a grid (also known as a *bitmap* or *raster*) of small squares, known as *pixels*, to represent graphics. Each pixel in a bitmap image has a specific location and color value assigned to it. For example, a bicycle tire in a bitmap image is made up of a collection of pixels in that location, with each pixel part of a mosaic that gives the appearance of a tire. When working with bitmap images, you edit pixels rather than objects or shapes.

Bitmap images are the most common electronic medium for continuous-tone images, such as photographs or images created in painting programs, because they can represent subtle gradations of shades and color. Bitmap images are resolution dependent—that is, they represent a fixed number of pixels. As a result, they can appear jagged and lose detail if they are scaled on-screen or if they are printed at a higher resolution than they were created for.

About resolution in bitmap images

Resolution is the number of dots or pixels per linear unit used to reproduce artwork and images. Output devices display images as groups of pixels. The resolution of vector graphics, such as Illustrator artwork, depends on the device used to display the artwork. The resolution of bitmap images, such as digital photographs, depends on both the display device and the inherent resolution of the bitmap image.

Pixel dimensions   The number of pixels along the height and width of a bitmap image. The display size of an image on-screen is determined by the pixel dimensions of the image plus the size and setting of the monitor. The file size of an image is proportional to its pixel dimensions.

A typical 13-inch monitor displays 640 pixels horizontally and 480 vertically. An image with pixel dimensions of 640 by 480 would fill this small screen. On a larger monitor with a 640 by 480 setting, the same image (with pixel dimensions of 640 by 480) would still fill the screen, but each pixel would appear larger. Changing the setting of this larger monitor to 1152 pixels by 870 pixels would display the image at a smaller size, occupying only part of the screen.

When preparing an image for online display (for example, a Web page that will be viewed on a variety of monitors), pixel dimensions become especially important. Because your image may be viewed on a 13-inch monitor, you'll probably want to limit the size of your image to a maximum of 640 pixels by 480 pixels.

Image resolution The number of pixels displayed per unit of printed length in an image, usually measured in pixels per inch (ppi). An image with a high resolution contains more, and therefore smaller, pixels than an image of the same printed dimensions with a low resolution. For example, a 1-inch-by-1-inch image with a resolution of 72 ppi contains a total of 5184 pixels (72 pixels wide x 72 pixels high = 5184). The same 1-inch-by-1-inch image with a resolution of 300 ppi would contain a total of 90,000 pixels.

Because they use more pixels to represent each unit of area, higher-resolution images usually reproduce more detail and subtler color transitions than lower-resolution images when printed. However, increasing the resolution of an image scanned or created at a lower resolution only spreads the original pixel information across a greater number of pixels and rarely improves image quality.

To determine the image resolution to use, consider the medium of final distribution for the image. If you're producing an image for online display, the image resolution only needs to match the typical monitor resolution (72 or 96 ppi). However, using too low a resolution for a printed image results in *pixelation*—output with large, coarse-looking pixels. Using too high a resolution (pixels smaller than what the output device can produce) increases the file size and slows the printing of the image.

Note: The Printing & Export panel of the Document Setup dialog box lets you define the output resolution for vector drawings. In Illustrator, output resolution refers to the number of line segments the PostScript interpreter uses to approximate a curve. (See "Changing the path output resolution" on page 369.)

Monitor resolution The number of pixels or dots displayed per unit of length on the monitor, usually measured in dots per inch (dpi). Monitor resolution depends on the size of the monitor plus its pixel setting. The typical resolution of a PC monitor is about 96 dpi, of a Mac OS monitor 72 dpi. Understanding monitor resolution helps explain why the display size of an image on-screen often differs from its printed size.

Printer resolution The number of ink dots per inch (dpi) produced by an imagesetter or laser printer. For best results, use an image resolution that is proportional to, but not the same as, printer resolution. Most laser printers have output resolutions of 300 dpi to 600 dpi and produce good results with images from 72 ppi to 150 ppi.

High-end imagesetters can print at 1200 dpi or higher and produce good results with images from 200 ppi to 300 ppi.

Screen frequency The number of printer dots or halftone cells per inch used to print grayscale images or color separations. Also known as screen ruling or line screen, screen frequency is measured in lines per inch (lpi)—or lines of cells per inch in a halftone screen.

The relationship between image resolution and screen frequency determines the quality of detail in the printed image. To produce a halftone image of the highest quality, you generally use an image resolution that is from 1.5 to at most 2 times the screen frequency. But with some images and output devices, a lower resolution can produce good results.

Note: Some imagesetters and 600-dpi laser printers use screening technologies other than halftoning. If you are printing an image on a nonhalftone printer, consult your service provider or your printer documentation for the recommended image resolutions.

About the work area

In Adobe Illustrator, the work area occupies the entire space within the Illustrator window and includes more than just the printable page containing your artwork. The printable and non-printable areas are represented by a series of solid and dotted lines between the outermost edge of the window and the printable area of the page.

Imageable area   The imageable area is bounded by the innermost dotted lines and represents the portion of the page on which the selected printer can print. Many printers cannot print to the edge of the paper.

Nonimageable area   The nonimageable area is between the two sets of dotted lines representing any nonprintable margin of the page.

Edge of the page   The page edge is indicated by the outermost set of dotted lines.

Artboard   The artboard is bounded by solid lines and represents the entire region that can contain printable artwork. By default, the artboard is the same size as the page, but it can be enlarged or reduced. The U.S. default artboard is 8.5" x 11", but it can be set as large as 227" x 227". You can choose to show or hide the artboard.

Scratch area   The scratch area is the area outside the artboard that extends to the edge of the 227-inch square window. The scratch area represents a space on which you can create, edit, and store elements of artwork before moving them onto the artboard. Objects placed onto the scratch area are visible on-screen, but they do not print.

Setting up the work area

Once you have created a document, you can then set up your work area to organize your work and streamline the workflow. For example, you can change the size of the artboard, tile your workspace, or move your page boundaries.

To open a new file:

1   Choose File > New, and then enter a name in the Name text box.

2   Select the CYMK or RGB color mode. (See "Color modes and models" on page 173.)

3 If necessary, enter a height and width for the artboard.

To create a new document without opening the New Document dialog box, press Ctrl+Alt+N (Windows) or Command+Option+N (Mac OS). The new, untitled document has the settings last used.

To open an existing file:

1 Choose File > Open.

2 Select the name of the file you want to open, and click Open.

To close a file and quit Illustrator:

1 Choose File > Exit (Windows) or File > Quit (Mac OS).

2 If the file has not yet been saved or named, the Save dialog box appears. To save the file, enter a name in the Name text box (if necessary) and then click OK.

To show or hide the artboard:

To show the artboard, choose View > Show Artboard; to hide the artboard, choose View > Hide Artboard.

To change the size of the artboard:

1 Choose File > Document Setup. Then choose Artboard from the pop-up menu at the top left of the Document Setup dialog box.

2 Do one of the following:

• Choose a preset size from the Size pop-up menu.

• Choose Custom from the Size pop-up menu, and enter the dimensions you want in the text boxes, up to 227 inches by 227 inches. You can change the units in the document (and therefore of the artboard size) by choosing a different unit from the Edit > Preferences > Units & Undo dialog box.

• Select Use Print Setup (Windows) or Use Page Setup (Mac OS) to set the size of the artboard to match the page size set in the Print Setup (Windows) or Page Setup (Mac OS) dialog box. The size of the artboard then changes anytime you choose a new page size in the Print/Page Setup dialog box.

3 Click OK.

Note: The artboard displays the maximum printable area but does not define the size of the printed page. The printable area of the page is derived from the printer driver and ppd of the printing device. You can only change page size settings if your printer will accept custom page sizes.

To change the size of the page:

Choose File > Print Setup (Windows) or File > Page Setup (Mac OS) and select a page type in the dialog box.

Note: The imageable area and page size are not limitations when printing to imagesetters that handle large media. Imagesetters can typically print to the edge of the page. The page size used by an imagesetter may be larger than the page size specified in Illustrator, enabling you to print bleeds, for example, that run past the edge of the page.

Tiling artwork and adjusting page boundaries

The artboard's dimensions do not necessarily match the paper sizes used by printers. As a result, when you print a file, the program divides the artboard into one or more rectangles that correspond to the page size available on your printer. Dividing the artboard to fit a printer's available page size is called *tiling*. Tiling is also used when you set up your file to view and print multiple pages.

You can also adjust the placement of the printable area of the page to control how artwork is printed.

For more information, see "Tiling artwork and adjusting page boundaries" in online Help.

About imported artwork

Placing artwork from other applications, such as Adobe Photoshop, into Adobe Illustrator is easily performed using various Adobe Illustrator commands.

Illustrator can import many common graphic file formats, including EPS, CorelDRAW™, FreeHand™, GIF, JPEG, PICT, TIFF, DXF, Adobe PDF, and PostScript® Level 1. In addition to these common graphic file formats, Illustrator can use artwork in any file format supported by an Adobe Photoshop-compatible file format plug-in filter, including Kodak Photo CD™, PNG, and TGA.

File Format	Import Methods	Considerations
AI	Open	Opens all Illustrator format files.
EPS	Open, Place	Placed files may be linked or embedded.
Adobe PDF	Open, Place	Specify which page of file you want to use. Placed files may be linked or embedded.
Photoshop	Open, Place	Supports Photoshop 2.5 and later. Placed files may be linked or embedded. Drag and drop artwork directly from Photoshop.
PICT	Open, Place	Placed files may be linked or embedded.
WMF/EMF	Open, Place	Placed files will be embedded. Drag and drop artwork directly from Microsoft Office.
DXF/DWG	Open, Place	Supports DXF releases 13, 14, and 2000. Placed files will be embedded.
FreeHand	Open, Place	Supports FreeHand versions 4.0, 5.0, 5.5, 7.0, and 8.0. (Japanese version supported to version 5.5.) Placed files will be embedded.
CorelDRAW	Open	Supports CorelDRAW versions 5.0, 6.0, 7.0, and 8.0.
CGM	Open, Place	Supports CGM versions 1, 2, and 3. Placed files will be embedded.
All raster formats supported by Photoshop-compatible filters	Open, Place	Supports the following formats: Amiga IFF, BMP, Filmstrip, GIF 89a, Kodak Photo CD, JPEG, PCX, Pixar, PNG, TIFF, and TGA.
Scalable Vector Graphics (SVG)/SVGZ	Open, Place	Placed files will be embedded.

File Format	Import Methods	Considerations
Text formats	Open, Place	Supports the following formats: plain text, MS RTF, MS Word 6.0, 95, 97, 98, and 2000. Vertical Japanese text in RTF and Word files will be imported as horizontal text. Placed files will be embedded.

Opening and placing artwork

You can use the Clipboard and drag-and-drop importing to bring images into Illustrator. (See "Moving, copying, and deleting objects" on page 125.) However, two commands are most commonly used when importing artwork created by other applications:

• The Open command opens a file created by another application as a new Adobe Illustrator file.

• The Place command places an image in an existing Illustrator file in one of two ways. Depending on the file format, the Place command creates a link to an external file by default and does not include a copy of the file in the Illustrator file. You can also deselect the Link option in the Place dialog box, which embeds (includes) a copy of the file in the Illustrator file.

Your document's color mode (CMYK or RGB) does not change when you open or place a file that uses a different color mode. Colors in the imported file convert to the document's color mode.

Note: Adobe Illustrator does not color-manage imported grayscale images. If you import a grayscale image that had a color profile in Adobe Photoshop, for example, the profile is discarded when the image is imported into Illustrator.

Opening files

When you open a file created by another application, it becomes a new Adobe Illustrator file. Vector artwork in the file you open is converted to Illustrator paths, which can be modified using any Illustrator tool; bitmap images can be modified using transformation tools, such as scale and rotate, and using image filters from the Illustrator Filter menu. (See "About vector graphics and bitmap images" on page 67.)

Files that have been saved in Portable Document Format (PDF) can be opened as Adobe Illustrator documents, without losing the ability to edit artwork with Illustrator tools and commands. Artwork stored in PDF format can also be placed into Illustrator files, as described in "Importing EPS and PDF files into Illustrator" on page 75.

To open a file created by Photoshop:

1 Choose File > Open.

2 Locate and select a Photoshop file, and click OK.

3 In the Photoshop Import dialog box, choose a method to import Photoshop layers to Illustrator:

• Select the Convert Photoshop Layers to Objects option to create a single layer in Illustrator containing objects that correspond to each Photoshop layer or clipping path. Only one clipping path will be imported, even if multiple clipping paths exist in the original file. Any opacity masks that were applied to the Photoshop layers appear in the Transparency palette when you select the corresponding objects.

Because not all Photoshop features (such as adjustment layers and layer effects) are supported, the Convert Photoshop Layers to Objects option may result in an image with a slightly altered appearance. If you want the image to appear as close as possible to the original image, you should choose the Flatten Photoshop Layers to a Single Image option.

• Select the Flatten Photoshop Layers to a Single Image option to flatten all Photoshop layers into a single image, and place the image on Layer 1 in the Illustrator file. The converted file retains clipping paths but no individual objects. Transparency is retained as part of the main image, but is not editable.

To open a file created by another application:

1 Choose File > Open.

2 Locate and select the file you want to open. If you don't see the name of the file you want, the file is stored in a format that Illustrator can't read. See "About imported artwork" on page 72 for a complete list of all the file formats you can open.

3 Click Open.

Note: If you open an EPS file that contains fonts not installed on your system, font substitution will occur when you print.

To open a file that has recently been used:

Choose File > Open Recent Files, and select the filename from the list.

Placing files

The Place command places files from other applications into Illustrator. Files can be *embedded*, or included in, the Illustrator file, or they can be linked to the Illustrator file. *Linked* files remain independent of the Illustrator file, resulting in a smaller Illustrator file. Depending on a preference you set for updating links, the linked image in the Illustrator file may change when the artwork in the linked file changes.

By default, the Link option is selected in the Place dialog box. If you deselect the Link option, the artwork is embedded in the Adobe Illustrator file, resulting in a larger Illustrator file. The Links palette lets you identify, select, monitor, and update objects in the Illustrator artwork that are linked to external files. (See "Managing linked and embedded images" on page 76.)

Placed bitmap images can be modified using transformation tools and image filters; placed vector artwork is converted to Illustrator paths (embedded images only).

If you place a Photoshop file and deselect the Link option, the Photoshop Import dialog box appears. For information on options in the Photoshop Import dialog box, see "Opening files" on page 73.

To place and link files created by other applications:

1 Open the Illustrator file into which you want to place the artwork.

2 Choose File > Place.

3 Locate and select the file you want to place. If you don't see the name of the file you want, the file has been saved in a format that Illustrator cannot read.

4 Do one of the following:

• To create a link between the artwork file and the Illustrator file, make sure the Link option is selected in the Place dialog box.

• To embed the artwork in the Illustrator file, deselect the Link option in the Place dialog box.

5 Click Place. The artwork is placed into the Illustrator file as either a linked or an embedded image, depending on the option you selected in the Place dialog box.

Importing EPS and PDF files into Illustrator

You can use Adobe Illustrator to edit artwork that was imported as Encapsulated PostScript (EPS) and Adobe Portable Document Format (PDF) file types.

You can import PDF and EPS files using these commands:

• The Open command to open a PDF or EPS file as a new Illustrator file.

• The Place command to place a PDF or EPS file in the current layer in an existing Illustrator file.

Important: To place an EPS image containing a gradient mesh object as an embedded file (that is, the Link option is deselected in the Place dialog box), the file should be saved as an EPS Level 1 PostScript file.

To open a PDF or EPS file as a new Adobe Illustrator file:

1 Choose File > Open.

2 Select the file you want to open, and click Open. If the file does not appear, for Files of Type, choose All Formats (Windows) or Show All Files (Mac OS).

To place PDF or EPS artwork into an Adobe Illustrator file:

1 Open the Adobe Illustrator file into which you want to place the artwork.

2 Choose File > Place, select the file you want to place, and click Place.

Placing EPS or PDF files in Illustrator with the Link option selected in the Place dialog box does not allow you to modify the linked object within the Illustrator file. To convert the elements in an EPS or PDF file to Illustrator objects that can be modified, deselect the Link option in the Place dialog box. Deselecting the Link option when you place the EPS or PDF file embeds the file and lets you edit each part of the artwork as a discrete object. (See "Editing artwork contained in linked files" on page 79.)

3 If you are placing a page from a PDF file that contains multiple pages, select the page you want to place, and click OK.

4 Adjust the placed artwork as needed.

Important: *If you import an EPS color that has the same name as a color in your document but with a different definition, Illustrator displays an alert. Choose Use Linked file's color to replace the color in your document with the EPS color in the linked file. All objects using this color in your document will get updated appropriately. Choose Use document's color to leave the swatch as is and resolve all color conflicts using the document's color. The EPS preview cannot be changed, so the preview may be incorrect, but it will print to the correct plates. Checking "Apply to All" will resolve all color conflicts, using the definition either of the document or the linked file, depending on which option you choose.*

Turning preview images on or off

If a placed file with the Link option selected was not saved with a preview image in the application that created it, it will not be visible in Adobe Illustrator when it is placed. Instead, an outlined box containing two diagonal lines appears and defines the artwork's dimensions. The box is placed into the center of the active window, in front of all other artwork in the file, and is selected.

If a placed file was saved with a preview image in the application that created it, you can see it in Preview view, and you can choose to display a preview image in Outline view.

To turn on and off the display of preview images in Outline view:

1 Choose File > Document Setup. Then choose Artboard from the pop-up menu at the top left of the Document Setup dialog box.

2 Click Show Images in Outline, and then click OK.

Note: Placed images with the appropriate resource always display in Preview view, regardless of the Show Images in Outline setting.

Managing linked and embedded images

The Links palette lets you identify, select, monitor, and update images that are linked to external files, or images that are embedded in the Illustrator file. In addition, you can determine if an image's link to an external file is broken or missing, get information about linked or embedded image characteristics, and open a linked image's original file and application to edit the image.

You can also use the Links palette to replace a linked image with another linked image. When you replace a linked image, the new image adopts the size, placement, and transformation status of the original linked image.

If you are color-managing artwork in a document, embedded EPS images are part of the document and therefore color-managed when sent to a printing device. In contrast, linked images are not color-managed, even if color management is turned on for the rest of the document. (See "About color management" on page 199.)

Important: *Occasionally you may encounter a warning when printing an Illustrator document containing embedded EPS images. If the application cannot find the original EPS image, you will be prompted to extract the EPS image. Select the Extract option in the dialog box; the image will be extracted into the same directory as the current document. Although the embedded file does not preview in the document, the file will now print correctly.*

Specifying how to update links

You can set a preference to specify how to update linked images when the original files change.

To specify how to update links:

1 Choose Edit > Preferences > Files & Clipboard.

2 Choose an update method from the Update Links pop-up menu:

- Automatically to have Illustrator update linked images automatically when the original files are modified.

- Manually to leave linked images unchanged when the original files are modified. You can use the Links palette to identify linked images whose originals have been modified and to update these images. (See "Using the Links palette" on page 77.)

- Ask When Modified to display a dialog box when the original files are modified. In the dialog box, click Yes to update the linked image or click No to leave it unchanged.

Using the Links palette

All linked or embedded images in the file are listed in the Links palette. Linked images whose originals have been modified since the image was placed (and which have not been updated) are identified with an exclamation point icon (⚠); linked images whose original files are missing are identified with a stop sign icon (⊘).

You can use the Links palette to quickly convert linked images into embedded images, using the Embed Image command.

To display the Links palette:

Choose Window > Show Links. Each linked or embedded image is identified by name and by a thumbnail display.

To select one or more links:

Choose from the following options:

- Click a link to select it.

- Shift-click to select a continuous range of links.

- Ctrl-click (Windows) or Command-click (Mac OS) to select a noncontinuous range of links.

- Ctrl+Alt (Windows) or Command+Option (Mac OS) and then click in the palette window to select a link by typing its name.

To display link information:

Do one of the following:

- Double-click a link to bring up the Link Information dialog box.

- Select a link, and choose Information from the Links palette menu.

To go to a linked object and select it:

1 Select a link in the Links palette display.

2 Choose one of the following:

- Click the Go to Link button ( ) at the bottom of the palette.

- Choose Go to Link from the Links palette menu.

The page containing the link is displayed, and the linked image is selected.

To replace a link with a new linked image:

1 Select a link in the Links palette.

2 Choose one of the following:

- Click the Replace Link button ( ) at the bottom of the palette.

- Choose Replace Link from the Links palette menu.

3 Select the file to replace the linked image in the Place dialog box, and click OK. The new image retains the size, placement, and transformation characteristics of the image that it replaced.

To update a link with the most recent data from the linked file:

1 Select one or more links in the Links palette display.

2 Choose one of the following to refresh the link with the most current version of the original file:

- Click the Update Link button ( ) at the bottom of the palette.

- Choose Update Link from the Links palette menu.

You can set a preference to automatically update links. See "Specifying how to update links" on page 77.

To change a linked image into an embedded image:

1 Select a linked image in the Links palette display.

2 Choose Embed Image from the Links palette menu.

Modifying the Links palette display

You can change the way that links are displayed in the Links palette using commands in the Links palette menu.

The palette can display icons of the links, or show different sized thumbnail images of the links. In addition, you can sort the display to show only those links that have missing or broken links with the original file, or those links that have been modified since the last update.

To change the links display icons or thumbnails:

1 Choose Palette Options from the Links palette menu.

2 In the Palette Options dialog box, select the type of icon or thumbnail you want displayed.

To sort the links display by name, kind, or status:

1 Select all or some of the links to sort in the Links palette display.

2 Choose one of the following from the Links palette menu to customize the links display by sorting:

• Sort by Names to alphabetize the links display.

• Sort by Kind to sort the display according to the type of file (for example, all JPEG files, all GIF files, all EPS files, and so on).

• Sort by Status to sort the display according to the linked or embedded status. Embedded images are listed first, followed by linked images.

To display links according to link type:

Choose one of the following from the Links palette menu:

• Show All to display all links in the file.

• Show Missing to display only links with missing or broken connections with the original file.

• Show Modified to display only links that have been changed after the last time the link was updated.

• Show Embedded to display only embedded images.

Editing artwork contained in linked files

When you make changes to a linked image using the application that created it, the changes are applied to the Illustrator file when the link is updated. (See "Specifying how to update links" on page 77.)

Note that if you replace a linked image with another image, any transformation attributes applied to it, such as scaling, rotating, or shearing, are retained and applied to the new image.

To edit a linked object from within the original file:

Do one of the following:

• Select the linked object, and choose Edit > Edit Original.

• Select a link in the Links palette display, and click the Edit Original button ( ) at the bottom of the palette.

• Select a link in the Links palette display, and choose Edit Original from the Links palette menu.

3

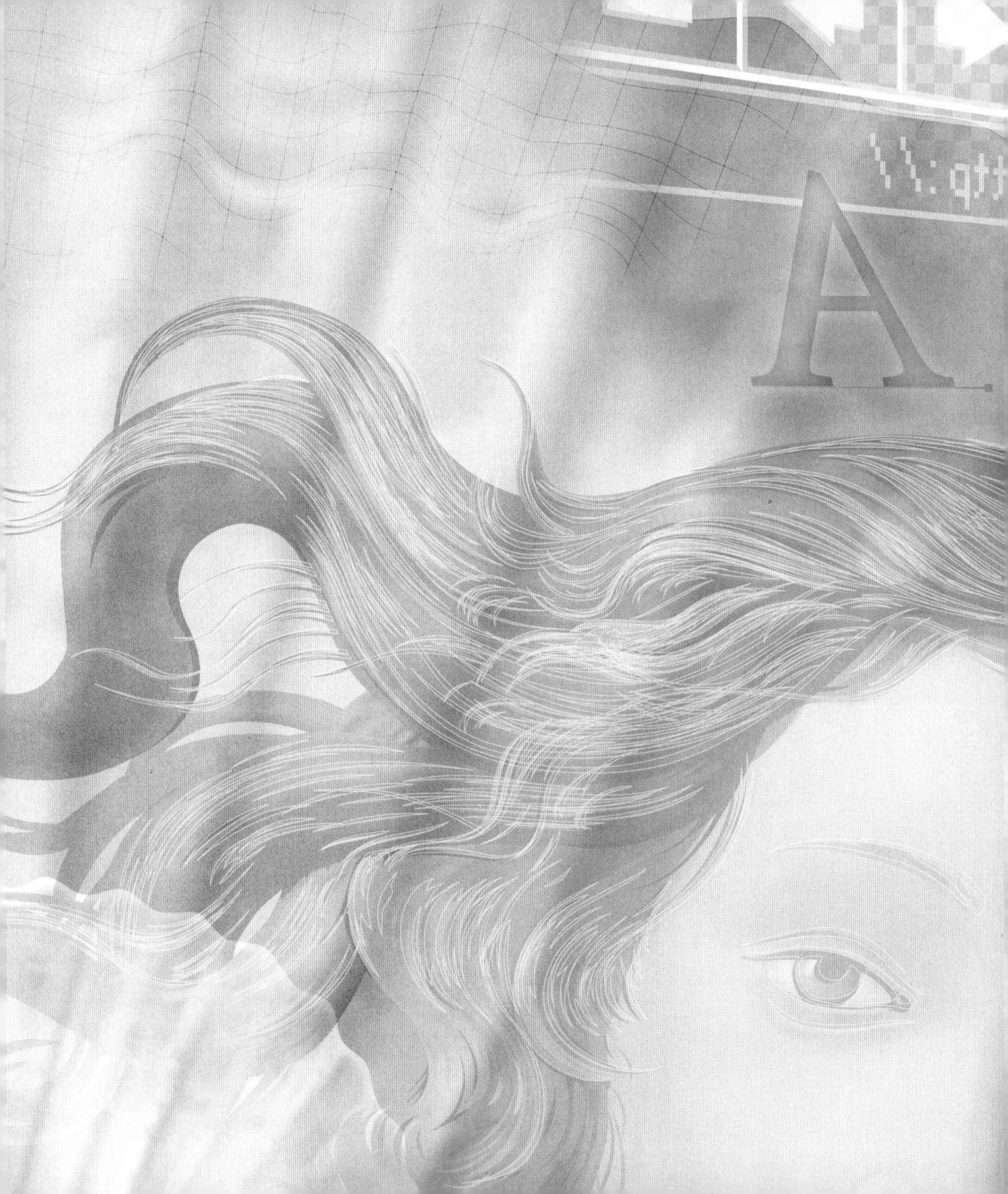
A

Chapter 3: Drawing

You draw and modify paths using a set of drawing tools and techniques common to Adobe Illustrator, InDesign, and Photoshop. Use Adobe Illustrator to draw paths or InDesign to draw paths, and freely copy and paste them between programs.

About paths

A path is made up of one or more straight or curved *segments*. The beginning and end of each segment is marked by *anchor points*, which work like pins holding wire in place. You change the shape of a path by editing its anchor points. You can control curves by dragging the *direction points* at the end of *direction lines* that appear at anchor points.

A path is either *open*, like an arc, or *closed*, like a circle. For an open path, the starting and ending anchor points for the path are called *endpoints*.

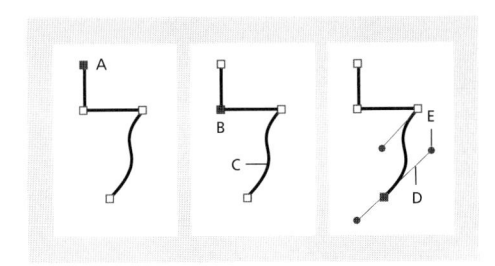

A. Selected (solid) endpoint B. Selected anchor point C. Curved path segment D. Direction line E. Direction point

Paths can have two kinds of anchor points—corner points and smooth points. At a *corner point*, a path abruptly changes direction. At a *smooth point*, path segments are connected as a continuous curve. You can draw a path using any combination of corner and smooth points. If you draw the wrong kind of point, you can always change it.

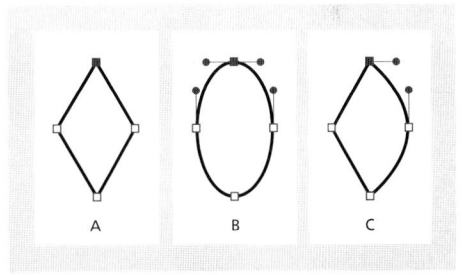

A. Four corner points B. Same point positions using smooth points C. Same point positions combining corner and smooth points

Don't confuse corner and smooth points with straight and curved segments. A corner point can connect any two straight or curved segments, while a smooth point always connects two curved segments.

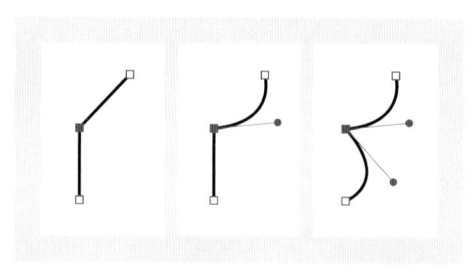

A corner point can connect both straight segments and curved segments.

Changing a tool pointer

You can change the appearance of the pointer from the tool pointer to a cross hair for more precise control. When the pointer is a cross hair, more of your artwork is visible. This is convenient when you're doing detailed drawing and editing.

To make a drawing tool pointer appear as a cross hair:

Do one of the following:

• Choose Edit > Preferences > General. Select Use Precise Cursors, and click OK.

• Press Caps Lock before you begin drawing with the tool.

Drawing and editing freeform paths

When you want to draw and edit freeform paths, use the pencil tool. You can also smooth out and erase segments of a freeform path with the smooth tool and erase tool.

Anchor points are set down as you draw with the pencil tool; you do not determine where they are positioned. However, you can adjust them once the path is complete. The number of anchor points set down is determined by the length and complexity of the path and by the tolerance values set in the Pencil Tool Preferences or Smooth Tool Preferences dialog box for either tool.

Note: You can draw and edit brushed paths with the paintbrush tool by using the same methods as for paths drawn with the pencil tool.

Drawing and editing with the pencil tool

The pencil tool lets you draw open and closed paths as if you were drawing with a pencil on paper. It is most useful for fast sketching or creating a hand-drawn look. Once you draw a path, you can immediately change it if needed.

To draw a freeform path with the pencil tool:

1 Select the pencil tool ( ).

2 Position the pointer where you want the path to begin, and drag to draw a path. The pencil tool displays a small *x* to indicate drawing a freeform path.

As you drag, a dotted line follows the pointer. Anchor points appear at both ends of the path and at various points along it. The path takes on the current paint attributes, and the path remains selected by default.

3 To continue the existing freeform path, make sure the path is selected, and then position the pencil tip on an endpoint of the path and drag.

To draw a closed path with the pencil tool:

1 Select the pencil tool.

2 Position the pointer where you want the path to begin, and start dragging to draw a path.

3 As you drag, hold down Alt (Windows) or Option (Mac OS). The pencil tool displays a small loop, and its eraser is solid, to indicate drawing a closed path.

4 When the path is the size and shape you want, release the mouse button (but not the Alt or Option key). After the path closes, release the Alt or Option key.

To connect a new path to an existing path:

Ctrl-drag (Windows) or Command-drag (Mac OS) from the current path onto the endpoint of the other path.

To change a path with the pencil tool:

1 If the path you want to change is not selected, select it with the selection tool ( ). Or Ctrl-click (Windows) or Command-click (Mac OS) the path to select it.

2 Position the pencil tool on or near the path to redraw, and drag the tool until the path is the desired shape.

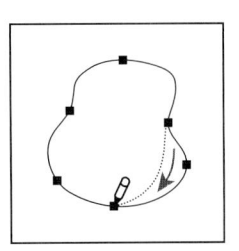

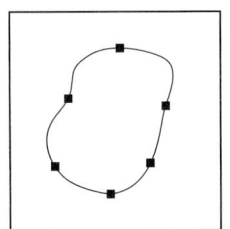

Using the pencil tool to edit a closed shape

Note: *Depending on where you begin to redraw the path and in which direction you drag, you may get unexpected results. For example, you may unintentionally change a closed path to an open path, change an open path to a closed path, or lose a portion of a shape.*

Smoothing the path with the smooth tool

The smooth tool lets you smooth out an existing stroke or section of a path. The smooth tool retains the original shape of the path as much as possible.

To use the smooth tool:

1 If the path to smooth is not selected, select it with the selection tool ( ). Or Ctrl-click (Windows) or Command-click (Mac OS) the path to select it.

2 Do one of the following:

• Select the smooth tool ( ).

• When the pencil or paintbrush tool is selected, hold down Alt (Windows) or Option (Mac OS) to change the pencil to the smooth tool.

3 Drag the tool along the length of the path segment you want to smooth out. The modified stroke or path may have fewer anchor points than the original.

4 Continue smoothing until the stroke or path is the desired smoothness.

Erasing the path with the erase tool

The erase tool lets you remove a portion of an existing path or stroke. You can use the erase tool on paths (including brushed paths), but not on text or meshes.

To use the erase tool:

1 Select the erase tool ( ).

2 Drag the tool along the length of the path segment you want to erase (not across the path). For best results, use a single, smooth, dragging motion.

Anchor points are added to the ends of the new paths.

Setting preferences for tools

You can set preferences for the pencil tool and smooth tool. The preferences include tolerances that control how sensitive the pencil and smooth tools are to the movement of your mouse or graphics-tablet stylus, and whether you want the path to remain selected after you draw it.

The tolerance is calculated in number of pixels. The larger the number of pixels you specify, the smoother and less complex are the paths.

Note: You can also set preferences for the paintbrush tool. (See "Drawing and editing brushed paths" on page 101.)

To set preferences for the pencil tool and smooth tool:

1 Double-click the pencil tool ( ) or smooth tool ( ).

2 Use the Fidelity and Smoothness sliders or enter values in the text boxes:

• Fidelity controls the distance (in pixels) in which curves can stray from the smoothed mouse or tablet data when using the tool. The lower the fidelity value, the more angular the curves; the higher the value, the smoother the curves.

• Smoothness controls the amount of smoothing (by percentage) applied when you use the tool. The lower the smoothness value, the coarser the path appears; the higher the value, the smoother the path.

3 To keep the path selected after you draw it, select Keep Selected. This option is selected by default.

4 To edit a path only when you are within a certain distance of it, select Edit Selected Paths, and enter a distance.

5 Click OK.

Drawing with the pen tool

Use the pen tool to draw a path that you can't draw using the simpler drawing tools. The pen tool lets you create straight lines and smooth, flowing curves with great precision.

Drawing straight segments

The simplest path you can draw with the pen tool is a straight line, made by clicking the pen tool to create two anchor points. By continuing to click, you create a path made of straight line segments connected by corner points.

To draw straight segments with the pen tool:

1 Select the pen tool ( ).

2 Position the tip of the pen point where you want the straight segment to begin, and click to define the first anchor point (do not drag). The anchor point remains selected (solid) until you add the next point.

Note: The first segment you draw will not be visible until you click a second anchor point. Also, if direction lines appear, you've accidentally dragged the pen tool; choose Edit > Undo and click again.

3 Click again where you want the segment to end. (Shift-click to constrain the segment's angle to multiples of 45 degrees.) This creates another anchor point.

4 Continue clicking the pen tool to create additional straight segments.

The last anchor point you add appears as a solid square, indicating that it is selected. Existing anchor points become deselected as you add more anchor points.

5 Complete the path by doing one of the following:

• To close a path, position the pen pointer over the first (hollow) anchor point. A small loop appears next to the pen tool ( ) when it is positioned correctly. Click to close the path.

• To leave the path open, Ctrl-click (Windows) or Command-click (Mac OS) anywhere away from all objects, or choose Edit > Deselect All, or select a different tool in the toolbox.

About direction lines and direction points

Before you draw and modify curved segments with the pen tool, it's important to understand two elements that are associated with anchor points on curves. When you use the direct-selection tool to select an anchor point connecting curved segments, the segments display *direction lines* which end in *direction points*. The angle and length of the direction lines determine the shape and size of the curved segments. Moving the direction points reshapes the curves. Direction lines don't print.

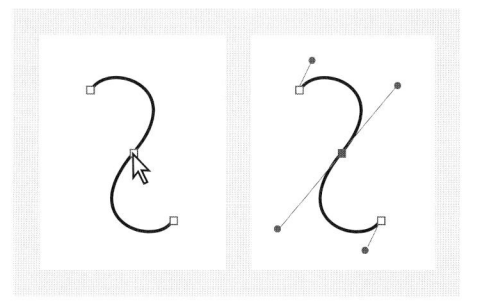

After selecting an anchor point (left), direction lines appear on any curved segments connected by the anchor point (right).

A smooth point always has two direction lines which move together as a single, straight unit. When you drag the direction point of either direction line on a smooth point, both direction lines move simultaneously, maintaining a continuous curve at that anchor point.

In comparison, a corner point can have two, one, or no direction lines, depending on whether it joins two, one, or no curved segments, respectively. Corner point direction lines maintain the corner by using different angles. When you drag a direction point on a corner point's direction line, the other direction line, if present, does not move.

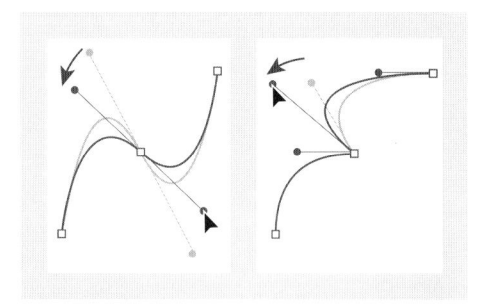

Adjusting direction lines on a smooth point (left) and a corner point (right)

Direction lines are always tangent to (perpendicular to the radius of) the curve at the anchor points. The angle of each direction line determines the slope of the curve, and the length of each direction line determines the height, or depth, of the curve.

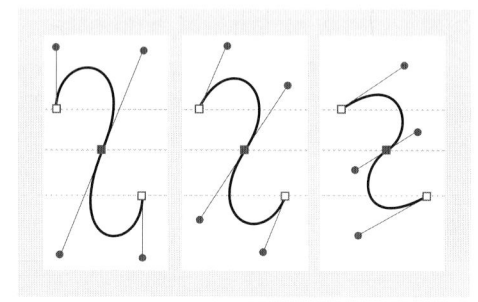

Moving and resizing direction lines changes the slopes of curves.

Drawing curved segments

You create curves by using the pen tool to add anchor points where a curve changes direction, and to drag the direction points that shape the curves.

Curves are easier to edit and your system can display and print them faster if you draw them using as few anchor points as possible. Using too many points can also introduce unwanted bumps in a curve. Instead, draw widely spaced anchor points, and practice shaping curves by adjusting the length and angles of the direction lines.

To draw a curved segment:

1 Select the pen tool ( ).

2 Position the pen tip where you want the curve to begin. Hold down the mouse button. The first anchor point appears, and the pen tip changes to an arrowhead ( ).

3 Drag to set the slope of the curve segment you're creating. In general, extend the direction line about one third of the distance to the next anchor point you plan to draw. Shift-drag to constrain the direction line to multiples of 45 degrees.

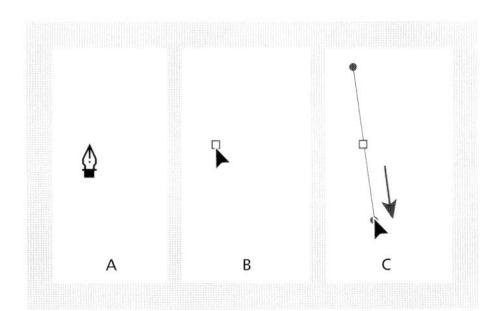

A. Positioning pen tool B. Starting to drag (mouse button pressed) C. Dragging to extend direction lines

4 Release the mouse button.

Note: The first segment will not be visible until you draw the second anchor point.

5 Position the pen tool where you want the curve segment to end, and then do one of the following:

- To create a "C"-shaped curve, drag in a direction opposite to the previous direction line.

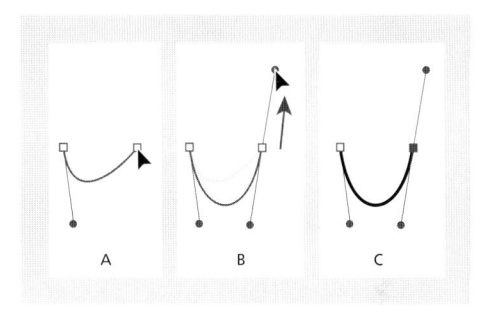

A. Starting to drag second smooth point B. Dragging away from previous direction line, creating a "C" curve C. Result after releasing mouse button

- To create an "S"-shaped curve, drag in the same direction as the previous direction line.

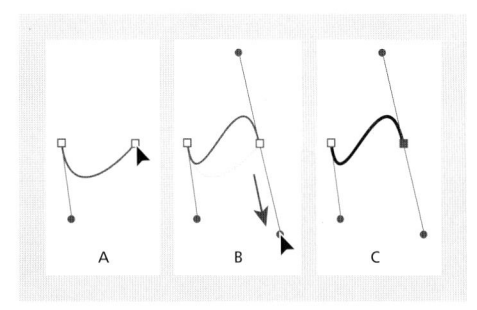

A. Starting to drag new smooth point B. Dragging in same direction as previous direction line, creating an "S" curve C. Result after releasing mouse button

6 Continue dragging the pen tool from different locations to create additional smooth points.

7 Complete the path by doing one of the following:

• To close the path, position the pen tool over the first (hollow) anchor point. A small loop appears next to the pen tip when it is positioned correctly. Click or drag to close the path.

• To leave the path open, Ctrl-click (Windows) or Command-click (Mac OS) anywhere away from all objects, or choose Edit > Deselect All, or select a different tool in the toolbox.

Mixing curves, corners, and straight segments as you draw

You can freely alter point types and direction lines as you draw a path. This is useful for interactively drawing straight and curved segments on a single path, or when you want to draw two curved segments that are connected by a corner point.

To draw a straight segment followed by a curved segment:

1 Using the pen tool ( ), click corner points in two locations to create a straight segment.

2 Position the pen tool over the selected endpoint. A convert-anchor-point icon ( ) appears next to the pen tool when it is positioned correctly. Drag a direction point at an end of the direction line that appears, to set the slope of the curved segment you'll create next.

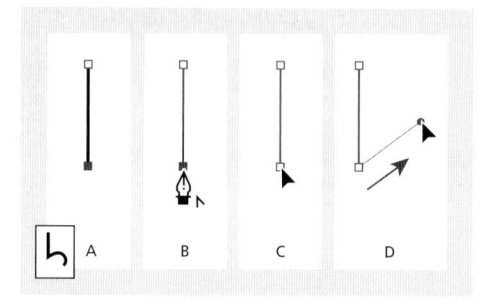

A. Straight segment completed B. Positioning pen tool over endpoint C. Beginning to drag D. Dragging direction point

3 Click or drag the third anchor point to complete the curve.

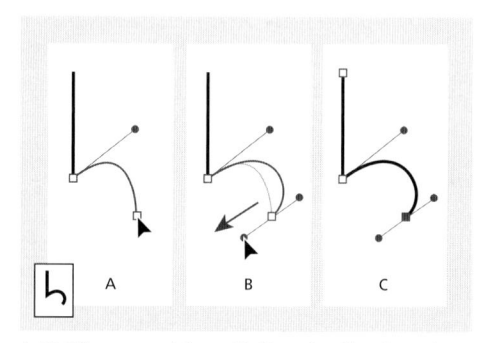

A. Holding pen tool down B. Dragging direction point C. New curve segment completed

To draw a curved segment followed by a straight segment:

1 Using the pen tool, drag to create the first smooth point of the curved segment.

2 Reposition the pen tool where you want the curved segment to end, drag to complete the curve, and release the mouse button.

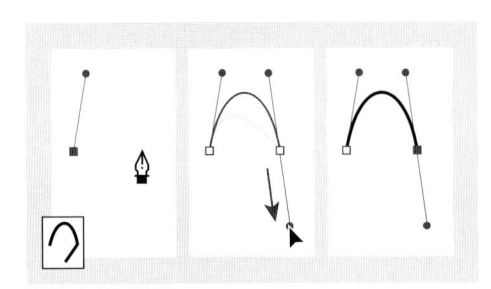

3 Position the pen tool over the selected endpoint. A convert-anchor-point icon ( ) appears next to the pen tool when it is positioned correctly. Click the anchor point to convert the smooth point to a corner point.

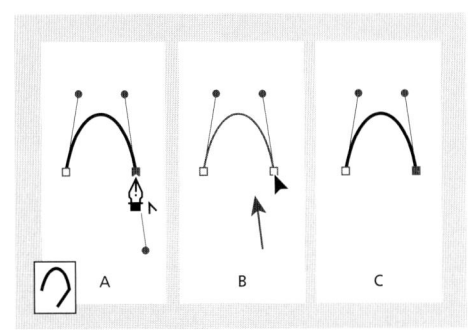

A. Positioning pen tool over existing endpoint B. Clicking endpoint C. Result after clicking

4 Click the next corner point to complete the straight segment.

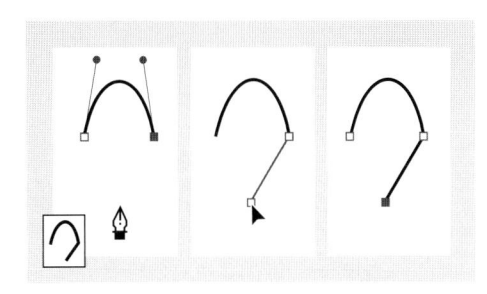

To draw two curved segments connected by a corner:

1 Using the pen tool, drag to create the first smooth point of a curved segment.

2 Reposition the pen tool, drag to create a curve with a second smooth point, and then press Alt (Windows) or Option (Mac OS) as you drag the direction point to set the slope of the next curve. Then release the key and the mouse button. This converts the smooth point to a corner point by splitting the direction lines.

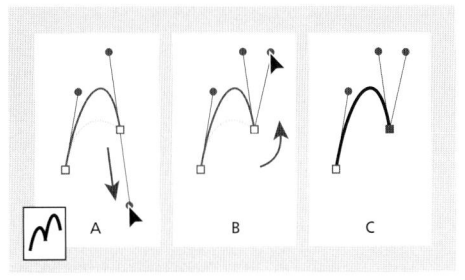

A. Dragging a new smooth point B. Pressing Alt/Option to split direction lines while dragging, and swinging direction point up C. Result after releasing mouse button

3 Reposition the pen tool where you want the second curved segment to end, and drag a new smooth point to complete the second curved segment.

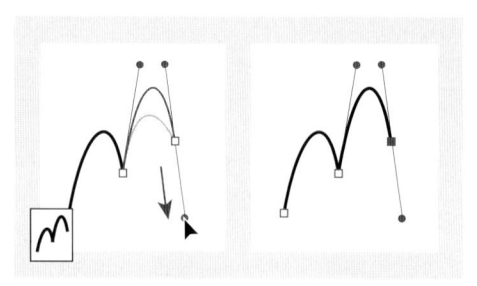

Dragging a new smooth point (left) to complete the second segment (right)

Adjusting path segments

You can change the shape of a path by adding, deleting, or moving the path's anchor points. To adjust a curved segment, you move one or more of its anchor points or direction points. You can also adjust a path by converting smooth points to corner points and vice versa.

Adding, deleting, and converting anchor points

You can add or delete anchor points on any path. Additional anchor points can give you more control over the path, or extend an open path. You can also connect two open paths. Similarly, you can delete anchor points to change the shape of a path or to simplify the path. It's a good idea to delete any unnecessary points to reduce the complexity of the path.

You can use the Path Simplify command to remove extra anchor points on a path without changing the path's shape. (See "Simplifying paths" on page 95.)

The pen tool automatically changes to the add-anchor-point tool or the delete-anchor-point tool as you position it over a selected path. The add-anchor-point tool adds the necessary type of point (corner or smooth) to preserve the existing shape of the path.

Note: You must delete anchor points by using the delete-anchor-point tool or the Path Simplify command. The Delete, Backspace, and Clear keys and the Edit > Cut or Edit > Clear commands always delete the entire path even if you select an anchor point on the path.

To add or delete an anchor point:

1 Using the direct-selection tool ( ), select the paths to which you want to add or delete anchor points.

2 Select the pen tool ( ), add-anchor-point tool ( ), or delete-anchor-point tool ( ). All of these tools share the same location in the toolbox; if necessary, position the pointer over the pen tool and drag to choose the tool you want.

3 Do one of the following:

• To add an anchor point using either the pen tool or the add-anchor-point tool ( ), position the pointer over a path segment and click.

• To delete an anchor point using either the pen tool or the delete-anchor-point tool, position the pointer over an anchor point and click.

To extend an open path or connect two open paths:

1 Using the pen tool, position the pointer over the endpoint of the open path you want to extend. A small slash appears next to the pointer ( ) when it's precisely positioned over the endpoint.

2 Click the endpoint.

3 Do one of the following:

• To create a corner point, position the pen tool where you want to end the new segment, and click. If you are extending a path that ends at a smooth point, the new segment will be curved by the existing direction line.

• To create a smooth point, position the pen tool where you want to end the new curved segment, and drag.

• To connect the path to another open path, click an endpoint on the other path. When you position the pen tool over the other path's endpoint, a small hollow point ( ) appears next to the pointer when it's precisely positioned.

To override automatic switching to the add- or delete-anchor-point tools:

Hold down Shift as you position the pen tool over the selected path or an anchor point. This is useful when you want to start a new path on top of an existing path. To prevent Shift from constraining the pen tool, release Shift before you release the mouse button.

To turn off automatic adding or deleting of anchor points:

1 Choose Edit > Preferences > General, or press Ctrl+K (Windows) or Command+K (Mac OS).

2 Under General Options, click Disable Auto Add/Delete to turn off the option. Then click OK.

To add anchor points using the Add Anchor Points command:

With the selection tool ( ), select the object and choose Object > Path > Add Anchor Points.

To convert between smooth points and corner points using the convert-anchor-point tool:

1 Using the direct-selection tool, select the path you want to modify.

To switch to the convert-anchor-point tool while the pen tool is selected, hold down Alt (Windows) or Option (Mac OS). With the convert-anchor-point tool selected, press Ctrl (Windows) or Command (Mac OS) to use the previous selection tool.

2 Select the convert-anchor-point tool.

3 Position the convert-anchor-point tool over the anchor point you want to convert, and do one of the following:

- To convert a corner point to a smooth point, drag a direction point out of the corner point.

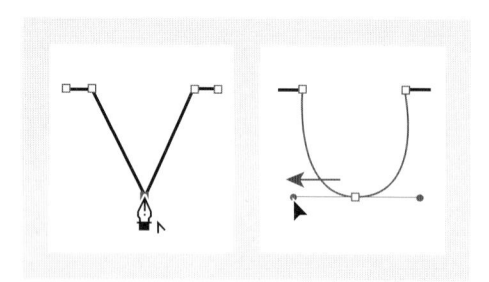

Dragging direction point out of a corner point to create a smooth point

- To convert a smooth point to a corner point without direction lines, click a smooth point.

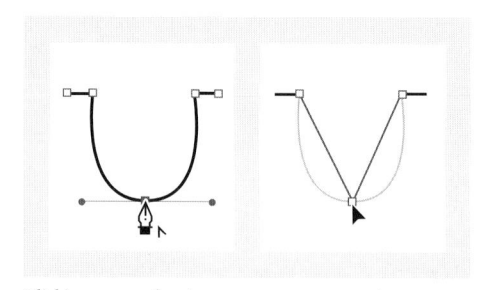

Clicking a smooth point to create a corner point

- To convert a corner point without direction lines to a corner point with independent direction lines, first drag a direction point out of a corner point (making it a smooth point with direction lines). Release the mouse button only (don't release any keys you may have pressed to activate the convert-anchor-point tool), and then drag either direction point.

- To convert a smooth point to a corner point with independent direction lines, drag either direction point.

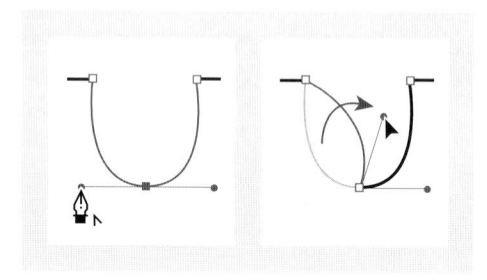

Converting a smooth point to a corner point

To temporarily switch from the convert-anchor-point tool to the last used selection tool, press Ctrl (Windows) or Command (Mac OS).

Adjusting straight and curved segments

You can modify the shape of a path by moving any of its anchor points or by moving the direction points of direction lines attached to a curve segment. Editing existing segments is slightly different from drawing them. Keep the following guidelines in mind as you adjust existing segments:

- If an anchor point connects two segments, moving that anchor point always changes both segments.

- When drawing with the pen tool, you can temporarily activate the direct-selection tool by holding down Ctrl (Windows) or Command (Mac OS) so that you can adjust segments you've already drawn.

• When you draw a smooth point with the pen tool, dragging the direction point changes the length of the direction line on both sides of the point. However, when you edit an existing smooth point with the direct-selection tool, you change the length of the direction line only on the side you're dragging.

To adjust a straight segment:

With the direct-selection tool ( ), drag the anchor point on either end of a segment. Shift-drag to constrain the adjustment to multiples of 45 degrees.

If you're simply trying to make a rectangle wider or narrower, it's easier to select it with the selection tool and resize it using one of the handles on the sides of its bounding box.

To adjust a curved segment:

1 Using the direct-selection tool ( ), select the anchor point on either end of a curved segment. Direction lines appear on the anchor point and on the adjacent anchor points, if present (some curved segments use just one direction line).

2 Do one of the following:

• Drag the anchor point. Shift-drag to constrain movement to multiples of 45 degrees.

• Drag a direction point. If you're adjusting a smooth point's direction lines, both direction lines revolve around the anchor point. Shift-drag to constrain the direction line angle to multiples of 45 degrees.

To split the direction lines of a smooth point, use the convert-anchor-point tool to drag them.

Using the reshape tool

The reshape tool lets you select one or more anchor points and sections of paths and then lets you adjust the selected points and paths globally. You can use the reshape tool to adjust paths containing many points while keeping the overall detail of the path intact. For example, if you have a drawing of a leaf with scallops along both edges, the reshape tool allows you to bend the leaf, keeping its overall smoothness, while retaining the scallops.

For more information on the reshape tool, see "Using the reshape tool" in online Help.

Simplifying paths

The Path Simplify command removes extra anchor points from a path without changing the shape of the path.

To simplify a path:

1 Select the path.

2 Choose Object > Path > Simplify.

3 For Curve Precision, enter a value between 0% and 100% to set how closely the simplified path should follow the original path. A higher percentage creates more points and a closer fit. Any existing anchor points are ignored except for endpoints of a curve and corner points (unless you enter a value for Angle Threshold).

4 For Angle Threshold, enter a value between 0 and 180 degrees to control the smoothness of corners. If the angle of a corner point is less than the angle threshold, the corner point is not changed. This option helps keep corners sharp, even if the value for Curve Precision is low.

5 Choose any of the following options:

• Straight Lines to create straight lines between the object's original anchor points. Corner points are removed if they have an angle greater than the value set in Angle Threshold.

• Show Original to show the original path behind the simplified path.

• Preview to show a preview of the simplified path and list the number of points in the original and simplified paths.

Splitting paths with the scissors tool

You may want to split paths that you have already created or that were created using the auto trace tool. Using the scissors tool, you can split an open path into two paths and split a closed path so that it becomes one or more open paths. You cannot split a type path.

To split a path and adjust it:

1 Select the path to see its current anchor points. (See "Selecting objects" on page 121.)

2 Select the scissors tool (✀).

3 Click the path where you want to split it.

When you split the path in the middle of a segment, two new endpoints are coincident (one on top of the other), and one endpoint is selected.

When you split the path at an anchor point, a new anchor point appears on top of the original anchor point, and one anchor point is selected.

4 Use the direct-selection tool (▶) to adjust the new anchor point or path segment.

Averaging anchor points

The Average command lets you move two or more anchor points (on the same path or on different paths) to a position that is the average of their current locations.

To average anchor points:

1 Use the direct-selection tool (▶) to select two or more anchor points. (See "Selecting objects" on page 121.)

2 Choose Object > Path > Average.

3 Choose to average along both axes, or the horizontal (x) axis only, or the vertical (y) axis only, and click OK.

Joining endpoints

The Join command connects the endpoints of an open path to create a closed path or joins the endpoints of two open paths.

If you join two coincident endpoints (endpoints on top of each other), they are replaced with a single anchor point. If you join two noncoincident endpoints, a path is drawn between the two points.

To join two endpoints:

1 Use the direct-selection tool ( ) to select the endpoints. (See "Selecting objects" on page 121.) If the endpoints are coincident (on top of each other), drag a marquee through both endpoints to select them.

2 Choose Object > Path > Join. A line is drawn, joining the two endpoints.

3 If the endpoints are coincident, select the Corner option (the default) or the Smooth option to specify the type of join you want.

4 Click OK.

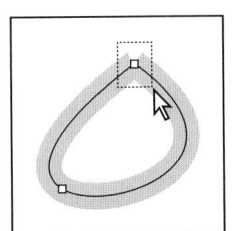

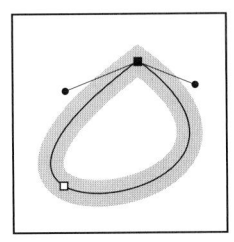

Drag a marquee through the coincident anchor points to select them, and choose the Join command.

Drawing shapes

You can create many objects in Adobe Illustrator by starting with basic shapes. The tools in Illustrator let you easily create rectangles, ellipses, polygons, spirals, and stars.

Drawing rectangles and ellipses

Adobe Illustrator provides two rectangle tools and one ellipse tool that let you quickly create these common graphic objects:

- The rectangle, rounded-rectangle, and ellipse tools let you draw rectangles (including squares) and ellipses (including circles) by dragging from one corner of the rectangle or edge of the ellipse to the opposite corner or edge.

- When a rectangle tool or the ellipse tool is selected, hold down Alt (Windows) or Option (Mac OS) to draw rectangles and ellipses by dragging from the center of the rectangle or ellipse outward.

When you create an object with a rectangle or the ellipse tool, a *center point* appears in the object. You can use this point to drag the object or to align the object with other elements in your artwork. The center point can be made visible or invisible, but it cannot be deleted.

To create a rectangle or ellipse by dragging from an edge:

1 Select the rectangle tool (□), the rounded-rectangle tool (◻), or the ellipse tool (○).

2 Position the pointer at one corner or edge of the shape you want to create, and drag diagonally until the shape is the desired size.

3 As you drag, you can do either of the following:

- To constrain the tool to multiples of 45 degrees, creating squares with the rectangle tool and circles with the ellipse tool, Shift-drag.

- To move a rectangle or ellipse as you draw it, hold down the spacebar.

To adjust corners of a rounded rectangle as you draw:

1 Select the rounded-rectangle tool.

2 Position the pointer where you want the rectangle to begin, and start dragging diagonally.

3 As you drag, you can do any of the following:

• Press or hold down Up Arrow or Down Arrow to change the corner radius. When the corners are the desired roundness, release Up Arrow or Down Arrow.

• Press Left Arrow to change to the minimum radius (most angular corners).

• Press Right Arrow to change to the maximum radius (most rounded corners).

4 Continue dragging with the rectangle tool until the rectangle is the desired size.

To create a rectangle or ellipse by dragging from the center:

1 Press Alt (Windows) or Option (Mac OS) with the rectangle tool, rounded-rectangle tool, or ellipse tool selected.

2 Position the pointer where you want the center of the shape to be, and drag diagonally to any corner or edge until the shape is the desired size. Shift-drag to constrain the tool to multiples of 45 degrees.

To draw a rectangle or ellipse by specifying dimensions:

1 Select a rectangle tool or the ellipse tool.

2 Click in the artwork to set the origin from which you want to create the shape. To draw rectangles and ellipses from the center of the point of origin, Alt-click (Windows) or Option-click (Mac OS).

By default, the Rectangle and Ellipse dialog boxes display the dimensions of the last rectangle or ellipse drawn. The unit of measure is determined by the unit of measure set in the Document Setup or Units & Undo Preferences dialog box.

3 In the Width text box, enter the width you want the shape to be.

4 In the Height text box, enter the height you want the shape to be, and click OK.

To create a square or circle, enter a value in the Width text box and then click the word Height; this copies the width value to the Height text box.

If you are drawing a rounded rectangle, enter the corner radius value you want the rectangle to have. The corner radius value represents the radius of a hypothetical circle drawn in the corner of the rectangle or square. The default corner radius is 12 points. A corner radius of 0 creates square corners.

Note: The corner style of the rectangle or square you draw is determined by the corner radius value you specify in either the Rectangle or General Preferences dialog box. Specifying a corner radius value in either dialog box updates the value in the other dialog box.

To display or hide the center points:

1 Choose Window > Show Attributes.

2 Click either the Show Center button (⊡) or the Don't Show Center button (☐).

Drawing polygons

The polygon tool draws an object with a specified number of sides of equal length, each side being the same distance from the center of the object.

To draw a polygon by dragging:

1 Select the polygon tool ( ).

2 Position the pointer at the center of the polygon you want to create, and drag until the polygon is the desired size.

3 As you drag, do any of the following:

• Drag the pointer in an arc to rotate the polygon.

• Shift-drag to constrain the tool to multiples of 45 degrees or to the angle specified in the Constrain Angle text box in the General Preferences dialog box.

• Hold down the spacebar to move the polygon.

• Press or hold down Up Arrow or Down Arrow to add or delete sides to the polygon.

To draw a polygon by specifying dimensions:

1 Select the polygon tool.

2 Click where you want to place the center of the polygon.

By default, the Polygon dialog box displays the dimensions of the last polygon you drew. The unit of measure is determined by the unit of measure set in the Document Setup or Units & Undo Preferences dialog box.

3 In the Radius text box, enter the distance from the center point to each line's endpoint.

4 Click the arrows or enter the number of sides in the Sides text box, and click OK.

Drawing spirals

The spiral tool creates a spiral-shaped object of a given radius and number of winds; that is, the number of turns that the spiral completes from start to finish.

To draw a spiral by dragging:

1 Select the spiral tool ( ).

2 Position the pointer at the center of the spiral you want to create, and drag until the spiral is the desired size.

3 As you drag, you can do any of the following:

• Drag the pointer in an arc to rotate the spiral.

• Shift-drag to constrain the tool to multiples of 45 degrees or to the angle specified in the Constrain Angle text box in the General Preferences dialog box.

• Hold down the spacebar to move the spiral.

• Press or hold down Up Arrow or Down Arrow to add or delete winds.

To draw a spiral by specifying dimensions:

1 Select the spiral tool, and click where you want to place the center of the spiral.

By default, the Spiral dialog box displays the dimensions of the last spiral you drew. The unit of measure is determined by the unit of measure set in the Document Setup or Units & Undo Preferences dialog box.

2 In the Radius text box, enter the distance from the center to the outermost point in the spiral.

3 In the Decay text box, enter the amount by which each wind of the spiral should decrease relative to the previous wind.

4 Click the arrows or enter the number of segments in the Segments text box. Each full wind of the spiral consists of four segments.

5 For Style, select the counterclockwise or clockwise option to specify the direction of the spiral, and click OK.

Drawing stars

The star tool creates a star-shaped object with a given number of points and size.

To draw a star by dragging:

1 Select the star tool (☆).

2 Position the pointer at the center of the star you want to create, and drag until the star is the desired size.

3 As you drag, you can do any of the following:

• Drag the pointer in an arc to rotate the star.

• Shift-drag to constrain the tool to multiples of 45 degrees.

• Hold down Ctrl (Windows) or Command (Mac OS) to hold the inner radius constant.

• Hold down Alt (Windows) or Option (Mac OS) to keep the sides of the star straight.

• Hold down the spacebar to move the star.

• Press or hold down Up Arrow or Down Arrow to add or delete sides to the star.

To draw a star by specifying dimensions:

1 Select the star tool.

2 Click where you want to place the center of the star. By default, the Star dialog box displays the dimensions of the last star you drew. The unit of measure is determined by the unit of measure set in the Document Setup or Units & Undo Preferences dialog box.

3 In the Radius 1 text box, enter the distance from the center to the innermost points.

4 In the Radius 2 text box, enter the distance from the center to the outermost points.

5 Click the arrows or enter the number of sides to the star in the Points text box, and click OK.

Drawing graphs

The graph tools and commands let you display and compare data visually. Once you have created a graph, you can customize it. You can create a number of different graph types: column, stacked column, bar, stacked bar, line, area, scatter, pie, and radar.

For more information on graphs, see "Using Graphs" in online Help.

Drawing and editing brushed paths

The Brushes palette in Illustrator contains four brush types—Calligraphic, Scatter, Art, and Pattern brushes—to use in adding art to paths. You can choose from the brush effects that have been preloaded into the Brushes palette. You can also modify these brushes, create brushes, or import a brush from the Brush Libraries to the Brushes palette.

Brushes that you create and store in the Brushes palette are associated only with the current file. Each Illustrator file can have a different set of brushes in its Brushes palette.

You can achieve the following effects using the four brush types:

• Calligraphic brushes create strokes that resemble strokes drawn with the angled point of a calligraphic pen, drawn along the center of the path.

• Scatter brushes disperse copies of an object (such as a ladybug or a leaf) along the path.

• Art brushes stretch an object or artwork (such as an arrow or dog bone) evenly along the length of the path.

• Pattern brushes paint a pattern—made of individual *tiles*—that repeats along the path. Pattern brushes can include up to five tiles, for the sides, inner corner, outer corner, beginning, and end of the pattern.

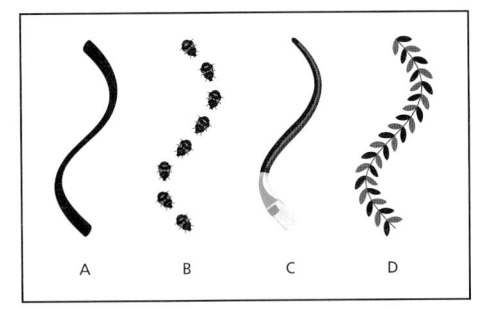

A. Calligraphic brush B. Scatter brush C. Art brush D. Pattern brush

Drawing a brushed path with the paintbrush tool

The paintbrush tool creates paths painted with a brush selected in the Brushes palette. You must select a brush in the Brushes palette to use the paintbrush tool.

To draw a path with the paintbrush tool:

1 Choose Window > View Brushes to display the Brushes palette, and select a brush from the Brushes palette.

2 Double-click the paintbrush tool ( ), set preferences, and click OK:

• In the Smoothness text box, enter a value (0% to 100%) for the percentage stroke and curve smoothness, or use the slider. The higher the value, the smoother the stroke or curve.

- In the Fidelity text box, enter the number of pixels (from 0.5 to 20) for the number of pixels the stroke can stray from the path to produce smooth curves, or use the slider. The higher the value, the smoother the stroke or curve.

- Select Fill New Brush Strokes to have paths drawn by the brush filled. When the option is unselected, paths are unfilled.

- Select Keep Selected to keep the path just drawn with the brush selected.

3 Position the tip of the paintbrush where you want the path to begin, and drag the paintbrush to draw the path. By default, the path is selected when you release the mouse button.

To draw a closed path with the paintbrush tool:

1 Select the paintbrush tool.

2 Position the pointer where you want the path to begin, and start dragging to draw a path.

3 As you drag, hold down Alt (Windows) or Option (Mac OS). The paintbrush tool displays a small loop to indicate drawing a closed path.

4 When the path is the size and shape you want, release the mouse button (but not the Alt or Option key). After the path closes, release the Alt or Option key.

To edit a brushed path with the paintbrush tool:

1 Select the path to edit with the selection tool (▶), or Ctrl-click (Windows) or Command-click (Mac OS) the path to select it.

2 Position the paintbrush tool on or near the path to redraw, and drag the tool until the path is the desired shape.

Creating a brushed path with a drawing tool

You can create a brushed path from any path created with an Illustrator drawing tool, including the pen or pencil tool or any of the basic shapes tools. You can then edit the brushed path as you would any path drawn with the tools.

To create a brushed path with a drawing tool:

1 Draw a path using a drawing tool, including the pen or pencil tool or a basic shape tool.

2 Choose a method for applying a brush to the path:

- Select the path that is to be brushed. In the Brushes palette, select a brush with which to brush the path.

- Drag a brush from the Brushes palette onto a path.

Note: To preserve brush stroke options previously applied to the object when applying a new brush, Alt-click (Windows) or Option-click (Mac OS) the new brush.

Modifying brushed paths

After you have applied a brush to a path, you can modify the attributes of the path in several ways.

To convert brushes in artwork to outlined paths:

1 Select the object or objects to convert.

2 Choose Object > Expand Appearance.

To remove a brush from a path:

1 Select the path to change.

2 Do one of the following:

• In the Brushes palette, choose Remove Brush Strokes from the palette menu or click the Remove Brush Strokes button ( ).

• In the toolbox or the Color palette, click the Stroke box and apply a stroke of None.

The brush is removed and the path remains.

Managing brushes

You can use the Brushes palette to organize your brushes.

To display the Brushes palette:

Choose Window > Show Brushes.

To display brushes by name:

Choose View By Name from the Brushes palette menu. A picture of the brush displays to the left of the name. The picture to the right of the name indicates the brush type.

To modify the type of brushes displayed:

From the Brushes palette menu, choose the type of brush to display in the palette. You can choose more than one brush.

To select all brushes not currently used in the file:

Choose Select All Unused from the Brushes palette menu. Only brushes that are not currently used in the active file are selected.

To move a brush in the Brushes palette:

Drag a brush to the new location in the Brushes palette. You can move brushes only within their type. (For example, you cannot move a Calligraphic brush to the Scatter brush area.)

To duplicate a brush in the Brushes palette:

1 Select a brush to duplicate. To select multiple brushes, Ctrl-click (Windows) or Command-click (Mac OS) each brush to duplicate. To select a range of brushes, Shift-click to define the range.

2 Do one of the following:

• Choose Duplicate Brush from the Brushes palette menu.

• Drag the selection to the New Brush button ( ) in the Brushes palette.

To delete a brush from the Brushes palette:

1 In the Brushes palette, select the brush to delete. To select multiple brushes, Ctrl-click (Windows) or Command-click (Mac OS) each brush to delete. To select a range of brushes, Shift-click to define the range.

2 Do one of the following:

• Choose Delete Brush from the Brushes palette menu.

• Click the Delete Brush button ( ) in the Brushes palette.

• Drag the selection to the Delete Brush button in the Brushes palette.

Creating brushes

You can create each of the four types of brushes in the Brushes palette. All brushes must be made up of simple open and closed path vectors. Brushes cannot have gradients, blends, other brush strokes, gradient meshes, bitmap images, graphs, placed files, or masks.

Art brushes and pattern brushes cannot include type. However, to achieve a brush stroke effect with type, create an outline of the type and then create a brush with the outline. (See "Modifying letterforms as graphic objects" on page 303.)

Creating a calligraphic brush

You can change the angle, roundness, and diameter of strokes painted with calligraphic brushes.

To create a calligraphic brush:

1 Click the New Brush button ( ) in the Brushes palette, or choose New Brush from the palette menu. Select New Calligraphic Brush and click OK.

2 In the Name text box, enter a name for the brush (up to 30 characters).

3 Specify values for the angle, roundness, and diameter of the brush (the preview in the dialog box reflects your settings):

• To set the ellipse angle of rotation, drag the arrowhead in the preview, or enter a value in the Angle text box.

• To set the roundness, drag a black dot in the preview away from or toward the center, or enter a value in the Roundness text box. The higher the value, the greater the roundness.

• To set the diameter, use the Diameter slider, or enter a value in the Diameter text box.

4 From each pop-up menu, choose the way in which you want to control variations in the angle, roundness, and diameter:

• Choose Fixed to use the value in the associated text box. For example, when the Diameter value is 20, Fixed always uses 20 for the brush diameter.

• Choose Random to use a random value within a specified range. When you choose Random, you also need to enter a value in the Variation text box, or use the Variation slider, to specify the range by which the brush characteristic can vary. For each stroke, Random uses any value between that in the text box for the brush characteristic plus or minus the Variation value. For example, when the Diameter value is 15 and the Variation value is 5, the diameter can be 10, or 20, or any value in between.

• Choose Pressure (if you will use the brush with a graphics tablet) to use a value determined by the pressure of your stylus. When you choose Pressure, you also need to enter a value in the Variation text box, or use the Variation slider. Pressure uses the value in the text box for the brush characteristic minus the Variation value for the lightest tablet pressure. It uses the value in the text box for the brush characteristic plus the Variation value for the heaviest pressure. For example, when the Roundness value is 75% and the Variation value is 25%, the lightest stroke is 50% and the heaviest stroke is 100%. The lighter the pressure, the more angular the brush stroke.

5 Click OK.

Creating a scatter brush

You use artwork from an illustration to define the scatter brush. You can change the size, spacing, scatter pattern, and rotation of objects painted on a path with scatter brushes.

To create a scatter brush:

1 Select the artwork to be used as a scatter brush.

2 Click the New Brush button ( ) in the Brushes palette, or choose New Brush from the palette menu. Select New Art Brush and click OK.

3 In the Name text box, enter a name for the brush (up to 30 characters).

4 Drag each Minimum slider or enter a value in each leftmost text box for the brush's size, spacing, scattering, and angle of rotation:

• Size controls the size of the objects.

• Spacing controls the amount of space between objects.

• Scatter controls how closely objects follow the path independently on each side of the path. The higher the value, the farther the objects are from the path.

• Rotation controls the angle of rotation of the objects.

5 From each pop-up menu, choose the way in which you want to control variations in the size, spacing, scattering, and rotation:

• Choose Fixed to use the value in the associated text box. For example, when the Scatter value is 50%, Fixed always uses 50% to scatter objects along the path.

• Choose Random to use a random value. When you choose Random, you also need to enter a value in the rightmost text box, or use the Maximum slider, to specify the range by which the brush characteristic can vary. For each stroke, Random uses any value between the Minimum and the Maximum value. For example, when the Minimum value is 50% and the Maximum value is 100% for Size, the objects' sizes can be 50%, or 100%, or any size in between.

- Choose Pressure (if you will use the brush with a graphics tablet) to use a value determined by the pressure of your stylus. When you choose Pressure, you also need to enter a value in the rightmost text box, or use the Maximum slider. Pressure uses the Minimum value for the lightest tablet pressure and the Maximum value for the heaviest pressure. The heavier the stroke, the larger the objects.

Note: To keep the same range of values between the two sliders, Shift-drag the sliders. To move the sliders an equal value apart or together, Alt-drag (Windows) or Option-drag (Mac OS) them.

6 Choose a relative orientation from the Rotation Relative To pop-up menu:

- For Page, the angle of rotation of scattered objects is relative to the page (0 degrees points to the top).

- For Path, the angle of rotation of scattered objects is relative to the path (0 degrees is tangent to the path).

7 Choose a method of colorization from the Method pop-up menu. (See "Choosing a colorization method" on page 108.)

8 Click OK.

To reset Random options for scatter brushes:

1 Select the scatter brush in the artwork.

2 Choose Options of Selected Object from the Brushes palette menu, or click the Options of Selected Object button ( ).

3 Make sure at least one brush characteristic is set to Random.

4 Click the Randomize button. (To see the effect of your changes on artwork, select Preview.) Click OK.

Creating an art brush

You use artwork from an illustration to define the art brush. You can change the direction and size of objects painted along a path with art brushes and also flip the objects along the path or across the path.

To create an art brush:

1 Select the artwork to be used as an art brush.

2 Click the New Brush button ( ) in the Brushes palette, or choose New Brush from the palette menu. Select New Art Brush and click OK.

3 In the Name text box, enter a name for the brush (up to 30 characters).

4 For Direction, click a button for the direction in which you want the art to be drawn as you drag the paintbrush. In each button, the arrowhead represents the end of the brush stroke.

When you drag the paintbrush in the artwork window, the art is drawn as follows:

- For ( ), the left side of the art is the end of the stroke.

- For ( ), the right side of the art is the end of the stroke.

- For ( ), the top of the art is the end of the stroke.

- For ( ), the bottom of the art is the end of the stroke.

5 For Size, enter a percentage by which to scale the art in the Width text box. To preserve the proportion, select Proportional.

6 To change the orientation of the art on the path, choose Flip Along or Flip Across.

7 Choose a method of colorization from the Method pop-up menu. (See "Choosing a colorization method" on page 108.)

8 Click OK.

Creating a pattern brush

To create a pattern brush, you can use pattern swatches in the Swatches palette or artwork from an illustration to define the tiles in the brush. When using swatches to define a pattern brush, you can use preloaded pattern swatches, or create your own Pattern swatches.

You can change the size, spacing, and orientation of pattern brushes. In addition, you can apply new artwork to any of the tiles in a pattern brush to redefine the brush.

To apply new art to tiles in existing pattern brushes, you select pattern swatches from the scroll list in the Pattern Brush Options dialog box. (The scroll list displays all the Pattern swatches available in the Swatches palette.)

To create a pattern brush using pattern swatches in the Swatches palette:

1 Click the New Brush button (⊟) in the Brushes palette, or choose New Brush from the palette menu. Select New Pattern Brush and click OK.

2 In the Name text box, enter a name for the brush (up to 30 characters).

3 Click a tile button for the tile you want to define. For example, to define the side tile, click the Side tile button (⊟).

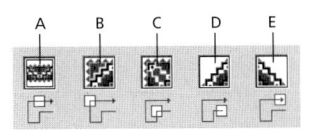

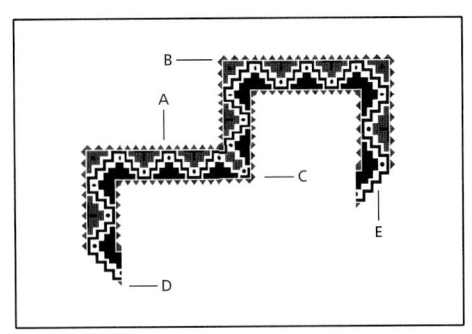

A. Side tile B. Outer Corner tile C. Inner Corner tile D. Start tile E. End tile

4 In the scroll list, select a Pattern swatch to apply to the selected tile.

The selected swatch appears in the selected tile button.

Note: To restore a pattern setting to its original value when modifying an existing Pattern brush, select Original from the scroll list.

5 Repeat steps 3 and 4 to apply Pattern swatches to other tiles as needed.

6 For Size, enter values for the scale (which preserves the proportion) and the spacing between tiles.

7 To change the orientation of the pattern on the path, choose Flip Along or Flip Across.

8 For Fit, choose how to fit the tiles on the path:

• Stretch to Fit lengthens or shortens the pattern tile to fit the object. This option can result in uneven tiling.

• Add Space to Fit adds blank space between each pattern tile to apply the pattern proportionally to the path.

• Approximate Path (for rectangular paths only) fits tiles to the closest approximate path without changing the tiles. This option applies the pattern slightly inside or outside the path, rather than centered on the path, to maintain even tiling.

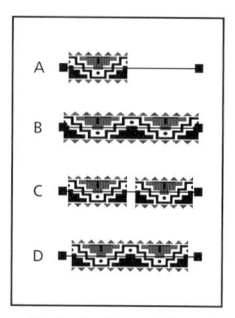

A. Default tile and Fit options
B. Stretch to Fit C. Add Space to Fit
D. Approximate Path

9 Choose a method of colorization from the Method pop-up menu. (See "Choosing a colorization method" on page 108.)

10 Click OK.

Note: After you define a Pattern brush with Pattern swatches, you can delete the Pattern swatches from the Swatches palette if you don't plan to use them for additional artwork.

To create a pattern brush using artwork from an illustration:

1 Create or display the artwork that you want to use as a Pattern brush. (See "Creating and working with patterns" on page 233.) Make sure to create artwork for each of the tiles in the Pattern brush, up to five tiles depending on the brush configuration desired.

2 In the Brushes palette, make sure the brushes are displayed by icon. (If necessary, choose View By Name from the palette menu to deselect name view.)

3 Drag the artwork to be used as the side tile onto the Brushes palette.

4 Select New Pattern Brush, and then click OK.

5 In the Name text box, enter a name for the brush (up to 30 characters), and then click OK.

6 Alt-drag (Windows) or Option-drag (Mac OS) artwork for additional tiles onto the appropriate section of the entry for the brush in the Brushes palette, and then click OK after adding each tile. The side tile already appears in the second section. Alt-drag or Option-drag artwork for the outer corner tile to the first section. Alt-drag or Option-drag artwork for the inner corner tile, start tile, and end tile to the remaining sections.

Choosing a colorization method

For Scatter, Art, and Pattern brushes, you can choose a method by which to colorize a brush.

To choose a colorization method:

1 With the options dialog box for the selected brush type open, choose an option from the Method pop-up menu:

• None displays colors as they appear in the brush in the Brushes palette. Choose None to keep a brush the same colors as in the Brushes palette.

• Tints displays the brush stroke in tints of the stroke color. Portions of the art that are black become the stroke color, portions that aren't black become tints of the stroke color, and white remains white. If you use a spot color as the stroke, Tints generates tints of the spot color. Choose Tints for brushes that are in black and white, or when you want to paint a brush stroke with a spot color.

• Tints and Shades displays the brush stroke in tints and shades of the stroke color. Tints and Shades maintains black and white, and everything between becomes a blend from black to white through the stroke color. Because black is added you may not be able to print to a single plate when using Tints and Shades with a spot color. Choose Tints and Shades for brushes that are in grayscale.

• Hue Shift uses the key color in the brush artwork, as shown in the Key Color box. (By default, the key color is the most prominent color in the art.) Everything in the brush artwork that is the key color becomes the stroke color. Other colors in the brush artwork become colors related to the stroke color. Hue Shift maintains black, white, and gray. Choose Hue Shift for brushes that use multiple colors. You can change the key color.

For information and samples about each choice, click Tips.

Note: You can experiment with different colorization methods to achieve the result you want.

To change the key color:

1 With the options dialog box for the selected brush type open, click the Key Color eyedropper.

2 Move the eyedropper to the preview in the dialog box, and click the color you want to use as the key color. The color in the Key Color box changes.

3 Click the eyedropper again to deselect it.

Modifying existing brushes

You can modify existing brushes. When you change the options of a brush, you can apply the changes to brush strokes already drawn in the artwork with the brush, or apply the changes to new strokes only. You can also change the brush stroke options of a selected object without affecting other objects in the artwork and without changing the brush's attributes.

To modify an existing brush:

1 Double-click the brush in the Brushes palette, or select the brush and choose Brush Options from the palette menu.

2 Choose an option for applying changes to pre-existing strokes:

• Click Apply To Strokes to change pre-existing strokes. (The modified brush will be applied to new strokes as well.)

- Click Leave Strokes to leave pre-existing strokes unchanged, and apply the modified brush to new strokes only.

3 Change options, and click OK.

To change options of a selected object without changing the brush attributes for all objects:

1 Select a brush in the artwork.

2 Choose Options of Selected Object from the Brushes palette menu, or click the Options of Selected Object button ( ) in the palette.

3 Change the options, and click OK. Only the selected objects are changed with the new options. Any other objects in the artwork that were painted with the brush remain with the original brush attributes. Attributes of the brush are not affected; the next time you use the brush, it uses the current attributes.

Note: *To reset changed objects to the original brush options, select the objects, apply a different brush to them, and then reapply the original brush.*

To modify brushes by dragging into your artwork:

1 Select a brush from the Brushes palette.

2 Drag the brush into your artwork.

3 Make the changes you want.

Drag the modified brush into the Brushes palette.

Using the brush libraries

You can import brushes from other Adobe Illustrator files into a palette associated with the current file using the Brush Libraries command. These libraries are stored in the Brush Libraries folder, located in the Illustrator 9.0 folder. You cannot add, delete, or edit brushes in a library; however, once you import a brush, you can change its attributes.

To import a brush from a Brush Library to the current Brushes palette:

1 Make sure the Brushes palette into which you want to import a brush is open.

2 Choose Window > Brush Libraries > *Brush Library name*. To locate a Brush Library not stored in the Brush Libraries folder, choose Window > Brush Libraries > Other Library.

3 Select the brush you want, and then do one of the following:

- Use the selected brush in the current artwork (recommended for one or two brushes at a time). Once you use it in the artwork, the brush is copied from the Brush Library to the Brushes palette.

- Drag the selected brush to the current Brushes palette (recommended for multiple brushes at a time).

- Choose Add to Brushes from the Brushes palette menu.

To have a Brush Library appear in the Brush Libraries menu:

1 Drag the Brush Library file into the Brush Libraries folder.

2 Restart Adobe Illustrator.

To create a Brush Library:

1 Create an Adobe Illustrator file containing the brushes you want in the Brush Library.

2 Save the file in the Brush Libraries folder.

3 Restart Adobe Illustrator.

Tips for using brushes

When you work with brushes, keep the following points in mind:

• You can often use Scatter brushes and Pattern brushes to achieve the same effect. However, one way in which they differ is that Pattern brushes follow the path exactly, while Scatter brushes do not.

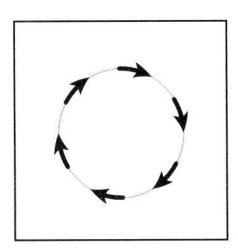

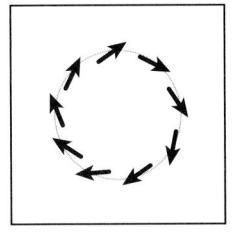

Arrows in a Pattern brush bend to follow the path; arrows remain straight in a Scatter brush.

• If you apply a brush to a closed path and want to control the placement of the end of the path, select the scissors tool and split the path. To change again, select the endpoints, choose Object >Path > Join, and use the scissors again. (See "Splitting paths with the scissors tool" on page 96.)

• To select all brush stroke paths in the current artwork, choose Edit > Select > Brush Strokes.

• For better performance when creating a brush from art that contains multiple overlapping paths filled with the same color and with no stroke, choose Unite from the Pathfinder palette before you create the brush.

Tracing artwork

There may be times when you want to base a new drawing on an existing piece of artwork. For example, you may want to create a graphic based on a pencil sketch drawn on paper or on an image saved in another graphics program. In either case, you can bring the image into Illustrator and trace over it. You can create a layer to use especially as a template.

You can trace artwork in the following ways, depending on the source of the artwork to trace and how you want to trace it:

• Use the auto trace tool to trace automatically any image you bring into Illustrator.

• Place any EPS, PDF, or image file into an Illustrator file as a template layer and manually trace over it using the pen or pencil tool. (See "Dimming and showing raster images on layers" on page 245.)

For details on using the auto trace tool, see "Tracing artwork" in online Help.

http://

A

4

Chapter 4: Working with Objects

Editing your artwork is made easy with tools that allow you to select, move, and arrange objects precisely. Tools are available that let you measure and align objects, group objects so that they are treated as a single unit, and selectively lock and hide objects. There are also commands for correcting your mistakes and reverting to an earlier saved version of your file.

Correcting mistakes

You can use the Undo command to correct mistakes you make while using the Adobe Illustrator program. You can even undo an operation after you choose the Save command (but not if you closed and then reopened the file). If an operation cannot be undone, the Undo command is dimmed.

Depending on how much memory is available, you can undo an unlimited number of the last operations you performed, in reverse order, by repeatedly choosing the Undo command. The Illustrator performance is usually not affected by the number of undo levels you choose; however, if you are trying to display complex artwork, you may receive a message asking you to reduce the number of undo levels because of insufficient memory.

You can also revert a file to the version that was last saved (but not if you closed and then reopened the file).

To undo or redo an operation:

Choose Edit > Undo or Edit > Redo. (Depending on the memory available to your system, you can choose Undo an unlimited number of times.)

To change the minimum number of undo levels:

1 Choose Edit > Preferences > Units & Undo.

2 Enter a value for Minimum Undo Levels, and click OK. The default undo level is 5.

To revert a file to the last saved version:

Choose File > Revert. You cannot undo this action.

Using rulers

Illustrator can display rulers, one along the top and one along the left side of the illustration window.

When you open a new file, the rulers are not visible, but you can display them at any time. These rulers are a tool for accurately placing and measuring objects on the artboard. As you scroll and zoom around the file, the rulers adjust accordingly.

To show or hide rulers:

Choose View > Show Rulers, or View > Hide Rulers.

Defining ruler units

The large tick marks on the rulers indicate the unit of measure (such as inches), and the small tick marks indicate increments of the unit of measure (such as 1/8 inch). When you magnify or reduce your view, the increments of the unit of measure reflect the change in magnification.

The default units of measure for the rulers are *points* (a point equals .3528 millimeter). You can change the unit of measure to inches, millimeters, centimeters, *picas* (a pica equals 12 points or 4.2333 millimeters), or pixels by using the Units & Undo panel of the Preferences dialog box or the Artboard panel of the Document Setup dialog box.

The unit of measure that you set for the rulers applies when you measure objects, move and transform objects, set grid and guides spacing, and create ellipses and rectangles. It does not affect the units in the Character and Paragraph palettes, which always display size, leading, vertical shift, line width, and line dash in the units set in the Type pop-up menu in the Units & Undo Preferences dialog box. (See "Setting type attributes" on page 293.)

To set the ruler unit of measure for all files:

1 Choose Edit > Preferences > Units & Undo.

2 From the General pop-up menu, choose the unit of measure you want to use, and click OK.

To set the ruler unit of measure for only the current file:

1 Choose File > Document Setup. Choose Artboard from the pop-up menu at the top left of the Document Setup dialog box.

2 From the Units pop-up menu, choose the unit of measure you want to use, and click OK.

Automatically converting unit values in text boxes

If you use a unit other than the preset unit to enter values, Illustrator converts it to the set unit. For example, entering **3cm** in a text box set to inches converts the value to 1.1811 inches.

You can also add, subtract, multiply, divide, define percentages, and perform other mathematical operations in any Illustrator text box that accepts numeric values. For example, when specifying the size of a rectangle, you can type **72 pt + 2cm** for the height. Illustrator performs the calculation and uses the result.

The following rules apply when entering unit values:

• You can use the following units and abbreviations in text boxes: inch, inches, in, millimeters, millimetres, mm, Qs (one Q equals 0.25 millimeter), centimeters, centimetres, cm, points, p, pt, picas, pc, pixel, pixels, and px.

• Units are in points by default unless a different unit of measure was set in Edit > Preferences > Units & Undo.

- When mixing picas and points, you can enter values as *Xp Y,* where *X* and *Y* are the number of picas and points (for example, 12p6 for 12 picas, 6 points).

- A value without a specified unit uses the default unit for that text box, unless it follows a value with a specified unit. For example, in a text box that uses inches by default, typing **3 + 6** would equal 3 inches plus 6 inches, or 9 inches. Typing **3cm + 6** would equal 3 centimeters plus 6 centimeters, or 3.5433 inches.

- You can use percentages in combination with units. For example, typing **3cm*50%** would equal 3 centimeters multiplied by 50%, or 1.50 cm. Typing **50pt + 25%** would equal 50 points plus 25% of 50 points, or 62.5 points.

Changing the ruler origin

The point where 0 appears on each ruler is called the *ruler origin.* When you open a file, the position of the ruler origin depends on the View option selected in the Artboard panel of the Document Setup dialog box. Generally, if you selected either the Single Full Page or the Tile Full Pages option, the default ruler origin is located at the lower left corner of page 1.

When you change the ruler setting, the new setting becomes the default for the file whenever that file is opened. You can change the origin for the rulers at any time. For example, you may be working on a 3-inch-by-5-inch card that is centered on an 8.5-inch-by-11-inch page. Setting the ruler origin to line up with the 3-by-5-inch artwork rather than the 8.5-by-11-inch page can make precision editing easier for you.

Note: *The position of the ruler origin affects the tiling of patterns, as well as the bounding box information for the Separation Setup command. (See "Specifying the printing bounding box in the separation" on page 389.)*

To change the ruler origin:

1 Move the pointer to the upper left corner of the rulers where the rulers intersect.

2 Do one of the following:

- Drag the pointer to where you want the new ruler origin. As you drag, a cross hair in the window and in the rulers indicates the changing ruler origin.

- Double-click the upper-left corner where the rulers intersect to restore the default settings.

Using the measure tool

The measure tool calculates the distance between any two points in the work area. When you measure from one point to another, the distance measured is displayed in the Info palette. The Info palette shows the horizontal and vertical distances from the *x* and *y* axes, the absolute horizontal and vertical distances, the total distances, and the angle measured.

All measurements except the angle are calculated in the unit of measure currently set in the Units & Undo Preferences dialog box or in the Artboard panel of the Document Setup dialog box. (See "Defining ruler units" on page 116.)

To measure the distance between two points:

1 Select the measure tool ( ).

2 Do one of the following:

• Click the two points to measure the distance between them.

• Click the first point and drag to the second point. Shift-drag to constrain the tool to multiples of 45 degrees.

Using guides and grids

To help align text and graphic objects on the page, you can use background grids or you can create and display alignment outlines called *guides*.

Grids normally appear as lines or dots behind the artwork, and they do not print. You use grids to lay out objects or elements symmetrically. Selected artwork and tools snap to the grid if Snap To Grid is turned on. Grid spacing, color, and style can be different for each file.

Note: When your document's viewing mode is Pixel Preview, the Snap to Grid command on the View menu changes to Snap to Pixel. For more information, see "Viewing artwork as pixels" on page 326.

Guides act as alignment tools. They also do not print. You can define any object as a guide to which you want to align artwork. Selected artwork and tools snap to guides when they are within tolerance of the guide. Guide color and style are the same for all files. (See "Setting guide and grid preferences" on page 119.)

Using guides

You can create two kinds of guides:

• *Ruler guides* are straight horizontal or vertical lines created with the ruler. These guides are the simplest to make and are useful for setting alignment lines across the length or width of the work area.

• *Guide objects* are objects (such as lines, rectangles, or any other artwork consisting of paths, except type) that are converted to guides. Using guide objects can help you plan and create your artwork around one or more objects. You can convert guide objects back into graphic objects at any point.

New guides are locked in place to orient your artwork. However, you can unlock a guide to select, move, delete, modify, or revert it to a graphic object.

By default, objects are aligned with guides whenever they are dragged within 2 pixels of the guide. (See "Moving, copying, and deleting objects" on page 125.)

To create a ruler guide:

1 If the rulers are not already displayed, choose View > Show Rulers.

2 Position the pointer on the left ruler for a vertical guide or on the top ruler for a horizontal guide. Press Alt (Windows) or Option (Mac OS) to switch the ruler guide from horizontal to vertical, and vice versa.

3 Drag the ruler guide into position.

To make working with multiple guides easier, place all guides on a single layer. You can then choose the layer to select all guides for moving or adjusting. (See "About layers" on page 241.)

To convert an object into a guide object:

1 Select an object, a group of objects, or any combination of objects and groups.

2 Choose View > Guides > Make Guides.

To move, delete, or release a guide:

1 Choose View > Guides > Lock Guides to lock or unlock the guide. When a guide is locked, a check mark appears next to the Lock Guides command.

2 Select the guide you want to move, delete, or release, and do one of the following:

• Move the guide by dragging or copying.

• Delete the guide by pressing Backspace or Del (Windows) or Delete (Mac OS), or by choosing Edit > Cut or Edit > Clear.

• Delete all guides at once by choosing View > Guides > Clear Guides.

• Release the guide object, turning it back into a regular graphic object, by choosing View > Guides > Release Guides.

To show or hide guides:

Choose View > Guides > Show Guides to show all guides or View > Hide Guides to hide them.

Using grids

You can choose between two grid styles—dots and lines—and you can change the color of the grid by using either predefined grid colors or colors you select using a color picker.

Spacing of grids is defined by two values: the distance between major lines, and the spacing between subdivisions. The visibility of the grid and snapping to the grid are controlled by the Show Grid command and the Snap to Grid command in the View menu.

Setting guide and grid preferences

Use the Guides & Grid preferences to set the color and style of guides and the grid, and grid spacing.

To set guide and grid preferences:

1 Choose Edit > Preferences > Guides & Grid.

2 Set options for guides and the grid:

• For Color, choose a color for guides, or the grid, or both. If you choose Other, click the color box, choose a color from the color picker, and click OK.

• For Style, choose a display option for guides, or the grid, or both.

• For Gridline Every, enter a new value (and unit of measure if necessary) for the spacing of primary gridlines.

- For Subdivisions, enter a value to subdivide the grid.

- For Grids in Back, select the option to display the grid behind all artwork; deselect the option to display the grid in front of all artwork.

3 Click OK.

Using Smart Guides

Smart Guides are temporary, "snap to" guides that help you create, align, edit, and transform objects relative to other objects. You can also use Smart Guides when rotating, scaling, and shearing objects. Objects can snap to locked objects and objects on locked layers.

You choose the point on the selected object at which you want to snap by selecting the object at that point. Illustrator determines additional points on artwork to create guides and snapping points. These points are determined by the last objects the cursor has passed over with the selected object.

You can create intersecting Smart Guides by passing over two Smart Guide lines, and then moving your selected object to the intersection point.

As you create, align, move, edit, and transform objects, Smart Guides appear from any anchor point on a nearby object over which the pointer recently passed. The direction, angle, tolerance, and appearance of Smart Guides are determined by settings in Preferences.

To turn Smart Guides on or off:

To turn Smart Guides on or off, choose View > Smart Guides. A check mark appears next to the command when Smart Guides are turned on.

To change Smart Guide preferences:

1 Choose Edit > Preferences > Smart Guides.

2 Specify options for Smart Guides:

- Select Text Label Hints to display information about the position the cursor is currently snapped to (such as *center*) as you manipulate the cursor.

- Select Construction Guides to see guidelines in the file as you use Smart Guides.

- Select Transform Tools to have Smart Guides help when you scale, rotate, and shear objects.

- Select Object Highlighting to highlight the object below the pointer as you drag around it.

3 Click a text box and set an angle at which you want guide lines drawn from the anchor points of a nearby object (the preview reflects your settings). You can set up to six angles. Do one of the following:

- Enter an angle in the selected Angles text box.

- Choose a set of angles from the Angles pop-up menu.

- Choose a set of angles from the pop-up menu and change one of the values in the text box to customize a set of angles.

4 Type a value in the Snapping Tolerance text box to specify the number of points the pointer must be from another object for Smart Guides to take effect. Then click OK.

How Smart Guides work

When Smart Guides are turned on and you move the cursor over your artwork, the cursor looks for objects, page boundaries, and intersections of construction guides to snap to that are within the tolerance range set in Smart Guides Preferences.

You can use Smart Guides in the following ways when you create, move, and transform objects:

• When you create an object with the pen or shape tools, use the Smart Guides to position the new object's anchor points relative to the other object.

• When you move an object, use the Smart Guides to align to the point on the object that you have selected. You can align to the anchor point at the corner of a selected object near the bounding box. To do so, select the object just inside the bounding box handle. If the tolerance is 5 points or greater, you can snap to the corner point from 5 points away. (See "Using the bounding box" on page 123.)

• When the Transform Tools option is selected in Smart Guides Preferences and you transform an object, Smart Guides appear to assist the transformation.

Note: When Snap to Grid is turned on, you cannot use Smart Guides (even if the menu command is selected).

Selecting objects

Before you can modify an object, you need to distinguish it from the objects around it. You do that by selecting the object with a selection tool. Once you've selected an object, or a part of an object, you can edit it by moving or copying, deleting, or adjusting paths.

Note: You can drag to move an object you have just selected with the selection, direct-selection, and group-selection tools, but not with the lasso or direct-lasso tools.

Using the selection tools

You select objects with the following selection tools:

• The selection tool ( ) lets you select entire paths, objects, and groups by selecting any spot on them (or within them if the path, object, or group is filled). When the selection tool is over an unselected path, object, or group, it changes to ( ). When it is over a selected path, object, or group, the tool changes to ( ). When it is over an anchor point, a hollow square appears next to the arrow ( ) or ( ), depending on whether the path, object, or group is selected or not.

• The direct-selection tool ( ) lets you select individual anchor points or segments on a path. All direction lines then appear on that part of the path for adjusting. When the direct-selection tool is over an unselected path or object, it changes to ( ). When it is over the anchor point of a selected path or object, it changes to ( ).

- The group-selection tool ( ) lets you select an object within a group, a single group within multiple groups, or a set of groups within the artwork. Each additional click adds all objects from the next group in the hierarchy. (See "Grouping and ungrouping objects" on page 133.)

- The lasso tool ( ) lets you select entire paths and objects by dragging around any part of the path.

- The direct-lasso tool ( ) lets you select individual anchor points or segments on a path by dragging around parts of a path. All direction lines then appear on that part of the path for adjusting.

To use the last-used selection, direct-selection, or group-selection tool when using any other tool (except these selection tools), hold down Ctrl (Windows) or Command (Mac OS).

To select an entire object or line:

1 Select the selection tool ( ) or the group-selection tool ( ).

2 Do one of the following:

- If the object is filled and you are in Preview view, click within the object.

Note: Clicking a filled object in Preview view selects the object only if the Use Area Select option in the General Preferences dialog box is selected. (See "Selecting filled objects" on page 123.)

- Click the path of the object.

- Click an anchor point of the object.

- Drag a dotted rectangle, called a *marquee*, around part or all of the object.

To select an entire object or line with the lasso tool:

1 Select the lasso tool ( ).

2 Drag around or across the object.

To select a segment:

Do one of the following:

- Select the direct-selection tool ( ), and then click within 2 pixels of the segment or drag a marquee over part of the segment.

- Select the direct-lasso tool ( ), and drag around part of the segment.

When you select a segment, all of the anchor points on the path are displayed, including all direction lines and direction points on that part of the path if the selected segment is curved. Direction points appear as filled circles; selected anchor points appear as filled squares; unselected anchor points appear as hollow squares.

To add or remove selections with the selection, direct-selection, or group-selection tool:

Hold down Shift while selecting or deselecting additional objects or segments.

To add or remove selections with the lasso or direct-lasso tool:

1 Do one of the following:

- Hold down Shift while selecting to add to the selection.

- Hold down Alt (Windows) or Option (Mac OS) to subtract from the selection.

Using the bounding box

When you select one or more objects with the selection tool, you see a bounding box around them. With the bounding box, you can move, rotate, duplicate, and scale objects easily by dragging the selection or a handle (one of the hollow squares surrounding the selected objects).

The bounding box creates a temporary border around the selected object. You see an outline of the selection as you drag it. When you release the mouse button, the object snaps to the current border created by the bounding box, and you see the object's outline move.

If you are working in Pixel Preview mode and want the object to snap to pixels when you drag it, turn off Use Preview Bounds in the General panel of the Preferences dialog box.

To move, duplicate, or scale objects, use the selection tool ( ).

Note: You can also move and scale selected objects, as well as perform other transformation actions, using the free transform tool, transformation tools, and the Transform palette. (See "Transforming selected objects" on page 139.)

If you rotate an object, its bounding box is also rotated. To reorient the bounding box to the page, choose Object > Transform > Reset Bounding Box.

To show or hide the bounding box:

Choose View > Show Bounding Box or View > Hide Bounding Box.

To move objects with the bounding box:

1 Select one or more objects using the selection tool.

2 Drag any part of the selection (but not a handle).

To rotate objects with the bounding box:

1 Select one or more objects using the selection tool.

2 Move the pointer near a corner handle so that it changes to a curve with arrows on both ends.

3 Drag the handle.

To duplicate objects with the bounding box:

1 Select one or more objects using the selection tool.

2 Alt-drag (Windows) or Option-drag (Mac OS) the selection (but not a handle).

Selecting filled objects

The Use Area Select option in the General Preferences dialog box determines whether you can select a filled object in Preview view by clicking anywhere within the area or whether you must click a path segment or anchor point. By default, the Use Area Select option is on. In some cases, you may want to turn off the Use Area Select option—for example, when you work with overlapping filled objects.

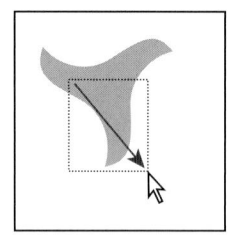

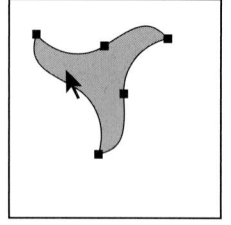

With Use Area Select option off, dragging selects points and segments within marquee. With Use Area Select option on, dragging selects object.

To turn the Use Area Select option on or off:

1 Choose Edit > Preferences > General.

2 Select or deselect the Use Area Select option, and click OK.

Selecting multiple objects

You can select several objects at a time and then move, paint, group, transform, or edit them using any editing tool.

You can also select objects based on their paint style, stroke color, stroke weight, style, blending mode, opacity, and whether they are masks, stray points, or brush strokes. For more information, see "Creating global colors and tints" on page 185.

Note: Objects that have been locked or hidden are not selected with the selection commands. (See "Locking and hiding objects" on page 134.)

To select or deselect multiple objects:

Do one of the following:

- With the selection tool, drag a marquee over all of the objects.
- With an object selected, Shift-drag a marquee over other objects to select.
- With the selection tool, select an object and then Shift-click to select additional objects.

To select or deselect all objects in a file:

Choose Edit > Select All or Deselect All to select or deselect all objects in a file.

To select all unselected objects, and deselect all selected objects:

Choose Edit > Select > Inverse.

To repeat the last type of selection you made:

Choose Edit > Select > Select Again.

To select all objects with the same attributes:

1 Select an object that has the attribute you want.

2 Choose Edit > Select, followed by a selection command:

Same Appearance Selects all objects with the same graphic style as the object you selected.

Same Fill & Stroke Selects all objects with the same paint style as the object you selected.

Same Fill Color Selects all objects with the same fill color as the object you selected.

Same Stroke Color Selects all objects with the same stroke color as the object you selected.

Same Stroke Weight Selects all objects with the same stroke weight as the object you selected.

Same Blending Mode Selects all objects with the same blending mode as the object you selected.

Same Opacity Selects all objects with the same opacity as the object you selected.

Masks Selects all mask objects.

Stray Points Selects all stray points.

Brush Strokes Selects all brush strokes.

Deselecting objects

You deselect objects when you no longer want to edit them. You can deselect one object, several objects, or all objects in your artwork.

To deselect objects when you are using a selection tool:

Do one of the following:

• To deselect everything in the file, click or drag at least 2 pixels away from any object, or choose Edit > Deselect All.

• To deselect part of a selection, Shift-click or Shift-drag over the path or segment you want to deselect.

Moving, copying, and deleting objects

You can move objects in your artwork by cutting them from one spot and pasting them into another, by dragging them, and by using the arrow keys, the Move dialog box, and the Transform Each dialog box. Dragging also enables you to copy objects between open Illustrator files and Photoshop files.

Note: You can also move objects using the Transform palette. (See "Using the Transform palette" on page 147.)

To set general preferences that affect how objects move:

1 Choose Edit > Preferences > General.

2 Choose options for Preferences:

• Enter an angle between 0 and 360 degrees in the Constrain Angle text box to rotate the x and y axes. The rotation of the axes determines how drawing and movement are constrained when you hold down Shift. (See "Rotating the x and y axes" on page 130.)

• Select Transform Pattern Tiles to specify whether you want to transform any patterns within objects when you apply a transformation such as scaling, rotating, or shearing. (See "Creating and working with patterns" on page 233.)

• Deselect Use Area Select to select objects underneath filled objects by clicking an anchor point or path segment (in Preview view). (See "Selecting filled objects" on page 123.)

3 Click OK.

Note: Smart Guides preferences also affect how objects move.

To set keyboard preferences that affect how objects move:

1 Choose Edit > Preferences > General.

2 In the Keyboard Increment text box, enter the distance you want each press of an arrow key to move a selection, and then click OK.

To move or copy an object by pasting:

1 Select one or more objects that you want to cut or copy.

2 Choose Edit > Cut or Edit > Copy.

Note: To copy a bitmap version of the selected object onto the Clipboard for pasting into Adobe Photoshop, choose Edit > Copy. (See "Using the Clipboard to copy artwork" on page 127.)

3 To paste an object into another file, open the file and choose one of the following commands:

- Edit > Paste to paste the objects into the center of the active window.

- Edit > Paste in Front to paste the object directly in front of the selected object.

- Edit > Paste in Back to paste the object directly in back of the selected object.

Note: The Paste in Front and Paste in Back commands paste the object in the same position on the new file's artboard as in the original file.

To move an object or a copy of an object by dragging:

1 Select the object.

You can also select multiple objects.

2 Position the pointer on an anchor point or path segment of the selected object. In Preview view, you can click anywhere on the object when the Use Area Select option is selected in General Preferences.

3 Drag the object to its new location. Shift-drag to constrain the object to multiples of 45 degrees.

You can use the Snap to Point command in the View menu to have the cursor snap to an anchor point or guide when you drag an object within 2 pixels of the anchor point or guide. Snap to Point is turned on when a check mark appears by the menu command.

To drag a copy of the object, press Alt (Windows) or Option (Mac OS) as you drag.

Note: You can use this technique to drag copies of objects between Illustrator and Photoshop files. (See "Using the drag-and-drop feature to copy artwork" on page 128.)

To move an object by using the arrow keys:

1 Select the object.

2 Press the arrow key for the direction in which you want to move the object.

The distance the object moves each time you press an arrow key is determined by the value specified in the Cursor Key text box in the General Preferences dialog box. The default distance is 1 point (1/72 of an inch, or .3528 millimeter).

To move a selection with the free transform tool:

1 With the selection tool (▶), select one or more objects to move.

2 Select the free transform tool (拒).

3 Drag any part of the selection (but not a handle).

To move or copy an object a specified distance and direction:

1 Select the object.

2 Choose Object > Transform > Move.

When an object is selected, you can also double-click the selection tool ( )—or press Enter or Return—to open the Move dialog box.

The Move dialog box displays the results of the last move or measure operation using the unit of measure set in the Units & Undo Preferences dialog box.

3 Do one of the following:

• Enter the horizontal and vertical distances that you want the object to move. Positive values move the object up and to the right of the *x* axis; negative values move the object down and to the left.

• Enter the distance and angle for the move. The angle you enter is calculated in degrees from the *x* axis. Positive angles specify a counterclockwise move; negative angles specify a clockwise move. You can also enter values between 180 and 360 degrees; these values are converted to their corresponding negative values (for example, a value of 270 degrees is converted to –90 degrees).

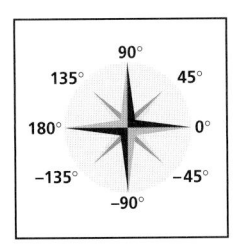

Directions relative to the x axis

Using the Clipboard to copy artwork

You can use the Clipboard to transfer selections between an Illustrator file and other Adobe products such as Adobe Photoshop, Adobe Streamline™, Adobe® Dimensions®, and Adobe Premiere®. The Clipboard is particularly useful for importing paths because paths are copied to the Clipboard as PostScript language descriptions.

When you copy a selection to the Clipboard, it is copied in PICT and, depending on which option you specify, as PDF or AICB (a format similar to EPS). Artwork copied to the Clipboard is pasted as PICT in most other applications.

However, some applications take the PDF version (such as Adobe InDesign) or the AICB version (such as Adobe Photoshop). PDF preserves transparency, whereas AICB breaks selections into many smaller opaque objects that give an overall look of transparency. If you choose AICB, you can also specify whether you want to preserve the overall appearance of the selection or copy the selection as a set of paths (which can be useful for Photoshop).

To specify copying preferences:

1 Choose Edit > Preferences > Files & Clipboard.

2 Select one or more of the following formats:

• PDF to copy the selection as PDF.

• AICB to copy the selection as AICB. You can then select whether to preserve the appearance or paths of the selection in AICB format.

3 Click OK.

To copy using the Clipboard:

1 Select the object or objects you want to copy in a non-Illustrator file. Then choose Edit > Copy.

2 In the Illustrator file to which you want to paste the object, choose Edit > Paste.

Note: Some file formats cannot be pasted into Illustrator, but they can be dropped into Illustrator by applications that support the drag-and-drop feature.

Using the drag-and-drop feature to copy artwork

The drag-and-drop feature lets you copy and move artwork between Illustrator and other applications.

In Windows, the other application must be OLE-compliant. To copy an OLE object that contains .psd data, use the OLE Clipboard. (See your Windows documentation.) Dragging vector artwork from Adobe Illustrator or from other applications that use the Illustrator Clipboard converts the artwork to a bitmap image (also called *raster* format).

In Mac OS, the application must support Macintosh Drag Manager.

To drag and drop selections of artwork between Illustrator and the desktop (Mac OS only):

1 Select the artwork you want to copy.

2 Drag the selection onto the desktop. Selections are copied to the desktop as a picture clipping, which can be dragged and dropped into the desired document. Picture clippings are converted to PICT format when dragged to the desktop.

To drag and drop artwork into a Photoshop image window:

1 Select the artwork you want to copy.

2 Open the Photoshop image into which you want to copy the selection.

3 Drag the selection toward the Photoshop window, and when a black outline appears, release the mouse button. To position the selection in the center of the Photoshop image, hold down Shift before dragging the selection.

To drag and drop artwork into Photoshop as paths:

1 Select the artwork you want to copy.

2 Open the Photoshop image into which you want to copy the selection.

3 Hold down Ctrl (Windows) or Command (Mac OS), and drag the selection to the Photoshop document. When you release the mouse button, the selection becomes a Photoshop path. By default, selected objects are copied as bitmap images to the active layer.

To drag and drop artwork into Illustrator from Photoshop:

1 Open the Photoshop image from which you want to copy.

2 Select the artwork you want to copy.

3 Hold down Ctrl (Windows) or Command (Mac OS), and drag the selection from Photoshop into the Illustrator file. When you release the mouse button, the selection becomes an Illustrator path. In Mac OS, dragging a selection from Photoshop to Illustrator converts the selection to an RGB image.

Note: If you're working with Adobe Photoshop 3.05 or earlier, you can drag from Photoshop into Illustrator, but you can't drag from Illustrator into Photoshop.

Aligning and distributing objects vertically and horizontally

The Align palette enables you to align selected objects along the axis you specify. You can align objects along the vertical axis, using the rightmost, center, or leftmost anchor point of the selected objects. Or you can align objects along the horizontal axis, using the topmost, center, and bottommost anchor points of the selected objects.

Note: Paragraph alignment of point type overrides the Align Objects options. (See "Specifying alignment options" on page 310.)

You can also distribute objects evenly along the horizontal axis or vertical axis.

In addition, you can distribute the space between objects evenly, both horizontally and vertically.

To align or distribute objects:

1 Select the objects to align or distribute.

2 Choose Window > Show Align.

In the Align palette, you see the Align Objects and Distribute Objects options. If you don't see the Distribute Spacing options, choose Show Options from the pop-up menu in the Align palette.

3 Click the button for the type of alignment or distribution you want.

Moving groups of objects

The Move option in the Transform Each dialog box moves objects in a selection in a specified or random direction. Use the Random option to give a slightly less rigid, more natural look to a group of items. For example, if you draw a brick wall and want the bricks to appear slightly offset from each other instead of perfectly aligned, you could select the Random option.

To move groups of objects:

1 Select the objects you want to move.

2 Choose Object > Transform > Transform Each.

3 In the Move Horizontal and Vertical text boxes, enter the distance you want to move the selected objects, or use the associated sliders. These numbers must be between –4000 and 4000 points and must not cause the objects to move beyond the edge of the artboard.

4 Do one of the following:

• To move the objects by the specified amounts, click OK.

• To move the objects randomly, but no more than the specified amounts, select the Random option. Then click OK.

Offsetting objects

You can create a replica of a path, set off from the selected path by a specified distance, by using the Offset Path command. This is useful when you want to create concentric shapes or make many replications of a path at a regular distance from the original path. You can create an offset path from a closed path or an open path; if created from a closed path, the new offset path appears at the specified distance outside or inside the original path.

You can apply the Offset Path command as a filter or as an effect. For more information on effects, see "Using effects" on page 271.

To create an offset path:

1 Do one of the following:

• To apply the command as a path command, select the paths you want to offset. Then choose Object > Path > Offset Path.

• To apply the command as an effect, select an object or group in the artwork, or target a group or layer in the Layers palette. (For more information on targeting, see "Targeting layers, groups, and objects to apply appearance attributes" on page 252.) Then choose Effect > Path > Offset Path.

2 Specify the offset distance, line join type, and miter limit. (For more information about line join type and miter limit, see "Creating line effects" on page 153.) Then click OK.

Deleting objects

Deleting an object removes it permanently.

To delete an object:

1 Select the object.

2 Press Backspace or Del (Windows) or Delete (Mac OS), or choose Edit > Clear or Edit > Cut.

Rotating the *x* and *y* axes

When you open a new file, the *x* and *y* axes are parallel to the horizontal and vertical sides of the window. You can rotate the axes by specifying an angle of constraint in the General Preferences dialog box.

Rotating the axes is useful if your artwork contains elements that are rotated to the same angle, such as a logo and text displayed on a 20-degree angle. Instead of rotating each element you add to the logo, you can simply rotate the axes by 20 degrees. Everything you draw is created along the new axes.

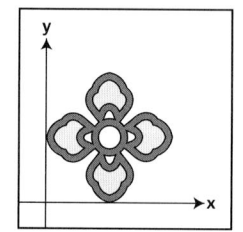

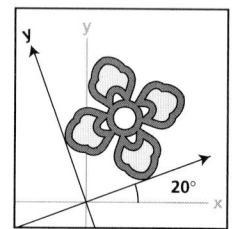

Object aligned with default axes and axes rotated 20º

You can then use the Shift key to constrain the movement of one or more objects so that they move in a precise horizontal, vertical, or diagonal direction relative to the current orientation of the *x* and *y* axes.

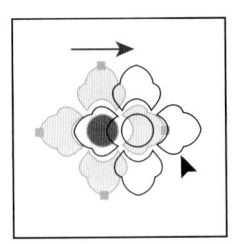

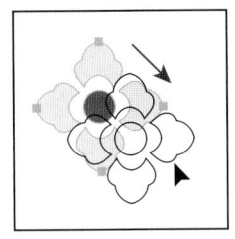

Hold down Shift while dragging or drawing to limit movement to the nearest 45º angle.

To rotate the axes:

1 Choose Edit > Preferences > General.

2 In the Constrain Angle text box, enter the angle at which you want the axes rotated. If you enter a positive number, the axes are rotated counter-clockwise. If you enter a negative number, the axes are rotated clockwise. Then click OK.

The rotation of the axes is saved in the Preferences file; it therefore affects new artwork in all files until you change its value or delete the Preferences file.

The following objects and actions are aligned along the new axes:

- Text and objects you draw with the graph tool.
- Scaling, reflecting, and shearing.
- Moving objects with the arrow keys.
- Any objects or operations to which you apply constraint (by holding down Shift while performing the action), limiting them to 45-degree multiples relative to the axes.
- The angle reported in the Info palette.
- Construction guides, which appear with Smart Guides.

The following objects and actions *are not* affected by the new axes:

- Objects that already exist.
- Rotating and blending.
- Drawing with the pencil or auto trace tool.

Stacking objects

The Adobe Illustrator program stacks successively drawn objects, beginning with the first object drawn. How objects are stacked determines how they are displayed when they overlap. In addition, stacking is important when you make masks. (See "Working with clipping masks" on page 167.)

You can change the stacking order (also called the *painting order*) of objects in your artwork at any time. By creating multiple layers in your artwork, you can also control how overlapping objects are displayed.

Note: *Grouping objects may affect the way the objects are stacked in relation to other, nongrouped objects in the artwork. (See "Grouping and ungrouping objects" on page 133.)*

Moving objects frontward or backward in a stack of objects

The Bring to Front and Send to Back commands let you move an object to the front or the back of the stack of objects on its layer. The Bring Forward and Send Backward commands let you move an object just one object forward or back in the stack of objects.

If the object is part of any type of group—including masked artwork, compound paths, text, and word wraps—the object is moved to the front or back of the group rather than the front or back of the entire layer.

To make an object the frontmost or backmost object in its group or on its layer:

1 Select the object you want to move.

2 Choose either Object > Arrange > Bring to Front or Object > Arrange > Send to Back.

To move an object one layer to the front or one layer to the back of a stack:

1 Select the object you want to move.

2 Choose either Object > Arrange > Bring Forward or Object > Arrange > Send Backward.

Pasting objects in front or in back of other objects

The Paste in Front and Paste in Back commands let you paste copies of objects directly on top of and behind the objects you select. This is useful if you want to move the copy a specified distance from the original location. These commands also let you paste the artwork into the same position in a new file as it was in the old file, relative to the page origin.

To move an object in front or in back of other objects in the stacking order:

1 Select the object you want to move.

2 Choose Edit > Cut. The selected object is temporarily deleted and is placed onto the Clipboard.

3 Select the object or objects in front or in back of where you want the cut object to appear.

4 Choose Edit > Paste in Front or Edit > Paste in Back.

The cut object is pasted into position. If no object was selected in step 3, the object is pasted on top of or in back of the stack.

If you paste more than one object, all pasted objects appear in front or in back of the selected artwork. However, the relative painting order among the individual pasted objects remains the same. If you are working with multiple layers in the file that you defined with the Layers palette, the layers may affect how objects are pasted. (See "Moving layers, groups, and objects between layers" on page 248.)

Pasting objects in the current layer

Pasted objects (even if copied from different layers) are placed directly in front or in back of all selected objects on the current layer if Paste Remembers Layers is turned off in the Layers palette menu. However, the relative painting order among the individual pasted objects remains the same.

When Paste Remembers Layers is on, objects are always pasted onto the layer where they originated. (See "Moving layers, groups, and objects between layers" on page 248.)

To paste objects into the current layer:

Make sure the Paste Remembers Layers is turned off in the Layers palette menu.

Grouping and ungrouping objects

You can combine several objects into a group so that the objects are treated as a single unit. You can then move or transform a number of objects without affecting their individual positions or attributes. For example, you might group the objects in a logo design so that you can move and scale the logo as one unit.

Groups can also be nested—that is, they can be grouped within other objects or groups to form larger groups.

To group or ungroup objects:

1 Select the objects to be grouped or ungrouped. Selecting part of an object and grouping it will group the entire object.

2 Choose either Object > Group or Object > Ungroup.

Selecting grouped objects

Once objects are grouped, selecting any part of the group with the selection tool or the lasso tool selects the entire group. If you are unsure whether an object is part of a group, select it with the selection tool.

The direct-selection tool and direct-lasso tool let you select a single path or object that is part of one group or several groups. If you have groups of objects within other groups, you can select the next group in the grouping hierarchy by using the group-selection tool. Each successive click adds another subset of grouped objects to the selection.

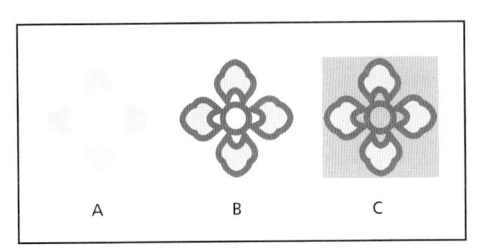

Three groups: Group A is part of group B, which in turn is part of group C.

To select grouped objects with the group-selection tool:

1 Select the group-selection tool ($\mathbb{k}^+$), and click the path you want to select.

2 Click the same place again to select successive groups until you have selected everything you want to include in your selection.

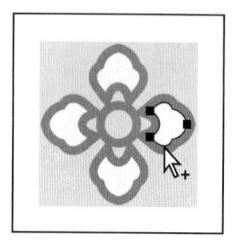

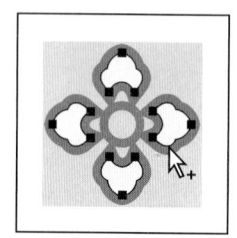

First click selects an object. Second click selects group A.

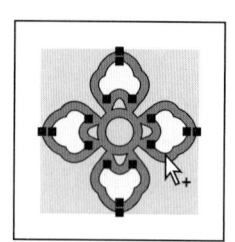

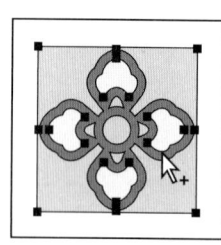

Third click selects next group (group B). Fourth click selects group C.

Grouping stacked objects

Grouped objects must be stacked in succession on the same layer of the artwork; therefore, grouping may change the layering of objects and their stacking order on a given layer. (See "Stacking objects" on page 131 and "About layers" on page 241.)

Grouped objects are stacked together behind the frontmost object in the group. If you group two objects that are separated by a nongrouped object in the stacking order, the nongrouped object is moved behind the grouped objects.

Locking and hiding objects

You can use the Lock and Hide commands to isolate parts of your artwork on which you do not want to work. Once an object is locked or hidden, it cannot be selected or modified in any way. These features are useful when you are working on objects that overlap. In addition, the Hide command makes objects temporarily invisible, and so may speed performance when you work on large or complex artwork.

Locked objects remain locked when files are closed and reopened. However, hidden objects reappear when files are reopened.

To lock or hide artwork:

Choose from the following options:

• To lock objects, select the objects and choose Object > Lock.

• To lock all unselected objects, press Alt (Windows) or Option (Mac OS) and choose Object > Lock.

• To hide a selected object, select the objects and choose Object > Hide Selection.

• To hide all unselected objects, press Alt (Windows) or Option (Mac OS), and choose Object > Hide Selection.

Note: You can lock or hide entire objects only. Selecting part of an object (anchor points or segments) and locking or hiding it affects the entire object.

To unlock all objects:

Choose Object > Unlock All. All previously locked objects are unlocked and selected. Any previously selected objects are deselected.

To show all objects:

Choose Object > Show All. All previously hidden objects are shown. Any previously selected objects are selected.

To unlock or show all objects within a selected group:

1 Select an unlocked and visible element within a group.

2 Hold down Alt (Windows) or Option (Mac OS) and choose either Object > Unlock All or Object > Show All.

5

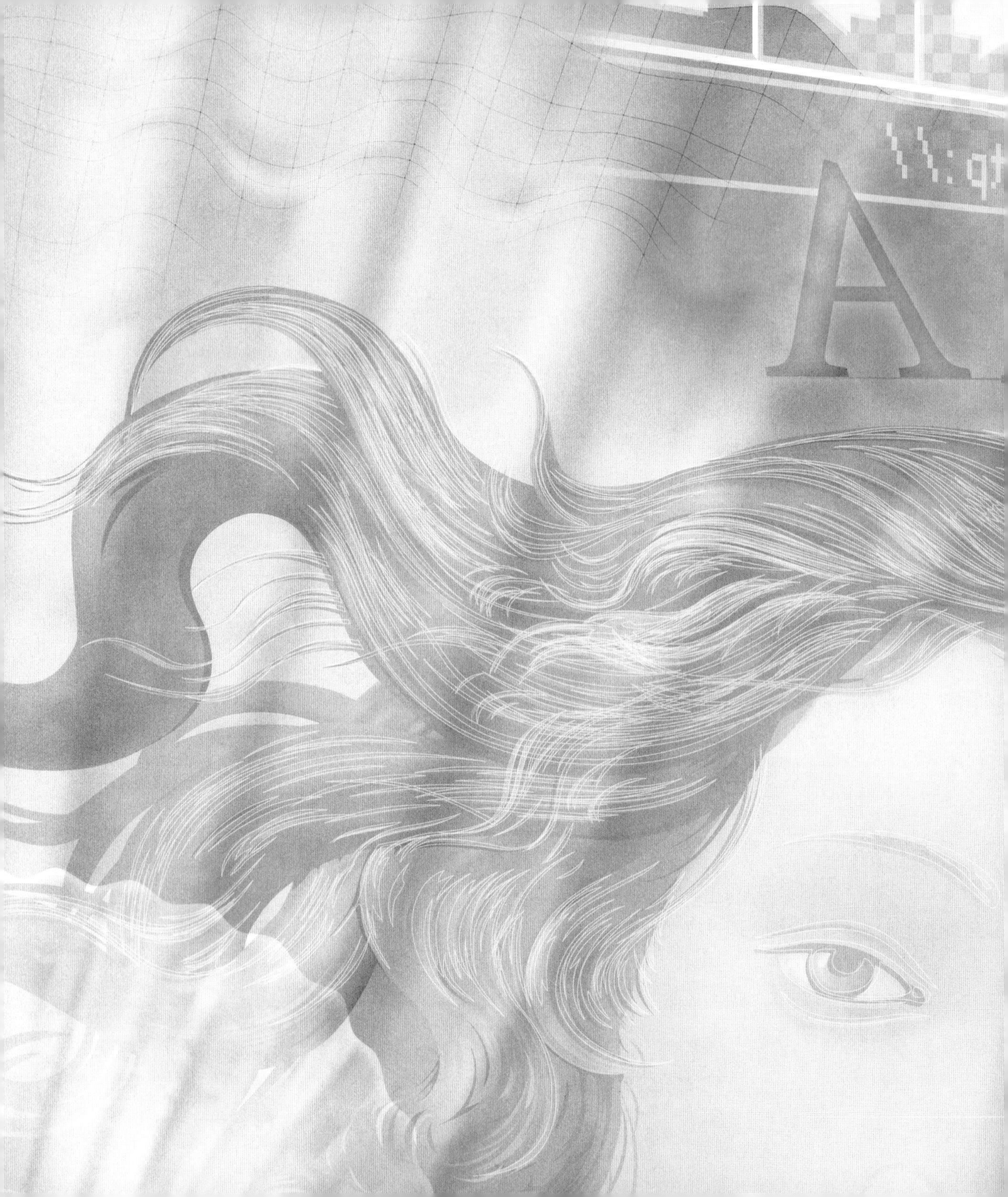
A

Chapter 5: Transforming and Distorting Shapes

You can easily modify an object's size, orientation, or shape by using tools and commands. You can also apply filters and effects to change an object's shape and path direction. And, by working with more than one object at a time, you can create complex designs using compound paths and masks.

Transforming selected objects

You can *transform* selected objects—that is, change their size, shape, and orientation by selecting one or more objects and then applying various transformation actions on them. For example, you can change the angle of an object by rotating it, or add perspective to an object by shearing it.

To transform an object, you can use the free transform tool, individual transformation tools, or the Transform palette:

• Use the free transform tool to rotate, scale, reflect, shear, and distort objects quickly.

• Use the transformation tools to change the size, shape, and orientation of selected objects. The transformation tools are the rotate tool, scale tool, reflect tool, and shear tool. You can also use individual transform dialog boxes to specify numeric values, to preview the transformation before applying it, and to select other transformation options.

• Use the Transform palette to modify selected objects by changing information in the palette. (See "Using the Transform palette" on page 147.)

As you transform objects, keep the following in mind:

• Transformation dialog boxes and commands can be opened for selected objects by using context-sensitive menus. To display context-sensitive menus, hold down the right mouse button (Windows) or Control-click (Mac OS) when the pointer is over the object.

• You can move and duplicate selected objects by using the bounding box. (See "Using the bounding box" on page 123.)

Defining the point of origin

All transformation actions perform their functions in relation to some fixed point on or around the object. This fixed point is called the *point of origin*. The default point of origin is the object's center point.

You can drag anywhere on an object with the free transform tool or an individual transformation tool to transform the object around the object's center. For example, you can drag an object to rotate it around its center, or you can set a new point of origin by clicking and then dragging to rotate it. You can also click a point of origin that you have set, and then drag it to a new position.

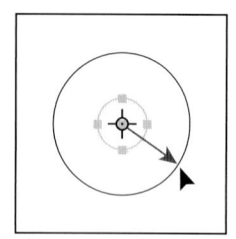

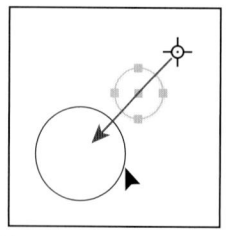

Object scaled from center and from new point of origin

When you transform an object or objects, the changes take place horizontally (along the *x* axis), vertically (along the *y* axis), or along both axes.

Rotating

Rotating an object turns it around a fixed point that you designate. The default point of origin is the object's center point. Copying while rotating is a useful way to create radially symmetrical objects, such as the petals of a flower.

To rotate with the bounding box:

1 With the selection tool, select the object or objects to rotate.

2 Move the pointer near a handle so that the pointer changes to a curve with arrows on both ends.

3 Drag the handle.

To rotate with the free transform tool:

1 With the selection tool ( ), select the object or objects to rotate.

2 Select the free transform tool ( ).

3 Position the pointer anywhere outside the bounding box. The pointer changes to ( ).

4 Drag until the selection is at the desired angle of rotation.

To rotate with the rotate tool:

1 With the selection tool, select the object or objects to rotate.

2 Select the rotate tool ( ).

3 Do one of the following:

• Drag to rotate around the object's center point.

• Click once to set the point of origin around which you want the object to rotate. Then move the arrowhead away from the point of origin and drag in a circular motion. Shift-drag to constrain the tool to multiples of 45 degrees.

• To rotate a copy of the object instead of the object itself, hold down Alt (Windows) or Option (Mac OS) after you start to drag.

• For finer control, drag farther from the object's point of origin.

To rotate by specifying an angle:

1 With the selection tool, select the object or objects to rotate.

2 Do one of the following:

• To set the center point as the point of origin, select the rotate tool ( ).

- To change the point of origin from which to rotate the object, select the rotate tool, and click where you want the new point of origin.

- To change the point of origin and specify the rotation angle in the Rotate dialog box, select the rotate tool, and Alt-click (Windows) or Option-click (Mac OS) the new point of origin.

- To specify the rotation angle in the Rotate dialog box, choose Object > Transform > Rotate, or double-click the rotate tool.

3 Enter the rotation angle, in degrees, in the Angle text box. Enter a negative angle to rotate the object clockwise; enter a positive angle to rotate the object counterclockwise.

4 Do one of the following:

- To rotate the object, click OK.

- To rotate a copy of the object, click Copy.

- To preview the effect before you apply it, select Preview.

- To place multiple copies of the object in a circular pattern around a point of origin, click Copy and then choose Object > Transform > Transform Again.

To rotate each object individually in a group:

1 Do one of the following:

- To apply the rotation as a transform command, select the object or objects to rotate. Then choose Object > Transform > Transform Each.

- To apply the rotation as an effect, select an object or group in the artwork, or target a group or layer in the Layers palette. (For more information on effects, see "Using effects" on page 271. For more information on targeting, see "Targeting layers, groups, and objects to apply appearance attributes" on page 252.) Then choose Effect > Distort & Transform > Transform.

2 In the Angle text box, enter the angle by which to rotate the selected objects, between –360 degrees and 360 degrees.

3 To preview the effect before you apply it, select Preview.

4 Do one of the following:

- To rotate the objects by the specified amount, click OK.

- To rotate the objects by a random amount, but by no more than the number of degrees specified in the Rotate text box, select Random, and click OK.

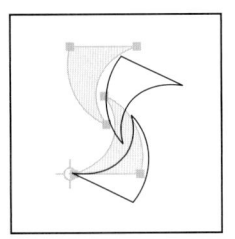

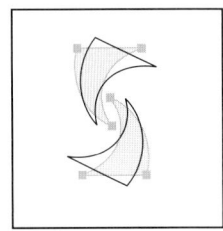

Rotate tool compared with the Transform Each and Transform commands, Rotate option

Scaling

Scaling an object enlarges or reduces it horizontally (along the *x* axis), vertically (along the *y* axis), or both horizontally and vertically, relative to the point of origin you designate. The default point of origin is the object's center point.

To scale with the bounding box:

1 With the selection tool, select the object or objects to scale.

2 Drag a handle until the selection is the desired size.

• Shift-drag the handle to preserve the proportion.

• Alt-drag (Windows) or Option-drag (Mac OS) to scale from the center of the bounding box (instead of the opposite handle).

To scale with the free transform tool:

1 With the selection tool, select the object or objects to scale.

2 Select the free transform tool ( ).

3 Drag a handle of the bounding box until the object is the desired size.

• Shift-drag the handle to preserve the proportion.

• Alt-drag (Windows) or Option-drag (Mac OS) to scale from the center of the bounding box (instead of the opposite handle).

To scale with the scale tool:

1 With the selection tool, select the object or objects to scale.

2 Select the scale tool ( ).

3 Do one of the following:

• Select the object, and drag to resize it around the center point.

• Click to set the point of origin from which you want the object to be resized, move the pointer away from the point of origin, and then drag to scale the object.

• Shift-drag to scale the object uniformly.

• To scale a copy of the object instead of the object itself, start dragging and then hold down Alt (Windows) or Option (Mac OS).

• For finer control over scaling, start dragging farther from the point of origin.

To scale by specifying scale factors:

1 With the selection tool, select the object or objects to scale.

2 Do one of the following:

• To set the center point as the point of origin, select the scale tool.

• To change the point of origin from which to scale the object, select the scale tool, and click the new point of origin.

3 To specify the scale percentage in the Scale dialog box, choose Object > Transform > Scale, or double-click the scale tool.

4 In the Scale dialog box, do one of the following:

• Select Uniform, and enter a percentage in the Scale text box to preserve the relative height and width of the object.

- Select Non-Uniform, and enter the horizontal and vertical scale factors as percentages to scale the height and width separately. The scale factors are relative to the specified point of origin and can be negative numbers.

- Select Scale Strokes & Effects to scale the line weights of all stroked paths (as specified in the Stroke palette), and scale any size-related effects, along with the objects.

You can also choose to scale stroke weights and effects automatically, whether you scale objects by dragging or by using the Scale dialog box. To scale stroke weights automatically, select Scale Strokes & Effects in the General Preferences dialog box, or choose the command from the Transform palette menu.

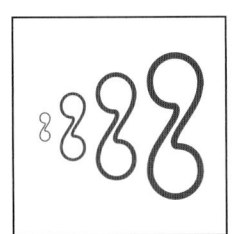

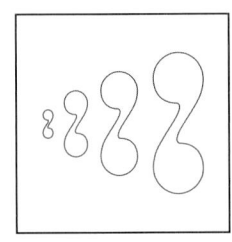

Scale Strokes & Effects option on and off

5 Do one of the following:

- To scale the object, click OK.

- To scale a copy of the object, click Copy.

- To preview the effect before you apply it, select Preview.

To scale objects individually in a group:

1 Do one of the following:

- To apply the command as a transform command, select the objects to scale. Then choose Object > Transform > Transform Each.

- To apply the command as an effect, select an object or group in the artwork, or target a group or layer in the Layers palette. (For more information on effects, see "Using effects" on page 271. For more information on targeting, see "Targeting layers, groups, and objects to apply appearance attributes" on page 252.) Then choose Effect > Distort & Transform > Transform.

2 In the Scale Horizontal and Vertical text boxes, enter the percentages by which to scale the selected objects.

3 Select Preview to preview the effect before you apply it.

4 Do one of the following:

- To scale the objects by the specified amounts, click OK.

- To scale the objects randomly, but by no more than the percentages specified in the Horizontal and Vertical text boxes, select Random, and click OK.

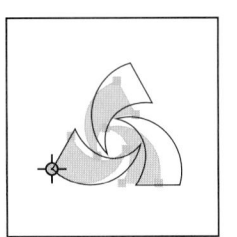

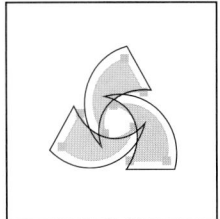

Scale tool compared with the Scale option in Transform Each dialog box

Reflecting

Reflecting an object flips the object across an invisible axis that you specify. Copying while reflecting lets you create a mirror image of an object.

To reflect with the free transform tool:

1 With the selection tool, select the object or objects to reflect.

2 Select the free transform tool ( ).

3 Drag a handle of the bounding box past the opposite edge or handle until the object is at the desired level of reflection.

To reflect with the reflect tool:

1 With the selection tool, select the object or objects to reflect.

2 Select the reflect tool ( ).

3 Position the pointer on one point along the invisible axis across which you want the reflection to occur, and click to set the point of origin. The pointer changes to an arrowhead.

4 Position the pointer at another point along the invisible axis, and do one of the following:

• Click to set a point across which to reflect the object. When you click, the selected object flips over the defined axis.

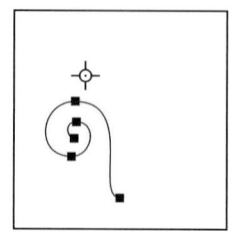

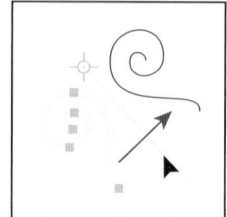

Click to set origin, then click again to reflect across axis.

• Adjust the axis of reflection by dragging instead of clicking. Shift-drag to constrain. As you drag, the invisible axis of reflection rotates around the point you clicked in step 3. When the image is in the desired position, release the mouse button.

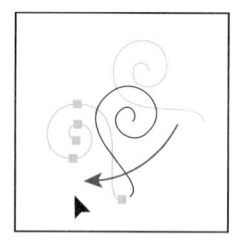

Drag reflect tool to rotate axis of reflection.

• For finer control over the reflection, drag farther from the object's point of origin.

To reflect by specifying an axis:

1 With the selection tool, select the object or objects to reflect.

2 Do one of the following:

• To set the center point as the point of origin, click the reflect tool.

• To change the point of origin from which to reflect the object, select the reflect tool and click where you want the new point of origin. To move the point of origin again, double-click where you want it to be.

3 To specify the reflect axis in the Reflect dialog box, choose Object > Transform > Reflect.

4 In the Reflect dialog box, select the axis across which you want the object to be reflected. You can reflect an object across a horizontal, a vertical, or an angled axis.

If you choose an angled axis, enter the desired angle of reflection, in degrees, relative to the *x* axis. Positive angles reflect the axis counterclockwise; negative angles reflect it clockwise.

5 Do one of the following:

• To reflect the object, click OK.

• To reflect a copy of the object, click Copy.

• To preview the effect before you apply it, select Preview.

Shearing

Shearing an object slants, or *skews*, the object along the axis you specify. Copying while shearing is useful for creating cast shadows.

To shear with the free transform tool:

1 With the selection tool, select the object or objects to shear.

2 Select the free transform tool ( ).

3 Start dragging a handle on the side of the bounding box (not a corner) and then hold down Ctrl+Alt (Windows) or Option+Command (Mac OS) as you drag until the object is at the desired perspective. Shift-drag to constrain the tool to multiples of 45 degrees.

To shear with the shear tool:

1 With the selection tool, select the object or objects to shear.

2 Select the shear tool ( ).

3 Do one of the following:

• Drag the object to shear by using the object's center point as the point of origin.

• Click to set the point of origin from which you want the object to be sheared. Then move the pointer away from the shear axis, and drag in the direction you want to shear the object.

• Shift-drag to constrain the tool.

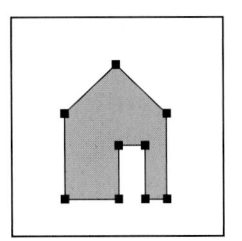

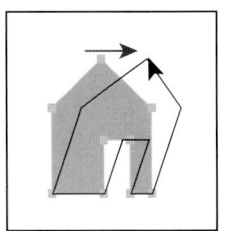

Select object. Then drag with the shear tool.

- To shear a copy of the object instead of the object itself, start dragging and then hold down Alt (Windows) or Option (Mac OS).

- For finer control over shearing, start dragging farther from the point of origin.

To shear by specifying an angle and an axis:

1 With the selection tool, select the object or objects to shear.

2 Do one of the following:

- To set the center point as the point of origin, click the shear tool.

- To change the point of origin from which to shear the object, select the shear tool and click where you want the point of origin.

3 To specify the shear angle and axis in the Shear dialog box, choose Object > Transform > Shear.

4 In the Shear dialog box, enter the new shear angle. The shear angle is the amount of slant to be applied to the object, relative to a line perpendicular to the shear axis. (Contrary to the way the program works with other transformation tools, the shear angle is calculated clockwise from the current axis.)

5 Specify the axis along which the object is to be sheared. You can shear an object along a horizontal, a vertical, or an angled axis.

If you choose an angled axis, enter the angle of the axis that you want, in degrees, relative to the *x* axis.

6 Do one of the following:

- To shear the object, click OK.

- To shear a copy of the object, click Copy.

- To preview the effect before you apply it, select Preview.

Distorting with the free transform tool

Distorting an object varies the size and shape of an object by dragging the corner points of the free transform tool's bounding box. As you drag the corner handles of the bounding box, the object's shape is distorted accordingly.

To distort with the free transform tool:

1 With the selection tool, select the object or objects to distort.

2 Select the free transform tool (昍).

3 Start dragging a handle on the corner of the bounding box (not a side) and then do one of the following:

- Hold down Ctrl (Windows) or Command (Mac OS) until the selection is at the desired level of distortion.

- Hold down Shift+Alt+Ctrl (Windows) or Shift+Option+Command (Mac OS) to distort in perspective.

Distorting in perspective

Resetting the bounding box angle

After you transform a selection, you can return the angle of the bounding box to its original orientation. You can do this after any transformation except shearing.

Choose Object > Transform > Reset Bounding Box.

Repeating transformations

Sometimes you may want to repeat the same transformation several times, especially when you are copying objects. The Transform Again command in the Object menu lets you repeat a move, scale, rotate, reflect, or shear operation as many times as you want, until you perform a different transform operation.

To repeat the previous transformation:

1 Make sure the object on which you want to repeat the transformation is selected.

2 Do one of the following:

• Choose Object > Transform > Transform Again.

• Press the right mouse button (Windows), or Control-click (Mac OS), and choose Transform Again from the context-sensitive menu.

Using the Transform palette

The Transform palette displays information about the location, size, and orientation of one or more selected objects. By entering new values, you can modify the selected objects. All values in the palette refer to the bounding boxes of the objects. You can also use commands in the Transform palette menu for such actions as flipping an object across the path or scaling the stroke weight.

To use the Transform palette:

1 Choose Window > Show Transform.

2 With the selection tool, select the object or objects to transform.

3 Enter options in the Transform palette:

• To select the reference point from which you are modifying the selection, click a handle on the square representing the object's bounding box.

• To change a selection to a horizontal orientation, enter a value in the X text box.

• To change a selection to a vertical orientation, enter a value in the Y text box.

• To change the width of a selection's bounding box, enter a value in the W text box.

• To change the height of a selection's bounding box, enter a value in the H text box.

• To rotate a selection, enter a new angle between 0 and 360 degrees in the Angle text box, or choose a value from the pop-up menu.

• To shear a selection, enter a value in the Shear text box, or choose a value from the pop-up menu.

4 Press Tab, Enter, or Return to apply the change.

To use commands in the Transform palette menu:

1 Choose Window > Show Transform.

2 With the selection tool, select the object or objects to transform.

3 Choose a command from the palette menu:

• To reflect a selection horizontally, choose Flip Horizontal.

• To reflect a selection vertically, choose Flip Vertical.

• To include the stroke when an object is transformed, choose Scale Strokes & Effects.

• To transform only the object, choose Transform Object Only.

• To transform only the pattern, choose Transform Pattern Only.

• To transform both the object and pattern, choose Transform Both.

Note: To ensure that values entered in the Info and Transform palettes include stroke weight and effects, choose Edit > Preferences > General, select the Display Preview Bounds option, and click OK.

Modifying shapes with filters and effects

Illustrator provides a variety of filters and effects for changing an object's shape and path direction. Using these commands as filters alters the original object's shape, whereas applying them as effects just changes the appearance of the object without altering the underlying structure of the object.

For more information, see "Using effects" on page 271.

Note: All of the following filters work with vector graphics only; you cannot use these filters with raster images.

Distorting with the Free Distort command

The Free Distort command lets you change the shape of a selection by dragging any of four corner points.

You can apply the Free Distort command as a filter or as an effect. For more information on effects, see "Using effects" on page 271.

To apply the Free Distort command:

1 Do one of the following:

• To apply the command as a filter, select an object. Then choose Filter > Distort > Free Distort.

• To apply the command as an effect, select an object or group in the artwork, or target a group or layer in the Layers palette. (For more information on targeting, see "Targeting layers, groups, and objects to apply appearance attributes" on page 252.) Then choose Effect > Distort & Transform > Free Distort.

2 Select Preview to preview the effect within the dialog box.

3 Drag one or more of the handles in the dialog box to distort the selection.

4 Click OK.

Rounding corners

The Round Corners command converts the corner points of an object to smooth curves.

You can apply the Round Corners command as a filter or as an effect. For more information, see "Using effects" on page 271.

To round corners on an object:

1 Do one of the following:

• To apply the command as a filter, select the object. Then choose Filter > Stylize > Round Corners.

• To apply the command as an effect, select an object or group in the artwork, or target a group or layer in the Layers palette. (For more information on targeting, see "Targeting layers, groups, and objects to apply appearance attributes" on page 252.) Then choose Effect > Stylize > Round Corners. Select Preview if you want to preview the effect.

2 Enter a value (in the unit of measure specified in the General Preferences dialog box) in the Radius text box to determine the curvature of the rounded curve, and click OK.

Making selections rectangular or elliptical

The Convert to Shape commands Rectangle, Rounded Rectangle, and Ellipse let you make objects appear to have this shape. These commands are useful when applied to a fill or stroke of an object with multiple fills or strokes. For more information, see "Using the Appearance palette" on page 261.

This command is only available as an effect. For more information, see "Using effects" on page 271.

To make objects rectangular or elliptical:

1 Make the selection to which you want to apply the Rectangle, Rounded Rectangle, or Ellipse command.

2 Choose Effect > Convert to Shape > Rectangle, Rounded Rectangle, or Ellipse.

3 Do one of the following:

• Select Absolute, and enter the height and width you want to make the selection.

• Select Relative and enter a value that represents how much higher and wider to make the selection than its current height and width. (Enter a negative value to make the selection shorter or narrower than its current height and width.)

4 If you are applying the Rounded Rectangle command, enter a value (in the unit of measure specified in the General Preferences dialog box) in the Corner Radius text box to determine the curvature of the rounded edge.

5 Click OK.

Punking and bloating

The Punk & Bloat command curves objects inward and outward from their anchor points.

You can apply the Punk & Bloat command as a filter or as an effect. For more information, see "Using effects" on page 271.

To bloat or punk an object:

1 Do one of the following:

• To apply the command as a filter, select the object to punk or bloat. Then choose Filter > Distort > Punk & Bloat.

• To apply the command as an effect, select an object or group in the artwork, or target a group or layer in the Layers palette. (For more information on targeting, see "Targeting layers, groups, and objects to apply appearance attributes" on page 252.) Then choose Effect > Distort & Transform > Punk & Bloat.

2 Drag the slider toward Punk to curve the object inward from its anchor points and move the anchor points outward; drag the slider toward Bloat to curve the object outward from its anchor points and move the anchor points inward. You can also enter a value, from –200% to 200%, in the Percentage text box.

3 To preview the effect before you apply it, select Preview, and click OK.

Roughening

The Roughen command moves anchor points in a jagged array from the original object, creating a rough edge on the object.

You can apply the Roughen command as a filter or as an effect. For more information, see "Using effects" on page 271.

To roughen an object:

1 Do one of the following:

• To apply the command as a filter, select the object to roughen. Then choose Filter > Distort > Roughen.

• To apply the command as an effect, select an object or group in the artwork, or target a group or layer in the Layers palette. (For more information on targeting, see "Targeting layers, groups, and objects to apply appearance attributes" on page 252) Then choose Effect > Distort & Transform > Roughen.

2 Select Relative to distort by a percentage of the size of the object or Absolute to distort a specific amount.

3 Set the size of the distortion by dragging the Size slider or entering a value in the Size text box.

4 Specify the details per inch by dragging the slider or entering a value between 0 and 100 in the Detail text box.

5 Select the type of distortion you want around each anchor point: Smooth (for soft edges) or Corner (for sharp edges).

6 To preview the effect before you apply it, select Preview, and click OK.

Scribbling and tweaking

The Scribble option randomly distorts objects by moving anchor points away from the original object. The Tweak option randomly distorts objects by moving anchor points on the selected object by an amount that you specify.

You can apply the Scribble and Tweak command as a filter or as an effect. For more information, see "Using effects" on page 271.

To scribble or tweak an object:

1 Do one of the following:

• To apply the command as a filter, select the object to scribble or tweak. Then choose Filter > Distort > Scribble and Tweak.

• To apply the command as an effect, select an object or group in the artwork, or target a group or layer in the Layers palette. (For more information on targeting, see "Targeting layers, groups, and objects to apply appearance attributes" on page 252.) Then choose Effect > Distort & Transform > Scribble and Tweak.

2 Select Relative to distort by a percentage of the size of the object or Absolute to distort a specific amount.

3 In the Horizontal and Vertical text boxes, enter the amount to move points or drag the sliders.

4 Select options for the anchor points:

• Anchor Points moves anchor points. Deselecting this option keeps anchor points anchored while a filter is applied to the rest of the object.

• "In" Control Points moves control points that lead into anchor points on the path.

• "Out" Control Points moves control points that lead out of anchor points on the path.

5 Because results vary, select Preview to preview the effect before you apply it, and click OK.

Note: Once you choose values, a different effect displays for both Scribble and Tweak when you select Preview.

Twirling

The Twirl command and the twirl tool rotate a selection more sharply in the center than at the edges.

You can apply the Twirl command as a filter or as an effect. For more information, see "Using effects" on page 271.

To twirl an object with the twirl tool:

1 Select the object to twirl.

2 Select the twirl tool ( ), and drag the object clockwise or counterclockwise.

To twirl an object with the twirl command:

1 Do one of the following:

• To apply the command as a filter, select the object to twirl. Then choose Filter > Distort > Twirl.

• To apply the command as an effect, select an object or group in the artwork, or target a group or layer in the Layers palette. (For more information on targeting, see "Targeting layers, groups, and objects to apply appearance attributes" on page 252.) Then choose Effect > Distort & Transform > Twirl.

2 Enter a value for the twirl angle, from −3600 to 3600 (a positive value twirls clockwise and a negative value twirls counterclockwise).

3 Click OK.

Adding drop shadows

The Drop Shadow command creates a three-dimensional shadow on any selected object. You can offset the drop shadow any distance from the object along the *x* or *y* axis, as well as vary the opacity, blending mode, blur, color, and darkness of the drop shadow.

You can apply the Drop Shadow command as a filter or as an effect. For more information, see "Using effects" on page 271.

To create a drop shadow:

1 Do one of the following:

• To apply the command as a filter, use a selection tool and select the object. Then choose Filter > Stylize > Drop Shadow.

• To apply the command as an effect, select an object or group in the artwork, or target a group or layer in the Layers palette. (For more information on targeting, see "Targeting layers, groups, and objects to apply appearance attributes" on page 252.) Then choose Effect > Stylize > Drop Shadow.

2 Choose a blending mode from the Mode menu. For more information, see "Selecting blending modes" on page 223.

3 Enter the amount of opacity you want for the shadow.

4 Enter the distance you want the drop shadow to be offset from the object on the *x* axis or the *y* axis (in the unit of measure set in the General Preferences dialog box).

5 Enter the distance from the edge of the shadow where you want any blurring to occur.

6 Do one of the following:

• Select Color, and click the color preview to specify a color for the shadow. For more information, see "Using the Color Picker" on page 191.

• Select Darkness, and enter the percentage darkness (percentage of black added) you want for the drop shadow. In a CMYK document, a value of 100% used with a selected object that contains a fill or stroke color other than black creates a multicolored black shadow. A value of 100% used with a selected object that contains only a black fill or stroke creates a 100% black shadow. A value of 0% creates a drop shadow the color of the selected object.

7 To place each shadow directly behind the object to which the shadow is applied, select Create Separate Shadows. Leaving this option unselected places all of the shadows together behind the bottom-most selected object.

8 Click OK.

Adding inner and outer glows

The Inner Glow and Outer Glow commands let you add glows that emanate from the inside or outside edges of the selection.

These commands are only available as effects. For more information, see "Using effects" on page 271.

To apply an inner or outer glow:

1 Select an object or group in the artwork, or target a group or layer in the Layers palette. For more information on targeting, see "Targeting layers, groups, and objects to apply appearance attributes" on page 252.

2 Choose Effect > Stylize > Inner Glow or Outer Glow.

3 Select Preview to preview the effect.

4 Choose a blending mode from the Mode menu. For more information, see "Selecting blending modes" on page 223.

5 Click the color preview next to the blending mode menu to specify a color for the glow. For more information, see "Using the Color Picker" on page 191.

6 Specify the amount of transparency you want for the glow. For more information, see "About transparency" on page 219.

7 If you are applying an inner glow, select a glow source option:

• Center to apply a glow that emanates from the center of the selection.

• Edge to apply a glow that emanates from the inside edges of the selection.

8 For blur, enter the distance from the center or edge of the selection where you want any blurring to occur.

9 Click OK.

Feathering edges

The Feather command softens the edges of an object by fading them to transparent over the distance you specify.

This command is only available as an effect. For more information, see "Using effects" on page 271.

To make the edges of an object fade from opaque to transparent:

1 Select the object whose edges you want to feather.

2 Choose Effect > Stylize > Feather.

3 Select Preview to display a preview of the results.

4 For Feather Radius, enter the distance over which you want the change from opaque to transparent to occur.

Creating line effects

Using the Zig Zag and Add Arrowheads commands, you can create wavy and zig zag effects and add various arrowhead styles to lines.

You can apply these commands as a filter or as an effect. For more information, see "Using effects" on page 271.

The Zig Zag command adds anchor points to an existing object and then moves some of the points to the left of (or upward from) the path and some to the right of (or downward from) the path. You can specify the number of anchor points to create and the distance to move them. You can also choose whether to create smooth anchor points for a wavy line effect, or corner anchor points for a jagged line effect.

The Add Arrowheads command lets you add an arrowhead or arrow tail to any selected line. If applied as a filter, the resulting arrows can be edited like any other object, but they do not move with the line to which they are attached. If applied as an effect, the arrows are similar to brush strokes. That is, the arrows change location, direction, and color along with the line, but they cannot be edited separately.

For information about creating stroked lines, see "Using the Stroke palette" on page 181.

To convert straight lines to Zig Zags:

1 Do one of the following:

• To apply the command as a filter, select the object you want to convert. Then choose Filter > Distort > Zig Zag.

• To apply the command as an effect, select an object or group in the artwork, or target a group or layer in the Layers palette. (For more information on targeting, see "Targeting layers, groups, and objects to apply appearance attributes" on page 252.) Then choose Effect > Distort & Transform > Zig Zag.

2 Select Relative to move points by a percentage of the size of the object or Absolute to move points a specific amount.

3 For Size, enter the distance you want to move points on the line, or drag the slider.

4 In the Ridges text box, enter the number of ridges per line segment you want, or drag the slider.

5 Select from the following options:

• Smooth to create smooth points, resulting in a wavy line.

• Corner to create corner points, resulting in a jagged line.

• Preview to preview the line.

6 Click OK.

To add arrowheads to a line:

1 Do one of the following:

• To apply the command as a filter, select a line to which you want to add arrowheads. Then choose Filter > Stylize > Add Arrowheads.

• To apply the command as an effect, select an object or group in the artwork, or target a group or layer in the Layers palette. (For more information on targeting, see "Targeting layers, groups, and objects to apply appearance attributes" on page 252.) Then choose Effect > Stylize > Add Arrowheads.

2 Choose from various arrowhead designs for each end of the line by clicking the forward icon or backward icon below the Start and End arrow boxes. The start and end of the line refer to the order in which the line was drawn.

3 To rescale the size of an arrowhead, enter the percentage you want in the Scale text box. This scales the arrowhead relative to the stroke weight of the line.

4 Click OK.

Blending shapes

The Adobe Illustrator blend tool and the Make Blend command let you create a series of intermediate objects and colors between two or more selected objects. You can blend between two open paths (such as two different lines), between two closed paths (such as a circle and a square), between gradients, or between other blends. Depending on the way you paint the objects you are blending, you can produce airbrush effects such as complex shading, highlighting, and contouring. The Blend filters can also be used to blend colors between filled objects.

You can edit blends that you created by moving, resizing, deleting, or adding objects. After you make editing changes, the artwork is automatically reblended.

About blending

One of the simplest uses for blending is to create and distribute shapes evenly between two objects. For example, you can create a series of evenly spaced bars using the blend tool or the Make Blend command.

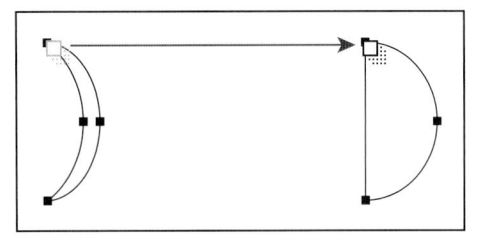

Two objects selected

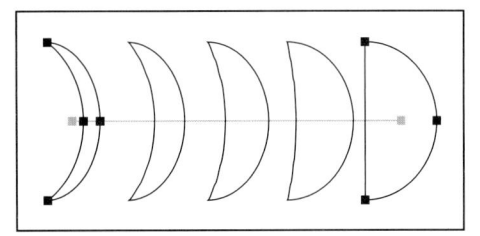

Blending distributes shapes evenly

You can also blend between two open paths to create a smooth transition between objects, or you can combine blends of colors and objects to create color transitions in the shape of a particular object.

The following rules apply to blending shapes and their associated colors:

• You can blend between an unlimited number of objects, colors, opacities, or gradients.

• Blends can be directly edited with tools such as the selection tools, the rotate tool, or the scale tool.

• A straight path is created between blended objects when the blend is first applied. You can edit the blend path by dragging anchor points and path segments. (See "Adjusting path segments" on page 92.)

• You cannot blend between gradient mesh objects.

• If you blend between one object painted with a process color and another object painted with a spot color, the blended shapes are painted with a blended process color. If you blend between two different spot colors, process colors are used to paint the intermediate steps. If, however, you blend between tints of the same spot color, the steps are all painted with percentages of the spot color.

• If you blend between two patterned objects, the blended steps will only use the fill of the object on the topmost layer.

• If you blend between objects that have blending modes specified with the Transparency palette, the blended steps will only use the blending mode of the top object.

• If you blend between objects with multiple appearance attributes (effects, fills, or strokes), Illustrator attempts to blend the options.

• By default, blends are created as knockout transparency groups, so that if any of the steps consist of overlapping transparent objects, these objects will not show through each other. You can change this setting by selecting the blend and deselecting Knockout Group in the Transparency palette.

• The Adobe Illustrator program automatically calculates the number of steps in a blend, unless you select Specify Steps in the Blend Options dialog box.

Creating blends

You create blends in Illustrator by clicking objects with the blend tool, or by selecting objects with a selection tool and using the Blend commands.

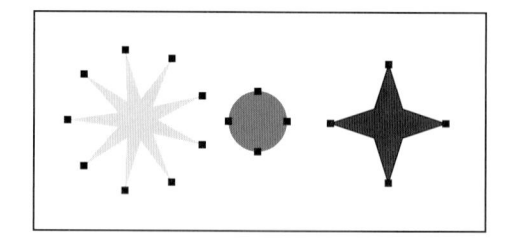

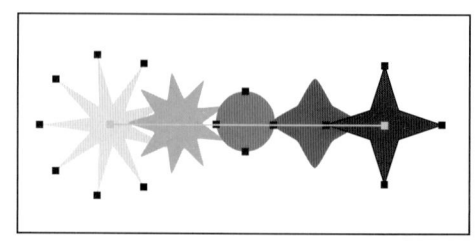

Multiple objects are clicked sequentially with the blend tool

Objects are blended relative to selected anchor points on each blended object. If the objects are unselected, or if you have only one anchor point selected, Illustrator automatically selects the two points from which the blend commences and finishes. You can also select two or more anchor points from which to blend by clicking anchor points with the blend tool. By selecting different anchor points on the objects, you can create the effect of rotating the blend from one point in an object to a selected point in the next object.

To create a blend with the blend tool:

1 Select the blend tool ( ).

2 Click objects to blend in sequential order. If you want to blend to a specific anchor point on an object, click the anchor point with the blend tool. If you are blending open paths, select an endpoint on each path.

3 When you are finished adding objects to the blend, you can click the blend tool again to start a new blend.

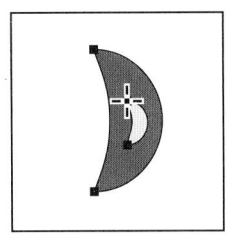

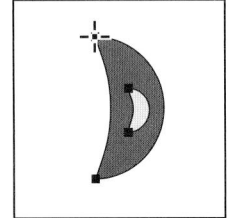

Click anchor point on first object with blend tool. Then click anchor point on second object.

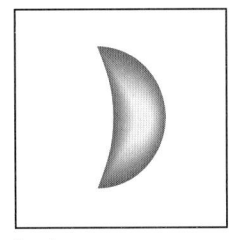

Result

To create a blend with the Make Blend command:

1 Select the objects to blend with any selection tool.

2 Choose Object > Blends > Make.

To release a blend:

1 Select the blend with any selection tool.

2 Choose Object > Blends > Release.

To change the number of steps between blends:

1 Choose Object > Blends > Blend Options.

2 Select from the following options in the Spacing pop-up menu:

• Specified Steps. Enter a value to specify the number of steps between the start and end of the blend.

• Specified Distance. Enter a value to specify the distance between the steps in the blend. The distance specified is measured from the edge of one object to the corresponding edge on the next object (for example, from the rightmost edge of one object to the rightmost edge of the next object).

• Smooth Color has the Adobe Illustrator program autocalculate the number of steps for the blends. If objects are filled or stroked with different colors, the steps are calculated to provide the optimum number of steps for a smooth color transition. If the objects contain identical colors, or if they contain gradients or patterns, the number of steps is based on the longest distance between the bounding box edges of the two objects.

To change the orientation of the blend to the path:

1 Choose Objects > Blends > Blend Options.

2 Select from the following options:

• Click the Align to Page button to orient the blend perpendicular to the x axis of the page.

• Click the Align to Path button to orient the blend perpendicular to the path.

Align to Page option applied

Align to Path option applied

Creating blends on paths

Once you create a blend, you can then apply the blend to a path. Applying a blend to a path is an easy way to wrap a blend around an object or create special effects in your artwork.

The blend follows the contours of the path in the orientation specified in the Blend Options dialog box. If Align to Path is selected, the alignment of the blend follows the contours of the path. If Align to Page (the default setting) is selected, the blend is aligned with the x axis of the page.

To apply a blend to a path:

1 Select a blend and hold down Shift to select a path.

2 Choose Object > Blends > Replace Spine.

To reverse the order of a blend on a path:

1 Select the blend.

2 Choose Object > Blends > Reverse Spine. The objects are ordered in reverse on the path.

To reverse the stacking order of a blend on a path:

1 Select the blend.

2 Choose Object > Blends > Reverse Front to Back. The objects are reversed in the stacking order on the path, so that those objects on the frontmost stacking order are moved to the back of the stacking order, and vice-versa. (See "Stacking objects" on page 131.)

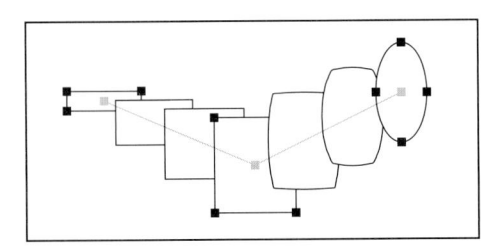

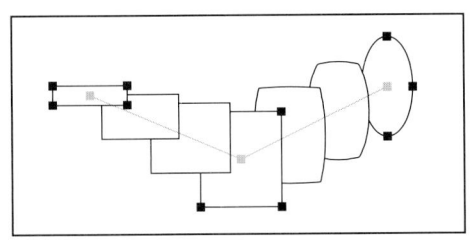

Original and with Reverse Front to Back command applied

Editing blends

You can move, delete, transform, edit anchor points and Bezier curves, or change colors on blends, using any of the editing tools available in the Adobe Illustrator program. When you edit a blend path, the changes take place interactively while you work.

Blending colors between filled objects

The Blend filters create a series of intermediate colors from a group of three or more filled objects, based on the objects' vertical or horizontal orientation, or on their stacking order. The filters do not affect strokes or unpainted objects. (See "Stacking objects" on page 131.)

To blend colors and opacities between filled objects:

1 Select three or more filled objects to blend.

2 Do one of the following:

• To fill the intermediate objects with gradated blends between the frontmost and backmost filled objects, choose Filter > Colors > Blend Front to Back.

- To fill the intermediate objects with gradated blends between the leftmost and rightmost filled objects, choose Filter > Colors > Blend Horizontally.

- To fill the intermediate objects with gradated blends between the topmost and bottommost filled objects, choose Filter > Colors > Blend Vertically.

Using the Pen and Ink filters

The Pen and Ink > Hatch Effects filter creates textured gradations, such as cross-hatching, and irregular random textures, such as wood grains, that you can apply to artwork to simulate the look of an ink pen drawing. A similar tool, called the Photo Crosshatch filter, can convert a bitmap photographic image into a series of hatched layers, so that it appears to be sketched by an ink pen. (See "Using the Photo Crosshatch filter" on page 282.)

The Hatch Effects filter converts a selected object into a mask and then draws lines or shapes behind it. The shapes created by the Hatch Effects filter are objects and can require significant program memory. Thus, consider applying Pen and Ink effects as the last step in creating your artwork: Make the entire drawing and paint it as desired. Then apply the hatch effects.

The *hatch* (or *hatch style*) is the design element of the Hatch Effects filter. The particular options associated with a hatch are called *hatch settings*. You can select from hatch settings supplied with the Adobe Illustrator program by using the Hatch Effects dialog box. You can also create your own hatched designs by drawing or selecting an object, naming it as a hatch in the New Hatch dialog box, and then applying it to artwork by using the Hatch Effects dialog box. Try experimenting with applying different hatches to your artwork before creating your own.

Applying a hatch effect

To apply a hatch effect to a selected object, you choose a hatch setting and its associated hatch style, modify the settings if desired, and apply them through the Hatch Effects dialog box. The Hatch Effects dialog box lets you adjust the hatch.

To fill an object with an existing ink pen hatch:

1 Select the object you want to fill with a hatch.

2 Choose Filter > Pen and Ink > Hatch Effects.

3 Choose a hatch from the Hatch pop-up menu and an effect from the Hatch Effect pop-up menu.

4 To improve the program's performance by turning off the hatch preview, deselect the Preview option at the lower right of the dialog box.

5 To adjust the number of hatch elements applied to the selection, drag the Density slider or enter values in the text box. To intensify the effect, click a gradation within the density adjustment bar.

6 To specify hatch uniformity or design characteristics, adjust sliders or enter values for Dispersion, Thickness, Scale, or Rotation.

Enter an angle along which to apply the effect by entering a value from -360 to 360 in the text boxes. Then drag the slider or enter values in the text boxes to specify a range, as follows:

• Dispersion, which controls the spacing of hatch elements, ranges from 0% to 300%.

• Thickness, or stroke weight, of the hatch elements ranges from 10 pts to 1000 pts. (This option is dimmed if the selection is unstroked.)

• Scale, which sets the size of the hatch elements, ranges from 10% to 1000%.

• Rotation, which sets the angle at which the hatch elements are applied, ranges from –180 degrees to 180 degrees.

7 Use the dial or text boxes to enter a value between -360 and 360 for effect variables as follows:

• Linear increases the effect progressively.

• Reflect varies the effect from the center of the object outward.

• Constant creates the same effect evenly across the shape.

• Symmetric varies the effect proportionately and evenly, for example, if applying hatches to round or cylindrical shapes.

• Random applies the effect irregularly.

• Fade specifies whether the hatch fades across the object. Choose the fade properties from the Fade pop-up menu: None for no fade, To White to fade the hatch to white, To Black to fade the hatch to black, or Use Gradient if the object is filled with a gradient and you want that gradient to define the fade's direction and colors.

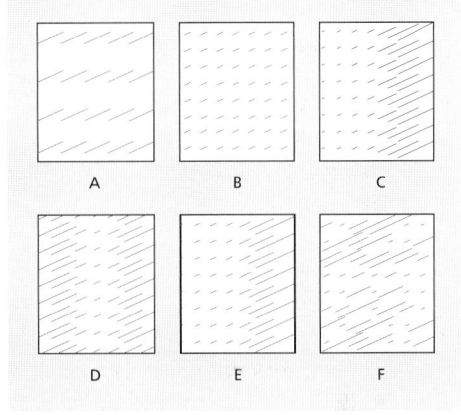

*A. Original hatch B. Constant C. Linear D. Reflect
E. Symmetric F. Random*

8 Select from the following color options for the hatch:

• Match Object's Color changes the hatch fill to the selection's fill.

• Keep Object's Fill Color applies the hatch in its original color on top of the object's fill color.

9 When you finish adjusting the hatch options, click OK.

Creating and saving hatches

You can create and save your own hatches or modify existing hatches and save them for reuse. To save hatches, you use either the New Hatch or the Hatch Effects dialog box.

To create a hatch:

1 Draw the objects you want to convert to a hatch design for the ink pen effect.

2 Select the artwork.

3 Choose Filter > Pen and Ink > New Hatch.

4 Click New. Enter a name for the new hatch and click OK.

5 To improve the program's performance, deselect Preview to turn off the preview of the hatch and click OK.

To modify an existing hatch:

1 Make sure that nothing is selected in the artwork.

2 Choose Filter > Pen and Ink > New Hatch.

3 Choose a hatch from the Hatch pop-up menu.

4 Click Paste and then click OK.

5 Edit the hatch as desired, and then select it.

6 Choose Filter > Pen and Ink > New Hatch.

7 Click New. Name the new hatch and click OK.

To save hatch settings:

1 Choose Filter > Pen and Ink > Hatch Effects.

2 Specify the hatch settings and any style options you want to save.

3 To save the settings in the file, click New. Enter a new name for the settings, and click OK.

To delete hatch settings:

1 Choose Filter > Pen and Ink > Hatch Effects.

2 Select the hatch settings and any style options you want to delete.

3 Click Delete, and then click OK.

To delete an existing hatch:

1 Choose Filter > Pen and Ink > New Hatch.

2 Choose a hatch from the Hatch pop-up menu.

3 Click Delete, and then click OK.

Using Pen and Ink hatch libraries

When using the Hatch Effects filter you may want to import hatches that you previously created in Illustrator, or save the current set of hatches you made into a hatch library. Hatch libraries are stored in the Illustrator 9.0 \ Plug-Ins \ Illustrator Filters \ Ink Pen folder.

Once you have opened a hatch library, all the hatches in the library are loaded into the Hatch Effects dialog and can be viewed in the Hatch Effect pop-up menu at the upper left corner of the dialog.

To load a pen and ink hatch library into Illustrator:

1 Choose Filter > Pen and Ink > Library Open.

2 In the dialog box, locate the hatch library you want to open and click OK. The hatch libraries are located in the Illustrator 9.0 \ Plug-Ins \ Illustrator Filters \ Ink Pen folder.

Once the new library has been loaded, use the Pen and Ink filter as described in "Applying a hatch effect" on page 160.

To save new hatches in an ink pen library:

1 Create new hatches as described in "Creating and saving hatches" on page 162.

2 Choose Filter > Pen and Ink > Library Save As.

3 In the dialog box, name the new file, save it in the Illustrator 9.0 \ Plug-Ins \ Illustrator Filters \ Ink Pen folder, and click OK.

Using the Pathfinder palette and Effect menu to modify shapes

The Pathfinder commands in the Pathfinder palette and Effect menu combine, isolate, and subdivide objects, and they build new objects formed by the intersections of objects.

To use the Pathfinder palette, you click a button in the palette that corresponds to the action you want to do. For more information on effects and the Effect menu, see "Using effects" on page 271.

Most Pathfinder commands create compound paths. A *compound path* is a group of two or more paths that are painted so that overlapping paths can appear transparent. Except where noted, the objects created by all Pathfinder commands are assigned the same paint style as the top object in the current layer's stack. (See "Stacking objects" on page 131 and "Working with compound paths" on page 166.)

You can choose Show Options from the Pathfinder palette menu to mix colors that overlap or adjoin using the Hard Mix, Soft Mix, and Trap options. (See "Using the Hard Mix and Soft Mix commands" on page 194 and "Step 3: Create a trap to compensate for misregistration on press" on page 385.)

Note: Applying Pathfinder commands to complex selections, such as blends, may require large amounts of RAM. If you are unable to use a Pathfinder command with Mac OS successfully, try increasing the memory allotted to the Adobe Illustrator program.

To use the Pathfinder commands:

Note: You cannot use Pathfinder commands with objects created using the gradient mesh tool.

1 Do one of the following:

• To apply the command from the Pathfinder palette, use a selection tool to select the objects to modify. Then choose Window > Show Pathfinder and click a Pathfinder command:

- To apply the Pathfinder command to multiple objects as an effect, first group the objects and target the group before applying the command. (For more information on targeting, see "Targeting layers, groups, and objects to apply appearance attributes" on page 252.) Then choose Effect > Pathfinder and choose a Pathfinder command:

Unite Traces the outline of all selected objects as if they were a single, merged object. The resulting shape takes on the paint attributes of the top object selected. Any objects inside the selected objects are deleted.

Intersect Traces the outline of all overlapping shapes in the selected objects, ignoring any nonoverlapping areas. This command works on two objects at a time.

Exclude Traces all nonoverlapping areas of the selected objects and makes overlapping areas transparent. Where an even number of objects overlap, the overlap becomes transparent. Where an odd number of objects overlap, the overlap becomes filled.

Minus Front Subtracts the frontmost selected objects from the backmost object. You can use this command to delete areas of an illustration by adjusting the stacking order. (See "Stacking objects" on page 131.)

Minus Back Subtracts the backmost selected objects from the frontmost object. You can use this command to delete areas of an illustration by adjusting the stacking order. (See "Stacking objects" on page 131.)

Divide Divides a piece of artwork into its component filled faces (a *face* is an area undivided by a line segment). The resulting faces can then be ungrouped and manipulated independently of each other.

You can choose to delete or preserve unfilled objects when applying the Divide command. See "Setting Pathfinder options" on page 165.

Trim Removes the part of a filled object that is hidden. It removes any strokes and does not merge objects of the same color.

Merge Removes the part of a filled object that is hidden. It removes any strokes and merges any adjoining or overlapping objects filled with the same color.

Crop Divides artwork into its component filled faces and then deletes all the parts of the artwork that fall outside the boundary of the topmost object. It also removes any strokes.

Outline Divides an object into its component line segments, or *edges*. Each edge can be ungrouped and independently manipulated. This command is useful for preparing artwork that needs a trap for overprinting objects.

You can choose to delete or preserve unfilled objects when applying the Outline command. See "Setting Pathfinder options" on page 165.

To repeat the most recent Pathfinder command:

Do one of the following:

- In the Pathfinder palette menu, choose Repeat Command, where Command is the most recently used command.

- Choose Effect > Apply <command>.

The command is applied with the most recently used settings.

Setting Pathfinder options

The Pathfinder Options dialog box lets you change the precision of Pathfinder commands and remove any redundant points created as a result of using Pathfinder commands. You can also control how the Divide and Outline commands affect unfilled objects.

Note: Pathfinder works best with filled and closed objects without strokes. Using Pathfinder with open and stroked paths may give you unexpected results.

To set Pathfinder options:

1 Choose Window > Show Pathfinder.

2 Choose Pathfinder Options from the Pathfinder palette menu.

3 Specify Pathfinder options:

- Enter a precision value in the Calculate Precision text box to affect the precision with which Pathfinder commands calculate when applied. The more precise the calculation, the more accurate the drawing and the more time is required to carry out a Pathfinder command. A more precise calculation may produce a more accurate drawing but carrying out a Pathfinder command will require more time.

- Select Remove Redundant Points to delete any points that are located directly on top of each other and that you created when using a Pathfinder command.

- Select Divide & Outline Will Remove Unpainted Artwork to delete any unfilled objects in the selected artwork that result from using the Divide or Outline command.

- To reset all options to their default settings, click Defaults.

4 Click OK.

Converting strokes to filled objects

The Outline Stroke command traces the outline of all stroked paths within the selected artwork and substitutes a filled object with the same width as the original stroked path. This commands lets you modify the outline of an object more than you could if it were only a stroke.

You can also use this command to create an overlay of your original artwork that strips out all stroked lines and replaces them with compound filled paths. The Outline Path command is useful when you prepare artwork for trapping color separations.

You can apply the Outline Stroke command as a filter or as an effect. For more information on effects, see "Using effects" on page 271.

To create an outline of your artwork:

1 Do one of the following:

- To apply the command as a Path command, select the artwork to outline. The artwork can contain filled and stroked paths; however, only stroked paths are outlined. Then choose Object > Path > Outline Stroke.

- To apply the command as an effect, select an object or group in the artwork, or target a group or layer in the Layers palette. (For more information on targeting, see "Targeting layers, groups, and objects to apply appearance attributes" on page 252.) Then choose Effect > Path > Outline Stroke.

The outline replaces the original artwork and is selected.

Cutting objects

The Slice command in the Object menu and the knife tool in the toolbox cut objects in a designated shape. When you use the Slice command, the object you cut must be ungrouped. The knife tool slices grouped and ungrouped objects.

The Slice command lets you use a selected object as a cookie cutter or stencil to cut through other objects. The Slice command slices overlapping objects into discrete shapes according to the selection's boundaries, and it discards the original selection.

The knife tool slices objects along a freehand path you draw with the tool, dividing objects into their component filled faces (a *face* is an area undivided by a line segment).

To cut objects by using the Slice command:

1 With the selection tool, select the object to use as a cutter, and position it so that it touches the object to cut. (To retain the original selection, save a copy elsewhere in your file.) The object cuts any filled object or objects that it's touching.

2 To cut the object, choose Object > Path > Slice. The shapes that result are ungrouped and selected.

To cut objects by using the knife tool:

1 Select the knife tool ( ).

2 Drag the pointer over the object. The knife cuts in a curved path.

To cut in a straight path, Alt-drag (Windows) or Option-drag (Mac OS) the knife tool.

Working with compound paths

Using the Compound Paths command enables you to create paths that have transparent interior spaces where the original objects overlapped (such as the interiors of the letters *o* and *g*). This method lets you create objects more complex than you could easily create using the drawing tools or Pathfinder commands.

Compound paths act as grouped objects. To select part of a compound path, you must use the direct-selection tool.

Important: *If you use complex shapes as compound paths, or if you use several compound paths in a file, you may have problems printing the file. If you experience printing problems, simplify or eliminate the compound paths.*

Creating and adjusting compound paths

When you are learning to create compound paths, you may find it helpful to work in Preview view or to open two windows so that you can preview your artwork in one window as you work in Outline view in the other window. Viewing both windows helps you understand how compound paths work.

Once you define objects as a compound path, all objects in the compound path take on the paint attributes of the backmost object in the stacking order. Releasing the compound path does not reapply the objects' previous paint attributes.

To create a compound path:

1 Make sure the objects you want to see through are in front of the background object in the painting order.

2 Use the selection tool, or drag a marquee to select all of the objects to include in the compound path.

3 Choose Object > Compound Paths > Make. You create a hole in the overlapping objects.

When you create a compound path, you can specify whether overlapping paths appear transparent or filled by clicking a Reverse Path Direction button in the Attributes palette.

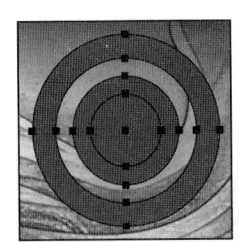

Compound path: Inner circle selected and Reversed option changed on inner circle

To release compound paths:

1 With the selection tool, select the compound path to release.

2 Choose Object > Compound Paths > Release.

To reverse paths within compound paths:

1 With the selection tool ( ), select the part of the compound path to reverse. Do not select the entire compound path.

2 Choose Window > Show Attributes.

3 Click the Reverse Path Direction Off button or the Reverse Path Direction On button.

Working with clipping masks

Clipping masks crop part of the artwork so that only a portion of the artwork appears through the shape or shapes you create. In Adobe Illustrator, you mask objects by using the Clipping Mask command.

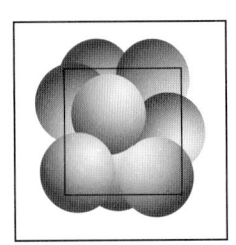

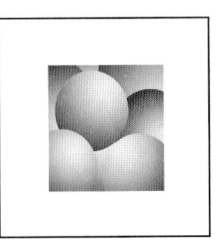

Masking object placed on top of artwork and Mask command applied

Important: *If you use complex shapes as masks, or if you use several masks in a file, you may have problems printing the file. If you experience printing problems, simplify or eliminate the masks.*

You can also make semitransparent clipping masks with the Transparency palette. (See "Creating opacity masks" on page 222.) And you can create clipping mask sets that mask multiple objects with the Layers palette. (See "Creating clipping masks" on page 253.)

To see whether an object is a mask:

1 With the selection tool, select the object.

2 Choose File > Document Info.

3 Choose Selection Only from the menu in the Document Info dialog box. The masking status of the selected object appears.

You can also select all masks in your artwork by using the Select Masks command. (See "Modifying and selecting masks" on page 168.)

Creating masks

A masking object can consist of a single path or a compound path.

To mask objects:

1 Draw or use the selection tool to select the object to use as a mask.

2 Make sure that the object is on top of the objects you want to mask.

When you mask objects on different layers, keep in mind that objects on intermediate layers become part of the masked artwork.

3 Select the mask and the objects you want masked.

4 Choose Object > Clipping Mask > Make. The mask loses its paint attributes and is assigned a fill and stroke value of None.

To undo the effects of a mask:

1 Use the selection tool or drag a marquee to select the objects you no longer want to use as a mask.

2 Choose Object > Clipping Mask > Release.

Because the mask was assigned a fill and stroke value of None, it is not visible unless you select it or assign it new paint attributes.

Modifying and selecting masks

Once you create a mask, the mask and the masked objects can be selected and modified as any other object. Masked objects are unlocked by default. You can lock the mask so that mask objects are secured together. By locking the mask, individual objects cannot be unintentionally moved with the direct-selection tool.

The Select Masks command finds and selects masks in the file. If there are no objects selected, the command selects all of the masks in your file. If objects are selected, the command deselects any objects that are not masks.

When you rasterize a mask, the full stroke value of the mask is displayed.

To select all masks in a file:

Choose Edit > Select > Masks.

To find out which objects are affected by a mask:

1 Select the group-selection tool.

2 Click the mask once to select it, and then continue clicking until all masked objects are selected.

To add an object to masked artwork:

1 Use the selection tool to select the object to add to the masked artwork, and drag it in front of the mask.

2 Choose Edit > Cut.

3 With the direct-selection tool, select an object within the masked artwork.

4 Choose either Edit > Paste in Front or Edit > Paste in Back. The object is pasted in front of or behind the selected object and becomes part of the masked artwork.

To remove an object from masked artwork:

1 With the direct-selection tool, select the object you want to remove.

2 Choose Edit > Cut.

To lock or unlock a mask:

1 With the direct-selection tool, select the mask to lock or unlock.

2 Choose either Object > Masks > Lock or Object > Masks > Unlock.

Filling and stroking masks

You can add a fill and stroke to a mask by setting these attributes using either the toolbox or the Color palette. (See "Applying color using the toolbox" on page 179 and "Using the Color palette" on page 180.)

To apply a fill and stroke to a mask:

1 With the direct-selection tool, select the mask you want to fill or stroke.

2 Use the Fill selection box or the Stroke selection box in the toolbox or Color palette to choose the mask's fill or stroke. If the Color palette is not visible, choose Window > Show Color.

3 Choose a fill color or stroke color for the mask.

6

Chapter 6: Applying Color

Applying colors, gradients, and patterns to artwork is a common Adobe Illustrator task, and one that requires some knowledge of color management for print media and for publishing on the Web. When applying color to artwork, keep in mind the final medium in which the artwork will be published, so as to use the correct color model and color definitions. Also, to ensure that colors are reproduced accurately in print and on-screen, verify that your monitor has been color-calibrated.

Adding color to artwork requires a combination of tools in Illustrator, including the Color palette, the Swatches palette, the Stroke palette, and the paint icons in the toolbox.

Color modes and models

A color mode In Illustrator determines the color model used to display and print Illustrator files. Illustrator bases its color modes on established models for describing and reproducing color. Common models include HSB (for hue, saturation, brightness); RGB (for red, green, blue); and CMYK (for cyan, magenta, yellow, black).

HSB model

Based on the human perception of color, the HSB model describes three fundamental characteristics of color:

- *Hue* is the color reflected from or transmitted through an object. It is measured as a location on the standard color wheel, expressed as a degree between 0° and 360°. In common use, hue is identified by the name of the color such as red, orange, or green.

- *Saturation*, sometimes called *chroma*, is the strength or purity of the color. Saturation represents the amount of gray in proportion to the hue, measured as a percentage from 0% (gray) to 100% (fully saturated). On the standard color wheel, saturation increases from the center to the edge.

- *Brightness* is the relative lightness or darkness of the color, usually measured as a percentage from 0% (black) to 100% (white).

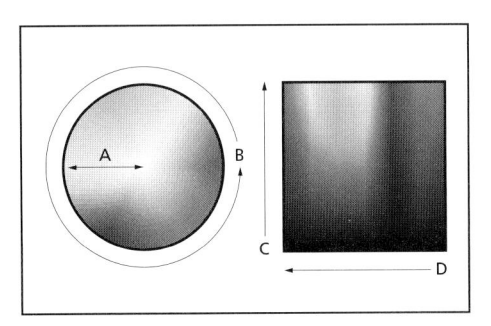

A. Saturation B. Hue C. Brightness D. All hues

RGB model

A large percentage of the visible spectrum can be represented by mixing red, green, and blue (RGB) colored light in various proportions and intensities. Where the colors overlap, they create cyan, magenta, and yellow.

RGB colors are called additive colors because you create white by adding R, G, and B together—that is, all light is reflected back to the eye. Additive colors are used for lighting, television, and computer monitors. Your monitor, for example, creates color by emitting light through red, green, and blue phosphors.

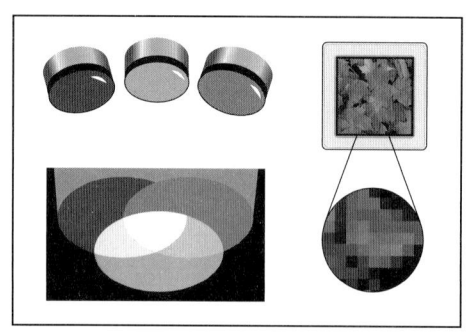

Additive colors (RGB)

How Illustrator uses the RGB model

You can work with color values using the RGB color mode, which is based on the RGB color model. In RGB mode, each of the RGB components can use a value ranging from 0 (black) to 255 (white). For example, a bright red color might have an R value of 246, a G value of 20, and a B value of 50. When the values of all three components are equal, the result is a shade of gray. When the value of all components is 255, the result is pure white; when all components have values of 0, the result is pure black.

Illustrator also includes a modified RGB color model called *Web Safe RGB*, which includes only those RGB colors that are appropriate for use on the Web.

CMYK model

Whereas the RGB model depends on a light source to create color, the CMYK model is based on the light-absorbing quality of ink printed on paper. As white light strikes translucent inks, a portion of the spectrum is absorbed. Color that is not absorbed is reflected back to your eye.

Combining pure cyan (C), magenta (M), and yellow (Y) pigments would result in black by absorbing, or subtracting, all colors. For this reason they are called *subtractive* colors. Black (K) ink is added for better shadow density. (The letter *K* came into use because black is the "key" color for registering other colors, and because the letter B also stands for blue.) Combining these inks to reproduce color is called *four-color process printing*.

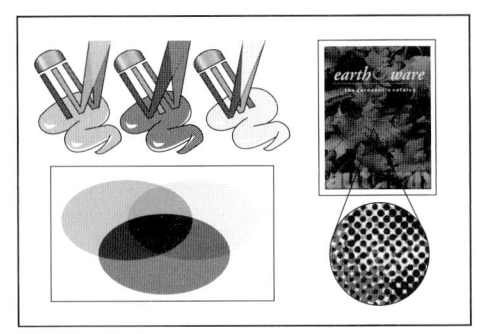

Subtractive color (CMYK)

How Illustrator uses the CMYK model

You can work with color values using the CMYK color mode, which is based on the CMYK color model. In CMYK mode, each of the CMYK process inks can use a value ranging from 0 to 100%. The lightest colors are assigned small percentages of process ink colors; darker colors have higher percentage values. For example, a bright red might contain 2% cyan, 93% magenta, 90% yellow, and 0% black. In CMYK objects, low ink percentages are closer to white, and high ink percentages are closer to black.

Use CMYK when preparing a document to be printed using process inks.

Grayscale model

Grayscale uses tints of black to represent an object. Every grayscale object has a brightness value ranging from 0% (white) to 100% (black). Images produced using black-and-white or grayscale scanners are typically displayed in grayscale.

Grayscale also lets you convert color artwork to high-quality black-and-white artwork. In this case, Adobe Illustrator discards all color information in the original artwork; the gray levels (shades) of the converted objects represent the luminosity of the original objects.

When you convert grayscale objects to RGB, the color values for each object are assigned that object's previous gray value. You can also convert a grayscale object to a CMYK object.

Color gamuts

The *gamut, or color space*, of a color system is the range of colors that can be displayed or printed. The spectrum of colors that can be viewed by the human eye is wider than any method of reproducing color.

The RGB gamut contains the subset of colors that can be viewed on a computer or television monitor (which emits red, green, and blue light). Some colors, such as pure cyan or pure yellow, can't be displayed accurately on a monitor. The smallest gamut is that of the CMYK model, which consists of colors that can be printed using process-color inks. When colors that cannot be printed are displayed on the screen, they are referred to as *out-of-gamut* colors (that is, they are outside the CMYK gamut).

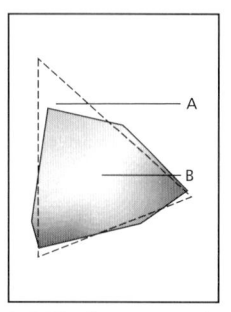

*A. RGB color gamut   B. CMYK color gamut
The extent of the RGB color gamut exceeds that of the CMYK color gamut.*

About spot and process color types

You can designate colors as either spot or process color types, which correspond to the two main ink types used in commercial printing. In the Swatches palette, you can identify the color type of a color using icons that appear next to the name of the color.

Spot colors

A *spot color* is a special premixed ink that is used instead of, or in addition to, CMYK process inks, and that requires its own printing plate on a printing press. Use spot color when few colors are specified and color accuracy is critical. Spot color inks can accurately reproduce colors that are outside the gamut of process colors. However, the exact appearance of the printed spot color is determined by combination of the ink as mixed by the commercial printer and the paper it's printed on, so it isn't affected by color values you specify or by color management. When you specify spot color values, you're describing the simulated appearance of the color for your monitor and composite printer only (subject to the gamut limitations of those devices).

For best results in printed documents, specify a spot color from a color-matching system supported by your commercial printer. Several color-matching system libraries are included with Illustrator; see "Loading colors from other color systems" on page 188.

Minimize the number of spot colors you use. Each spot color you create will generate an additional spot color printing plate for a printing press, increasing your printing costs. If you think you might require more than four colors, consider printing your document using process colors.

Process colors

A *process color* is printed using a combination of four standard process inks: cyan, magenta, yellow, and black (CMYK). Use process colors when a job requires so many colors that using individual spot inks would be expensive or impractical, such as when printing color photographs. Keep the following guidelines in mind when specifying a process color:

• For best results in a printed document, specify process colors using CMYK values printed in process-color reference charts, such as those available from a commercial printer.

• The final color values of a process color are its values in CMYK, so if you specify a process color using RGB, those color values will be converted to CMYK when you print color separations. These conversions will work differently if you turn on color management; they'll be affected by the profiles you've specified.

• Don't specify a process color based on how it looks on your monitor unless you have set up a color management system properly and you understand its limitations for previewing color.

• Avoid using process colors in documents intended for online viewing only, because CMYK has a smaller color gamut than a typical monitor.

Using spot and process colors together

Sometimes it's practical to print process and spot inks on the same job. For example, you might use one spot ink to print the exact color of a company logo on the same pages of an annual report where photographs are reproduced using process color. You can also use a spot color printing plate to apply a varnish over areas of a process color job. In both cases, your print job would use a total of five inks—four process inks and one spot ink or varnish.

Important: *If an object contains spot colors and overlaps another object containing transparency features, undesirable results may occur when exporting to EPS format or creating color separations. To prevent problems you should convert spot colors to process colors before attempting to export the file or create color separations.*

Comparing global and non-global process colors

Illustrator lets you specify a process color as either global or non global. Global process colors remain linked to a swatch in the Swatches palette, so that if you modify the swatch of a global process color, all objects using that color are updated.

Global process colors make it easier to modify color schemes without locating and adjusting each individual object. This is especially useful in standardized, production-oriented documents such as magazines.

Non-global process colors do not automatically update throughout the document when the color is edited. Process colors are non-global by default; a non-global process color can be changed to a global process color using the Swatch Options dialog box.

Global and non-global process colors only affect how a particular color is applied to objects, never how colors separate or behave when you move them between applications.

Working with swatches and unnamed colors

You must create spot colors as named swatches stored in the Swatches palette, so that you and your prepress service provider can uniquely identify each resulting spot color printing plate. In comparison, printing any process color requires no more than four inks, so you can use process colors either as swatches or as unnamed colors.

Swatches A swatch appears in the Swatches palette with a name you specify, making a color, gradient, pattern, or tint easy to locate and edit.

Note: Although colors from swatch libraries are named, they aren't saved as named swatches in your document unless you add them to the Swatches palette before you apply them to objects.

Unnamed colors You can create colors faster when you don't have to name them. However, unnamed colors are more difficult to edit later because they do not appear on the Swatches palette. When many objects use unnamed colors, document colors can be difficult to maintain because you must locate and select each individual object to edit its color.

You can create a swatch from any unnamed color. See "Adding, duplicating, and deleting swatches" on page 184.

Applying color

When you create an object or when you want to change the paint attributes of an existing object in Illustrator, you use a combination of the Fill and Stroke boxes in the toolbox, the Color palette, the Gradient palette, and the Swatches palette.

To apply colors to artwork:

1 Select an object's fill or stroke using one of the following:

• Select the object and then click the Fill or Stroke box in the toolbox. (See "Applying color using the toolbox" on page 179.)

• Click the Color button in the toolbox, or choose Window > Show Color. (For information about the toolbox, see "Applying color using the toolbox" on page 179.) Select the object, and click the Fill or Stroke box in the Color palette.

2 Apply a color to the selected fill or stroke, or a gradient to a fill, using one of the following:

- In the Color palette, mix a color using the Grayscale, RGB, Web-safe RGB, HSB, or CMYK sliders, or select a color from the color bar. (See "Using the Color palette" on page 180.)

Hold down the Shift key, and click on the color bar to cycle through the Grayscale, RGB, Web-safe RGB, HSB, or CMYK sliders.

- Double-click the Fill or Stroke box in the toolbox to display the Adobe Color Picker. You can then pick a color in the Color Picker dialog box. (See "Using the Color Picker" on page 191.)

- Choose Window > Show Swatches, and select a predefined color or gradient. (See "Using the Swatches palette" on page 182.)

- Choose Window > Swatch Libraries, and select a predefined color library. (See "Using the Swatch Libraries command" on page 188.)

- Drag a color or gradient to the artwork. (See "Applying color by dragging and dropping" on page 180.)

- Use the paint bucket or eyedropper tool to copy attributes between objects. (See "Copying attributes between objects" on page 193.)

- If you are stroking the object or path, choose line attributes. (See "Using the Stroke palette" on page 181.)

Applying color using the toolbox

Use the Fill and Stroke boxes in the toolbox to select an object's fill and stroke, to swap the fill color with the stroke color, and to return the fill and stroke to their default colors.

To switch between fill and stroke as the active selection, press x on the keyboard. To swap the fill and stroke colors of a selected object, press Shift+x.

Below the Fill and Stroke boxes are the Color, Gradient, and None buttons. You use these buttons to change the selected fill or stroke to a color, to change a fill to a gradient, or to remove the fill or stroke from the selected object.

To change fill or stroke attributes using the toolbox:

1 Select an object using any selection tool.

2 Do one of the following:

- Click the Swap Fill and Stroke button (↰), or press Shift+x to swap colors between the fill and the stroke.

- Click the Default Fill and Stroke button (▣) to return to the default color settings (white fill and black stroke).

- Click the Color button (□) to change the currently selected stroke or fill to the last-selected solid color in the Color palette.

- Click the Gradient button (▣) to change the currently selected fill to the last-selected gradient in the Gradient palette.

- Click the None button (⊘) to remove the object's fill or stroke.

- Double-click the Fill or Stroke button to choose a color with the Color Picker. See "Using the Color Picker" on page 191.

💡 *Use keyboard shortcuts to switch to Color, Gradient, or None: Press < to change the selection to a color; > to change the selection to a gradient; and / to change to None.*

Using the Color palette

You use the Color palette to apply color to an object's fill and stroke, and also to edit and mix colors —either colors that you create or colors that you selected from the Swatches palette, from an object, or from a color library.

To edit the fill or stroke color using the Color palette:

1 Select an object using any selection tool.

2 Choose Window > Show Color.

3 Select the Fill box or Stroke box in the Color palette or in the toolbox.

4 Do one of the following:

- Position the pointer over the color bar (the pointer turns into the eyedropper), and click.

- Choose an RGB, Web-safe RGB, HSB, CMYK, or Grayscale color model from the Color palette menu, and use the sliders to change the color values. You can also enter numeric values in the text boxes next to the color sliders.

An exclamation point inside a yellow triangle in the Color palette when using HSB or RGB color indicates that you have chosen an out-of-gamut color—that is, a color that cannot be printed using CMYK inks. The closest CMYK equivalent appears next to the triangle. Click the CMYK equivalent to substitute it for the out-of-gamut color.

A cube above the yellow triangle in the Color palette when using RGB, HSB, or CMYK color indicates that you have not chosen a Web-safe color. Click the cube to substitute the closest Web-safe color.

- Adjust the Tint slider if using a global color from the Swatches palette.

Applying color by dragging and dropping

An easy way to paint an object is to drag a color directly from the Fill box or Stroke box in the toolbox, the Color palette, or the Gradient palette and drop the color onto the object, or to drag a swatch from the Swatches palette and drop it on an object. Dragging and dropping lets you paint objects without first selecting them. You can also drag and drop colors from the Swatches palette to the Fill box or Stroke box in the toolbox, the Color palette, or the Gradient palette.

When you drag, the color is applied to either the object's fill or stroke, depending on whether the Fill box or Stroke box is currently selected. (For example, if you drag a red color to an unselected object when the stroke box in the toolbox is selected, the object's stroke is painted red.)

Using the Stroke palette

Stroke attributes are available only when you stroke a path. These attributes, available in the Stroke palette, control whether a line is solid or dashed, the dash sequence if it is dashed, the stroke weight, the miter limit, and the styles of line joins and line caps.

Use the Stroke palette to select stroke attributes, including the thickness (weight) of the stroke, how the stroke is capped and joined, and whether a stroke is solid or dashed.

To set stroke attributes using the Stroke palette:

1 With any selection tool, select the object with the stroke attributes you want to change.

2 Click the Stroke box in the toolbox to select the object's stroke.

3 Choose Window > Show Stroke.

4 To specify a stroke weight, enter the desired weight in the Weight text box or choose a value from the pop-up menu. You can enter a value in inches (in), millimeters (mm), centimeters (cm), or picas (pi), and Illustrator converts it to an equal value in points.

The stroke weight determines the thickness of the stroke, in points. Illustrator strokes a path by centering the stroke on the path; half of the stroke appears on one side of the path, and the other half of the stroke appears on the other side of the path.

If you enter a weight of 0, the stroke is changed to None.

5 Select from the following options:

• Butt Cap for stroked lines with squared ends.

• Round Cap for stroked lines with semicircular ends.

• Projecting Cap for stroked lines with squared ends that extend half the line width beyond the end of the line. This option makes the weight of the line extend equally in all directions around the line.

6 Select one of the following options:

• Miter Join for stroked lines with pointed corners. Enter a miter limit between 1 and 500. The miter limit controls when the program switches from a mitered (pointed) join to a beveled (squared-off) join. The default miter limit is 4, which means that when the length of the point reaches four times the stroke weight, the program switches from a miter join to a bevel join. A miter limit of 1 results in a bevel join.

• Round Join for stroked lines with rounded corners.

• Bevel Join for stroked lines with squared corners.

• Dashed Line for a dashed line; then specify a dash sequence by entering the lengths of dashes and the gaps between them in the Dash Pattern text boxes. As with the stroke weight, you can enter a value in inches (in), millimeters (mm), centimeters (cm), or picas and Illustrator converts it to an equal value in points.

The numbers entered are repeated in sequence so that once you have established the pattern, you don't need to fill in all the text boxes. Dash patterns are specified in points.

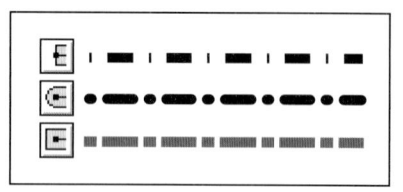

Effects of line cap styles on dashed lines with dash gap of 1, 6, 10, 6

Using the Swatches palette

You can control all document colors and gradients from the Swatches palette alone. Use it to create, name, and store colors and gradients for instant access. When a selected object's fill or stroke contains a color or gradient applied from the Swatches palette, the applied swatch is highlighted in the Swatches palette.

About swatch types

The Swatches palette stores the following types of swatches:

Colors Icons on the Swatches palette identify the spot ( ) and process ( ) color types, and HSB ( ), RGB ( ), or CMYK ( ) color modes. If the RGB or CMYK color is a spot color, a dot appears in the corner of the icon.

Tints A percentage value next to a swatch in the Swatches palette indicates a tint of a spot or process color. See "Creating global colors and tints" on page 185.

Gradients An icon on the Swatches palette indicates a gradient.

Patterns An icon on the Swatches palette filled with a pattern indicates the specific pattern type.

None The None swatch removes the stroke or fill from an object. You can't edit or remove this swatch.

Registration Registration (⊕) is a built-in swatch that causes objects filled or stroked with it to print on every separation from a PostScript printer. For example, registration marks use the Registration color so that printing plates can be aligned precisely on a press. You can edit the Registration color by double-clicking it in the Swatches palette. You can't remove this swatch.

You can also add any colors from any swatch library to the Swatches palette so that they are saved with your document. (See "Applying color using the toolbox" on page 179.)

Working with the Swatches palette

You can add colors and gradients to the Swatches palette by dragging them from the Color palette, from the Gradient palette, or from the toolbox Fill and Stroke boxes to the Swatches palette. You can add a pattern to the Swatches palette by dragging it from the artwork or by selecting it and choosing Edit > Define Pattern. (See "Creating and working with patterns" on page 233.)

New colors, gradients, or patterns that you create and store in the Swatches palette are associated only with the current file. Each new Adobe Illustrator file can have a different set of swatches stored in its Swatches palette. Swatches stored in the RGB Startup file or CMYK Startup file are loaded into all new Illustrator documents, depending on which color mode you select when you create the new document. (See "Creating a custom startup file" on page 190.)

To choose a color, gradient, or pattern from the Swatches palette:

1 Choose Window > Show Swatches.

2 Click a color, gradient, or pattern swatch in the Swatches palette. The selected color, gradient, or pattern appears in the Color palette and in the Fill box or Stroke box in the toolbox, and it is applied to any selected object.

To modify the swatch display:

1 Choose Window > Show Swatches.

2 Choose one of the following display options from the pop-up menu:

• Name displays a small swatch next to the name of the swatch. The icons to the right of the name show the color model (CMYK, RGB, and so on), and whether the color is a spot color, global process color, non-global process color, registration color, or none.

• Small Swatch or Large Swatch displays only the swatch. A triangle with a dot in the corner of the swatch indicates that the color is a spot color. A triangle without a dot indicates a global process color.

To modify the type of swatches displayed:

1 Choose Window > Show Swatches.

2 Click one of the following buttons at the bottom of the Swatches palette:

• Show All Swatches ( ) displays all color, gradient, and pattern swatches.

• Show Color Swatches ( ) displays only process color and spot color swatches.

• Show Gradient Swatches ( ) displays only gradient swatches.

• Show Pattern Swatches ( ) displays only pattern swatches.

To select all swatches not currently used in the file:

1 Choose Window > Show Swatches.

2 Choose Select All Unused from the pop-up menu. Only swatches that are not currently used in the active file are selected.

To sort swatches by swatch type or by name:

1 Choose Window > Show Swatches.

2 Choose from the sorting options in the pop-up menu:

• Sort by Name sorts all swatches alphabetically by name.

• Sort by Kind sorts all swatches in ascending order by swatch type: colors, gradients, and patterns.

Adding, duplicating, and deleting swatches

You can add color swatches to the Swatches palette by dragging and dropping colors on the palette or by using commands in the Swatches palette. To duplicate swatches, use the commands in the Swatches palette or drag the swatch onto the New Swatch button.

To add a color to the Swatches palette:

1 In the Color palette, Gradient palette, or the Fill box and Stroke box in the toolbox, select the color or gradient you want to add to the Swatches palette.

2 Do one of the following:

• Click the New Swatch button ( ) at the bottom of the Swatches palette.

• Choose New Swatch from the pop-up menu in the Swatches palette. Enter a name in the Swatch Name text box, choose Process Color or Spot Color from the Color Type pop-up menu, and click OK.

• Drag the color or gradient to the Swatches palette, positioning the pointer where you want the new swatch to appear.

• Ctrl-drag (Windows) or Command-drag (Mac OS) a color to the Swatches palette to create a spot color. You can also press Ctrl (Windows) or Command (Mac OS) while clicking the New Swatch button to create a spot color.

To duplicate a swatch in the Swatches palette:

1 Select the swatch you want to duplicate. To select multiple swatches, hold down Ctrl (Windows) or Command (Mac OS) and click each swatch. To select a range of swatches, hold down Shift and click to define the range.

2 Do one of the following:

• Choose Duplicate Swatch from the pop-up menu.

• Drag the swatches to the New Swatch button on the bottom of the palette.

To replace a swatch in the Swatches palette:

Hold down Alt (Windows) or Option (Mac OS) and drag the color or gradient from the Color palette, Gradient palette, or the Fill box and Stroke box in the toolbox to the Swatches palette, highlighting the swatch you want to replace.

Important: Replacing an existing color, gradient, or pattern in the Swatches palette globally changes artwork in the file containing that swatch color with the new color, gradient, or pattern. The only exception is for a process color that does not have the Global option selected in the Swatch Options dialog box.

To delete a swatch from the Swatches palette:

1 Select the swatch you want to delete. To select multiple swatches, hold down Ctrl (Windows) or Command (Mac OS) and click each swatch. To select adjacent swatches, hold down Shift and click to define the range.

2 Delete the selected swatches in one of the following ways:

• Choose Delete Swatch from the pop-up menu.

• Click the Delete Swatch button (🗑) at the bottom of the palette.

• Drag the selected swatches to the Delete Swatch button.

Note: When you delete a spot color or global process color swatch (or a pattern or gradient containing a spot or global process color), all objects painted with those colors will be converted to the non-global process color equivalent.

Editing swatches

You can change individual attributes of a swatch—such as its name, color mode, color definition, whether it is process or spot, or whether a process color can be changed globally—using the Swatch Options dialog box.

Any swatch can be named in Adobe Illustrator; for example, you can change the name of a CMYK process color, and it still prints and separates with each of its CMYK values intact.

To edit a swatch:

1 Choose Window > Show Swatches.

2 Select a swatch, and do one of the following:

• Double-click the swatch.

• Choose Swatch Options from the pop-up menu in the Swatches palette.

3 Enter the relevant information in the Swatch Options dialog box:

• Enter a name in the Swatch Name text box.

• Choose Spot Color or Process Color from the Color Type pop-up menu. Both spot colors and process colors can be changed globally.

• Click Global if you want changes to the selected process color to be applied globally throughout the document. (For more information, see "Comparing global and non-global process colors" on page 177.)

• Choose CMYK, RGB, Web-safe RGB, HSB, or Grayscale from the Color Mode pop-up menu and change the color definition (if desired) using the color sliders or text boxes at the bottom of the palette.

4 Click OK.

Note: When separated, each spot color is converted to a process color by default, unless you deselect the Convert to Process option in the Separation Setup dialog box. (See "Separating spot colors as process colors" on page 392.)

Creating global colors and tints

You can make global color changes in an individual file either by selecting all objects with the characteristics you want to change, or by editing or replacing global process color or spot color swatches in the Swatches palette.

The Tint slider in the Color palette is used to modify a global color's intensity. The tint range is from 0% to 100%; the lower the number, the lighter the tint will be.

To modify the tint of a global process color or spot color:

1 Do one of the following to select a global color:

• Click an object and select the appropriate fill or stroke.

• Click a color swatch in the Swatches palette.

Important: To ensure that a process color is global, make sure the Global option is selected in the Swatch Options dialog box. (See "Editing swatches" on page 185.)

2 In the Color palette, drag the Tint slider or enter a tint value in the Tint Percentage text box.

To save a tint in the Swatches palette:

1 Create a tint by modifying the swatch.

2 Save the tint in the Swatches palette using one of the following:

• Drag the Fill or Stroke box in the toolbox to the Swatches palette.

• Click the New button in the Swatches palette.

The tint is saved with the same name as the base color, but with the tint percentage added to the name. For example, if you saved a color named "Sky Blue" at 51 percent, the swatch name would be "Sky Blue 51%."

Important: Tints of the same color are linked together, so that if you edit a tint swatch, all associated tint swatches (and the objects painted with those swatches) are also changed.

To select all objects with the same properties:

1 Do one of the following:

• To select all objects with the same fill, stroke, and stroke weight, select an object with these attributes or choose the fill, stroke, and stroke weight attributes from the Color palette, Swatches palette, or Stroke palette. Then choose Edit > Select > Same Paint Style.

• To select all objects with the same fill or stroke color, select an object with that fill color or choose the fill color from the Color palette or Swatches palette. Then choose Edit > Select > Same Fill Color or Edit > Select > Same Stroke Color.

• To select all objects with the same stroke weight, select an object with that stroke weight or choose the stroke weight from the Stroke palette. Then choose Edit > Select > Same Stroke Weight.

• To apply the same selection options using a different object (for example, if you have already selected all red objects using the Same Fill Color command and now you want to search for all green objects), select a new object and then choose Edit > Select > Select Again.

To change a color throughout a file:

Replace a color swatch in the Swatches palette using one of the following options:

• Alt-drag (Windows) or Option-drag (Mac OS) a swatch from the Swatches palette over the swatch you want to replace.

• Alt-drag (Windows) or Option-drag (Mac OS) a color from the Color palette over the swatch you want to replace in the Swatches palette.

- Alt-drag (Windows) or Option-drag (Mac OS) a color from the Fill box or the Stroke box over the swatch you want to replace in the Swatches palette.

- Double-click the swatch and edit the color in the Swatch Options dialog box.

Adding colors from other documents and merging swatch names

When you copy objects from one document to another, any swatches (global process colors, spot colors, patterns, or gradients) contained in the object are added to the destination document's Swatches palette. If swatches in the two documents have the same name, but different color values, a warning dialog appears and you can choose to either add the duplicate swatch or merge the swatches together and use only one set of color values.

If the color spaces of the source file from which you are copying or dragging the object do not match the color spaces of the destination document, the color spaces will be determined by options that you select in the Color Settings dialog box. (See "Producing Consistent Color" on page 199.)

You can also merge swatches together using the Merge Swatches command. When you merge swatches together, all objects painted with either of the swatch colors will be updated with the merged swatch color.

To add color, gradient, or pattern swatches from one document to another:

1 Copy an object into the current document using drag-and-drop, copy-and-paste, or the Place command. You can also use the Swatch Libraries command to add new swatch palettes. (See "Using the Swatch Libraries command" on page 188.)

2 If one or more swatches have the same name (but with different color values), select from the following options in the Swatch Conflict dialog box:

- Add Swatches adds the new swatch to the Swatches palette, appending the word *copy* to the name of the new swatch.

- Merge Swatches combines the two swatches into a single swatch, using the color value of the destination document's swatch.

3 If there are multiple naming conflicts, select the Apply to All check box to automatically apply the selected method (either adding swatches or merging swatches) to all naming conflicts in the document. This prevents the Swatch Conflict dialog box from appearing for each naming conflict in the document.

To merge multiple colors in the Swatches palette:

1 In the Swatches palette select two or more swatches to merge. Press Shift and click to select a range of swatches; press Ctrl (Windows) or Command (Mac OS) and click to select non-contiguous swatches.

2 Choose Merge Swatches from the Swatches palette menu. The first selected swatch name and color value replaces all other selected swatches.

Using the Swatch Libraries command

The Swatch Libraries command lets you import colors, gradients, and patterns from other Adobe Illustrator files into a palette. It also lets you import entire color libraries from other color systems, such as the PANTONE Process Color System.

When you import color libraries into Adobe Illustrator, the colors in the library are permanent. You must copy a color in a color library to the Swatches palette to modify it.

Loading colors from other files

Use the Swatch Libraries > Other Library command to import colors, gradients, and patterns from other Adobe Illustrator files. When you select a file using the Swatch Libraries > Other Library command, all of the source file's spot and process colors, gradients, and patterns are added to a new palette.

To import colors, gradients, or patterns from other files:

1 Choose Window > Swatch Libraries > Other Library.

2 Select the file from which you want to import swatches, and click Select.

To add colors from the other file's library into the Swatches palette:

1 Select one or more swatches in the library:

- Click to select a single swatch.
- Shift-click to select a range of swatches.
- Ctrl-click (Windows) or Command-click (Mac OS) to select noncontiguous swatches.

2 Do one of the following:

- Drag and drop the selected swatches from the library to the Swatches palette.
- Choose Add to Swatches from the library palette's pop-up menu.

If you select a file whose color mode is different than the current document, the colors will be converted into the closest equivalent color in the destination document's color mode.

Loading colors from other color systems

The Swatch Libraries command lets you select from a range of color libraries—including the PANTONE® Process Color System, Toyo™ Ink Electronic Color Finder™ 1050, the Focoltone® color system, the Trumatch™ color swatching system, the DIC Process Color Note, and libraries created especially for Web use. Each color system that you select appears in its own Swatch Library palette.

Spot colors from color libraries, as are all spot colors, are converted to process colors when separated unless you deselect the Convert to Process option in the Separation Setup dialog box. (See Chapter 16, "Producing Color Separations.")

To load predefined custom color libraries into Illustrator:

1 Choose Window > Swatch Libraries.

2 Select the color system you want from the submenu. The color system that you select appears as a tabbed palette.

To make a custom color library appear each time Illustrator is started:

1 Select a custom color swatch library.

2 Choose Persistent from the swatch library palette's pop-up menu. The library will now automatically open in the same position each time the Illustrator application is started.

To select a swatch by its name or number:

1 Select the Swatches palette or a swatch library of a particular color system (for example, the PANTONE color system).

2 Choose Show Find Field from the Swatches menu.

3 In the Find text box, type the name or the number of a swatch to select it. (For example, in the PANTONE Process library palette you can type **11-7 CVS** to select PANTONE swatch 11-7.)

Choosing a custom color system

The Swatch Libraries command supports various color systems, including the following:

PANTONE® Used for printing inks. Each PANTONE color has a specified CMYK equivalent. To select a PANTONE color, first determine the ink color you want, using either the *PANTONE Color Formula Guide* or an ink chart obtained from your printer. PANTONE books are available from printers and graphic arts supply stores.

You can select from PANTONE Coated, PANTONE Uncoated, PANTONE Process, PANTONE ProSim custom colors, PANTONE Internet Color System Library, and PANTONE Digital Color System.

TRUMATCH Provides predictable CMYK color matching with more than 2000 achievable, computer-generated colors. TRUMATCH colors cover the visible spectrum of the CMYK gamut in even steps. The TRUMATCHCOLORFINDER displays up to 40 tints and shades of each hue, each originally created in four-color process and each reproducible in four colors on electronic imagesetters. In addition, four-color grays using different hues are included.

FOCOLTONE Consists of 763 CMYK colors. FOCOLTONE colors help avoid prepress trapping and registration problems.

A swatch book with specifications for process and spot colors, overprint charts, and a chip book for marking up layouts are available from FOCOLTONE.

TOYO Color Finder 1050 Consists of more than 1000 colors based on the most common printing inks used in Japan. The *TOYO Color Finder 1050 Book* contains printed samples of Toyo colors and is available from printers and graphic arts supply stores.

ANPA-COLOR Commonly used for newspaper applications. The *ANPA-COLOR ROP Newspaper Color Ink Book* contains samples of the ANPA colors.

DIC Color Guide Commonly used for printing projects in Japan.

Creating a custom startup file

Adobe Illustrator provides two different startup files: a startup file for the CMYK color mode and a startup file for the RGB color mode. When you create a new document, you are asked to choose a color mode for the new document. Depending on the startup file you choose (CMYK or RGB), your new document will contain the default settings for that particular startup file: brushes, swatches, gradients, patterns, and styles. The startup files are called Adobe Illustrator Startup_CMYK and Adobe Illustrator Startup_RGB, respectively, and are found in the Plug-ins folder inside the Adobe Illustrator application folder.

You can create a custom startup file that defines the contents of the Swatches palette by default, including any custom color libraries that you want to appear in the Swatches palette. In this way, you can have easy access to the patterns, gradients, brushes, graph designs, colors, and color libraries that you use most frequently. By adding these elements to one or both of the startup files, you make them available in every new Adobe Illustrator file you create.

In addition, any files you create have the same Document Setup and Page Setup settings as those found in the CMYK or RGB startup files, and they use the same zoom level, window size, viewing preferences, and scroll position as that of the startup file when it was last saved.

To create a custom startup file:

1 Make a backup copy of the current default startup file, Adobe Illustrator Startup_CMYK or Adobe Illustrator Startup_RGB, and then save the backup file outside of the Plug-ins folder. This action saves the original startup file in case you need it again. The startup files are located in the Plug-ins folder in the Adobe Illustrator application folder.

2 Open one of the default startup files (either CMYK or RGB, depending on which type of document you intend to use) as a template for the custom startup file. This file contains squares filled with the default colors, patterns, and gradients available in the Swatches palette.

3 Delete any existing colors, patterns, and gradients you don't want to retain. Note that you must delete them from their respective palettes as well as from the artwork in the startup file.

4 Add new paint style attributes to the startup file as follows:

• Create any colors, patterns, and gradients you want. You can also import swatches using the Swatch Libraries command and then move the swatches you want in the startup file into the default Swatches palette. (See "Loading colors from other files" on page 188.)

- Save any graph designs that you want available in your files using the Graph Design dialog box. (See "Using Graphs" in online Help.) As with the new paint style attributes, add the graphs to the artwork in the startup file so you can see and refer to the graphs later if necessary.

5 Select the options you want as default settings in the Page Setup and Document Setup dialog boxes, as well as the view preferences, the ruler origins, and the page origins.

Save the new file as Adobe Illustrator Startup _CMYK or Adobe Illustrator Startup_RGB, and place it inside the Plug-ins folder.

Important: *Make sure that you select the correct type of startup file (that is, CMYK or RGB) and that you save it with the exact name for its color mode. Also, you must quit the Illustrator application and restart it before the new startup settings are applied to a new document.*

Using the Color Picker

You can use the Color Picker to select the fill or stroke color by choosing from a color spectrum or by defining colors numerically. In addition, you can select colors based on the HSB, RGB, and CMYK color models (see "Color modes and models" on page 173.)

To display the Color Picker:

Do one of the following:

- Double-click the fill or stroke color selection box in the toolbox.

- Double-click the active color selection box in the Color palette.

Specifying a color using the color field and color slider

With the HSB, RGB, and CMYK color modes, you can use the color field and the color slider in the Color Picker dialog box to select a color. The color slider displays the range of color levels available for the selected color component (for example, R, G, or B). The color field displays the range for the remaining two components—one on the horizontal axis, one on the vertical.

For example, if the current color is black and you click the red component (R) using the RGB color model, the color slider displays the range of color for red (0 is at the bottom of the slider and 255 is at the top). The color field displays the values for blue along its horizontal axis, for green along its vertical axis.

To choose a color:

1 Click a component next to the HSB, RGB, or CMYK values.

2 Click the Only Web Colors option to display only Web-safe colors in the Color Picker.

3 Select a color:

- Drag the white triangles along the slider.

- Click inside the color slider.

- Click inside the color field.

When you click in the color field, a circular marker indicates the color's position in the field.

As you adjust the color using the color field and color slider, the numerical values change to reflect the new color. The color rectangle to the right of the color slider displays the new color in the top section of the rectangle. The original color appears at the bottom of the rectangle.

Specifying a color using numeric values

In the Color Picker, you can select a color in any of the four color models by specifying numeric values for each color component.

To specify colors using numeric values:

Do one of the following:

• In CMYK color mode (this is the mode PostScript printers use), specify each component value as a percentage of cyan, magenta, yellow, and black.

• In RGB color mode (this is the mode your monitor uses), specify component values from 0 to 255 (0 is black, and 255 is the pure color).

• In HSB color mode, specify saturation and brightness as percentages; specify hue as an angle, from 0° to 360°, that corresponds to a location on the color wheel. (See "Color modes and models" on page 173 for information on the color wheel.)

Recognizing nonprintable or non-Web-safe colors

Some colors in the RGB and HSB color models, such as neon colors, cannot be printed, because they have no equivalents in the CMYK model. When you select a nonprintable color, an alert triangle with an exclamation point appears in the Color Picker dialog box and in the Color palette. The closest CMYK equivalent is displayed below the triangle. (See "Color gamuts" on page 175.)

Printable colors are determined by the printing values you enter for the selected ink set in the CMYK Setup dialog box.

A cube above the yellow triangle indicates that you have not chosen a Web-safe color.

To select the closest CMYK equivalent for a nonprintable color:

Click the alert triangle that appears in the Color Picker dialog box or the Color palette.

To select the closest Web-safe equivalent for a non-Web-safe color:

The closest Web-safe equivalent color appears next to the cube. Click the cube to substitute the closest Web-safe color.

Modifying colors

Illustrator provides a wide variety of tools to modify and edit colors in your file. You can use the paint bucket and eyedropper tools to copy paint attributes from one object to another.

Copying attributes between objects

You can use the eyedropper tool to copy appearance and color attributes—including transparency, live effects, and other attributes—from any object in an Illustrator file, from a paint swatch, or from anywhere on the desktop, including from another application. You can then use the paint bucket tool to apply the current attributes to an object. Together these tools let you copy attributes from one object to another.

By default, the eyedropper and paint bucket tools affect all attributes of an object. You can use the tool's options dialog box to change the object's attributes. You can also use the eyedropper tool and paint bucket tool to copy and paste type attributes. (See "Copying type attributes between objects" on page 300.)

To copy attributes using the eyedropper tool:

1 Select the object with the attributes you want to change.

2 Select the eyedropper tool ( ).

3 Click the object that has the attributes you want to sample with the eyedropper tool. The selected object is automatically updated with the attributes of the sampled object.

To copy attributes from the desktop to Illustrator using the eyedropper tool:

1 Select the object whose attributes you want to change.

2 Select the eyedropper tool.

3 Click anywhere on the document and continue to hold down the mouse button.

4 Without releasing the mouse button, move the pointer over the object on your computer's desktop whose attributes you want to copy. When directly over the object, release the mouse button.

Important: When you copy an object's characteristics from the desktop, the eyedropper tool only copies the RGB color from the screen, even if the object in another application is colored in the CMYK color mode.

To apply attributes using the paint bucket tool:

1 Select the paint bucket tool ( ).

2 Click any object to apply the saved attributes.

If you are working in Outline view or if the object is stroked and not filled, be sure to click the object's outline.

To toggle between the eyedropper tool and the paint bucket tool, press Alt (Windows) or Option (Mac OS) while either tool is selected.

To change the attributes affected by the paint bucket or eyedropper tool:

1 Double-click the paint bucket or eyedropper tool.

2 Select the attributes you want to copy with the eyedropper tool, then apply with the paint bucket tool and click OK.

Using the Hard Mix and Soft Mix commands

The Hard Mix and Soft Mix commands let you control the mix of overlapping fill colors. (See "Step 2: Select overprint options for overlapping colors" on page 383.)

Important: You can also control the mix of overlapping colors using the blending modes in the Transparency palette. Blending modes provide many options for controlling overlapping colors, and should always be used for artwork containing spot colors, patterns, gradients, text, or other complex artwork.

You can apply the Hard Mix and Soft Mix commands as Pathfinder commands or effects. Pathfinder effects should always be used on groups or layers; for individual objects, use the Pathfinder commands in the Pathfinder palette. For more information on using effects, see "Using effects" on page 271.

• The Hard Mix command combines colors by choosing the highest value of each of the color components. For example, if Color 1 is 20% cyan, 66% magenta, 40% yellow, and 0% black; and Color 2 is 40% cyan, 20% magenta, 30% yellow, and 10% black; the resulting hard color is 40% cyan, 66% magenta, 40% yellow, and 10% black.

• The Soft Mix command makes the underlying colors visible through the overlapping artwork, and then divides the image into its component faces. You specify the percentage of visibility you want in the overlapping colors.

Note: Applying either the Hard Mix or Soft Mix command to objects removes their strokes and groups the objects.

In most cases, applying the Hard Mix or Soft Mix command to objects painted using a mix of process and spot colors converts the color to CMYK. In the case of mixing a non-global process RGB color with a spot RGB color, all spot colors are converted to a non-global process RGB color.

If you overlap multiple objects, all overlapping objects are given the visibility level you select.

To mix colors by selecting each highest CMYK component value (Hard Mix):

1 Do one of the following:

• To mix colors between individual objects using the Hard Mix Pathfinder command, select the objects whose fill colors you want to mix, and choose Window > Show Pathfinder. Next, choose Show Options from the pop-up menu in the Pathfinder palette. Then click the Hard Mix button at the bottom of the palette.

• To apply the command to a group or layer as an effect, select a group in the artwork, or target a group or layer in the Layers palette. (For more information on targeting, see "Targeting layers, groups, and objects to apply appearance attributes" on page 252.) Then choose Effect > Pathfinder > Hard Mix.

To mix colors by specifying a mixing rate (Soft Mix):

1 Do one of the following:

• To mix colors between individual objects using the Soft Mix Pathfinder command, select the objects whose fill colors you want to mix, and choose Window > Show Pathfinder. Next, choose Show Options from the pop-up menu in the Pathfinder palette. Then click the Soft Mix button at the bottom of the palette.

• To apply the command to a group or layer as an effect, select a group in the artwork, or target a group or layer in the Layers palette. (For more information on targeting, see "Targeting layers, groups, and objects to apply appearance attributes" on page 252.) Then choose Effect > Pathfinder > Soft Mix.

2 Enter a value between 1% and 100% in the Mixing Rate text box to determine the percentage of visibility you want in the overlapping colors, and click OK.

Using filters to modify colors

Illustrator filters provide shortcuts for changing color attributes or blending colors between objects.

Using the Adjust Colors and Convert filters

The Adjust Colors filter lets you change the color values in objects, as well as the tint of global colors. You can also use the Convert filters to convert objects between grayscale and your document's color mode.

To adjust colors using the Adjust Colors filter:

1 Select the objects whose colors you want to adjust.

2 Choose Filter > Colors > Adjust Colors.

3 Select Convert and then a color mode. If the document is an RGB document, you can select between RGB and Grayscale; if the document is CMYK, you can select between CMYK and Grayscale.

4 Select Fill or Stroke (or both) to adjust the fill or stroke or both.

5 Drag the sliders or enter values in the color value text boxes.

6 Click Preview to preview the effect and click OK.

To convert an object to a different color mode using a Convert filter:

1 Select the object you want to convert.

2 Convert the object to grayscale or to your document's color mode:

• If the document is a CMYK document, choose Filter > Colors > Convert to Grayscale or Filter > Colors > Convert to CMYK.

• If the document is an RGB document, choose Filter > Colors > Convert to Grayscale or Filter > Colors > Convert to RGB.

Saturating and desaturating colors

The Saturate filter darkens or lightens the colors of selected objects by increasing or decreasing the percentages of color values or the percentage tint of spot colors. You set the desired percentage using the Saturate dialog box.

To saturate or desaturate colors:

1 Select the objects whose colors you want to saturate or desaturate.

2 Choose Filter > Colors > Saturate.

3 Drag the slider or enter a value from –100% to 100% to specify the percentage by which to decrease or increase the color or the spot color tint.

4 Click Preview to preview the effect and click OK.

Inverting colors

The Invert Colors filter creates a color negative (or inverse) of the selected object. When you invert an object, its color values are converted to the inverse of the color values of the original.

To invert colors:

1 Select the objects whose colors you want to invert.

2 Choose Filter > Colors > Invert Colors.

7

Chapter 7: Producing Consistent Color

When your document must meet color standards set by clients and designers, viewing and editing color consistently becomes critical, all the way from scanning source images to creating final output. A color management system reconciles color differences among devices so that you can be reasonably certain of the colors your system ultimately produces.

Why colors sometimes don't match

No device in a publishing system is capable of reproducing the full range of colors viewable to the human eye. Each device operates within a specific color space which can produce a certain range, or *gamut*, of colors.

The RGB (red, green, blue) and CMYK (cyan, magenta, yellow, and black) color models represent two main categories of color spaces. The gamuts of the RGB and CMYK spaces are very different; while the RGB gamut is generally larger (that is, capable of representing more colors) than CMYK, some CMYK colors still fall outside the RGB gamut (see "Color gamuts" on page 175 for an illustration). In addition, different devices produce slightly different gamuts within the same color model. For example, a variety of RGB spaces can exist among scanners and monitors, and a variety of CMYK spaces can exist among printing presses.

Because of these varying color spaces, colors can shift in appearance as you transfer documents between different devices. Color variations can result from different image sources (scanners and software produce art using different color spaces), differences in brands of computer monitors, differences in the way software applications define color, differences in print media (newsprint paper reproduces a smaller gamut than magazine-quality paper), and other natural variations, such as manufacturing differences in monitors or monitor age.

About color management

Because color-matching problems result from various devices and software using different color spaces, one solution is to have a system that interprets and translates color accurately between devices. A color management system (CMS) compares the color space in which a color was created to the color space in which the same color will be output, and makes the necessary adjustments to represent the color as consistently as possible among different devices.

The following components are integral to a color-managed workflow:

Device-independent color space To successfully compare different device gamuts and make adjustments, a color management system must use a reference color space—an objective way of defining color. Most CMSs use the internal CIE (Commission Internationale d'Eclairage) LAB color model, which exists independently of any device and is large enough to reproduce any color visible to the human eye. For this reason, CIE LAB is considered *device-independent*.

Color management engine Different companies have developed various ways to manage color. To provide you with a choice, a color management system lets you choose a *color management engine* that represents the approach you want to use. Sometimes called the *color management module (CMM)*, the color management engine is the part of the CMS that does the work of reading and translating colors between different color spaces.

Color profiles The CMS translates colors with the help of *color profiles*. A profile is a mathematical description of a device's color space, that is, how the reference CIE values of each color in the color space map to the visual appearance produced by the device. For example, a scanner profile tells a CMS how your scanner "sees" colors so that an image from your scanner can be translated into the CIE color space accurately. From the CIE space, the colors can then be translated accurately again, via another profile, to the color space of an output device. Illustrator 9.0 uses ICC profiles, a format defined by the International Color Consortium (ICC) as a cross-platform standard.

Rendering intents No single color translation method can manage color correctly for all types of graphics. For example, a color translation method that preserves correct relationships among colors in a wildlife photograph may alter the colors in a logo containing flat tints of color. Color management engines provide a choice of *rendering intents*, or translation methods, so that you can apply a method appropriate to a particular graphical element. For descriptions of the rendering intents available to Illustrator, see "Specifying a rendering intent" on page 209.

Note: Don't confuse color management with color correction. A CMS won't correct an image that was saved with tonal or color balance problems. It provides an environment where you can evaluate images reliably in the context of your final output.

Creating a viewing environment for color management

Your work environment influences how you see color on your monitor and on printed output. For best results, control the colors and light in your work environment by doing the following:

• View your documents in an environment that provides a consistent light level and color temperature. For example, the color characteristics of sunlight change throughout the day and alter the way colors appear on your screen, so keep shades closed or work in a windowless room. To eliminate the blue-green cast from fluorescent lighting, consider installing D50 (5000 degree Kelvin) lighting. Ideally, view printed documents using a D50 lightbox.

- View your document in a room with neutral-colored walls and ceiling. A room's color can affect the perception of both monitor color and printed color. The best color for a viewing room is polychromatic gray. Also, the color of your clothing reflecting off the glass of your monitor may affect the appearance of colors on-screen.

- Match the light intensity in the room or lightbox to the light intensity of your monitor. View continuous-tone art, printed output, and images on-screen under the same intensity of light.

- Remove colorful background patterns on your monitor desktop. Busy or bright patterns surrounding a document interfere with accurate color perception. Set your desktop to display neutral grays only.

- View document proofs in the real-world conditions under which your audience will see the final piece. For example, you might want to see how a housewares catalog looks under the incandescent light bulbs used in homes, or view an office furniture catalog under the fluorescent lighting used in offices. However, always make final color judgements under the lighting conditions specified by the legal requirements for contract proofs in your country.

Setting up color management

Illustrator 9.0 simplifies the task of setting up a color-managed workflow by gathering most color management controls in a single Color Settings dialog box. Rather than adjusting each control manually, you can choose from a list of predefined color management settings. Each predefined configuration includes a set of color management options designed to produce consistent color for a common publishing workflow, such as preparation for Web or domestic prepress output. These predefined configurations can also serve as starting points for customizing your own workflow-specific configurations.

Illustrator 9.0 also introduces the use of color management policies, which determine how to handle color data that does not immediately match your current color management workflow. Policies are designed to clarify the color management decisions that you need to make when you open a document or import color data into an active document.

Keep in mind that you must specify color management settings *before* opening or creating files in order for the settings to take effect in those files.

Note: *Illustrator 9.0 supports color management for files that use either the RGB or CMYK color model. Illustrator 9.0 does not support color management for the grayscale color model or for spot colors. If a file containing a grayscale object (defined in tints of black) is opened or imported into Illustrator, that object will retain its grayscale qualities but will not be color-managed.*

To open the Color Settings dialog box:

Choose Edit > Color Settings.

To display helpful descriptions of the terminology and options in the dialog box, position the mouse over a section heading or menu item. These descriptions appear in the lower area of the dialog box.

Using predefined color management settings

Illustrator offers a collection of predefined color management settings, each with corresponding color profile and conversion options designed to preserve consistent color for a particular publishing workflow under typical conditions. In most cases, the predefined settings will provide sufficient color management for your needs.

Use the following guidelines to determine whether or not you need to use color management:

• You might not need color management if your production process is tightly controlled for one medium only. For example, you or your prepress service provider may prefer to tailor CMYK images and specify color values for a known, specific set of printing conditions.

• You can benefit from color management when you have more variables in your production process. Color management is recommended if you anticipate reusing color graphics for print and online media, using various kinds of devices within a single medium (such as different printing presses), if you manage multiple workstations, or if you plan to print to different domestic and international presses. If you decide to use color management, consult with your production partners—such as graphic artists and prepress service providers—to ensure that all aspects of your color management workflow integrate seamlessly with theirs.

To choose a predefined color management setting:

1 Choose Edit > Color Settings.

2 For Settings, choose a configuration option:

Emulate Adobe® Illustrator® 6.0 Emulates the color workflow used by Illustrator 6.0 and earlier. This configuration does not recognize or save color profiles in documents. When you choose this configuration, the Assign Profile and soft-proofing commands are not available, and color management options in the Print dialog box are not available.

Color Management Off Uses minimal color management settings to emulate the behavior of applications that do not support color management. Use this option for content that will be output on video or as onscreen presentations.

Emulate Photoshop 4 Emulates the color workflow used by Adobe Photoshop 4.0 and earlier.

U.S. Prepress Defaults Manages color for content that will be output under common press conditions in the U.S.

Europe Prepress Defaults Manages color for content that will be output under common press conditions in Europe.

Japan Prepress Defaults Manages color for content that will be output under common press conditions in Japan.

Web Graphics Defaults Manages color for content that will be published on the World Wide Web.

ColorSync Workflow (Mac OS only) Manages color using the ColorSync 3.0 CMS with the profiles chosen in the ColorSync control panel. This color management configuration is not recognized by Windows systems, or by earlier versions of ColorSync.

When you choose a predefined configuration, the Color Settings dialog box updates to display the specific color management settings associated with the configuration.

About working spaces

Among other options, predefined color management settings specify the default color profiles to be associated with the RGB and CMYK color models. Central to the color management workflow, these default profiles are known as the RGB and CMYK *working spaces*, respectively. The working spaces specified by predefined settings represent the color profiles that will produce the best color fidelity for several common output conditions. For example, the U.S. Prepress Defaults setting uses a CMYK working space that is designed to preserve color consistency under standard Specifications for Web Offset Publications (SWOP) press conditions.

A working space acts as the default color profile for newly created documents that use the associated color model. For example, if Adobe RGB (1998) is the current RGB working space, each new RGB document that you create will use colors within the Adobe RGB (1998) gamut. Working spaces also define the destination gamut of documents converted to the RGB or CMYK color model.

Using color management policies

When you specify a predefined color management setting, Illustrator sets up a color management workflow that will be used as the standard for all documents and color data that you open or import. For a newly created document, the color workflow operates relatively seamlessly: the document uses the working space profile associated with its color model for creating and editing colors, and the profile is usually embedded in the saved document to provide color translation information for the destination output device.

However, some existing documents may not use the working space that you have specified, and some existing documents may not be color-managed. It is common to encounter the following exceptions to your color-managed workflow:

• You might open a document or import color data from a document that has not been color-managed and lacks a profile altogether. This is often the case when you open a document created in an application that either does not support color management or has color management turned off.

- You might open a document or import color data from a document that contains a color profile different from the current working space. This may be the case when you open a document that has been created using different color management settings, or a document that has been scanned and assigned with a scanner profile.

In either case, Illustrator must decide how to handle the color data in the document. A *color management policy* looks for the color profile associated with an opened document or imported color data, and compares the profile (or lack of profile) with the current working space to make default color management decisions. If the profile matches the working space, the colors are automatically brought into the color management workflow that you have specified, using the working space profile. If the profile is missing or does not match the working space, Illustrator displays a message that alerts you to the mismatch situation and, in many cases, lets you specify how to handle the colors in question.

The following table provides a summary of the policy decisions you may be prompted to consider when opening or importing mismatched color data:

Mismatch situation	Policy options that may be available
Opening non-color-managed document without color profile	• Use working space for editing but not saving; do not color-manage document. • Use working space for editing, and save working space with document. • Use another color profile for editing, and save profile with document.
Opening document with color profile that does not match working space	• Use profile (instead of working space) for editing, and save profile with document. • Convert colors to working space, and save working space with document. • Discard profile, and do not color-manage document.
Importing color data into destination document	• Import and convert numeric values of source colors to color space of destination document in order to preserve color appearances. • Import and preserve numeric values of source colors.

The predefined color management workflows are set to display warning or option messages when a default color management policy is about to be implemented. Although you can disable the repeated display of some of the messages, it is highly recommended that you continue to display all policy messages, to ensure the appropriate color management of documents on a case-by-case basis. You should only turn off message displays if you are very confident that you understand the default policy decision and are willing to accept it for all documents that you open. You cannot undo the results of a default policy decision once a document has been saved.

To turn off the display of a policy message:

In the message dialog box, select the Don't Show Again option if it is available.

To reset the display of policy messages that have been disabled:

1 Choose Edit > Preferences > General.

2 Click Reset All Warning Dialogs, and click OK.

Customizing color management settings

Although the predefined settings should provide sufficient color management for most publishing workflows, you may sometimes want to customize individual options in a configuration. For example, you might want to change the CMYK working space to a profile that matches the proofing system used by your service bureau.

It's important to save your custom configurations so that you can reuse and share them with other users who use the same color management workflows; for more information, see "Saving and loading custom color management settings" on page 210. The color management settings that you customize in the Color Settings dialog box have an associated preferences file called *AI Color Settings,* located inside the Illustrator folder (Windows) or in the Preferences folder in your System Folder (Mac OS)

To customize color management settings:

1 Choose Edit > Color Settings.

2 To use a preset color management configuration as the starting point for your customization, choose that configuration from the Settings menu.

3 Specify the desired color settings. (As you make adjustments, the Settings menu option changes to Custom by default.) Refer to the following sections for detailed customization instructions.

Specifying working spaces

In a color-managed workflow, each color model must have a working space associated with it. At times you may want to customize the RGB or CMYK working space to reflect a workflow that uses a particular output or display device. For more information, see "About working spaces" on page 203.

Illustrator 9.0 ships with a standard set of color profiles that have been recommended and tested by Adobe Systems for most color management workflows. By default, only these profiles appear under the working space menus. To display additional color profiles that you have installed on your system, select Advanced Mode at the top of the Color Settings dialog box. To appear under a working space menu, a color profile must be bi-directional, that is, contain specifications for translating both into and out of color spaces. For information on installing color profiles, see "Adding device profiles to the color management system" on page 213.

For the RGB color model, the following standard working space options are available:

Adobe RGB (1998) Provides a fairly large gamut (range) of colors and is well-suited for documents that will be converted to CMYK. Use this space if you need to do print production work with a broad range of colors.

sRGB IEC61966-2.1 Reflects the characteristics of the average PC monitor. This standard space is endorsed by many hardware and software manufacturers, and is becoming the default color space for many scanners, low-end printers, and software applications. This space is recommended for Web work but not for prepress work (because of its limited color gamut).

Apple RGB Reflects the characteristics of the Apple Standard 13-inch monitor, and is used by a variety of desktop publishing applications, including Adobe Photoshop 4.0 and earlier. Use this space for files that you plan to display on Mac OS monitors, or for working with legacy (older) desktop publishing files.

ColorMatch RGB Matches the native color space of Radius Pressview monitors. This space provides a smaller gamut alternative to Adobe RGB (1998) for print production work.

Monitor RGB Sets the RGB working space to the current color profile of your monitor. Use this setting if other applications in your workflow do not support color management. If a color management configuration that specifies Monitor RGB is shared with another user working on a different system, the configuration uses that system's monitor profile as the working space.

ColorSync RGB (Mac OS only) Matches the RGB space specified in the control panel for Apple ColorSync 3.0 or later. If a color management configuration specifying this setting is shared with another user working on a different system, the configuration uses that system's ColorSync RGB space as the working space.

For the CMYK color model, the following standard working space options are available:

Euroscale (Coated) Uses specifications designed to produce quality separations using Euroscale inks under the following printing conditions: 350% total area of ink coverage, positive plate, bright white coated stock.

Euroscale (Uncoated) Uses specifications designed to produce quality separations using Euroscale inks under the following printing conditions: 260% total area of ink coverage, positive plate, uncoated white offset stock.

Japan Standard Uses specifications designed to produce quality separations using Japan Standard inks under the following printing conditions: 300% total area of ink coverage, positive plate, coated publication-grade stock.

U.S. Sheetfed Coated Uses specifications designed to produce quality separations using U.S. inks under the following printing conditions: 350% total area of ink coverage, negative plate, bright white coated stock.

U.S. Sheetfed Uncoated Uses specifications designed to produce quality separations using U.S. inks under the following printing conditions: 260% total area of ink coverage, negative plate, uncoated white offset stock.

U.S. Web Coated (SWOP) Uses specifications designed to produce quality separations using U.S. inks under the following printing conditions: 300% total area of ink coverage, negative plate, coated publication-grade stock. This profile was created using the TR001 characterization data.

U.S. Web Uncoated Uses specifications designed to produce quality separations using U.S. inks under the following printing conditions: 260% total area of ink coverage, negative plate, uncoated white offset stock.

ColorSync CMYK (Mac OS only) Matches the CMYK space specified in the control panel for Apple ColorSync 3.0 or later. If a color management configuration specifying this setting is shared with another user working on a different system, the configuration uses that system's ColorSync CMYK space as the working space

Specifying color management policies

Each predefined color management configuration sets up a color management policy for each color model and displays warning messages to let you override the default policy behavior on a case-by-case basis. If desired, you can change the default policy behavior to reflect a color management workflow that you use more often. For more information on policies, see "Using color management policies" on page 203.

To customize color management policies:

1 In the Color Settings dialog box, under Policies, choose one of the following to set the default color management policy for each color model:

• Off if you do not want to color-manage imported or opened color data.

• Preserve Embedded Profiles if you anticipate working with a mix of color-managed and non-color-managed documents, or with documents that use different profiles within the same color model.

• Convert to Working Space if you want to color-manage all documents using the current working spaces.

For detailed descriptions of the default behaviors associated with each policy option, see the table following this procedure.

2 Select either, both, or neither of the following:

• Ask When Opening to display a message whenever the embedded color profile in a newly opened document does not match the current working space. You will be given the option to override the policy's default behavior.

• Ask When Pasting to display a message whenever color profile mismatches occur as colors are imported into a document (via pasting, drag-and-drop, placing, and so on). You will be given the option to override the policy's default behavior.

It is strongly recommended that you keep both options selected. Deselecting the options causes Illustrator to implement default policy behavior without notification.

Policy option	Default color management behavior
Off	• No profiles are saved with new documents. • If opened document's profile does not match current working space, profile is discarded and not saved with document. • If opened document's profile matches current working space, profile is preserved and saved with document. • For color data imported into same color model, numeric values of colors are preserved. • For color data imported into different color model, colors are converted to destination document's color space.
Preserve Embedded Profiles	• Working space profile is saved with new documents. • If opened document's profile does not match current working space, profile is preserved and saved with document. • If opened document does not contain a profile, working space is used for editing but not saved with document. • For color data imported within same color model between either a non-color-managed source or destination, or from a CMYK document into a CMYK document, numeric color values are preserved. • For all other import cases, colors are converted to destination document's color space.

Policy option	Default color management behavior
Convert to Working Space	• Working space profile is saved with new documents. • If opened document's profile does not match current working space, document is converted to working space; working space is saved with document. • If opened document does not contain a profile, working space is used for editing but not saved with document. • For color data imported within same color model between either a non-color-managed source or destination, numeric color values are preserved. • For all other import cases, colors are converted to destination document's color space.

Customizing advanced color management settings

When you select Advanced Mode at the top of the Color Settings dialog box, you have the option of further customizing settings used for color management.

Specifying a color management engine

The color management engine specifies the system and color-matching method used to convert colors between color spaces. For more information, see "About color management" on page 199.

The following standard engine options are available. If you have installed additional color management engines, they may also appear as options.

Adobe (ACE) Uses the Adobe color management system and color engine. This is the default setting for most preset color configurations.

Apple ColorSync Uses the color management system provided by Apple Computer, Inc. for Mac OS computers.

Microsoft ICM Uses the color management system provided by Microsoft Corporation for Windows 98 and Windows 2000 computers.

Specifying a rendering intent

Translating colors to a different color space usually involves an adjustment of the colors to accommodate the gamut of the destination color space. Different translation methods use different rules to determine how the source colors are adjusted; for example, colors that fall inside the destination gamut may remain unchanged, or they may be adjusted to preserve the original range of visual relationships as translated to a smaller destination gamut. These translation methods are known as *rendering intents* because each technique is optimized for a different intended use of color graphics.

Note: The result of choosing a rendering intent depends on the graphical content of documents and on the profiles used to specify color spaces. Some profiles produce identical results for different rendering intents. Differences between rendering intents are apparent only when you print a document or convert it to a different working space.

The following rendering intent options are available:

Perceptual This intent aims to preserve the visual relationship between colors in a way that is perceived as natural to the human eye, although the color values themselves may change.

Saturation Appropriate for office and presentation graphics, this intent aims to create vivid color at the expense of accurate color. It scales the source gamut to the destination gamut but preserves relative saturation instead of hue, so when scaling to a smaller gamut, hues may shift. This rendering intent is suitable for business graphics, where the exact relationship between colors is not as important as having bright saturated colors.

Absolute Colorimetric Leaves colors that fall inside the destination gamut unchanged. This intent aims to maintain color accuracy at the expense of preserving relationships between colors. When translating to a smaller gamut, two colors that are distinct in the source space may be mapped to the same color in the destination space.

Relative Colorimetric This intent is identical to absolute colorimetric except for the following difference: relative colorimetric compares the *white point* (extreme highlight) of the source color space to that of the destination color space and shifts all colors accordingly. Relative colorimetric can be more accurate if the image's profile contains correct white point information. This is the default rendering intent used by all predefined color management configurations.

Using black-point compensation

The Use Black Point Compensation option controls whether to adjust for differences in black points when converting colors between color spaces. When this option is enabled, the full dynamic range of the source space is mapped into the full dynamic range of the destination space. When disabled, the dynamic range of the source space is simulated in the destination space; although this mode can result in blocked or gray shadows, it can be useful when the black point of the source space is lower than that of the destination space.

The Use Black Point Compensation option is selected for all predefined color management configurations. It is highly recommended that you keep this option selected.

Saving and loading custom color management settings

When you create a custom color management configuration, you should name and save the configuration to ensure that it can be reused and shared with other users. You can also load previously saved color management configurations into the Color Settings dialog box.

To save a custom color management configuration:

1 In the Color Settings dialog box, click Save.

2 Name your color settings file, and click Save.

To ensure that Illustrator displays the saved configuration in the Settings menu of the Color Settings dialog box, save the file in the Color Settings folder (the default location when you first open the Save dialog box).

To load a color management configuration:

1 In the Color Settings dialog box, click Load.

2 Locate and select the desired color settings file, and click Load.

When you load a custom color settings file, it appears as the active choice in the Settings menu of the Color Settings dialog box. If you choose a different option from the Settings menu, you must reload the custom settings file in order to access it again.

Soft-proofing colors

In a traditional publishing workflow, you print a hard proof of your document to preview how the document's colors will look when reproduced on a specific output device. In a color-managed workflow, you can use the precision of color profiles to soft-proof your document directly on the monitor. You can display an onscreen preview of how your document's colors will look when reproduced on a particular output device.

Keep in mind that the reliability of the soft proof is highly dependent upon the quality of your monitor, your monitor profile, and the ambient lighting conditions of your work station. For information on creating a monitor profile, see "Creating an ICC monitor profile" on page 214.

Note: The soft-proofing commands are not available when the Emulate Adobe Illustrator 6.0 setting is chosen in the Color Settings dialog box.

To display a soft proof:

1 Choose View > Proof Setup, and choose the output display that you want to simulate:

• Choose Custom to soft-proof colors as displayed on a specific output device. Then follow the instructions outlined in the next procedure to set up the custom proof.

• Choose Macintosh RGB or Windows RGB to soft-proof colors using either a standard Mac OS or Windows monitor as the proof profile space that you want to simulate.

• Choose Monitor RGB to soft-proof colors using your current monitor color space as the proof profile space.

2 Choose View > Proof Colors to toggle the soft-proof display on and off. When soft proofing is on, a checkmark appears next to the Proof Colors command.

To create a custom proof setup:

1 Choose View > Proof Setup > Custom.

2 In the Proof Setup dialog box, for Profile, choose the color profile for the device for which you want to create the proof.

3 If you chose a proof profile using the document's current color model, do one of the following:

• Select Preserve Color Numbers to simulate how the document will appear without converting colors to the proof profile space.

• Deselect Preserve Color Numbers to simulate how the document will appear if colors are converted to the proof profile space in an effort to preserve the colors' visual appearances. Then specify a rendering intent for the conversion; for more information, see "Specifying a rendering intent" on page 209.

4 Click OK.

Changing the color profile of a document

In some cases you may want to use the Assign Profile command to assign a different color profile to a document with an existing profile, or remove the existing profile altogether. For example, you may want to prepare the document for a different output destination, or you may want to correct a policy behavior that you no longer want implemented on the document. The Assign Profile command is recommended only for advanced users.

Note: The Assign Profile command is not available when the Emulate Adobe Illustrator 6.0 setting is chosen in the Color Settings dialog box.

To reassign or discard the profile of a document:

1 Choose Edit > Assign Profile.

2 Select one of the following:

• Don't Color Manage This Document to remove the existing profile from the document. Select this option only if you are sure that you do not want to color-manage the document.

• Working <*color model: working space*> to assign the working space profile to a document that either uses no profile or a profile different from the working space.

• Profile to reassign a different profile to a color-managed document. Choose the desired profile from the menu. Illustrator assigns the new profile to the document without converting colors to the profile space.

3 Click OK.

Embedding profiles in saved documents

By default, a document for which you have specified color management will have its profile embedded upon saving in a file format that supports embedded ICC profiles. These formats include the native Illustrator format (.ai), PDF, JPEG, TIFF, and the native Photoshop format (.psd). Profiles are not saved by default with non-color-managed documents.

You can change the default behavior to embed or not to embed profiles as you save a document. Changing the default behavior, however, is recommended only for advanced users who are very familiar with color management.

To change the embedding behavior of a profile in a document:

1 Choose File > Save. Name the document, specify a file format, and click Save.

2 In the file format options dialog box that appears, select or deselect Embed Color Profile.

3 Click OK to save the document.

Obtaining, installing, and updating color profiles

Precise, consistent color management requires accurate ICC-compliant profiles of all of your color devices. For example, without an accurate scanner profile, a perfectly scanned image may appear incorrect in another program, simply due to any difference in gamuts between the scanner and the program displaying the image. This misleading representation may cause you to make unnecessary, time-wasting, and potentially damaging "corrections" to an already satisfactory image. With an accurate profile, a program importing the image can correct for any gamut differences and display a scan's actual colors.

Once you obtain accurate profiles, they will work with all applications that are compatible with your color-management system. You can obtain profiles in the following ways, with the most precise methods listed first:

• Generate profiles customized for your specific devices using professional profiling equipment.

- Obtain a profile created by the manufacturer. Unfortunately, such profiles do not account for individual variations that naturally occur among machines (even identical models from the same manufacturer) or from age.

- Substitute an available profile that may be appropriate given information you have about the device's gamut. For example, many Mac OS scanners have been optimized for an Apple RGB monitor gamut, so you might try using an Apple monitor profile for these devices. Be sure to proof images created with the profile before using the profile in production. This workaround is unlikely to produce results suitable for professionally color-managed work.

Adding device profiles to the color management system

The Illustrator installer lets you choose from manufacturer-supplied device profiles for some commonly used equipment. This is useful if you don't have access to hardware-based calibration tools. It is not possible for the installer to supply profiles for all devices. If the installer did not install a profile for your device, create one or contact the device manufacturer to obtain one.

To minimize confusion when working with profiles, delete any profiles for devices not used by you or your workgroup.

In Mac OS, you can organize the ColorSync Profiles folder by creating additional folders within it, or adding aliases to other folders.

To add profiles to your system:

Do one of the following:

- In Windows NT or 2000, copy profiles into the WinNT\System32\Color folder.

- In Windows 98, copy profiles into the Windows\System\Color folder.

- In Mac OS, copy profiles into the ColorSync Profiles folder in the System Folder (ColorSync 2.5 or later), or System Folder/Preferences/ColorSync™ Profiles (ColorSync versions earlier than 2.5).

Note: *If you use ColorSync 2.5 but have used earlier versions, some profiles may still be stored in System Folder/Preferences/ColorSync™ Profiles on your hard disk. For compatibility with ColorSync 2.5 or later, store profiles in the ColorSync Profiles folder in the System Folder.*

Updating profiles

The color reproduction characteristics of a color device change as it ages, so recalibrate devices periodically and generate updated profiles. Profiles should be good for approximately a month depending on the device. Some monitors automatically compensate for phosphor aging.

Also, recalibrate a device when you change any of the factors that affect calibration. For example, recalibrate your monitor when you change the room lighting or the monitor brightness setting.

Creating an ICC monitor profile

Your monitor will display color more reliably if you use color management and accurate ICC profiles. The Adobe Gamma utility, which is automatically installed into your Control Panels folder, lets you calibrate and characterize your monitor to a standard and then save the settings as an ICC-compliant profile available to any program that uses your color management system. This calibration helps you eliminate any color cast in your monitor, make your monitor grays as neutral as possible, and standardize image display across different monitors.

Although Adobe Gamma is an effective calibration and profiling utility, hardware-based utilities are more precise. If you have a hardware-based utility that can generate an ICC-compliant profile, you should use that instead of Adobe Gamma.

Depending on your workflow scenario, an ICC monitor profile can be either a source profile, a destination profile, or both.

Note: *Adobe Gamma can characterize, but not calibrate, monitors used with Windows NT. In addition, the ICC profile you create with Adobe Gamma can be used as the system-level profile in Windows NT. Its ability to calibrate settings in Windows 98 depends on the video card and video driver software. In such cases, some calibration options documented here may not be available.*

Calibrating versus characterizing a monitor

Profiling software such as Adobe Gamma can both characterize and calibrate your monitor. When you *characterize* your monitor, you create a profile that describes how the monitor is currently reproducing color. When you *calibrate* your monitor, you bring it into compliance with a predefined standard; adjusting your monitor so that it displays color using the graphics arts standard white point color temperature of 5000 kelvin is an example of calibration.

Determine in advance the standard to which you are calibrating so that you can enter the set of values for that standard. Coordinate calibration with your workgroup and prepress service provider to make sure you're all calibrating to the same standard.

About monitor calibration settings

Monitor calibration involves adjusting video settings, which may be unfamiliar to you. A monitor profile uses these settings to precisely describe how your monitor reproduces color.

Brightness and contrast The overall level and range, respectively, of display intensity. These parameters work just as they do on a television. Adobe Gamma helps you set an optimum brightness and contrast range for calibration.

Gamma The brightness of the midtone values. The values produced by a monitor from black to white are nonlinear—if you graph the values, they form a curve, not a straight line. Gamma defines the value of that curve at halfway between black and white. Gamma adjustment compensates for the nonlinear tonal reproduction of output devices such as monitor tubes.

Phosphors The substance that monitors use to emit light. Different phosphors have different color characteristics.

White point The RGB coordinates at which red, green, and blue phosphors at full intensity create white.

Guidelines for creating an ICC monitor profile

The following guidelines can help you create an accurate monitor profile.

You may find it helpful to have your monitor's user guide handy while using Adobe Gamma.

• You don't need to calibrate your monitor if you've already done so using an ICC-compliant calibration tool such as Adobe Gamma and haven't changed your video card or monitor settings.

• If you have the Mac OS Gamma control panel (included with Adobe Photoshop 4.0 and earlier) or the Monitor Setup utility (included with PageMaker® 6.0) for Windows, remove it; it is obsolete. Use the latest Adobe Gamma utility instead.

• Make sure your monitor has been turned on for at least a half hour. This gives it sufficient time to warm up for a more accurate color reading.

• Make sure your monitor is displaying thousands of colors or more.

• Remove colorful background patterns on your monitor desktop. Busy or bright patterns surrounding a document interfere with accurate color perception. Set your desktop to display neutral grays only, using RGB values of 128. For more information, see the manual for your operating system.

• If your monitor has digital controls for choosing the white point of your monitor from a range of preset values, set those controls before starting Adobe Gamma. Later, in Adobe Gamma, you'll set the white point to match your monitor's current setting. Be sure to set the digital controls before you start Adobe Gamma. If you set them after you begin the calibration process in Adobe Gamma, you'll need to begin the process again.

• Monitor performance changes and declines over time; recharacterize your monitor every month or so. If you find it difficult or impossible to calibrate your monitor to a standard, it may be too old and faded.

Calibrating with Adobe Gamma

The ICC profile you get using Adobe Gamma uses the calibration settings to describe how your monitor reproduces color.

To use Adobe Gamma: 1 Do one of the following to start the Adobe Gamma utility:

• In Windows, double-click Adobe Gamma, located in the Program Files\Common Files\Adobe\Calibration folder on your hard drive.

• In Mac OS, from the Apple menu, choose Control Panels > Adobe Gamma.

2 Do one of the following:

• To use a version of the utility that will guide you through each step, select Step by Step, and click OK. This version is recommended if you're inexperienced. If you choose this option, follow the instructions described in the utility. Start from the default profile for your monitor if available.

• To use a compact version of the utility with all the controls in one place, select Control Panel, and click OK. This version is recommended if you have experience creating color profiles.

Any time while working in the Adobe Gamma control panel, you can click the Wizard (Windows) or Assistant (Mac OS) button to switch to the wizard for instructions that guide you through the same settings as in the control panel, one option at a time.

8

Chapter 8: Using Transparency, Gradients, and Patterns

When you create artwork in Illustrator, by default it appears solid; that is, it has an opacity of 100 percent. The Transparency palette lets you vary an object's opacity and other characteristics to create a range of effects. You can blend colors in different ways between overlapping objects, create masks that change the shape and transparency of objects, or knock out shapes below selected objects.

About transparency

The Transparency palette lets you vary the degree of transparency of an object, a group of objects, or a layer from 100% opacity (completely solid) to 0% opacity (completely transparent). When you decrease an object's opacity, the underlying artwork becomes visible through the surface of the object.

Using commands in the Transparency palette, you can also create special effects, such as knocking out underlying colors, or creating graduated transparencies on blends. For example, you can use the Knockout option in the Transparency palette to have an overlapping stroke knock out the color of the underlying fill.

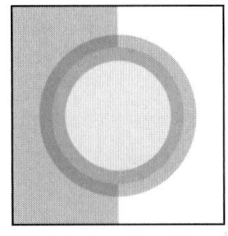

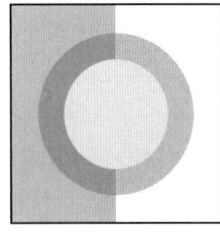

Filled circle and overlying stroke without Knockout Group option and with Knockout Group option applied.

You should keep the following in mind when you are applying transparency effects to artwork:

• By default, the entire object (both the stroke and the fill) is affected by transparency commands. To change the transparency of only the fill or only the stroke, you can select the fill or stroke in the Appearance palette. You can then apply transparency effects to the selected fill or stroke using the Transparency palette.

- Use the Layers palette to target an object, group of objects, or layer to apply transparency effects. (See "Using Layers" on page 241.) This is the only way to ensure that the effect is applied only to the artwork you want to target.

- To export files containing transparent objects to other applications, you can export the file in the Photoshop file format to maintain transparency on layers. (See "Exporting Illustrator files containing transparent artwork" on page 351.) Alternatively, you can use the Save or Export commands to export to other file formats; however, transparent objects will be flattened according to settings in the Transparency panel of the Document Setup dialog box.

Using grouped objects with the Transparency palette

By default the Transparency palette acts on objects, but you can also use it to create unique transparency effects at the group or layer level.

If you simply select objects and change the opacity setting, the selected objects' opacity will change relative to the others. Any overlapping areas will show an accumulated opacity.

In contrast, if you target a group that has been created with the Group command and then change the opacity, the group is treated as a single object by the Transparency palette and the opacities within the group do not change. Only objects *outside* the group are made transparent relative to the group.

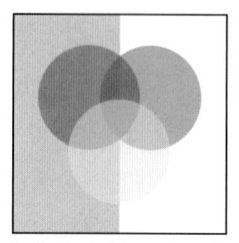

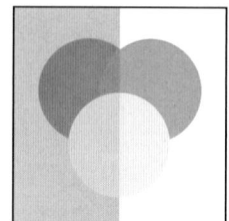

Individual objects selected and set to 50% opacity. Group selected and set to 50% opacity.

Using the Transparency palette

You use the Transparency palette to specify the opacity and blending mode of objects, to create opacity masks, or to "knock out" a portion of one object with the overlying portion of another object.

To display the Transparency palette:

Choose Window > Show Transparency.

Displaying the Transparency Grid

You can display a checkered background grid that lets you more easily view the areas of the artwork that are transparent when you are working on the artwork.

To show or hide the Transparency Grid:

Choose View > Show Transparency Grid, or View > Hide Transparency Grid.

Setting transparency preferences

You use the Document Setup dialog box to set transparency preferences. Using these settings, you can change the size or color of the Transparency Grid, or you can adjust the quality or printing speed of transparent artwork.

To set transparency preferences:

1 Choose File > Document Setup.

2 Choose Transparency from the menu at the top of the Document Setup dialog box.

3 In the Grid Size menu, choose the desired checkerboard size.

4 In the Grid Colors drop-down menu, choose an option:

• Light, Medium, or Dark to display a grayscale grid.

• A color option to display the grid in a preset color.

• To create a custom color for the Transparency grid, click either of the color swatches to the right of the Grid Colors drop-down menu. In the color-picker, select a color, and then click OK.

5 Check the Simulate Colored Paper option to simulate colors as if the artwork were printed on colored paper. For example, if you were to draw a blue object on a yellow artboard background, the object would appear green.

6 Use the Quality/Speed slider to adjust the degree of rasterization of transparent artwork when printing or exporting. For a detailed description of this feature, see "Specifying rasterization settings with the Quality/Speed slider" on page 368.

7 Click OK to close the Document Setup dialog box.

Specifying transparency

To change the transparency of an object, group, or layer, you target the artwork and then adjust the Opacity slider in the Transparency palette. You can adjust the opacity from 0% (fully transparent) to 100% (fully opaque).

The only way to precisely target an object, group, or layer is to select the artwork using the Layers palette. When you select the object, group, or layer, a thumbnail of the selected artwork appears in the Transparency palette.

When you make transparency changes on a targeted layer, the changes are targeted on the layer container itself. The transparency change is applied to the layer as a whole, not to objects on the layer.

To specify the opacity of an object:

1 Select the desired object in the artwork, or target the object or group in the Layers palette.

2 In the Transparency palette, drag the Opacity slider to control the transparency of the object.

To specify the opacity of one or more groups or layers:

1 In the Layers palette, click the target icon of the desired layer or group. To select more than one layer or group, hold down Shift, and click their target icons.

2 In the Transparency palette, drag the Opacity slider to control the transparency of the targeted layers and groups.

Creating opacity masks

An *opacity mask* lets you mask underlying artwork, using the change in luminosity of the overlying artwork to affect objects beneath. Any colors, patterns, or gradients contained in the mask are visible on the underlying artwork.

You create the opacity mask from the topmost shape in the selected set of objects. If you select only one object, a blank opacity mask is created.

When you create an opacity mask, a thumbnail of the mask appears next to the thumbnail of the object being masked. By default, the mask and the object are linked together, shown by a link between the thumbnails. When the artwork and mask are linked, they move together as a unit in the artwork.

To create an opacity mask:

1 Select the objects that you want masked. Ensure that the object you want to use as the masking shape appears at the front of the artwork. The topmost selected object will be used as the mask.

2 Choose Make Opacity Mask in the Transparency palette menu.

To remove or disable a transparency mask:

1 Make sure that the mask you want to release is currently selected.

2 Do one of the following:

• Choose Release Opacity Mask in the Transparency palette menu to remove the mask.

• Choose Disable Opacity Mask in the Transparency palette menu to deactivate the mask without removing it. To reactivate the mask, choose Enable Opacity Mask from the Transparency palette menu.

To edit an opacity mask:

1 Do one of the following to enter mask-editing mode:

• Click on the mask thumbnail in the Transparency palette.

• Alt-click (Windows) or Option-click (Mac OS) on a mask thumbnail to view only the mask in the document window.

2 Use any of the Illustrator editing tools and techniques to edit the mask. Changes made to the mask will be immediately visible in the Transparency palette.

3 Click the artwork thumbnail in the Transparency palette to exit mask-editing mode.

Note: You can also add artwork to an opacity mask without entering mask-editing mode. Select the artwork to be added, together with an already-masked object, and click Mask.

To unlink a mask from the artwork:

Do one of the following:

• Click the link symbol (🔗) between the artwork thumbnail and the mask thumbnail in the Transparency palette. Click the area between the thumbnails again to relink the mask and artwork.

• Choose Unlink Opacity Mask in the Transparency palette menu. To relink the mask, choose Link Opacity Mask in the Transparency palette menu.

Inverting the values of an opacity mask

When you select an opacity mask, the Invert Mask button becomes visible. The Invert Mask command is used to invert the opacity values of a mask. Areas outside of the mask artwork are also inverted, so that they appear fully transparent rather than fully opaque.

To invert the opacity of a mask, or to return an inverted mask to its original state:

1 Select the masked artwork.

2 Click the Invert Mask option. Deselect the Invert Mask option to return the mask to the original state.

To make all masks inverted by default:

1 Choose New Opacity Masks Are Inverted from the Transparency palette menu. All new masks created in the Transparency palette will now have inverted values.

Selecting blending modes

You can blend the colors between two superimposed objects by using the blending modes in the Transparency palette.

Blending modes let you vary the ways that the colors of objects blend with the colors of underlying objects.

It's helpful to think in terms of the following colors when visualizing a blending mode's effect:

• The *base color* is the underlying color in the artwork.

• The *blend color* is the color of the selected object, group, or layer.

• The *resulting color* is the color resulting from the blend.

To specify the blending mode of an object:

1 Target the desired object, group, or layer.

2 In the Transparency palette, choose a blending mode from the menu.

The following sections describe each of the blending modes.

Normal Paints the selection with the blend color, without interaction with the base color. This is the default mode.

Multiply Looks at each color component (CMYK and spot colors in CMYK documents, or RGB and spot colors in RGB documents), and multiplies the base color by the blend color. The resulting color is always a darker color. Multiplying any color with black produces black. Multiplying any color with white leaves the color unchanged. The effect is similar to drawing on the page with multiple magic markers.

Screen Looks at each color component, and multiplies the inverse of the blend and base colors. The resulting color is always a lighter color. Screening with black leaves the color unchanged. Screening with white produces white. The effect is similar to projecting multiple slide images on top of each other.

Overlay Multiplies or screens the colors, depending on the base color. Patterns or colors overlay the existing artwork while preserving the highlights and shadows of the base color. The base color is not replaced but is mixed with the blend color to reflect the lightness or darkness of the original color.

Soft Light Darkens or lightens the colors, depending on the blend color. The effect is similar to shining a diffused spotlight on the artwork.

If the blend color (light source) is lighter than 50% gray, the artwork is lightened, as if it were dodged. If the blend color is darker than 50% gray, the artwork is darkened, as if it were burned in. Painting with pure black or white produces a distinctly darker or lighter area but does not result in pure black or white.

Hard Light Multiplies or screens the colors, depending on the blend color. The effect is similar to shining a harsh spotlight on the artwork.

If the blend color (light source) is lighter than 50% gray, the artwork is lightened, as if it were screened. This is useful for adding highlights to artwork. If the blend color is darker than 50% gray, the artwork is darkened, as if it were multiplied. This is useful for adding shadows to artwork. Painting with pure black or white results in pure black or white.

Color Dodge Looks at the color components in the artwork, and brightens the base color to reflect the blend color. Blending with black produces no change.

Color Burn Looks at the color components in the artwork, and darkens the base color to reflect the blend color. Blending with white produces no change.

Darken Looks at the color components in the artwork, and selects the base or blend color—whichever is darker—as the resulting color. Areas lighter than the blend color are replaced, and areas darker than the blend color do not change.

Lighten Looks at the color components in the artwork, and selects the base or blend color—whichever is lighter—as the resulting color. Areas darker than the blend color are replaced, and areas lighter than the blend color do not change.

Difference Looks at the color components, and subtracts either the blend color from the base color or the base color from the blend color, depending on which has the greater brightness value. Blending with white inverts the base color values; blending with black produces no change.

Exclusion Creates an effect similar to but lower in contrast than the Difference mode. Blending with white inverts the base color components. Blending with black produces no change.

Hue Creates a resulting color with the luminance and saturation of the base color and the hue of the blend color.

Saturation Creates a resulting color with the luminance and hue of the base color and the saturation of the blend color. Painting with this mode in an area with no saturation (gray) causes no change.

Color Creates a resulting color with the luminance of the base color and the hue and saturation of the blend color. This preserves the gray levels in the artwork and is useful for coloring monochrome artwork and for tinting color artwork.

Luminosity Creates a resulting color with the hue and saturation of the base color and the luminance of the blend color. This mode creates an inverse effect from that of the Color mode.

Note: The Difference, Exclusion, Hue, Saturation, Color, and Luminosity modes do not blend spot colors.

Isolating blending modes

When you apply blending modes to objects in a group, the effects of the blending modes are normally seen on any objects beneath the group.

You can use the Isolate Blending command to change the behavior of blending modes so that only members of the selected group are affected and objects beneath the group are unaffected by the blending modes.

Note: The Isolate Blending command is only useful when used on groups or layers containing objects that have a blending mode other than Normal applied to them. The command also works on individual objects that have had blending modes other than Normal applied to overlapping strokes or fills.

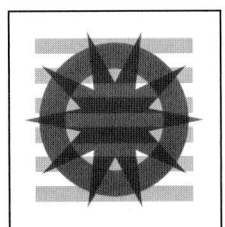

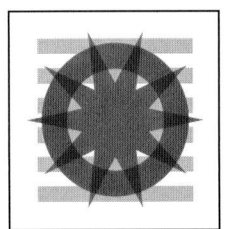

Group selected without Isolate Blending and same group with Isolate Blending option applied.

To isolate blending modes:

1 In the Layers palette, target a group or layer containing two or more objects to which blending modes are applied. You can also select individual objects with overlapping strokes or fills to which different blending modes have been applied.

2 In the Transparency palette, click Isolate Blending.

Isolating a layer lets you preview the way it will look against other layers in Photoshop after export.

Using the Transparency palette to create knockouts

Using the Knockout Group option in the Transparency palette, you can make every object of a group "knock out"—that is, visually block out—the objects it overlays in the group.

When you use the Knockout Group option, only artwork within the selected group is visually knocked out. Objects beneath the selected group are still visible relative to the group.

As you click on the Knockout Group option, it cycles through three states: on (selected), off (deselected), and neutral. The neutral knockout option lets you group artwork without interfering with the knockout behavior determined by the enclosing layer or group. If you want to ensure that a group of transparent objects will never knock each other out, use the off option.

All three knockout options can also be used to control the interaction of transparent fills and strokes within an object. To do this, select or target the object before choosing a Knockout Group option.

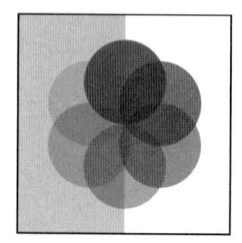

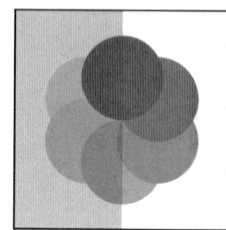

Group with Knockout Group option off and with Knockout Group option on.

When you use the Opacity and Mask Define Knockout Shape option, the knockout effect is proportional to the object's opacity. In the areas of the mask that are close to 100% opacity, the knockout effect is strong. In the areas with less opacity, the knockout effect is weaker. For example, if you use a gradient mask as a knockout group, the underlying object will be knocked out progressively, as if it were being shaded by a gradient.

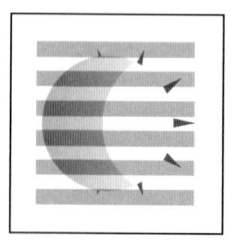

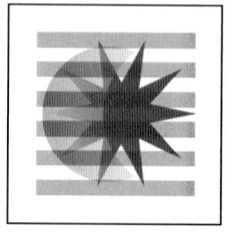

Circle with blending mode, opacity mask, and Knockout Group option applied; Opacity and Mask Define Knockout Shape option applied to circle.

To knock out objects within a group or layer:

1 Target the group or layer in the Layers palette.

2 In the Transparency palette, click Knockout Group until the option is selected.

To prevent objects from knocking out within a knockout group or layer:

1 Select the objects and group them using the Object > Group command.

2 Target the newly created group in the Layers palette.

3 In the Transparency palette, click Knockout Group until the option is deselected.

Applying a gradient, gradient mesh, or pattern opacity mask to an object

You can also use the Transparency palette to create an opacity mask of virtually any artwork imaginable, including a gradient, gradient mesh, or pattern. When you apply the opacity mask to an object, the characteristics of the masking artwork—for example, a pattern or a gradient—appear as a transparent addition to the object's surface.

To apply a gradient, gradient mesh, or pattern opacity mask to an object:

1 Select an object on which to apply the mask.

2 Shift-select an existing gradient, gradient mesh, or pattern in your artwork. Make sure that the gradient, gradient mesh, or pattern is topmost and overlying the object on which you want to apply the mask.

3 In the Transparency palette menu, choose Make Opacity Mask.

About gradients, gradient meshes, and blends

Depending on the effect you want, you can choose different ways to apply blends or color gradients to objects.

To apply a graduated blend of colors as you would apply any other color, you can create a gradient fill. You use the Gradient palette or the gradient tool to apply a gradient; applying a gradient in this way does not transform the object. Creating a gradient fill is a good way to create a smooth color gradation across one or more objects.

In contrast, the gradient mesh tool transforms a path object (or a bitmap image) into a single, multicolored object. When an object is transformed into a gradient mesh object, you create smooth shifts in color that can be precisely adjusted and manipulated—the color is controlled by a mesh that can be moved and adjusted to vary the color shift from one part of the object to another. The gradient mesh tool provides the most precise method for shifting colors within a single object.

You can create blends of colors, opacities, and shapes between objects using the Blend command or the blend tool. You can select the beginning and ending shapes, opacities, and colors, and have Illustrator create the intermediate steps to create the final blend.

Creating and working with gradient fills

A *gradient fill* is a graduated blend between two or more colors or tints of the same color. You use the Gradient palette to create your own gradients and—in combination with the Color palette and Swatches palette—to modify existing gradients. You can also add intermediate colors to a gradient to create a fill defined by multiple blends among colors.

Gradient colors can be assigned as CMYK process color, RGB process color, or a spot color. When a gradient is printed or separated, mixed-mode gradient colors are all converted to CMYK process color. (See "Printing gradients, gradient mesh objects, color blends, and transparencies" on page 370.)

To create a gradient:

1 Select an object with a selection tool, and click the Fill box in the toolbox to select the object's fill.

2 To apply a gradient, do one of the following:

• Choose Window > Show Gradient, and click the Gradient Fill box at the upper left of the Gradient palette. (If the Gradient Fill box is not displayed, choose Show Options from the pop-up menu in the Gradient palette.)

• Click the Gradient button in the toolbox.

• Click a gradient swatch in the Swatches palette.

3 To define the starting color of a gradient, click the left square below the gradient bar and then do one of the following:

• Alt-click (Windows) or Option-click (Mac OS) a color swatch in the Swatches palette.

• Create a color using the sliders or the color bar in the Color palette.

• Drag a color from the Color palette or the Swatches palette to the square below the gradient bar.

Note: If you create a gradient between spot colors, you must deselect Convert to Process in the Separation Setup dialog box to print the gradient in individual spot color separations. (See "Printing gradients as separations" on page 383.)

4 To define the ending color of the gradient, click the right square below the gradient bar. Then choose the color you want as described in step 3.

5 Choose Linear or Radial from the pop-up menu to indicate the type of gradient you want. With a radial gradient, the beginning point of the gradient defines the center point of the fill, which radiates outward to the endpoint.

6 To adjust the beginning point or endpoint of the gradient, drag the squares located below the bar. To adjust the midpoint of the gradient (the point at which the colors are at 50%), drag the diamond icon located above the bar.

7 Enter the angle of direction for the gradient in the Angle text box. The angle can range from -180 to 180 degrees. (The angle option is not available when a radial gradient is chosen.)

8 To save the gradient, do one of the following:

• Drag the completed gradient from the Gradient palette to the Swatches palette.

- Drag the gradient from the Fill box in the toolbox to the Swatches palette.
- Click the New Swatch button in the Swatches palette.

Modifying gradients

You can modify gradients by adding colors to make blends from multiple colors or by adjusting the endpoints and midpoints of the gradients.

Gradient colors are defined by a series of stops in the gradient bar. A *stop* is the point at which a gradient changes from one color to the next and is identified by a square below the gradient bar. The squares in the Gradient palette display the color currently assigned to each gradient stop.

It's a good idea to fill an object with the gradient you plan to adjust so that you can preview the effect on the artwork as you adjust the gradient.

To add intermediate colors to a gradient:

Do one of the following:

- Drag and drop a color from the Swatches palette or the Color palette onto the gradient bar in the Gradient palette.
- Click anywhere below the gradient bar to define another color square. You can then select a color and adjust the square as you would any other starting or ending color. To delete an intermediate color, drag the square off the gradient bar.

Adjusting gradients with the gradient tool

Once you have filled an object with a gradient, the gradient tool lets you modify the gradient by "repainting" the fill along an imaginary line you drag. This tool lets you change the direction of a gradient, change the beginning point and endpoint of a gradient, and apply a gradient across multiple objects.

To use the gradient tool:

1 Select an object whose gradient you want to modify.

2 Select the gradient tool ( ).

3 Position the pointer where you want to define the beginning point of the gradient, and drag across the object in the direction you want the gradient to be painted. Hold down Shift to constrain the tool to multiples of 45 degrees.

4 Release the mouse button where you want to define the endpoint of the gradient.

To apply a gradient across multiple objects:

1 Fill each object with a gradient using the Gradient palette, the Swatches palette, or the paint bucket tool.

2 Select all of the objects.

3 Select the gradient tool ( ).

4 Position the pointer where you want to define the beginning point of the gradient, and drag across the objects in the direction you want the gradient to be painted.

5 Release the mouse button where you want to define the endpoint of the gradient.

Creating multicolored objects with the gradient mesh tool

The gradient mesh tool, the Create Gradient Mesh command, and the Expand command can all be used to transform an object into a *mesh object*. A mesh object is a single, multicolored object on which colors can flow in different directions, and transition smoothly from one point to another.

By creating a fine mesh on an object and manipulating the color characteristics at each point in the mesh, you can precisely manipulate the coloring of the mesh object. You can also apply color to four mesh points at the same time by clicking the patch between them, to create broad color changes on part of the object.

About gradient meshes

When you create a mesh object, multiple lines called *mesh lines* crisscross the object and provide a way to easily manipulate color transitions on the object. By moving and editing points on the mesh lines, you can change the intensity of a color shift, or change the extent of a colored area on the object.

At the intersection of two mesh lines is a special kind of anchor point called a *mesh point*. Mesh points appear as diamonds and have all of the same properties as anchor points but with the added capability of accepting color. You can add and delete mesh points, edit the mesh points, or change the color associated with each mesh point.

Anchor points also appear in the mesh (differentiated by their square rather than diamond shape), and can be added, deleted, edited, and moved as with any anchor points in Illustrator. Anchor points can be placed on any mesh line; you can click an anchor point and drag its direction lines to modify it. (See "About direction lines and direction points" on page 87.)

The area between any four mesh points is called the *mesh patch*. You can also change the color of the mesh patch using the same techniques as changing colors on a mesh point.

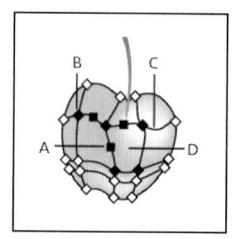

A. Anchor point *B.* Mesh point
C. Mesh line *D.* Mesh patch

Tips for creating mesh objects

You can create a mesh object out of any path object, or any bitmap image (such as a photographic image imported from Adobe Photoshop). There are a few important guidelines to keep in mind when creating mesh objects:

• You cannot create mesh objects from compound paths, text objects, or linked EPS files.

• Once a mesh object has been created, it cannot be converted back to a path object.

- When converting complex objects, use the Create Gradient Mesh command for the best results.

- When converting simple objects, use either the gradient mesh tool or the Create Gradient Mesh command. However, if you want to add a highlight to a particular spot, use the gradient mesh tool and click at the point you want the highlight to appear.

- To create a mesh object with a regular pattern of mesh points and mesh lines, use the Create Gradient Mesh command.

- When converting complex objects, Illustrator can add hidden anchor points to maintain the shape of a line. If you want to edit, add, or delete one or more of these anchor points, use the add-anchor-point tool or the delete-anchor-point tool.

- To improve performance and speed of redrawing, keep the size of mesh objects to a minimum. Complex mesh objects can greatly reduce performance. Therefore, it is better to create a few small, simple mesh objects than to create a single, complex mesh object.

Creating a mesh object

Use the gradient mesh tool or the Create Gradient Mesh command to convert objects to mesh objects. You can also use the Expand command to convert radial or linear gradient path objects into mesh objects.

To create a gradient mesh object with the gradient mesh tool:

Choose the gradient mesh tool ( ) and click a filled object. The object is converted to a gradient mesh object with the minimum number of mesh lines.

To create a gradient mesh object with the Create Gradient Mesh command:

1 Select a filled object.

2 Choose Object > Create Gradient Mesh.

3 Enter the number of horizontal rows of mesh lines to create on the object in the Rows text box.

4 Enter the number of vertical columns of mesh lines to create on the object in the Columns text box.

5 Select the direction of the highlight from the Appearance pop-up menu:

- To Center creates a highlight in the center of the object.

- To Edge creates a highlight on the edges of the object.

- Flat applies the object's original color evenly across the surface, resulting in no highlight.

6 Enter a percentage of white highlight to apply to the mesh object. A value of 100% applies maximum white highlight to the object; a value of 0% applies no white highlight to the object.

Creating a mesh object using the Expand command:

1 Select an object containing a radial or linear gradient fill.

2 Choose Object > Expand.

3 Select the Gradient Mesh option in the Expand dialog box and click OK. The selected object is converted to a mesh object that takes the shape of the gradient, either circular (radial) or rectangular (linear).

Editing mesh objects

Once you have created a mesh object, you can adjust or edit its mesh points, anchor points, and mesh lines. Anchor points can be added with the add-anchor-point tool or deleted with the delete-anchor-point tool on any mesh line.

To add or delete mesh points and mesh lines:

1 Select the gradient mesh tool ( ).

2 Do one of the following:

• To add a mesh point colored with the current fill color, click anywhere in the mesh object. The corresponding mesh lines extend from the new mesh point to the edges of the object. Clicking on an existing mesh line adds a single intersecting mesh line.

• To add a mesh point without changing to the current fill color, press Shift and click.

• To delete a mesh point and the corresponding mesh lines, Alt-click (Windows) or Option-click (Mac OS) directly on the mesh point.

To edit a mesh point:

1 Select the gradient mesh tool and click directly on a mesh point. Direction lines appear on the mesh point.

2 Do one of the following:

• Drag the direction points on the direction lines to edit the mesh point as you would any anchor point. For more information about editing anchor points, see "About direction lines and direction points" on page 87.

• Shift-drag a direction point to move all direction lines from the mesh point at once.

• Use the direct-selection tool, the convert-selection-point tool, or the transformation tools to edit mesh points.

To move a mesh point:

1 Select the gradient mesh tool.

2 Do one of the following:

• Click a mesh point and drag to freely move the point and the connecting mesh lines.

• Press Shift and drag the mesh point to constrain the movement to follow a mesh line. This is a convenient way to move a mesh point along a curved mesh line without distorting the mesh line.

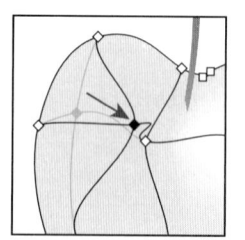

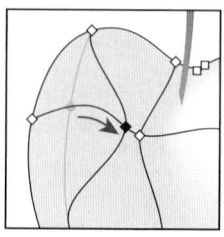

Dragging to move mesh point and Shift-dragging with the gradient mesh tool to constrain to mesh line

Adjusting colors on gradient mesh objects

Colors are added to gradient mesh objects using the Color palette, by dragging and dropping colors, or by using the paint bucket tool. When you select and color a mesh point, the mesh point and surrounding area are colored with the current fill color. When you click over a mesh patch, all four mesh points surrounding the patch are colored. You can also use color filters to change the color of mesh points.

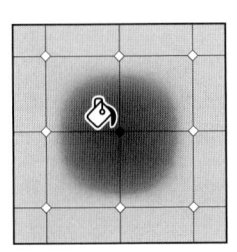

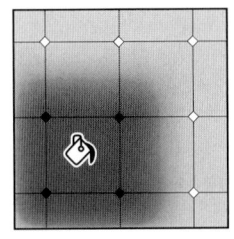

Adding color to a mesh point and to a mesh patch

Once color is applied to parts of a mesh object, you can change the shape and extent of the colored areas by editing the mesh points, anchor points, and mesh lines. (See "Editing mesh objects" on page 232.)

To add color to a mesh point or mesh patch with the Color palette:

1 Select a mesh point or mesh patch with the gradient mesh tool ( ) or the direct-selection tool ( ).

2 Do one of the following:

• In the Color palette, select a color using the sliders or the color bar.

• In the Swatches palette, select a swatch.

To add color to a mesh point or mesh patch by dragging and dropping:

Do one of the following:

• Drag a color from the Color palette directly over a mesh point or mesh patch and release the mouse button.

• Drag a swatch color from the Swatches palette directly over a mesh point or mesh patch and release the mouse button.

To add color to a mesh point or mesh patch with the paint bucket:

1 Select the paint bucket tool.

2 Click directly on a mesh point or a mesh patch. The point or patch is colored with the current fill color.

Creating and working with patterns

To create a pattern, you create artwork you want to use as a pattern and then drag the artwork to the Swatches palette or use the Edit > Define Pattern command. You can use paths, compound paths, or text with solid fills (or no fill) for a pattern, or you can design a pattern from scratch with any of the tools in the Adobe Illustrator program. (However, you cannot use patterns, gradients, blends, brushstrokes, gradient meshes, bitmap images, graphs, placed files, or masks in a pattern.) You can customize any pattern by resizing the pattern, moving or transforming it, or coloring its objects.

Note: The Illustrator Extras folder on the Adobe Illustrator CD includes pattern and texture libraries. In addition, the Adobe Illustrator Startup_CMYK and Startup_RGB files and the Adobe Illustrator 9.0/Libraries folder contain a smaller collection of these patterns.

Patterns intended for filling objects (*fill patterns*) differ in design and tiling from patterns intended to be applied to a path with the Brushes palette (*brush patterns*). For best results, use fill patterns to fill objects and brush patterns to outline objects.

How patterns tile

When designing patterns, it helps to understand how Adobe Illustrator tiles patterns:

• Patterns tile from left to right from the ruler origin (by default, the bottom of the artwork) to the top of the artwork. Typically, only one tile makes up a fill pattern. Brush patterns can consist of up to five tiles—for the sides, outer corners, inner corners, and the beginning and end of the path. The additional corner tiles enable brush patterns to flow smoothly at corners.

• Fill patterns tile perpendicular to the *x* axis. In contrast, brush patterns tile perpendicular to the path (with the top of the pattern tile always facing outward). Also, corner tiles rotate 90 degrees clockwise each time the path changes direction.

• Fill and brush patterns also tile differently in relation to the *pattern bounding box*—an unfilled and unstroked rectangle backmost in the artwork. For fill patterns, the bounding box acts as a mask; fill patterns tile only the artwork within the pattern's bounding box. In contrast, brush patterns tile artwork within the bounding box and protruding from or grouped with it.

Constructing simple patterns and defining patterns

To create a pattern, you create artwork that you want to use as a pattern tile and then drag it to the Swatches palette.

To create a pattern:

1 Create artwork for the pattern following "Guidelines for constructing patterns" on page 235.

2 To make the pattern less complex so that it prints more rapidly, remove any unnecessary detail from the pattern artwork, and group objects that are painted with the same color so that they are adjacent in the stacking order.

3 Optionally, to control the spacing between pattern elements or to clip out portions of the pattern, draw a pattern bounding box (an unfilled rectangle) around the artwork you want to use as a pattern. Choose Object > Arrange > Send to Back to make the rectangle the backmost object. To use the rectangle as a bounding box for a brush or fill pattern, fill and stroke it with None.

4 Use the selection tool to select the artwork and bounding box (if any) that will make up the pattern tile.

5 Do one of the following:

• Choose Edit > Define Pattern, and enter a name in the New Swatch dialog box.

• Choose Window > Show Swatches, and then drag the artwork to the Swatches palette.

To name a pattern in the Swatches palette:

1 Double-click a pattern swatch.

2 Enter the new pattern name in the Swatch Name text box, and click OK.

Guidelines for constructing patterns

Follow these general guidelines for constructing pattern tiles:

• As you create your pattern tile, zoom in on the artwork to align elements more accurately, and then zoom out from the artwork for the final selection.

• For greatest efficiency in previewing and printing, a fill pattern tile should be about 1/2 inch to 1 inch square. Side tiles for brush patterns should be no larger than 1/2 inch to 1 inch high by 1 inch to 2 inches wide; the corner tiles must be the same height as the side tiles and should be square.

• The more complex the pattern, the smaller the selection used to create it should be; however, the smaller the selection (and the pattern tile it creates), the more copies are needed to create the pattern. Thus, a 1-inch-square tile is more efficient than a 1/4-inch-square tile. If you are creating a simple pattern, you can include multiple copies of the object within the selection intended for the pattern tile.

• To create simple line patterns, layer stroked lines of varying widths and colors and place an unfilled and unstroked bounding box behind the lines to create a pattern tile.

• To make an organic or textural pattern appear irregular, vary the tile artwork subtly, not dramatically, for a more realistic effect. You can use the Roughen filter in the Distort menu to control variations.

• To ensure smooth tiling, close paths before defining the pattern.

• Enlarge your artwork view, and check for flaws before defining a pattern.

• If you draw a bounding box around the artwork, make sure that the box is a rectangle, that it is the backmost object of the tile, and that it is unfilled and unstroked. To have Illustrator use this bounding box for a brush pattern, do not fill or stroke the box and make sure that nothing protrudes from it.

Follow these additional guidelines when creating brush patterns:

• When possible, confine artwork to an unpainted bounding box so that you can control how the pattern tiles. (See "How patterns tile" on page 234.)

• Corner tiles must be square and have the same height as side tiles to align properly on the path. If you plan to use corner tiles with your brush pattern, align objects in the corner tiles horizontally with objects in the side tiles so that the patterns tile correctly.

- Create special corner effects for brush patterns using corner tiles.

For more information on constructing patterns and creating corner tiles for brush patterns, see "Creating and working with patterns" in online Help.

Modifying patterns

You can modify a pattern by editing the artwork and then replacing the old pattern in the Swatches palette with the new artwork. If you replace an old pattern with a new pattern, any new and existing objects painted with that pattern are painted with the new definition rather than with the old definition.

To modify an existing pattern:

1 Make sure that nothing is selected in your artwork.

2 Choose Windows > Show Swatches, and select the pattern swatch you want to modify.

3 Drag the pattern swatch onto your artwork.

4 Select artwork in the pattern tile, and edit the tile. (To do this, use the direct-selection tool or group-selection tool, or ungroup the pattern.)

5 Select the pattern tile.

6 Alt-drag (Windows) or Option-drag (Mac OS) the modified pattern on top of the old pattern swatch in the Swatches palette. The pattern is replaced in the Swatches palette and is updated in the current file.

Moving patterns

Patterns begin tiling from the ruler origin and continue to tile in a left-to-right sequence, from bottom to top, until the object is filled. To adjust where all patterns in your artwork begin tiling, you can change the file's ruler origin.

To move all of the patterns within a file:

1 Choose View > Show Rulers.

2 Move the selection pointer to the box in the upper left corner where the rulers intersect.

3 As you drag into the window, two intersecting lines, indicating the ruler origin, follow the pointer. When the ruler origins are positioned as desired, release the mouse button. (See "Changing the ruler origin" on page 117.)

Transforming pattern-filled objects

If an object that you want to transform is filled with a pattern, you can choose to transform only the pattern, transform only the object, or transform the pattern and the object simultaneously.

Once you have transformed a fill pattern, all patterns that you subsequently apply are transformed the same way. To return fill patterns to their original states, select another paint style and then reselect the desired pattern.

You can transform fill patterns using the dialog box associated with a transformation tool. Regardless of the method you choose, turning this option on or off in any dialog box updates the option in all dialog boxes. (See "Moving, copying, and deleting objects" on page 125.)

To transform a pattern and object using a transformation tool:

1 Use the selection tool to select the pattern-filled object.

2 Double-click the transformation tool you want to use.

3 Select one or both of the following options:

• Patterns to transform the pattern tiles.

• Objects to transform the object.

4 Enter the desired transformation values in the text boxes and click OK.

To transform patterns using the mouse:

1 Select the pattern-filled object.

2 Hold down the tilde key (~) and drag.

3 Release the mouse button when the transformation is as desired.

Important: The borders of the object appear to be transformed while dragging with the mouse, but when the mouse button is released the borders snap back to their original configuration, leaving only the pattern transformed.

To select the Transform Pattern Tiles preferences option:

1 Choose Edit > Preferences > General.

2 Select Transform Pattern Tiles to select Pattern Tiles automatically in the transformation dialog boxes, and click OK.

Changing gradients, blends, and patterns into filled objects

The Expand command can convert gradients, blends, patterns, and styles into filled objects. This command can be particularly useful if you are having difficulty printing objects that contain these effects. The Expand command can also convert fills and strokes into individual objects, and can convert gradients into mesh objects. (See "Creating a mesh object" on page 231.)

To convert fills or strokes into objects:

1 Select a filled or stroked object, or an object that has been both filled and stroked.

2 Choose Object > Expand.

3 Do one of the following:

• To expand only the fill, select the Fill check box.

• To expand only the Stroke, select the Stroke check box.

• To expand both the fill and the stroke, select both check boxes.

4 Click OK.

To convert gradients, blends, and patterns into objects:

1 Select objects that have blends, or objects that have been filled or stroked with a gradient or pattern.

2 Choose Object > Expand.

3 Do one of the following:

• If you are expanding a complex object, select the Object option, and click OK.

• If you are expanding a gradient, select the Specify Objects option, enter the number of steps to which you want to convert the gradient, and click OK.

Hold down Alt (Windows) or Option (Mac OS) as you choose Object > Expand to expand a gradient using the last number of steps entered in the Expand dialog box.

To convert gradients, blends, and patterns into a gradient mesh:

1 Select objects that have blends or objects that have been filled or stroked with a gradient or pattern.

2 Choose Object > Expand.

3 In the Expand Gradient To box, click Gradient Mesh.

9

Chapter 9: Using Layers

Layers are useful for organizing your work into distinct levels, which you can edit and view as individual units. You can also use the Layers palette to apply appearance attributes to layers, groups, and objects.

About layers

Every document contains at least one layer. Layers act like clear sheets containing one or more objects. Where there are no overlapping filled objects, you can see through any layer to the layer below.

Creating multiple layers in your document lets you easily control how artwork is printed, organized, displayed, and edited. You can create and modify objects on any layer without affecting the artwork on any other layer.

Once you create layers, you can work with them in various ways, such as duplicating and reordering them, creating layers within layers, and merging, flattening, and adding objects to them. You can even create template layers, which you can use to trace artwork. In addition, you can import layers from Photoshop.

Nesting layers, groups, and objects in the Layers palette

To help you organize your artwork, you can create layers, groups, and objects within layers. Each of these can be displayed and selected through the Layers palette.

The following guidelines apply to the hierarchy in the Layers palette:

- You can create any number of layers, groups, and objects.

- Layers can contain other layers, groups, and objects.

- Only layers can exist at the top level of the hierarchy.

- Groups can contain other groups and objects, but not layers.

- Applying a command such as Lock or Hide to a layer or group locks or hides everything within the layer or group but preserves its previous settings. For example, assume Group A and Group B are in Layer 1, and that you apply the Hide command to Group A and then to Layer 1. Everything in Layer 1 is hidden, including Group A (which had the Hide command applied to it) and Group B (which did not have the Hide command applied to it). If you then apply the Show command to Layer 1, Group A remains hidden, but Group B is visible again.

- Moving a layer or group moves every layer, group, and object within it.

How objects appear in layers and groups

Within each layer and group, objects are stacked according to their stacking order. (See "Stacking objects" on page 131.)

Grouped objects are on the same layer. If you group objects from different layers, all objects are placed on the layer of the frontmost object in the group.

Using the Layers palette

You can use the Layers palette to do any of the following to layers, groups, and objects:

• Select, create, and delete them.

• Hide and lock them.

• Merge and flatten them.

• Apply appearance attributes, styles, effects, and transparency to them. For more information, see "About appearance attributes, styles, and effects" on page 259 and "About transparency" on page 219.

• Choose options for determining how they are displayed and printed.

The current layer, group, or object displays a triangle (◥) in the Layers palette. New art is placed in the current layer or group or above the current object.

To display the Layers palette:

Choose Window > Show Layers.

The Layers palette lists the layers in a file, starting with the frontmost layer. The current layer, group, or object is indicated by a triangle (◥) to the right of its name. If the background color of the layer is dark, the triangle is white instead of black.

Any object you create with a drawing or object tool is placed onto the current layer or group. (Objects created by other means, such as a filter, are placed with the objects they are based on.)

To select a layer, group, or object on which to work:

Do one of the following:

• Click the name of the layer, group, or object you want on the Layers palette. (If necessary, click the small triangle (▶) to the left of the layer or group name to expand it so you can view its contents.)

• Ctrl+Alt-click (Windows) or Option+Command-click (Mac OS) anywhere in the layer list. When you see a heavy black border around the list, type the name or number of the layer you want to select. You can omit prefixes. For example, you can type **30** to go to "Layer 30."

Once you select a layer, group, or object, it is highlighted and the current-layer indicator (◥) appears at the far right of the layer, group, or object name in the palette.

To add an object to a group:

1 Display the group and objects contained in it using the Layers palette.

2 In the Layers palette, select an object in the group.

3 Create the object in the document. The object is added to the group above the object you selected in the Layers palette.

To select all objects on one or more layers or groups in the artwork:

1 Do one of the following in the Layers palette:

• Alt-click (Windows) or Option-click (Mac OS) a layer name.

• Alt-drag (Windows) or Option-drag (Mac OS) through the layer names to select all objects on the selected layers.

• Click to the far right of the layer or group name (where the selection indicator appears) to select everything within the layer or group.

Note: Hold down Shift while making a selection to add to or subtract from the selection.

To select multiple layers, groups, or objects at the same level in the Layers palette:

Do one of the following:

• Click a layer, group, or object in the Layers palette, and then shift-click another layer, group, or object in the palette to select them and all the ones between.

• Ctrl-click (Windows) or Command-click (Mac OS) layers, groups, or objects in the Layers palette to select or deselect noncontiguous layers, groups, or objects.

To change the palette view:

1 Choose Palette Options from the Layers palette menu.

2 Specify the palette view:

• Select Show Layers Only to hide groups and objects in the Layers palette.

• For Row Size, select the size in which to display layer, group, and object thumbnails (if available). For a custom size, select Other, and enter a value between 12 and 100.

• For Thumbnails, select which combination of layers, groups, and objects to display.

Viewing layers, groups, and objects

By selecting options in the Layers palette and Layer Options dialog box, you can control the ways in which selected layers, groups, and objects are displayed in the artwork.

You can also expand or collapse a layer in the Layers palette to display or hide the contents of that layer, whether the contents are further layers, groups, or objects. You can continue expanding layers and groups to display individual objects.

To expand or collapse a layer, or group:

Click the triangle (▶) to the left of the layer or group name. If the layer or group has no contents, no triangle appears, and the item cannot be expanded.

Hiding or displaying layers, groups, and objects

You cannot view or edit hidden layers, groups, and objects. Hiding an element, such as a layer, hides all the elements it contains, such as groups and objects.

To hide or display a layer, group, or object:

Click the eye icon to the left of the layer, group, or object name. This turns off the Show option in the Layer Options dialog box. Click the eye area again to redisplay the item.

Hiding a layer or group hides all layers, groups, and objects within it as well.

To hide all unselected layers (and their contents if displayed):

1 Do one of the following:

• If no other layer is currently hidden, select the layer, group, or object you want to view, and choose Hide Others from the Layers palette menu.

• Alt-click (Windows) or Option-click (Mac OS) the eye icon.

To display all layers:

Choose Show All Layers from the Layers palette menu.

Locating objects on layers

The Locate Object/Locate Layer command lets you quickly find where an object in your artwork is located in the layer hierarchy in the Layers palette.

If necessary, the view in the Layers palette is expanded or scrolled to display the layer, group, or object on which your artwork is located.

To locate an object in the Layers palette:

1 Select the object in the artwork you want to locate in the Layers palette. If you select more than one object, the top object in the stacking order is located.

2 Choose Locate Object from the Layers palette menu. (If the Show Layers Only option is selected, this command is changed to Locate Layer.)

Choosing a layer color

Selecting a different color for each layer makes it easy to distinguish layers in your artwork as you work. By default, the first layer is light blue, the second layer is red, the third layer is green, and each subsequent layer is a different color. By changing the color, you can contrast the layer's color with the artwork's colors on the layer. For example, if your artwork is primarily blue, you can set the layer color to red so that you can see the layer selection marks more clearly as you work on the layer.

The layer color is indicated by a square (■) to the far right of the chosen layer in the Layers palette, and to the far right of the group or object in the Layers palette if you select a group or object in the artwork.

To specify a selection color for a layer:

1 In the Layers palette, choose the layer for which you want to specify a selection color.

2 Choose Options for <*layer name*> from the Layers palette menu, or double-click a layer name.

3 Select a color from the Color pop-up menu, and click OK. Or double-click the color sample to open the Color dialog box.

Displaying layers, groups, and objects in Outline or Preview view

Displaying a layer, group, or object in Outline view is equivalent to choosing the Outline command from the View menu—all artwork is displayed as outlines. Displaying in Preview view shows how the layer, group, or object will look when printed or shown online. (See "Viewing artwork as paths" on page 59.)

To display a layer, group, or object in Outline view:

Do one of the following:

• Ctrl-click (Windows) or Command-click (Mac OS) the eye icon to the left of the layer name.

• Deselect the Preview option in the Layer Options dialog box.

• Choose Preview Others from the Layers palette menu.

To display all unselected layers in Outline view:

1 Do one of the following:

• Select the layer or layers you want to display in Preview view. Then choose Outline Others from the Layers palette menu.

• Alt+Ctrl-click (Windows) or Option+Command-click (Mac OS) the eye icon.

To display all layers in Preview view:

Choose Preview All Layers from the Layers palette menu.

Dimming and showing raster images on layers

The Dim Images To option in the Layer Options dialog box makes raster images on a given layer appear dimmed on-screen. This option dims raster images to make it easier to edit objects on top of the image. You can use this option as a design guide with raster images, for laying out artwork on top of them, or using them as a template you can trace over.

Raster images on template layers appear the same in both Outline and Preview views. Raster images on regular layers appear as frames in Outline view.

To dim a raster image on the screen:

1 In the Layers palette, choose the layers that contain the raster images you want to dim.

2 Choose Options for <*layer name*> from the Layers palette menu, or double-click the layer in the palette.

3 Select Dim Images To, enter a value for the percentage (0% to 100%) by which you want images dimmed, and click OK.

Images are dimmed on the screen, but not when they are printed or exported to another format.

To show raster images on template layers:

1 Choose File > Document Setup.

2 Select the Show Images In Outline option, and click OK.

Creating layered artwork

Every new Adobe Illustrator file contains one layer named by default "Layer 1." You can create any number of layers in your file. The number of layers a file can have is limited only by your computer's memory.

Once a layer is created, you can then set options, such as whether the layer displays or prints. By default, layers are named according to the order in which they were created.

After you create layers, you can duplicate, move, nest, merge, flatten, and hide them, make them nonprintable, and move objects between them.

To create a layer:

1 Do one of the following:

• Click the New Layer button ( ) on the bottom of the Layers palette or choose New Layer from the Layers palette menu to create a layer with default options. The new layer is created above the current layer, group, or object.

• Click the New Sublayer button ( ) on the bottom of the Layers palette or choose New Sublayer from the Layers palette menu to create a layer with default options. The new layer is created inside the selected layer.

• Ctrl-click (Windows) or Command-click (Mac OS) the New Layer button to create a layer on top of the layer list.

• Alt+Ctrl-click (Windows) or Command+Option-click (Mac OS) the New Layer button to create a layer below the selected layer.

• Choose New Layer from the Layers palette menu. The Layer Options dialog box appears.

• Alt-click (Windows) or Option-click (Mac OS) the New Layer button. The Layer Options dialog box appears.

• Drag a layer, group, or object onto the New Layer or New Sublayer button to create a copy of the selected layer, group, or object.

2 If you want, specify layer options as described in "Specifying layer, group, and object options" on page 246.

Specifying layer, group, and object options

The Options for <"layer, group, or object name"> command lets you specify options for the selected layer, group, or object in the Layers palette.

To specify options for a layer, group, or object in the Layers palette:

1 Do one of the following:

• Create a new layer as described in "Creating layered artwork" on page 246.

• Select a layer, group, or object in the Layers palette, and choose Options for *<layer, group, or object name>* from the Layers palette menu.

• Double-click a layer, group, or object in the Layers palette.

2 To change the default name, enter a name in the Name text box.

3 To change the layer's color, select a color from the Color pop-up menu. (See "Choosing a layer color" on page 244.) (This option is not available for groups and objects.)

4 Select other options for the layer, group, or object:

• Template to make the layer a template layer. (See "Creating template layers" on page 254.) When the option is selected, the template layer icon replaces the eyeball icon, and the layer becomes locked. (This option is only available for layers.)

• Show to display or hide the layer, group, or object. (See "Hiding or displaying layers, groups, and objects" on page 243.)

• Preview to display the layer in Preview or Outline view. When the option is unselected, the eyeball changes to a hollow eyeball to indicate that layer is in Outline view. (This option is only available for layers.)

• Lock to prevent a layer, group, or object from being edited. When the option is selected, the lock icon appears to the left of the layer name. (See "Locking layers, groups, and objects" on page 250.)

• Print to make the layer printable or nonprintable. When the option is unselected (and the layer is nonprintable), the layer name is displayed in italics. (See "Making selected layers, groups, or objects nonprintable" on page 250.) (This option is only available for layers.)

• Dim Images To to dim placed or rasterized images according to the value (0% to 100%) you enter in the text box. (See "Dimming and showing raster images on layers" on page 245.) (This option is only available for layers.)

5 Click OK.

Creating layers automatically

The Release to Layers command creates a new layer for each object in the selected layer or group. The resulting layers are located within the selected layer or group.

If you are using the Release to Layers command on complex groups such as a blend between two objects, you need to ensure that the group is selected in the Layers palette, rather than just the top-most layer. For more information, see "Targeting layers, groups, and objects to apply appearance attributes" on page 252.

To place objects on separate layers:

1 Select the layer or group in the Layers palette.

2 Do one of the following:

• To separate each object onto its own layer, choose Release to Layers from the Layers palette menu. For example, assume Layer 1 contains a series of circles, one next to the other. This command places each circle on its own layer. This is useful for creating motion animation effects when you export the frames, by showing each frame with the object in a new position.

- To separate objects cumulatively onto layers, hold down the Shift key and choose Release to Layers from the Layers palette menu. For example, assume Layer 1 contains a circle, a square, and a triangle. This command creates three layers, one with a circle, square, and triangle; one with a circle and square; and one with just a circle. This is useful for creating cumulative animation effects when you export the frames, showing one object, then each additional object, for a kind of "typewriter" effect.

You can export layers as Flash frames to create a Flash animation. You can select the Write Layers option when exporting in Photoshop file format to create a GIF animation with Photoshop.

Moving layers, groups, and objects between layers

You can move layers, groups, and objects from one layer to another (including to hidden layers) by dragging them in the Layers palette or cutting groups or objects from one layer in the artwork and pasting them into another. You can also reorder the layers, groups, and objects in your artwork. When you move a layer, or group, all layers, groups, and objects within it move too.

The Paste commands can be used to move objects between layers. With the Paste commands, objects cut or copied from different layers, groups, or objects are pasted together onto the selected layer by default. You cannot move groups or objects to the top level.

With the Paste Remembers Layers option on, objects are always pasted onto the layer from which they originated. If no layer exists with the original name, a layer is created and the objects are pasted onto the new layer.

The Reverse Order command lets you reverse the order of selected layers, groups, and objects within the same layer.

To ensure that objects are pasted onto the layer from which they originated:

1 Choose Paste Remembers Layers from the Layers palette menu.

To move an object to a different layer using the Paste commands:

1 Make sure that Paste Remember Layers is not selected in the Layers palette menu.

2 Select the object that you want to move, either in the artwork or by using the Layers palette.

3 Choose Edit > Cut.

4 Select any object on the layer to which you want to move the cut object, or select the layer or group name in the Layers palette.

5 Choose one of the following commands:

- Edit > Paste pastes the object into the center of the artwork as the frontmost object on the current layer or group.

- Edit > Paste in Front pastes the object into its original position in the artwork, in front of the topmost selected object. If the selected object is in a group, the pasted selection becomes part of the group.

- Edit > Paste in Back pastes the object into its original position in the artwork, behind the backmost selected object. If the selected object is in a group, the pasted selection becomes part of the group. If Paste Remember Layers is selected, the object is pasted onto the layer from which it originated.

Once the object is pasted, you can move it and use the commands in the Object menu to change the stacking order of the object on its new layer.

To move a layer, group, or object to a different level using the Layers palette:

1 Drag the layer, group, or object to another level in the layer hierarchy. The layer can be visible or hidden. If necessary, expand the layer hierarchy before dragging.

An indicator bar shows where the dragged layer, group, or object will be placed. If you drop the item directly on top of a layer or group, the item is added at the top level inside the layer or group. If you drag the item between layers, groups, or objects, it is added between them.

To copy selected items to a different layer or group

Alt-drag (Windows) or Option-drag (Mac OS) the colored dot next to the layer, group, or object you want to copy, and drop it into another layer or group. The layer or group can be visible or hidden. If necessary, expand the layer hierarchy before dragging.

Note: To move the object to a locked layer, hold down Ctrl (Windows) or Command (Mac OS) after starting to drag.

To reverse the order of selected layers, groups, and objects in a layer:

1 In the Layers palette, select the layers, groups, and objects you want to reverse within the layer.

2 Choose Reverse Order from the Layers palette menu.

Duplicating, merging, and collecting layers, groups, and objects

Duplicating a layer, group, or object places a new layer, group, or object above the currently selected one and duplicates all the options and contents of the original. The duplicate contains copies of all the artwork on the original.

For example, if you duplicate a layer that contains layers, groups, objects, and clipping sets, the duplicated layer will contain all those things as well.

When you merge layers, groups, or objects, their contents are merged into the current layers or group. (If the current layer or group is locked or hidden, the selections are merged into the top selected layer or group that isn't locked or hidden.) The objects on the merged selections retain their original stacking order.

The Collect in New Layer command moves all selected layers, groups, and objects in the Layers palette into a new layer.

To duplicate a layer, group, or object:

1 In the Layers palette, select the layers, groups, or objects you want to duplicate.

2 Do one of the following:

• Choose Duplicate <selection> from the Layers palette menu.

• Drag the selection to the New Layer button (🗔) or New Sublayer button (🗔) at the bottom of the palette.

To merge layers, groups, or objects:

1 Select the layers, groups, or objects that you want to merge into a single layer or group.

2 Choose Merge Selected from the Layers palette menu.

To move all selected layers, groups, or objects into a new layer:

1 Select the layers, groups, or objects that you want to move into a new layer.

2 Choose Collect in New Layer from the Layers palette menu.

Locking layers, groups, and objects

Locking a layer, group, or object has an effect similar to that of choosing the Lock command from the Object menu—you cannot select or edit artwork on that selection in any way. When a layer, group, or object is locked, the cursor becomes a pencil with a slash (✘) when it's over the page, and a lock (🔒) appears in the edit column on the left side of the Layers palette. When unlocked, the edit column appears empty.

Locking a layer or group locks all of the layers, groups, and objects within it in the palette.

To lock or unlock a layer, group, or object:

Click the edit column button (🔒) to the left of the layer, group, or object name. This turns on the Lock option in the Layer Options dialog box. Click again to unlock the layer.

To lock all unselected layers, groups, or objects:

1 Do one of the following:

• Select the layers, groups, or objects you want to edit. Then choose Lock Others from the Layers palette menu.

• Alt-click (Windows) or Option-click (Mac OS) the edit column to the left of the layer you want to change.

To unlock all layers, groups, and objects:

Do one of the following:

• Choose Unlock All Layers from the Layers palette menu.

• Hold down Alt (Windows) or Option (Mac OS) and click the lock icon or the empty edit column for any layer.

Making selected layers, groups, or objects nonprintable

Illustrator provides several ways to make layers, groups, or objects nonprintable. You can deselect the eye icon to hide a layer, group, or object, or you can deselect the Print option in the Options dialog box to make layers and their contents unprintable.

Hiding a layer, group, or object is useful for printing only the segments of your artwork that you want to proof. For example, you could put all type in a document on a single layer and then print only that layer for proofing. Hidden layers, groups, and objects do not print or export.

For layers that you don't normally print, such as annotations, you can make use the Print option in the Layer Options dialog box. Layers with the Print option unselected do not print even when they are visible, but they do export.

For layers, groups, or objects that you do not want to print or export, you can create a template layer by selecting the Template option in the Layer Options dialog box. Template Layers do not print or export, even when visible.

To make a layer, group, or object nonprintable from any application by hiding it:

In the Layers palette, select the layer, group, or object and click the eye icon ( ) to the left of the name to hide it.

To make layers nonprintable from Illustrator using the Options dialog box:

1 Do one of the following:

• In the Layers palette, select the layer that you don't want to print, and choose Options for <layer name> from the palette menu.

• Double-click the name of the layer in the palette.

2 Deselect the Print option, and click OK. The layer name is displayed in italics.

Deleting layers, groups, and objects

You can remove a layer, group, or object by removing it from the Layers palette. Deleting removes from the file all objects on that layer or in that group.

For example, if you delete a layer that contains layers, groups, objects, and clipping sets, all those things will be deleted along with the layer.

Before you delete a layer, group, or object, hide all the other layers so that you can check what's on the remaining layer or group and verify that there are no objects on it that you don't want deleted.

To delete a layer, group, or object:

1 Select the layer, group, or object in the Layers palette.

2 Do one of the following:

• Click the Trash button ( ) at the bottom of the Layers palette.

• Drag the layer onto the Trash button at the bottom of the Layers palette.

• Choose Delete <layer name> from the Layers palette menu.

Flattening artwork

In flattened artwork, all visible top-level layers are merged into the selected top-level layer. The following guidelines apply to the Flatten Artwork command:

- If you flatten a hidden layer that contains artwork, you can choose to delete the artwork along with the hidden layer or make all artwork visible and flatten it into one layer. In most cases, you won't want to flatten a file until you finish editing individual layers.

- Any special attributes in the top-level layers, such as transparency and clipping masks, are lost.

- Any layers are converted into groups to preserve effects contained in them.

To merge specific layers without deleting hidden layers, select the layers you want to merge, and then choose Merge Layers from the Layers palette menu. (See "Duplicating, merging, and collecting layers, groups, and objects" on page 249.)

To flatten artwork:

1 Make sure all the layers you want to flatten are visible.

2 Select the layer into which you want to flatten the artwork. You cannot flatten artwork into layers that are hidden, locked, or templates.

Note: *Regardless of the layer you select, the options for the layer and the stacking order of the artwork don't change.*

3 Choose Flatten Artwork from the Layers palette menu.

If artwork is present on a hidden layer, a dialog box appears to allow you to choose whether to make all artwork visible and flatten it into one layer, or delete the artwork along with the layer.

Targeting layers, groups, and objects to apply appearance attributes

You can apply appearance attributes such as styles, effects, and transparency to layers, groups, and objects with the Layers palette. When an appearance attribute is applied to a layer or group in the Layers palette, any artwork created on or moved to that layer or group takes on that appearance. For more information, see "About appearance attributes, styles, and effects" on page 259.

For example, if you apply a style that has a drop shadow to Layer 2 in your artwork, anything you create on Layer 2 will have a drop shadow. If you move an object from Layer 2 to another layer, that object will no longer have the drop shadow.

The following icons on the right side of a layer, group, or object in the Layers palette indicates whether any appearance attributes are applied to it or whether it is targeted:

- (○) indicates the layer, group, or object is not targeted and has no appearance attributes applied to it.

- (◎) indicates the layer, group, or object is targeted but has no appearance attributes applied to it.

- (◉) indicates the layer, group, or object is not targeted but has appearance attributes applied to it.

• (◉) indicates the layer or group is targeted and has appearance attributes applied to it. Also appears for any object that is targeted and has appearance attributes more complex than a single fill and stroke applied to it.

To target a layer, group, or object in the Layers palette:

1 Click the target icon (○ or ◉) in the Layers palette for the layer, group, or object to which you want to apply the appearance attribute.

2 Use the Styles, Appearance, or Transparency palette or effects listed under the Effect menu to apply appearance attributes to the layer, group, or object in the Layers palette.

To move, copy, or delete appearance attributes from a layer, group, or object.

1 Select the layer, group, or object in the Layers palette.

2 Do one of the following:

• To move the appearance attributes, drag the appearance icon (◉ or ◉) from the selected layer, group, or object onto the layer, group, or object to which you want to apply it. Layers and groups lose all appearance attributes, and objects lose all appearance attributes except a single fill and stroke.

• To copy the appearance attributes, Alt-drag (Windows) or Option-drag (Mac OS) the appearance icon from the selected layer, group, or object onto the layer, group, or object to which you want to apply it.

• To delete the appearance attributes, drag the appearance icon from the selected layer, group, or object onto the Trash button (🗑) at the bottom of the Layers palette. Layers and groups lose all appearance attributes, and objects lose all appearance attributes except a single fill and stroke.

Creating clipping masks

A *clipping mask* is an object or group of objects whose shape masks artwork below it so that only artwork within the shape is visible—in effect, clipping the artwork to the shape of the mask. You can create a clipping mask to control how artwork on a layer is hidden and revealed.

A *clipping set* is a collection of items in the Layers palette consisting of one or more levels (such as a layer and a group), one or more clipping masks, and one or more objects that are masked by the clipping masks.

The following guidelines apply to clipping masks:

• A clipping mask and the objects to be masked must be in the same layer or group in the Layers palette.

• A top-level layer cannot be a clipping mask. However, you can put a clipping mask inside a top-level layer along with artwork to be masked below it.

- The first object in the layer or group becomes the clipping mask for everything that is a subset of the layer or group the clipping mask is in. For example, if a clipping mask is the first item in Layer 1, all objects in layers and groups within Layer 1 are masked. However, objects in Layer 2 are not masked, because Layer 2 is not a subset of Layer 1.

- Objects in the clipping path are indicated with a dotted line in the Layers palette.

- Regardless of its previous attributes, a clipping mask object changes to an object with no fill or stroke.

- The clipping mask and the artwork you want to mask must be in the same layer or group in the Layers palette. For example, Layer 3 could consist of a clipping mask and two objects you want to mask.

- The clipping mask is always at the top of the clipping set. Moving the mask does not change the appearance or masking.

To create a clipping set:

1 In the Layers palette, select the layer or group that contains the object or group that you want to become the clipping set. The topmost object will be the clipping mask.

2 Click the Make/Release Clipping Mask button ( ) at the bottom of the Layers palette, or choose Make Clipping Mask from the Layers palette menu.

To convert a clipping mask back to an object:

1 Select the layer or group that contains the clipping mask.

2 Click the Make/Release Clipping Mask button ( ) at the bottom of the Layers palette, or choose Release Clipping Mask from the Layers palette menu.

The clipping mask is converted to an object with the default fill and stroke.

Creating template layers

Create a template layer whenever you want to base a new illustration on an existing piece of artwork and, for example, trace over it or build an illustration from it. (See "Tracing artwork" on page 111.)

A template layer is locked, dimmed, and previewed. Template layers remain visible in Outline view. When a template layer is in Outline view, all raster images display as dimmed and in normal color. Images in PICT format display in color. Template layers neither print nor export.

You can create a template from an existing layer or as a new layer.

To create a template layer:

1 Do one of the following:

• Choose New Layer from the Layers palette menu; or double-click the name of the layer to be a template; or Alt-click (Windows) or Option-click (Mac OS) the New Layer button ( ) in the palette. Click Template in the Layer Options dialog box, and click OK. The Preview, Lock, and Print options are then dimmed.

• Select a layer to be a template, and choose Template from the palette menu.

• Choose File > Place, and click Template. A new template layer, with the default name "Template *filename*," appears below the current layer in the palette. Link the placed image if you want. (See "Placing files" on page 74.)

The eye icon is replaced by the template icon, and the layer becomes locked.

Importing and exporting Adobe Photoshop layers

When you import a Photoshop file that has multiple layers, the layers are flattened and appear as one layer in the Illustrator file. You can import Adobe Photoshop files using the Place command. (See "Placing files" on page 74.)

When you export layers, you can flatten them into one layer or preserve the individual layers so you can work with them in the Photoshop file. You can export Illustrator layers to Photoshop using the Export command. (See "About exporting artwork" on page 349.) Template layers aren't exported.

To import Adobe Photoshop layers as a flattened Illustrator layer:

1 If the Layers palette is not displayed, choose Window > Show Layers, and then create or select the layer where you want the image to appear.

2 Choose File > Place.

3 Locate and select the Photoshop file you want to import.

4 Click Open (Windows) or Place (Mac OS).

If the Photoshop file had multiple layers, the layers are flattened in Illustrator. The Photoshop image appears as a selected object on the layer you specified.

To export Adobe Illustrator layers to Adobe Photoshop:

1 If the Layers palette is not displayed, choose Window > Show Layers, and then create or show the layers you want to export.

2 Choose File > Export.

3 Select the folder where you want to save the file, and rename the file. Changing the filename ensures that your original artwork is preserved on disk.

4 Choose Photoshop 5 from the Save as Type (Windows) or Format (Mac OS) menu.

5 Click Export, and choose from the following options:

• To change the color format, select a format from the Color Model pop-up menu.

- To set the resolution for the bitmap image, choose a resolution or type a number in the Other text box. (See "About resolution in bitmap images" on page 68.)

- To smooth jagged edges around the bitmap image, select Anti-Alias. (Anti-aliasing may cause small type or thin lines to look blurry.)

- To export individual layers, select Write layers. This is useful for creating animations, where each layer can act as a separate frame for the animation. Select Write Nested Layers to preserve the hierarchical relationship in the layers.

- To include hidden layers, select Hidden Layers.

- To include an ICC color management profile, select Embed ICC Profile.

- To preserve Illustrator layers when the file is exported to Photoshop, select Write Layers. (To flatten the layers so they appear as one layer in Photoshop, deselect Write Layers.)

6 Click OK.

The Illustrator layers appear as raster objects in the Photoshop file, and you can work with them in the Photoshop Layers dialog box.

10

Chapter 10: Using Appearance Attributes, Styles, and Effects

You can apply appearance attributes to any object, group, or layer by using effects and the Appearance and Styles palettes. Appearance attributes do not change the underlying objects to which they are applied and they can be modified or removed at any time.

About appearance attributes, styles, and effects

Appearance attributes are properties that affect the look of an object without altering its underlying structure. If you apply an appearance attribute to an object and later edit or remove that attribute, it does not change the underlying object or any other attributes applied to the object.

Fills, strokes, transparency, and effects are all types of appearance attributes. For example, you can fill a rectangle with yellow, apply the Roughen effect (a version of the Roughen command that applies an appearance attribute), save and close the document, reopen it, and remove the color and Roughen effect. The resulting object is still a rectangle.

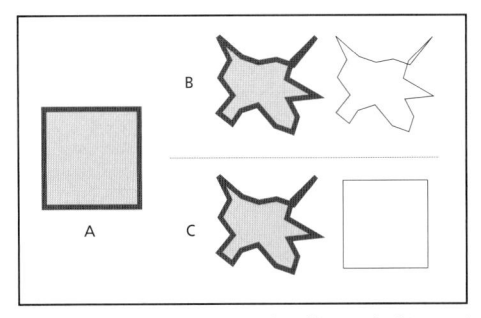

A. Original object B. With Roughen filter applied in Preview and Outline views C. With Roughen effect applied in Preview and Outline views

The appearance attributes of the current selection are listed in the Appearance palette so that you can select and edit them.

A *style* is a named set of appearance attributes. The Styles palette lets you store and apply a set of appearance attributes to objects, groups, and layers. This gives you a fast and consistent way to change the look of artwork in documents. If the style is replaced (that is, if any appearance attributes that make up the style are changed and the new attributes are saved as that style), all objects with that style change to the new appearance.

Effects are a type of appearance attribute and are listed under the Effect menu. Most effects have the same function and name as commands found elsewhere in the application. However, the version of the command found under Effects does not change the underlying object, only its appearance. You can distort, rasterize, and modify any path using any number of effects, but the original size, anchor points, and shape of the path never changes—only the way it looks. The underlying object remains editable, and an effect's parameters can be changed at any time.

For example, if you apply the Twirl command listed under the Filter menu to an ellipse and then save, close, and reopen the document, you cannot remove the twirl from the ellipse. The object has been changed and is no longer an ellipse. But if you apply the Twirl command listed under the Effect menu, you can use the Appearance palette to remove the Twirl appearance attribute at any time, and the object returns to the way it looked before you applied the Twirl effect—an ellipse.

Using appearance attributes

An *appearance attribute* is a property you can reedit at any time without changing the basic structure of the object to which it is applied.

For example, you can draw a circle and then apply a color change, transparency, and a Zig Zag effect (from the Effect menu). The color, transparency, and Zig Zag effect are all editable because they affect only the appearance of the circle; they don't alter the circle itself. You can modify or even remove any of these attributes at any time, and the object remains a circle. But if you apply the Zig Zag filter from the Filter menu, the underlying object is changed and is no longer a circle.

You can apply appearance attributes to the following:

• Objects and groups in the artwork. For more information, see "Applying styles" on page 267.

• Objects, groups, and layers with the Layers palette. Any objects added to those groups and layers look as specified by those appearance attributes. For more information, see "Targeting layers, groups, and objects to apply appearance attributes" on page 252.

• Styles with the Styles palette. A *style* is a named set of appearance attributes. For more information, see "Using styles" on page 265.

About the Appearance palette

To help you work more easily with appearance attributes, the Appearance palette displays the following types of attributes, which you can edit:

• Fill lists all fill attributes (fill type, color, transparency, and effects).

• Stroke lists some stroke attributes (stroke type, brush, color, transparency, and effects). All other stroke attributes are displayed in the Strokes Palette.

• Transparency lists opacity and blending mode.

• Effects lists commands in the Effect menu. See "Using effects" on page 271.

- Using the Appearance palette

The following are guidelines for viewing and editing appearance attributes with the Appearance palette:

- The upper part of the Appearance palette (above the black line) shows the current selection in the artwork. If a group is fully selected, it also shows the group. In addition, the upper part of the palette shows any group or layer that contains the selection if that group or layer has appearance attributes.

- (▫) indicates the selection in the artwork has at least one fill or stroke applied to a layer or group that contains the selection.

- (●) indicates the selection in the artwork has at least one effect applied to a layer or group that contains the selection.

- (▦) indicates the selection in the artwork has transparency applied to a layer or group that contains the selection.

- The lower part of the Appearance palette lists effects in the order in which they are applied. It lists fills and strokes in stacking order (front to back). It also shows transparency attributes.

- When you modify the appearance attributes of a style, the attributes and selection to which they apply are disassociated from the style and the set is unnamed in the Appearance palette. For information on styles, see "Applying styles" on page 267.

- You can expand the view of a fill or stroke to display all the appearance attributes applied to it.

- You can change the order of any appearance attributes in the Appearances palette.

- If the selection includes a group, the Appearance palette contains a Contents listing. If the selection includes a type object (container for editable text), the Appearance palette contains a Text listing. If the selections includes a gradient mesh, the Appearance palette contains a Mesh Points listing. You can change the order in which attributes are applied by moving the Contents, Text, or Mesh Points listings within the palette.

- You can add additional fills and strokes. For example, you could create an appearance that includes a wide blue stroke and then add a narrower, dashed yellow stroke on top of that. Or you could create an appearance that includes multiple fills that interact with each other through different effects, opacities, and blending modes.

- You can change the order of effects. For example, if you apply the Punk and Bloat effect and then apply the Roughen effect, you can drag Roughen above Punk and Bloat in the palette. This applies the Roughen effect before the Punk and Bloat effect.

- You can define effects for the fill and stroke separately. An effect applies to the entire selection by default.

To display the Appearance palette:

Choose Window > Show Appearance.

To apply appearance attributes to an object by dragging:

Drag the appearance icon from the top left corner of the Appearance palette onto an object. The object does not have to be selected first.

To expand or collapse a fill or stroke:

Click the triangle (▶) to the left of the fill or stroke in the Appearance palette.

To reorder appearance attributes:

1 Do one of the following:

• Select an object in the artwork whose appearance attributes you want to change.

• Target an object, group, or layer in the Layers palette. For more information, see "Targeting layers, groups, and objects to apply appearance attributes" on page 252.

• Select a style in the Styles palette. For more information, see "Using the Styles palette" on page 268.

2 Select the appearance attribute you want to reorder in the Appearance palette.

3 Drag the appearance attribute up or down in the palette. (If necessary, click the triangle next to a fill or stroke to display the appearance attributes applied to the fill or stroke. This lets you apply an effect to a particular stroke but not to a fill, for example.) When the outline of the appearance attribute you are dragging appears in the position you want, release the mouse button.

4 If the appearance attributes were part of a style, they are unlinked from that style. In this case, you can do any of the following:

• Relink them to the style, replacing the style's previous appearance attributes. For more information, see the instructions for modifying a style in "Using the Styles palette" on page 268.

• Create a new style. For more information, see the instructions for modifying a style in "Using the Styles palette" on page 268.

• Leave the appearance attributes unlinked to any style.

To edit appearance attributes:

1 Do one of the following:

• Select an object or group in the artwork whose appearance attributes you want to change.

• Target an object, group, or layer in the Layers palette. For more information, see "Targeting layers, groups, and objects to apply appearance attributes" on page 252.

• Select a style in the Styles palette. For more information, see "Using the Styles palette" on page 268.

2 In the Appearance palette, double-click the attribute you want to modify. This action displays the appropriate dialog box or palette.

3 Edit the attribute in the dialog box or palette.

4 If the appearance attributes were part of a style, they are unlinked from that style. In this case, you can do any of the following:

• Relink them to the style, replacing the style's previous appearance attributes. For more information, see the instructions for modifying a style in "Using the Styles palette" on page 268.

• Create a new style. For more information, see the instructions for modifying a style in "Using the Styles palette" on page 268.

• Leave the appearance attributes unlinked to any style.

To add another fill or stroke:

1 Do one of the following:

• Select an object or group in the artwork whose appearance attributes you want to change.

• Target an object, group, or layer in the Layers palette. For more information, see "Targeting layers, groups, and objects to apply appearance attributes" on page 252.

• Select a style in the Styles palette. For more information, see "Using the Styles palette" on page 268.

2 Do one of the following in the Appearance palette:

• Choose Add New Fill or Add New Stroke from the palette menu.

• Select a fill or stroke and click the Duplicate Selected Item button ( ) or choose Duplicate Item from the palette menu.

• Drag the appearance attribute onto the Duplicate Selected Item button in the palette.

3 Select the new fill or stroke in the Appearance palette.

4 Specify the properties you want for the fill or stroke.

5 If the appearance attributes were part of a style, they are unlinked from that style. In this case, you can do any of the following:

• Relink them to the style, replacing the style's previous appearance attributes. For more information, see the instructions for modifying a style in "Using the Styles palette" on page 268.

• Create a new style. For more information, see the instructions for modifying a style in "Using the Styles palette" on page 268.

• Leave the appearance attributes unlinked to any style.

To duplicate an appearance attribute:

1 Do one of the following:

• Select an object or group in the artwork whose appearance attributes you want to change.

• Target an object, group, or layer in the Layers palette. For more information, see "Targeting layers, groups, and objects to apply appearance attributes" on page 252.

• Select a style in the Styles palette. For more information, see "Using the Styles palette" on page 268.

2 In the Appearance palette, select the attribute you want to duplicate.

3 Do one of the following:

• Click the Duplicate Selected Item button ( ) in the palette or choose Duplicate Item from the palette menu.

• Drag the appearance attribute onto the Duplicate Selected Item button in the palette.

4 If the appearance attributes were part of a style, they are unlinked from that style. In this case, you can do any of the following:

• Relink them to the style, replacing the style's previous appearance attributes. For more information, see the instructions for modifying a style in "Using the Styles palette" on page 268.

- Create a new style. For more information, see the instructions for modifying a style in "Using the Styles palette" on page 268.

- Leave the appearance attributes unlinked to any style.

To remove an appearance attribute:

1 Do one of the following:

- Select an object or group in the artwork whose appearance attributes you want to change.

- Target an object, group, or layer in the Layers palette. For more information, see "Targeting layers, groups, and objects to apply appearance attributes" on page 252.

- Select a style in the Styles palette. For more information, see "Using the Styles palette" on page 268.

2 In the Appearance palette, select the appearance attribute you want to remove.

3 Remove the appearance attribute from the Appearance palette:

- Select the attribute and choose Remove Item from the palette menu.

- Select the attribute and click the Trash button (🗑) in the palette.

- Drag the attribute to the Trash button.

4 If the appearance attributes were part of a style, they are unlinked from that style. In this case, you can do any of the following:

- Relink them to the style, replacing the style's previous appearance attributes. For more information, see the instructions for modifying a style in "Using the Styles palette" on page 268.

- Create a new style. For more information, see the instructions for modifying a style in "Using the Styles palette" on page 268.

- Leave the appearance attributes unlinked to any style.

To remove all appearance attributes or all except a single fill and stroke:

1 Do one of the following:

- Select an object or group in the artwork whose appearance attributes you want to change.

- Target an object, group, or layer in the Layers palette. For more information, see "Targeting layers, groups, and objects to apply appearance attributes" on page 252.

- Select a style in the Styles palette. For more information, see "Using the Styles palette" on page 268.

2 Remove the attributes from the Appearance palette:

- To remove all appearance attributes, including any fill or stroke, choose Clear Appearance from the palette menu or click the Clear Appearance button (⊘) in the palette.

- To remove all appearance attributes except a single fill and stroke, choose Reduce to Basic Appearance from the palette menu or click the Reduce to Basic Appearance button (⊙) in the palette.

3 If the appearance attributes were part of a style, they are unlinked from that style. In this case, you can do any of the following:

• Relink them to the style, replacing the style's previous appearance attributes. For more information, see the instructions for modifying a style in "Using the Styles palette" on page 268.

• Create a new style. For more information, see the instructions for modifying a style in "Using the Styles palette" on page 268.

• Leave the appearance attributes unlinked to any style.

To specify whether the current appearance attributes are applied to new objects:

Do one of the following:

• To apply only a single fill and stroke to new objects, select New Art Has Basic Appearance from the palette menu.

• To apply all of the current appearance attributes to new objects, deselect New Art Has Basic Appearance from the palette menu.

To choose whether the color applied to a targeted layer or group overrides the color of objects in that layer or group:

Do one of the following:

• To remove the fill and stroke color from objects in the layer or group when applying color to that layer or group, select Layer/Group Overrides Color from the Appearance palette menu.

• To retain the fill and stroke color of objects in the layer or group when applying color to that layer or group, deselect Layer/Group Overrides Color from the Appearance palette menu.

To modify a style:

1 Choose Window > Show Styles to display the Styles palette if necessary. For more information, see "Using styles" on page 265.

2 In the Styles palette, Select a style you want to redefine. (If you've already selected a style and changed its appearance attributes, proceed to step 4.)

3 Modify the style, using the Appearance palette if necessary.

4 Rename or replace the style:

• Choose New Style from the Styles palette menu, enter a name for the style, and click OK. The new style appears at the bottom of the list in the Styles palette.

• To replace the existing style with the one you modified, choose Replace "(style name)" from the Appearance palette menu. All selections with that style applied change to the new style.

Using styles

A style is a named set of appearance attributes, such as color, transparency, fill patterns, effects, and transformations. (For more information on appearance attributes, see "Using appearance attributes" on page 260. For more information on effects, see "Using effects" on page 271.)

By applying different styles, you can quickly change the entire appearance of an object. For example, you can first apply a style that makes an object look distorted and yellow and gives it a drop shadow. You can then apply a different style that instead makes the object look resized and blue and gives it an outer glow.

The Styles palette lets you create, name, save, and apply sets of appearance attributes. Applying a style to an object, group, or layer lets you change the appearance of an object without changing the object itself. Moreover, all the changes you apply with styles are completely reversible at any time.

This means you can apply a style that distorts and roughens the shape of an object, save your file, close it, reopen it at a later date, and by removing the style, go back to the original shape of the object.

For example, if you apply the Roughen filter from the Filter menu to a simple rectangle that has four control points, the resulting object might have 50 control points. If you create a style that contains the Roughen effect from the Effect menu as one of its attributes and apply that style to a rectangle, it will look like a roughened rectangle; however, the resulting object will have the same four control points of the original rectangle to which the style is applied.

The following guidelines apply to styles:

- You can apply a style to an object, group, or layer. This includes bitmap images and most type objects, as well as vector graphics. (Bitmap images must be embedded in the document, and you can't apply styles to type objects made with outline-protected fonts or bitmap fonts.)

- You can apply named styles to type objects, but not to the text characters within the type objects. Within type objects that have styles applied, text remains fully editable.

Note: If you attempt to apply a style to text within a type object, the current fill and stroke are applied, along with the transparency specified by the style. Any additional fills or strokes, brushes, or effects are not applied. Modifying a style applied to text within a type object does not change the appearance of the text characters.

- Each style can contain any combination of color, fill, stroke, pattern, effect (that is, any command listed under the Effect menu), transparency, blend mode, gradient, transformation, and the like.

- Each style can contain multiple attributes, such as colors, fills, strokes, effects (commands listed under the Effect menu), and transformations. For example, you can have three fills in a style, each with a different opacity and blend mode that defines how the various colors interact. Similarly, you can have multiple strokes in a style to make complex stroke designs.

- You can save and name a style in the Styles palette and then apply it to objects, groups, and layers. For more information, see "Targeting layers, groups, and objects to apply appearance attributes" on page 252.

- Styles are nondestructive changes. That is, objects, groups, and layers with styles applied are fully editable at any time, and you can edit such objects, groups, and layers back to their underlying properties at any time.

- You can save and apply all effects (commands listed under the Effect menu) as styles. However, commands with the same name but not under the Effect menu cannot be saved as styles, and applying them will change the object.

- Changing an attribute of a selection that has a style applied to it disassociates the style from the selection, but retains all of the other attributes.

- Redefining a style applies the change to all objects, groups, or layers that have that style associated with them.

Applying styles

The following guidelines describe what happens when you apply styles to objects, groups and layers:

- If you apply a style to an object, the new style replaces any style or appearance attributes the object had before.

- If you apply a style to multiple objects at the same time, the style is applied to each object.

- You can apply a style to a group of objects. This requires targeting the group. In this case, the appearance attributes are applied not to the objects in the group, but to the group itself. Anything in the group or added to it takes on that style in addition to any appearance attributes or styles it already has.

Take the example of two circles grouped together. The first circle has a blue fill and the second has a red fill. Neither has a stroke. Assume you have a style named "Green Outline" that consists of no fill, but a green stroke. When you apply this style to the group, the style is applied in addition to any appearance attributes that the individual circles have. In this case, the first circle keeps its blue fill and the second circle keeps its red fill, but they both gain a green stroke. Any object added to this group takes on the green stroke as well. This means you can apply changes not just to the objects inside the group, but to the group itself.

- Applying a style to a layer is similar to applying it to a group. For example, assume you have a style that consists of 50% opacity. If you apply the style to a layer, all objects on or added to that layer will be 50% opaque.

- When applying a style to a group or layer, you can control where in the painting order the styles of the original objects appear. For example, assume you have two objects grouped together—one with a green fill and one with a blue fill—and you apply a style that has a red fill and a yellow stroke. You can put the green and blue fills of the objects in front of the red fill and yellow stroke of the style, behind the fill and stroke of the style, behind the fill but in front of the stroke of the style, and so on.

- You can apply a style to an object in the artwork or to an object, group, or layer by targeting it the Layers palette. When applied with the Layers palette, any objects moved to that group or layer take on that style in addition to whatever other appearance attributes they have directly applied to them. Moving them off that group or layer in the Layers palette removes those appearance attributes. For more information, see "Targeting layers, groups, and objects to apply appearance attributes" on page 252.

Using the Styles palette

The Styles palette lets you apply styles to objects, groups, and layers.

To display the Styles palette:

1 Choose Window > Show Styles.

2 Choose a view for the style swatches:

- Swatch View to display a scrollable list of thumbnail examples of styles.

- Small List View to display a scrollable list of named styles with a small thumbnail example of each.

- Large List View to display a scrollable named list of styles along with a large thumbnail example of each.

To apply a style to a selection:

1 Do one of the following:

- Select an object in the artwork.

- Target an object, group, or layer in the Layers palette. For more information, see "Targeting layers, groups, and objects to apply appearance attributes" on page 252.

2 Apply the style from the Styles palette:

- Select a style you want from the list.

- Drag the style onto an object.

- Copy and apply a style using the eyedropper and paint bucket tools. Depending on what you specify in the Paint Bucket/Eyedropper Options dialog box, you can copy and paste the entire style or selected attributes.

To apply a style to an object by dragging:

Drag a style from the palette onto an object. The object does not have to be selected first.

To create or modify a style:

1 Do one of the following:

- Create or select an object in the artwork.

- Select a style in the Styles palette to start with a set of attributes.

- Start with no object or style selected.

2 Specify the appearance attributes you want, such as the fill, stroke, and the like. You can use the Appearance palette to help specify and order the appearance attributes. For more information, see "Using appearance attributes" on page 260.

3 Do one of the following:

- To create a new style with a default name, click the New Style button (◨) at the bottom of the Styles palette.

- To create a new style with a default name, drag the appearance icon from the top left corner of the Appearance palette into the Styles palette or onto the New Style button at the bottom of the Styles palette.

- To create a new style with a default name, drag the object with the appearance attributes you want into the Styles palette or onto the New Style button at the bottom of the Styles palette.

- To create a new style with a new name, choose New Style from the Styles palette menu, enter a name for the style, and click OK. The new style appears at the bottom of the list in the Styles palette.

- To create a new style with a new name, Alt-click (Windows) or Option-click (Mac OS) the New Style button, enter the name of the style, and click OK.

- To replace a style, choose Replace "(style name)" from the Appearance palette menu. All objects, groups, and layers with that style applied change to the new style.

- To replace a style, Alt-drag (Windows) or Option-drag (Mac OS) the object from the artwork onto a style in the Styles palette.

- To replace a style, Alt-drag (Windows) or Option-drag (Mac OS) the appearance icon from the top left corner of the Appearance palette onto a style in the Styles palette.

To create a new style by merging existing styles:

1 In the Styles palette, Ctrl-click (Windows) or Command-click (Mac OS) to select all the styles you want to merge.

2 Choose Merge Styles from the palette menu.

3 The new style contains all the attributes of the selected styles and is added to the end of the list of styles in the palette.

To change the order of styles:

1 Select a style in the Styles palette.

2 Drag the style up or down in the palette. When the outline of the style you are dragging appears in the position you want, release the mouse button.

To rename a style:

1 Do one of the following:

- Double-click the style in the Styles palette.

- Choose Style Options from the palette menu.

2 Enter the name of the style, and click OK.

To replace one style with another:

1 Alt-drag (Windows) or Option-drag (Mac OS) the style you want to use onto the style you want to replace.

The replaced style keeps its name but takes on all the appearance attributes of the style you dragged onto it. All selections with the original style applied have the replaced style applied instead.

To duplicate a style:

1 In the Styles palette, Select a style you want to copy.

2 Choose Duplicate Style from the Styles palette menu, enter a name for the style, and click OK.

The new style appears at the bottom of the list in the Styles palette.

To disassociate a style from a selection:

1 Select the object, group, or layer that has the style applied to it.

2 Disassociate the style:

• Choose Break Link to Style from the Styles palette menu, or click the Break Link to Style button ( ) in the palette.

• Change any appearance attribute of the selection (such as a fill, stroke, transparency, or effect).

To delete a style:

1 In the Styles palette, Select a style you want to delete.

2 Delete the style:

• Choose Delete Style from the Styles palette menu.

• Click the Trash button ( ) in the palette.

• Drag the style onto the Trash button in the palette.

Using style libraries

You can import styles from other files into a palette associated with the current file using the Style Libraries command. These libraries are stored in the Style Libraries folder, located in the application folder. You cannot add, delete, or edit styles in a library; however, once you import a style, you can change its attributes using the Appearance palette.

Be sure to explore the Illustrator Extras folder on the application CD for libraries containing other styles.

To import a style from a Style Library to the current Styles palette:

1 Make sure the Styles palette into which you want to import a style is open.

2 Choose Window > Style Libraries > *Style Library name*. To locate a Style Library not stored in the Style Libraries folder, choose Window > Style Libraries > Other Library.

3 Select a style you want, and then do one of the following:

• Use the selected style in the current artwork (recommended for one or two styles at a time). Once you use it in the artwork, the style is copied from the Styles Library to the Styles palette.

• Drag the selected style to the current Styles palette (recommended for multiple styles at a time).

To have a Styles Library appear in the Styles Libraries menu:

1 Drag the Styles Library file into the Styles Libraries folder.

2 Restart the program.

To create a Styles Library:

1 Create a file containing the styles you want in the Styles Library.

2 Save the file in the Styles Libraries folder.

3 Restart the program.

Using effects

The commands listed under the Effect menu alter the appearance of an object without changing the underlying object itself.

For example, you can apply the Roughen command listed under Effect, transform the object with the rotate tool, scale it, and fill it with a 50% opaque red. You can then edit the roughen amount or remove it entirely, without the rotation, scale, or color or previous shape of the object being affected.

The following guidelines apply to effects:

• Effects include many commands also found under other menus in the application, including distortion filter commands, Photoshop filter commands, Add Arrowheads, Drop Shadow, Round Corners, rasterization commands, Pathfinder commands, Create Text Outlines, Outline Stroke, and transformations. For more information on each of these, see the individual command.

• Only the version of the commands listed under the Effect menu are reeditable. For instance, applying the Roughen command from the Filter menu alters the underlying object; applying the Roughen command from the Effect menu does not.

• Effects include several commands unique to the Effect menu, such as Feather, Outer Glow, Inner Glow, and the Convert to Shape commands. For more information on these, see the individual commands.

• You can apply any number of effects to an object.

• You can apply effects to type objects, but not to the text characters within the type objects.

• Effects are automatically added to the appearance attributes for the object to which you apply them.

• You can select and edit effects applied to an object, group, layer, or style using the Appearance palette.

• Because effects are listed in the Appearance palette, you can save them as part of a style.

• Because they are part of an appearance and can be saved as a style, effects remain fully editable when you apply the effect or style. This means you can add, remove, or edit any of these effects as part of an appearance or style at any time without altering the underlying object.

To apply an effect:

1 Do one of the following:

• To apply the effect to an object, select an object in the artwork.

• To apply the effect to an object, group, or layer, target it in the Layers palette. For more information, see "Targeting layers, groups, and objects to apply appearance attributes" on page 252.

• To apply the effect to a stroke or fill, select the stroke or fill in the Appearance palette. For more information, see "Using appearance attributes" on page 260.

- To apply the effect to a style, select a style in the Styles palette. For more information, see "Using styles" on page 265.

2 Choose a command from the Effect menu.

3 Specify settings, and apply the effect.

4 If you selected a style, the appearance attributes are unlinked from that style. In this case, you can do any of the following:

- Relink them to the style, replacing the style's previous appearance attributes. For more information, see the instructions for modifying a style in "Using the Styles palette" on page 268.

- Create a new style. For more information, see the instructions for modifying a style in "Using the Styles palette" on page 268.

- Leave the appearance attributes unlinked to any style.

To edit or remove an effect:

Edit or remove the effect as described in "Using appearance attributes" on page 260.

11

Chapter 11: Working with Bitmap Images

Much of the work you do with the Adobe Illustrator program may involve using bitmap images. Illustrator provides many features that allow you great flexibility in working with bitmap images.

Using bitmap images

You can do the following with bitmap images:

• Place an image into a file. (See "Placing files" on page 74.)

• Use the Links palette to see information about the image. (See "Managing linked and embedded images" on page 76.)

• Trace images using the auto trace tool. (See "Tracing artwork" on page 111.)

• Create bitmap artwork with a transparent background using the Rasterize filter. By using the Transparent option in the Rasterize filter, you create an alpha channel (as in the Adobe Photoshop application). The transparent background also provides superior anti-aliasing of the rasterized artwork than does using a clipping mask to mask the background.

• Create a clipping mask in the Rasterize filter to make the background appear transparent. (See "Working with clipping masks" on page 167.)

• Use the Rasterize dialog box to convert vector objects (including paths and text objects) into an image, and choose other options for the image. You can also change the color model for the image by reselecting Rasterize and changing the color. (See "Changing vector graphics into bitmap images" on page 275.)

• Colorize 1-bit images. (See "Colorizing 1-bit images" on page 276.)

• Use bitmap filters and filter effects. (See "Choosing a filter or filter effect" on page 280.)

• Use the Object Mosaic filter to convert the pixels to a collection of colored squares. Then you can use Illustrator tools. (See "Using the Object Mosaic filter" on page 281.)

• Apply the Photo Crosshatch filter, which gives a photographic image the appearance of a pen drawing. (See "Using the Photo Crosshatch filter" on page 282.)

Changing vector graphics into bitmap images

The Rasterize command converts vector objects into bitmap images. You can apply the Rasterize command from the Object menu to convert objects to bitmap images, or apply the command from the Effect menu to convert only the appearance of the objects.

Once objects are converted by either method, you can apply plug-in filters, such as those designed for Adobe Photoshop, to the image as you would with any placed image. However, you cannot apply vector tools and commands (such as the type tools and the Pathfinder commands) to modify the bitmap image.

To create a bitmap version of artwork:

1 Do one of the following:

• To convert one or more objects to a bitmap image, select the objects and choose Object > Rasterize.

• To apply a bitmap appearance as an effect, select an object or group in the artwork, or target a group or layer in the Layers palette. (For more information on effects, see "Using effects" on page 271. For more information on targeting, see "Targeting layers, groups, and objects to apply appearance attributes" on page 252.) Then choose Effect > Rasterize > Rasterize.

2 Choose an image format for the conversion from the Color Model pop-up menu. You can generate an RGB or CMYK color image (depending on the color mode of your document), a grayscale image, or a 1-bit image (which may be black-and-white or black-and-transparent, depending on the background option selected).

3 Choose a resolution from the Resolution area: Screen for monitor output, Medium for laser printer output, High for imagesetter output. Or type a value in the Other text box.

In the Rasterize dialog box, resolution is measured in ppi (pixels per inch). For more information about units of measure, see "About resolution in bitmap images" on page 68.

4 In the Background area, select White to make the object's background opaque, or Transparent to make the background transparent. If you select Transparent, you create an alpha channel (for all images except 1-bit images). The alpha channel is retained if the artwork is exported into Photoshop.

5 To create a bitmap image mask that makes its background appear transparent, select Create Clipping Mask, and then click OK. (See "Working with clipping masks" on page 167.)

Note: You do not need to create a clipping mask to mask the background if you have selected Transparent in the previous step.

6 To smooth the jagged edges around the bitmap image when it's converted, select the Anti-Alias option.

Note: The Anti-Alias option can take longer to rasterize. Also, text and thin lines may look blurred.

7 To add pixels as padding around the object, enter a value in the Add Around Object text box.

Colorizing 1-bit images

You can add color to 1-bit images using the Color palette.

To colorize a 1-bit image:

1 Select the image. Make sure the Fill button is selected, and no stroke is applied.

2 Use the Color palette to paint the image with black, white, a process color, or a spot color.

Using filters and filter effects on bitmap images

Some commands in Adobe Illustrator let you apply a special look to bitmap images. For example, you can apply an impressionistic or mosaic look, apply lighting changes, distort images, and produce many other interesting visual results.

For descriptions of individual filters and filter effects, see "About filters and filter effects for bitmap images" in online Help.

Most of these commands are listed both under the Filter menu and the Effect menu, letting you apply the command either as a filter or a filter effect. The versions of the commands listed under Filter alter the structure of the objects to which they are applied. You can apply these commands only to bitmap images.

The commands listed under Effect change only the appearance of the object without changing the object's underlying structure, letting you modify the settings of the command or remove the command at any time. You can apply these commands to bitmap images and also to vector objects, including paths and type. For more information, see "Using effects" on page 271.

Filters and filter effects don't work on linked bitmap images. If you apply a filter or filter effect to a linked bitmap image, it is applied to an embedded copy of the image instead of to the original. For information on linked and embedded images, see "Opening and placing artwork" on page 73.

About plug-in filters

Adobe Illustrator supports plug-in filters and filter effects from Adobe products such as Adobe Photoshop and from non-Adobe software developers. Once installed, most plug-in filters and filter effects appear in the Filter and Effect menus and work the same as built-in filters.

For information on installing and developing these plug-in modules, see "Using plug-in modules" on page 61. For information on effects, see "Using effects" on page 271.

Previewing and applying filters and filter effects

To use a filter or filter effect, choose the appropriate submenu command from the Filter or Effect menu. The last filter or filter effect chosen appears at the top of the menu.

The commands in the top part of the menu can be applied to vector images, with the exception of Pen and Ink > Photo Crosshatch. The commands in the bottom part of the menu can be applied to bitmap images, but not to 1-bit (black-and-white) images. All the bitmap filters and filter effects work on RGB and grayscale images. The following filters and filter effects do not work with CMYK images: Artistic, Brush Strokes, Distort, Sketch, Stylize, Texture, and Video.

You can specify the settings to be used when you use filters to apply raster effects to vector objects. For more information on effects, see "Using effects" on page 271.

Some commands let you preview the result before applying the command. Because applying a filter or filter effect—especially to large bitmap images—can be time-consuming, use the Preview box to save time and prevent unintended results.

Note: Some bitmap images take more memory to process. Make sure Illustrator has enough RAM allocated for performing tasks and for the scratch disk—temporary disk space used to work with bitmap images.

To set raster options for filter effects:

1 Choose Effect > Rasterize > Rasterize Effect Settings.

2 Enter values or select options, and then click OK. The options are the same as those used to rasterize an object. For details on the options, see "Changing vector graphics into bitmap images" on page 275.

To preview and apply a filter or filter effect:

1 Select a bitmap image on which to apply the command.

2 Choose a filter from the submenu in the Filter menu or a filter effect from the Effect menu. If a filter or filter-effects name has an ellipsis, a dialog box appears.

3 If a dialog box appears, enter values or select options.

4 To preview the result with the filter's preview box, do either of the following:

• Drag in the image window to center a specific area of the bitmap image in the preview box.

• Move the cursor inside the preview box to activate the hand tool to see part of the image that is not visible. Drag to see the bitmap image. Use the + or – button under the preview box to zoom in or zoom out of the preview. A flashing line beneath the preview size indicates that Illustrator is still rendering the preview.

5 Click OK to apply the filter.

When a filter or filter effect takes some time to be applied, you see a progress dialog box that indicates the time remaining until the filter is applied.

Loading bitmap images and textures

Some commands let you load other bitmap images, such as textures and displacement maps, to use with a filter or filter effect. These commands include Glass and Rough Pastels.

You can apply the Glass and Rough Pastel command as a filter or as an effect. For more information on effects, see "Using effects" on page 271.

To load bitmap images and textures:

1 Choose one of the following:

• Filter > Artistic > Rough Pastels.

• Effect > Artistic > Rough Pastels.

• Filter> Distort > Glass.

• Effect > Distort > Glass.

2 Choose Load Texture from the Texture pop-up menu.

3 Open the texture bitmap image.

4 Click OK in the filter or effect dialog box to apply the settings.

Using texture and glass surface controls

Some commands included in Illustrator have texturizing options, such as the Glass, Rough Pastels, Grain, and Fresco commands. The texturizing options can make a bitmap image appear as though painted onto various textures, such as canvas and brick, or viewed through glass blocks.

You can apply these command as a filter or as an effect. For more information on effects, see "Using effects" on page 271.

To use texture and glass surface controls:

1 From the Filter or Effect menu, choose Artistic > Rough Pastels; Artistic > Fresco; Distort > Glass; or Texture > Grain.

2 Choose a texture type from the Texture pop-up menu (if available), or choose Load Texture from the Texture pop-up menu to specify a file.

3 Drag the Scaling slider (if available) to enlarge or reduce the effect on the bitmap image's surface.

4 Choose other available options:

• Drag the Relief slider (if available) to adjust the depth of the texture's surface.

• From the Light Direction pop-up menu (if available), choose the direction from which you want the light to appear.

• Select Invert (if available) to reverse the surface's light and dark colors.

5 Click OK to apply the settings.

Improving performance with filters and filter effects

Some filters and filter effects can be memory intensive, especially when applied to a high-resolution bitmap image. Use the following techniques to improve performance when applying these commands:

• Change the settings. Some commands, such as Glass, are extremely memory-intensive. Try different settings to increase its speed.

• If you plan to print to a grayscale printer, convert a copy of the bitmap image to grayscale before applying filters. Note, however, that in some cases, applying a filter to a color bitmap image and then converting it to grayscale may not have the same effect as applying the same filter to a grayscale version of the image.

Choosing a filter or filter effect

The Illustrator filters and filter effects fall into the following general categories. In addition, third-party filters appear at the bottom of the Filter menu. For more information on effects, see "Using effects" on page 271.

Artistic filters and effects Give a bitmap image the appearance of different media for a more organic (and less computer-generated) look. (See "Using texture and glass surface controls" on page 279.)

Blur filters and effects Soften a bitmap image and are useful for retouching images. Blur filters and effects smooth transitions by averaging the pixels next to the hard edges of defined lines and shaded areas where significant color transitions occur in a bitmap image.

Brush Strokes filters and effects Give a bitmap image a fine-arts look by using different brush and ink stroke effects.

Distort filters and effects Geometrically distort a bitmap image and can be used to create 3-D or other plastic effects.

Pixelate filters and effects Sharply define a selection by clumping pixels of similar color values in cells. (See "Using the Color Halftone command" on page 280.)

Sharpen filter and effects Focus a blurry image by increasing the contrast of adjacent pixels.

Sketch filters and effects Add a fine-arts and hand-drawn look to a bitmap image.

Stylize filters and effects Produce a painted or impressionistic look on a selection by displacing pixels and by finding and heightening contrast in an image.

Texture filters and effects Apply texturing effects to an image, including effects that add grain, paint, glass, or texture to a bitmap image. (See "Using texture and glass surface controls" on page 279.)

Video filters and effects Include the National Television Standards Committee (NTSC) Colors and De-Interlace commands. NTSC Colors restricts the gamut of colors to those acceptable for television reproduction, to prevent oversaturated colors from bleeding across television scan lines. De-Interlace smooths moving bitmap images captured on video by removing either the odd or the even interlaced lines in a video image. The command gives you the option of replacing the discarded lines by duplication or interpolation.

Using the Color Halftone command

The Color Halftone command simulates the effect of using an enlarged halftone screen on each channel of the bitmap image. (Color information channels are created automatically when you open a new image. The image's color mode determines the number of color channels created.) For each channel, the command divides the image into rectangles and replaces each rectangle with a circle. The circle size is proportional to the brightness of the rectangle. To use the Color Halftone command, you specify a screen-angle value for each channel of the image.

You can apply the Color Halftone command as a filter or as an effect. For more information on effects, see "Using effects" on page 271.

To use the Color Halftone command:

1 Do one of the following:

• To apply the command as a filter, choose Filter > Pixelate > Color Halftone.

• To apply the command as an effect, select an object or group in the artwork, or target a group or layer in the Layers palette. (For more information on targeting, see "Targeting layers, groups, and objects to apply appearance attributes" on page 252.) Then choose Effect > Pixelate > Color Halftone.

2 Enter a value in pixels, from 4 to 127, for the maximum radius of a halftone dot.

3 Enter a screen-angle value (the angle of the dot from the true horizontal) for each channel, as follows:

• Grayscale bitmap images use only Channels 1.

• In RGB bitmap images, Channel 1, 2, and 3 correspond to the red, green, and blue channels.

• In CMYK bitmap images, the four channels correspond to the cyan, magenta, yellow, and black channels, respectively.

• Click Defaults to return all the screen angles to their default values.

4 Click OK.

Using the Object Mosaic filter

The Object Mosaic filter creates sharp definition in an image by clustering pixels of similar color values together into individual tiles. You can control the tile size, the spacing between tiles, and the total number of tiles, and you can preserve the proportions of the original image when creating the mosaic copy.

The Object Mosaic filter works with any bitmap image format that Illustrator can place, and with bitmap images created with the Rasterize command. The Object Mosaic filter creates a tiled vector version of the bitmap image. You can choose to keep the original image or delete it.

To create a tiled effect on a copy of a bitmap image:

1 Select a bitmap image.

2 Choose Filter > Create > Object Mosaic.

The dimensions of the bitmap image are displayed at the top left of the Object Mosaic dialog box.

3 Choose from the following options:

• To set the width and height of the mosaic in points, enter values for New Size.

• To set the distance in points between each tile in the mosaic, enter values for Tile Spacing.

• To set the number of tiles horizontally and vertically in the mosaic, enter values for Number of Tiles.

- To lock the width or height dimensions to those of the original bitmap image, choose Width or Height for the Constrain Ratio option. Choosing Width calculates the appropriate number of tiles to use for the width of the mosaic, based on the original number of tiles for the width. Choosing Height calculates the appropriate number of tiles to use for the height of the mosaic, based on the original number of tiles for the height.

- To have the result appear as a color or grayscale image, select Color or Gray.

- To change the size of the image by percentages of width and height, select Resize Using Percentages and enter new percentages in the Width and Height text boxes.

- To delete the original bitmap image, select Delete Raster.

- To make tiles square, using the number of tiles specified in Number of Tiles, click Use Ratio.

4 Click OK.

Using the Photo Crosshatch filter

The Photo Crosshatch filter can convert a photographic image, or any rasterized image, into a hatched ink pen image. The filter converts the photo into a series of overlapping hatch layers, each hatch layer representing different lightness areas of the original photo. Since there are many hatch layers overlapping where the image is darkest, and few where the image is lightest, the result is a simulated crosshatched drawing of the original photographic image.

Note: You can apply various hatch filters to images, to give the image the appearance of a pen drawing. (See "Using the Pen and Ink filters" on page 160.)

To convert a rasterized image into a crosshatched drawing:

1 Select a rasterized image.

2 Choose Filter > Pen and Ink > Photo Crosshatch.

3 Enter the number of hatch layers to create in the Hatch Layers text box. The maximum number of layers is 8. Each hatch layer receives a distribution of the lightness values between 0 and 255. For example, if you enter a Hatch Layer of 4, the first layer contains lightness values of 0 to 64, the second values of 0 to 128, the third values of 0 to 192, and the fourth values of 0 to 255.

4 Use the slider under the histogram to adjust the weighting of the threshold levels toward light or dark. The histogram shows how many pixels of the hatched image fall into each value of lightness between 0 and 255. Use the middle slider to skew the threshold levels on each level toward light (by moving the slider to the right) or dark (by moving the slider to the left). Adjust the end sliders to moderate the highest levels of light (the rightmost slider) and dark (the leftmost slider).

5 Use the sliders on the left side of the dialog box to adjust options as follows:

• Density adjusts the number of hatch elements applied to the selection, from .5 pt to 10 pts.

• Dispersion Noise controls the spacing of hatch elements, from 0 to 300%.

• Thickness controls the stroke weight of the hatch elements, from .1 pt to 10 pts. (This option is dimmed if the selection is unstroked.)

• Max. Line Length sets the length of the hatch elements, from 5 pts to 999 pts.

• Rotation Noise sets the amount of random rotation of objects within the hatch layers, from –360 degrees to 360 degrees.

• Rotation Variance sets the amount that each layer is rotated from the previous layer, from 0 to 100%.

• Top Angle sets the angle of rotation for the top-most hatch layer, from –360 degrees to 360 degrees.

6 Click OK.

12

Chapter 12: Using Type

Among the most powerful aspects of Adobe Illustrator are the type features. You can quickly change type size, shape, and scale; you can flow type precisely into virtually any shape of object; and you can flow type horizontally or vertically along differently shaped pathways.

About using type in Illustrator

No matter which language version you are using, Adobe Illustrator provides a wide range of multi-national language features—from spell-checking and hyphenation support for numerous European languages to advanced typography features for Chinese, Japanese, and Korean (CJK) text.

Note: Your operating system must support the languages in which you wish to work. Consult your system software manufacturer for more information.

The range of type tools in Illustrator make it easy to flow text into shapes and place type along a path in your artwork, such as along a circle or irregular path that you create. To enhance your designs, you can also paint type with colors and patterns, apply effects and styles, or transform type into entirely new shapes.

You can enter type or import type into your artwork from another application. Adobe Illustrator imports and exports vertical text files, such as MS Word or RTF, as horizontal. Vertical text is imported into Illustrator horizontally, and vertical text is exported from Illustrator horizontally.

Creating type

Using the type tools, you can create horizontal or vertical type anywhere in a file. In addition, you can flow text into shapes or onto paths in a variety of ways: You can enter type in a containing column or rectangle, inside an irregularly shaped object, and inside or along a path.

Entering type at a point

The horizontal and vertical type tools are used to enter type anywhere in the Illustrator work area, without needing to define a bounding area for the type. Entering type this way, for example, is useful for adding a caption to an illustration.

To enter horizontal or vertical type at a specific point:

1 Select the type tool (T) or the vertical type tool (|T). The pointer changes to an I-beam within a dotted box.

The small horizontal line near the bottom of the I-beam marks the position of the type *baseline*. The baseline is the line on which the type rests.

2 Click where you want the type to begin.

Important: Be sure not to click an existing object, because doing so converts the object into a container or path for the type. If an existing object is located where you want to enter type, lock or hide the object or enter the type away from the object and reposition the type over the object afterward.

3 Enter the type you want. Press Enter or Return to begin a new line of type.

Selecting type

The type or vertical type tool's I-beam pointer lets you select individual characters, words, and paragraphs, and lets you change the type's attributes. To select all of the type on a path or in a type container, use the selection tool on the path or type container. (See "Selecting objects" on page 121.)

By default, Type Area Select is selected in the Type & Auto Tracing Preferences dialog box. You can reset your preferences to select type from the baseline.

To select characters and words:

1 Select any type tool.

2 Do one of the following:

• Drag to select the type you want to change. (Shift-drag to extend or reduce the selection.)

• Position the pointer in a word, and double-click to select that word.

• Position the pointer at the beginning of a paragraph, and press Shift+Ctrl+Up Arrow (Windows) or Shift+Command+Up Arrow (Mac OS) to select the previous paragraph. With the pointer at the end of a paragraph, press Shift+Ctrl+Down Arrow (Windows) or Shift+Command+Down Arrow (Mac OS) twice to select the next paragraph.

• Press Shift+Ctrl+Right Arrow (Windows) or Shift+Command+Right Arrow (Mac OS) to select one word to the right. Press Shift+Ctrl+Left Arrow (Windows) or Shift+Command+Left Arrow (Mac OS) to select one word to the left.

To select blocks of type:

1 Select any type tool.

2 Do one of the following:

• Drag to select the type you want to change. (Shift-drag to extend or reduce the selection.)

• Position the I-beam pointer in a paragraph, and triple-click to select the entire paragraph.

• Click the type with a type tool, and then choose Edit > Select All to select all the type on the type path or in the type container.

To set the preference for selecting type from the baseline:

1 Choose Edit > Preferences > Type & Auto Tracing.

2 Deselect the Type Area Select option, and click OK.

To select type from the baseline:

1 Use the selection tool (▶) or direct-selection too (▶) to select the type path. You see the text baseline.

2 Click the baseline to select it.

Entering horizontal or vertical type in a rectangle

You can use the type or vertical type tool to define a text rectangle into which you enter type. This method is useful when you want to create one or more columns of text, such as for a brochure. You can also create a rectangle with the rectangle tool and then use any type tool to convert it to a text rectangle.

Once you've entered type, you can change the shape and size of the text rectangle.

To create a text rectangle using a type tool:

1 Select the type tool (T) or the vertical type tool (IT). The pointer changes to an I-beam within a dotted box.

2 Drag diagonally to define the text rectangle. The text rectangle you create is unpainted (not filled or stroked). Text rectangles are not visible in Preview view or when printing, unless filled or stroked with color. (See "Using the Color palette" on page 180.)

When you release the mouse button, the pointer reverts to an I-beam. (In Outline view, a rectangle appears with an insertion point at the top left corner of the text rectangle.)

3 Enter the type. The type wraps to fit inside the defined area.

4 Press Enter or Return to begin a new paragraph.

If you enter more type than can fit within the rectangle, a small box containing a plus symbol (+) appears near the bottom of the rectangle when in Outline view or when the text rectangle or type is selected. The plus symbol is positioned at the end of the baseline of the last visible line of type.

You can adjust the size of the rectangle to accommodate the type using either the bounding box or the direct-selection tool. When you adjust the size or shape of the rectangle, the text reflows within the adjusted shape.

Note: If you select objects, point text, or path text in addition to a text rectangle, scaling with the bounding box will cause all objects, including the area text, to be rescaled.

You can also create a linked copy of the rectangle to force extra type to flow into another text rectangle or object. (See "Linking type containers" on page 306.)

To change the size or shape of a text rectangle using the bounding box:

1 Select the selection tool ( ).

2 Select the text rectangle to adjust.

3 Drag a handle of the selection until the text rectangle is the desired size or shape. Shift-drag to maintain the proportion.

To change the size or shape of a text rectangle using the direct-selection tool:

1 Select the direct-selection tool ( ).

2 If the type is selected, click outside the rectangle to deselect it.

3 Position the pointer on the edge of the text container you want to adjust. Do not select any type baselines.

4 Click to select an edge or corner of the text rectangle, and drag to adjust the rectangle's shape. Shift-drag to constrain the tool to multiples of 45 degrees (constraining makes it easier to retain the shape of a rectangle).

Adjusting the text rectangle using the direct-selection tool is easiest when you're in Outline view.

Entering horizontal or vertical type in an object

You can use any object as an area within which to enter type. If the object is an open path, the program draws an imaginary line between the endpoints of the path to define the object for the type, just as it does to paint open paths.

To create only area type or to create area type on an open path, you can use the type or vertical area-type tools exclusively. If, however, you want to create several kinds of type, you should use the type tool or the vertical type tool. When you move a type tool over different kinds of objects, the type tool appropriate to the specific object (for example, an area-type tool or a path-type tool) appears.

To enter type in an object:

1 Select the type tool (T) or the area-type tool (T) if the object is a filled open path.

2 Position the pointer on the path, and click. An insertion point appears.

When you turn an object into a type path, the path becomes unstroked and unfilled, even if the path was originally stroked or filled. When the entire text object is selected, any changes to the paint settings affect only the type, not the path.

3 Enter some type.

As with text rectangles, if you enter more type than can fit within the area, in Outline view and in Preview view (only when text is selected), a small box with a plus symbol (+) appears near the bottom of the area.

You can paint the path after you enter type by selecting the path with the direct-selection tool and using the Color palette or Swatches palette.

Entering horizontal or vertical type along a path

You can enter type that flows along the edge of an open or a closed path. The path can be regularly or irregularly shaped. When you enter type along a path, the path is no longer stroked or filled. You can paint it later if you want, without affecting the paint attributes of the type.

Entering horizontal type on a path results in letters that are perpendicular to the baseline. Entering vertical type on a path results in text orientation parallel to the baseline.

To toggle between the type tool and the vertical type tool when another type tool is currently selected, Shift-click.

To enter horizontal type along a path:

1 Select the type tool (T) or the path-type tool (🖉).

2 Position the pointer on the path, and click. An insertion point appears on the path.

3 Enter the type you want. Type appears along the path, perpendicular to the baseline.

To enter vertical type along a path:

1 Select the vertical type tool (IT) or the vertical-path-type tool (🖉).

2 Choose Standard from the Direction pop-up menu in the Character palette.

3 Position the pointer on the path, and click. An insertion point appears on the path.

4 Enter the type you want. Type appears along the path, parallel to the baseline.

Note: For 1-byte vertical CJK text, Roman characters rotate by default.

To move type along a path:

1 Use the selection tool (▶) or the direct-selection tool (▷) to select the type path if it is not already selected.

2 Position the pointer on the I-beam in the type.

3 Use the selection tool to move the selected type along the path. Be careful not to drag across the path.

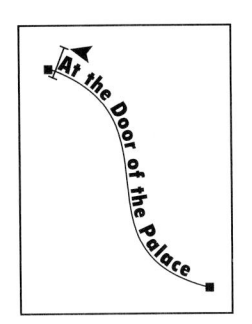

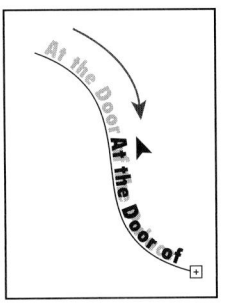

Position pointer on I-beam. Then drag to move type.

💡 *To align horizontal type evenly along a path, enter a negative baseline shift value in the Character palette so that the type runs along the center of the path. This method creates an even flow of type along the curve. (See "Specifying baseline shift" on page 298.)*

To flip the direction of the type along a path:

1 Select the selection tool (▶).

2 Position the pointer precisely on the I-beam.

3 Do one of the following:

- Drag the I-beam across the path.
- Double-click the I-beam.

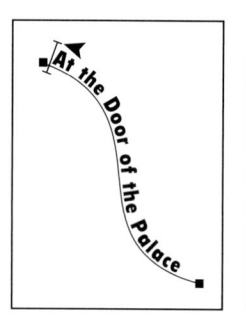

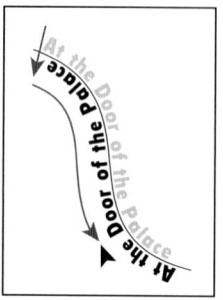

Position pointer on I-beam. Then drag across path to flip type.

> The initial direction of type flows in the order that points were added to the path. If you want your text to flow from left-to-right without having to flip the I-beam, construct your paths in that order.

To move type across a path without changing the direction of the type, use the Baseline Shift option in the Character palette. (See "Specifying baseline shift" on page 298.) For example, if you created type that runs from left to right across the top of a circle, you can enter a negative number in the Baseline Shift text box to drop the type so that it flows inside the top of the circle.

Deleting empty type paths from artwork

The Delete Empty Text Paths option in the Cleanup dialog box lets you delete unused type paths and containers from your artwork. Doing so makes your artwork more efficient and easier to print. You can create empty type paths, for example, by inadvertently clicking the type tool in the artwork area and then choosing another tool.

To delete an empty type path from your artwork:

1 Choose Object > Path > Cleanup.

2 Select Delete Empty Text Paths, and click OK.

Using or modifying multiple master fonts

Illustrator supports the Adobe multiple master font technology and provides special options for working with those fonts.

Multiple master fonts are customizable Type 1 fonts whose typeface characteristics are described in terms of linear design axes such as weight, width, style, and optical size. Multiple master fonts include a number of primary instances. For example, Myriad® includes 15 primary instances, ranging from 215LT 300CN (Light condensed) to 830BL 700SE (Black SemiExtended). Standard Type 1 fonts are single master fonts, which means they are adjustable in style only (for example, Roman, bold, italic).

When you create a multiple master font, the font is available only when the file for which it was created is open. To have a multiple master font instance always available for Illustrator and other applications, you must first create it in Adobe® Type Manager®.

To modify a multiple master font from within Illustrator:

1 Using the type tool (T), select the text that uses a multiple master font.

2 Display the Multiple Master design palette using one of the following methods:

• Choose Type > MM Design.

• Click the MM Design tab in the Character palette.

3 Edit the font as described in the documentation included with your multiple master font.

Showing hidden characters

As you work with type, nonprinting characters are embedded into the file to indicate keyboard actions or states, such as spaces, returns (line breaks), and tabs. These characters include hard returns (line breaks), soft returns (line breaks), tabs, spaces, nonbreaking spaces, double-byte characters (including spaces), discretionary hyphens, other nonprinting characters, and end of text.

These characters are by default hidden. To help you format and edit type, you can make the characters visible.

To show hidden characters:

Choose Type > Show Hidden Characters. A check mark appears next to the menu command. To hide visible characters, choose the command to remove the check mark.

Setting type attributes

The Adobe Illustrator program gives you precise control over type attributes, including font, type size, leading, kerning, tracking, baseline shift, horizontal and vertical scale, spacing, and letter orientation. You can either set type attributes before you enter new type or reset them to change the appearance of existing, selected type. You can also set attributes for several type paths and type containers at once, if they are all selected.

You change the type attributes using the Character and Paragraph palettes. Some of the type attributes also have separate submenus or palettes so that you do not have to open the Character or Paragraph palette to change only one attribute. In addition, some attributes can be changed using keyboard shortcuts. For a complete list of shortcuts, see the *Adobe Illustrator Quick Reference Card*.

To apply a value in the Character or Paragraph palette to the selected type without moving to the next text box in the palette, press Enter or Return. To apply a value and then highlight the value just edited, press Shift+Enter or Shift+Return. To apply a value and move to the next text box in the palette, press Tab.

To open the Character or Paragraph palette:

Choose either Type > Character or Type > Paragraph.

To show character options in the Character palette:

Choose Type > Character, and then choose Show Options from the Character palette menu.

To show multilingual and orientation options in the Character palette:

Choose Type > Character, and then choose Show Multilingual from the Character palette menu.

Choosing a font family

A *font family* is a complete set of characters, letters, and symbols of a particular typeface design. For example, the font used in this paragraph is Minion®.

You can choose a font from the Character palette, or you can choose Type > Font and choose from the submenu.

You do not see fonts in their respective faces in the palette or submenu, even when you have a utility that shows typefaces installed (such as Adobe Type Reunion®).

Note: When you open an Illustrator file on a Japanese system, the Font Details dialog box appears, showing the font format and Tsume information format for fonts used in the file. If the fonts in the file are different from those available on your system, the Font Issues dialog box appears, providing information about font substitution.

To choose a font from the Character palette:

1 Do one of the following:

• Select any type container or type path using a selection tool.

• Select a block of type using a type tool.

2 Choose Type > Character.

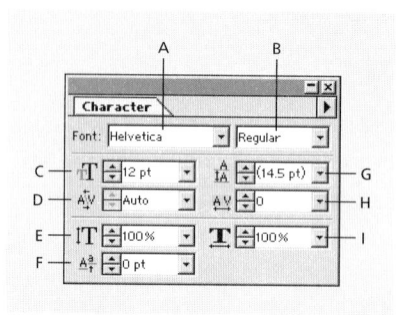

*A. Family B. Style C. Font size D. Kerning
E. Vertical scale F. Baseline shift G. Leading
H. Tracking I. Horizontal scale*

3 Do one of the following:

• In the Font text box, type the name of the font family you want to use. In the Style text box, enter the type style (for example, Bold, Condensed, Italic). As you type, the name of the first font or style beginning with that letter appears. Continue typing the name until the correct font or style name appears.

• Choose a font and style from the pop-up menu in which you see styles (to the right of the Font text box).

Note: Font styles are not available for Kanji fonts.

4 Press Enter, Return, or Tab to apply the new font.

To choose a font from the Type menu:

1 Do one of the following:

• Select any type container or type path using a selection tool.

• Set an insertion point or select a range of text using the type tool (T) or the vertical-type tool (|T).

2 Choose Type > Font. A check mark appears next to the selected font.

3 Drag to choose the font family you want. If more than one style of the font is installed, you see a submenu, which contains a list of styles available for the font family you choose.

4 Select the style you want. The font you choose becomes the active font.

Note: When using 2-byte fonts, you can switch between showing a font's name in a 2-byte script or showing the font in its English name by selecting or deselecting the Show Font Names in English option in the Type & Auto Tracing Preferences dialog box.

Choosing a type size

You can choose the type size in the Character palette, or from the Size submenu in the Type menu, or by using keyboard commands. The default type size is 12 points. Type size units can be set to points, inches, millimeters, or Q in the Units & Undo Preferences dialog box.

To choose a type size in the Character palette:

1 Do one of the following:

• Select any type container or type path using a selection tool.

• Set an insertion point or select a range of text using the type tools.

2 Choose Type > Character. The Character palette opens, displaying the currently selected type size in the Font Size text box.

If the selection contains fonts of more than one size, the text box is blank.

3 Choose a new type size from the Size pop-up menu. You can also press Up Arrow or Down Arrow to change the size, or enter the size in the Font Size text box and press Enter, Return, or Tab.

To choose a type size from the Type menu:

1 Do one of the following:

• Select any type container or type path using a selection tool.

• Set an insertion point or select a block of type using a type tool.

2 Choose Type > Size. A check mark appears next to the current type size in the Size submenu.

3 Do one of the following:

• Select a new type size from the Size submenu.

• If the desired type size does not appear in the Size submenu, choose Other to display the Character palette. Enter a value in the Size text box, and press Enter, Return, or Tab.

• To decrease the point size, press Shift+Ctrl+< (Windows) or Shift+Command+< (Mac OS). The point size changes by the increment set in the Size/Leading text box in the Type & Auto Tracing Preferences dialog box. The default is 2 points.

To change type size units:

1 Choose Edit > Preferences > Units & Undo.

2 In the Type pop-up menu, choose the type units you want to use, and click OK.

Finding and replacing fonts

The Find Font command creates a list of all the fonts in your file and allows you to search for and replace them (including the font's type style) by name. This command also lets you save the list of fonts as a separate file, which can be useful for a service bureau that is printing the file.

To find and replace fonts in your file:

1 Choose Type > Find Font.

2 Do one of the following:

• Select the Multiple Master, Standard (Chicago, Geneva, Monaco, New York, Courier, Souvenir, Symbol, Hobo, Helvetica*, and Times*), Roman, Type 1, TrueType™, CID, or OTF (OpenType® font) option to display these fonts. To display multiple master fonts, you must click the Multiple Master *and* Type 1 options (multiple master fonts are Type 1 fonts).

• Choose System from the Replace Font From pop-up menu to make all fonts currently installed on your system (as filtered through the previous options you chose) available as replacements.

• Choose Document from the Replace Font From pop-up menu to limit the fonts you can use as replacements to those already in your file.

3 Select a font name from the Fonts in Document list. Illustrator selects the next instance of that font in your file.

4 Click Find Next to find the next instance of the font.

5 Select the font you want to use as a replacement from the Replace Font From list, and do one of the following:

• Click Change to change just that instance of the selected font.

• Click Change All to change all instances of the selected font.

When there are no more instances of a font in your file, that font name is removed from the list of fonts to find.

6 To save a list of all fonts found in the file, click Save List, enter a filename and location in the Save Font List As text box, and click Save.

7 Click Done.

Specifying leading

Leading determines the amount of vertical space between baselines. Leading is always measured in units specified in the Type pop-up menu in the Units & Undo Preferences dialog box; the default units are points. If a line of type contains characters with different leading values, the line's leading is set to the greater of the two values.

You can adjust leading in the Character palette or directly from the keyboard. The default Auto-Leading option sets the leading at 120% of the type size. For example, 10-point type would have a leading value of 12 points (120% of 10 points).

To change the leading value using the Character palette:

1 Do one of the following:

• Select any type container or type path using a selection tool.

• Select a block of type using the type tools.

2 Choose Type > Character.

3 Enter a value in the Leading text box, or choose a value from the pop-up menu.

4 Press Enter or Return.

Note: To set the leading to the same value as the font size, double-click the Leading icon. To reset a setting to its default value, Ctrl-click (Windows) or Command-click (Mac OS) the associated icon in the palette.

To specify leading before a paragraph:

1 Do one of the following:

• To apply leading to a single paragraph in text, use the type tool to click anywhere in the paragraph.

• To apply leading to all paragraphs in a type container, use the selection tool to select the entire type container.

2 Choose Type > Paragraph.

3 Do one of the following:

• Click the Space Before Paragraph button and enter a value in the text box.

• Press Up Arrow or Down Arrow to increase or decrease the leading value.

4 Press Enter, Return, or Tab.

Note: You can specify leading before a paragraph with Area Type only.

Specifying kerning and tracking

Kerning controls the spacing between two characters. You can control kerning manually, or you can turn on the kerning built into a font by the font designer. (See "Spacing characters with auto-kerning" on page 298.) *Tracking* inserts uniform spacing between more than two characters in selected type. Use tracking to adjust the spacing of a word or an entire block of type.

Positive kerning or tracking values move characters apart; negative kerning or tracking values move characters closer together. Kerning and tracking values are measured in units that are 1/1000 of an *em space*. The width of an em space is relative to the current type size. In a 1-point font, 1 em corresponds to 1 point; in a 10-point font, 1 em corresponds to 10 points. Because kerning units are 1/1000 em, 100 kerning units in a 10-point font are equivalent to 1 point.

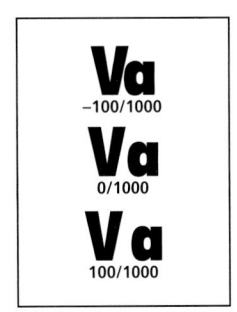

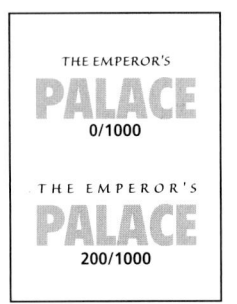

Kerning values, and tracking values ("The Emperor's")

To change the kerning or tracking value using the Character palette:

1 Set an insertion point between two characters for kerning or select type for tracking using the type tools.

2 Choose Type > Character.

3 Do one of the following:

• Click the Kerning button and enter a value in the Kerning text box.

• Click the Tracking button and enter a value in the Tracking text box.

4 Press Enter, Return, or Tab.

To view the kerning value between two characters:

1 Set an insertion point between two characters whose kerning value you want to view, using the type tools.

2 Choose Window > Show Info.

The Info palette displays the total spacing value for the two characters. For example, if the Info palette displays *109 = 100 + 9/1000 em*, the characters have 9/1000 em kerning and the word has 100/1000 em tracking.

Spacing characters with auto-kerning

To use a font's kerning information to space characters, you can select the Auto-Kerning option in the Character palette. Many Roman fonts contain information about the spacing of character pairs. For example, the spacing between an *A* and a *W* often is less than the spacing between an *A* and an *F*.

You can also choose a specific kerning value, rather than Auto-Kerning, in the Character palette until you finish creating your type. Then select the type and apply auto-kerning to it.

To apply auto-kerning to existing type in a file:

1 Choose Edit > Select All.

2 Choose Type > Character, and choose Auto from the Kerning pop-up menu or type **Auto** in the text box.

To turn auto-kerning off:

Choose Type > Character, and enter **0** in the Kerning text box.

Specifying baseline shift

Baseline shift controls the distance that type appears from its baseline, either raising or lowering the selected type. The Baseline Shift option lets you create subscripts or superscripts or move path type above or below a path without changing the direction of the type flow. For example, using the path-type tool on a circle positions type above the circle. Using the Baseline Shift option, you can move the type inside the circle without changing the type's orientation.

A positive value moves type above the baseline; a negative value moves it below the baseline. Baseline shift is measured by points unless you change the option set in the Type pop-up menu in the Units & Undo Preferences dialog box.

To specify baseline shift using the Character palette:

1 Select a type container or type path using a selection tool, or select a block of type using the type tools.

2 Choose Type > Character. If the Baseline Shift button ( ) is not visible, choose Show Options from the Character palette menu.

3 Enter a value in the Baseline Shift text box, or press Up Arrow or Down Arrow to increase or decrease baseline shift.

4 Press Enter or Return.

Adjusting horizontal or vertical scale

Horizontal scale and *vertical scale* specify the proportion between the height and width of the type relative to the baseline. Unscaled characters have a value of 100%. You can adjust scale to compress or expand selected characters in both width and height.

Scaling type using a transformation tool affects the type's horizontal scale as well as the type size, leading, indentation, and baseline shift. You can return type scaled using a transformation tool to its original horizontal scale by setting the horizontal scale to 100%.

Note: *Depending on the value you enter when you use vertical type, the horizontal scale may make the text appear narrower, because it functions relative to the baseline. The opposite is true for vertical scale.*

To adjust the horizontal or vertical scale of type:

1 Select any type container or type path using a selection tool, or select a range of text using the type tools.

2 Choose Type > Character. If the Horizontal Scale ( ) or Vertical Scale ( ) pop-up menus are not visible, choose Show Options from the Character palette menu.

3 Enter a percentage in the Horizontal Scale or the Vertical Scale text box.

4 Press Enter or Return.

Adjusting spacing using the keyboard

You can set the increments in which baseline shift and kerning/tracking values increase or decrease when you use keyboard shortcuts. The default key increment values are 2 points for size/leading, 2 points for baseline shift, and 20/1000 of an em space for kerning/tracking.

Settings in the Type & Auto Tracing Preferences and General Preferences dialog boxes control the keyboard shortcuts.

The type units preference determines the units for font size, leading, and baseline shift.

To change keyboard increments:

1 Choose Edit > Preferences > Type & Auto Tracing.

2 Enter the values you want in the Size/Leading, Baseline Shift, and Tracking text boxes, and click OK.

To change the cursor key increment value:

1 Choose Edit > Preferences > General.

2 Enter the value you want in the Cursor Key text box, and click OK.

To change type units:

1 Choose Edit > Preferences > Units & Undo.

2 Choose a type unit from the Type pop-up menu, and click OK.

The default type unit is *points* (a point equals 1/72 of an inch). You can choose inches, millimeters, or Q (a Q equals 0.25 millimeter).

Painting type

You can paint type, the type container, or the type path. You may want to paint the container to create a background for your type, or paint the type path as a visual base for the type.

To paint type, a type container, or a type path:

1 Do one of the following:

- To paint the type, use the selection tool (▶) to select the type.

- To paint a type container or type path, use the direct-selection tool (▷) or the group-selection tool (▷⁺) and click the path or object.

Do not select the baselines.

- Use a type tool to select characters, words, or paragraphs.

2 Choose either Window > Show Color or Window > Show Swatches.

3 Paint the type or type path as desired. (See "Using the Color palette" on page 180 and "Using the Swatches palette" on page 182.)

Note: You can't use a gradient swatch as a fill for type, but you can apply gradient effects to type.

Copying type attributes between objects

You can use the eyedropper tool to copy—or *sample*—the character, paragraph, fill, and stroke attributes from type in an Illustrator file. You can then use the paint bucket tool to apply the copied attributes to other type.

By default, the eyedropper and paint bucket tools affect all attributes of a type selection, including appearance attributes. To customize the attributes you want affected by these tools, use the Paint bucket/Eyedropper dialog box.

Note: When you select an entire type path or container, the fill, stroke, character, and paragraph attributes of that object are copied and applied to the new text. When you select a portion of text, only the fill, stroke, and character attributes are copied.

To copy type attributes to selected text objects:

1 With the selection tool or any type tool, select the type container, type path, or a portion of text to which you want attributes copied.

2 Select the eyedropper tool.

3 Click the text from which you want attributes copied. The text can be unselected, locked, or in an inactive artwork file. The attributes are applied to the selected type, and that type remains selected.

To copy type attributes using the paint bucket tool:

1 Select the paint bucket tool (🖌).

2 Click the type path or type container, or drag to select a portion of text, to which you want attributes applied. The paint bucket displays a small *t* next to it, to indicate you are copying type attributes.

The attributes are applied to the selected type.

💡 *To toggle between the eyedropper tool and the paint bucket tool, press Alt (Windows) or Option (Mac OS) when either tool is selected.*

To change type attributes:

1 Double-click the paint bucket or the eyedropper tool.

2 Select or deselect the attributes for the eyedropper to copy and the paint bucket to apply.

• To expand or collapse the list of attributes for each characteristic (for example, Paragraph), click the triangle to the left of the list.

• To select or deselect all the attributes for each characteristic, click the group option.

• To select or deselect individual attributes for a characteristic, click the attribute.

3 Click OK.

For a description of each attribute, see the appropriate sections in this guide.

Transforming type

The selection tool lets you select an entire type path or type container so that you can transform the type along with the path or container. You can also transform individual type containers within linked type containers.

To transform type including its path:

1 Do one of the following:

• To transform all of the type, use the selection tool (▶) to select the type path or type container, or click its baseline.

• To transform individual type containers in a series of linked type containers, use the direct-selection tool (▷) to select the linked type containers you want to transform. Make sure the baselines appear, indicating that the type is selected within the containers.

Note: To transform the type path or type container without transforming the type, use the direct-selection tool to select just the path. Make sure that the baselines do not appear, indicating type is deselected.

2 Select the rotate (↻), scale (▣), or shear (↗) tool to transform the type container and its path.

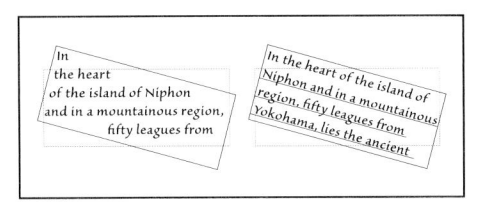

Rotated type container only compared to rotated type container and type

Changing text orientation

You can change the direction of individual characters as well as the flow of an entire block of text, using type tools, the Character palette, or the Text Orientation command.

Enter vertical type along a path or in an object by using vertical-type tools in the toolbox. (See "Creating type" on page 287.)

Change the direction of individual characters or change the entire orientation of a block of text using the Character palette or the Text Orientation command.

Changing character direction using the Character palette

You can change the direction of individual characters or portions of a vertical text block using the Direction pop-up menu in the Character palette.

Changing character direction maintains the original orientation of the text (for example, vertical text remains in a vertical orientation), but the direction of the individual character or portions of text are rotated 90 degrees.

To change the direction of type:

1 Select the text whose direction you want to change.

2 Choose Type > Character. If the multilingual options aren't visible, choose Show Multilingual from the Character palette menu.

3 Choose a direction from the Direction pop-up menu.

• Standard orients text characters in line with the axis of the page.

• Rotate rotates Roman fonts and other one-byte characters 90 degrees from standard.

• Tate Chu Yoko rotates the selected block of text (1- or 2-byte characters) in the plane opposite from the rest of the text.

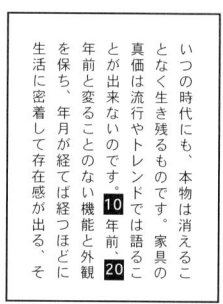

Vertical text in Standard direction and with Tate Chu Yoko option applied

Changing text orientation using the Text Orientation command

The Text Orientation command lets you change text from a horizontal orientation to a vertical orientation, and vice versa.

To change a text block orientation from horizontal to vertical, and vice versa:

1 Select a text block with any selection tool.

2 Choose either Type > Type Orientation > Horizontal or Type > Type Orientation > Vertical.

Using the Wari-Chu (divided note) option

The Wari-Chu option in the Character palette decreases the type size of selected text to a percentage of the original and stacks the type—horizontally or vertically, according to the orientation—on two lines.

Regardless of the point size of wari-chu text, the number of wari-chu lines is always two.

Selected text without and with Wari-Chu option applied

Note: *The Wari-Chu option does not work with path type and does not affect type entered on open or closed paths.*

To create a divided note with the Wari-Chu option:

1 Using any type tool, select the type to be divided.

2 Choose Type > Character. If the multilingual options are not visible, choose Show Multilingual from the Character palette menu.

3 Select the Wari-Chu option.

4 To change the wari-chu type size (as a percentage of the original point size), enter a percentage in the Scale text box (below the Wari-Chu option). The default is 50%.

Changing the shape of letterforms

You can change the appearance of type objects (text containers or text paths) by applying styles and effects, or you can convert the letterforms to outlines that you can edit as paths.

Applying styles and effects to type objects

When you apply styles and effects to type objects, their appearance changes, but the characters they contain remain editable as text. (See "About appearance attributes, styles, and effects" on page 259.)

Note: *You can't apply styles and effects to editable text. Attempting to apply a style to text changes only its stroke, fill, and transparency (and has no effect if the text uses bitmap fonts or outline-protected fonts such as Kanji fonts). The text is not linked to the style and the appearance of the text does not change if the style is modified.*

Modifying letterforms as graphic objects

The Create Outlines command (and the same command as an effect—Outline Object) lets you turn type into a set of compound paths that you can edit and manipulate as you would any other graphic object. (For more information on effects, see "Using effects" on page 271.) Create Outlines and Outline Object are useful for changing the look of large display type, but they are rarely useful for body text or other type at small sizes.

These commands get font outline information from the actual Type 1, TrueType, or OpenType font files installed on your system. When you create outlines from type, characters are converted in their current positions; they retain all graphics formatting such as their stroke and fill.

Note: You can't convert bitmap fonts or outline protected fonts to outlines.

When you convert type to outlines, the type loses its *hints*—instructions built into outline fonts to adjust their shape so that your system displays or prints them optimally at a wide range of sizes. Therefore, if you plan to scale the type, do so by adjusting its point size before converting it to outlines.

You must convert all the type in a selection to outlines; you cannot convert a single letter within a string of type. To convert a single letter into an outline, create a separate piece of type containing only that letter.

To convert type to path outlines:

1 Do one of the following:

• To apply the Create Outline command, select the type you want to convert. Then choose Type > Create Outlines.

• To apply the Outline Object command, select an object or group in the artwork, or target a group or layer in the Layers palette. (For more information on targeting, see "Targeting layers, groups, and objects to apply appearance attributes" on page 252.) Then choose Effect > Path > Outline Object.

If you select type outlines and choose Object > Compound Paths > Release, you can use the outlines as type containers.

To use several outlined letters as a mask:

1 Select all of the letters.

2 Choose Object > Compound Paths > Make.

3 Mask the letters. (See "Working with clipping masks" on page 167.)

Working with columns of text

Adobe Illustrator provides several commands that make creating and working with columns or blocks of type easy. The various features enable you to import and export text from non-Illustrator files, link text so that it flows from one column to another, create sets of columns for text, wrap text so that it flows around a piece of artwork, and speed up the display of type when you don't need to read the text in your artwork.

Note: When you are importing or exporting text, make sure that the fonts used in the file are available on the system where the text will be displayed or printed. Missing fonts and font styles—including fonts that have the same name but different formats (Type 1, TrueType, OCF or CID)—may cause unexpected results. On Japanese systems, differences in character sets may prevent text that was entered in Windows from appearing on-screen in Mac OS.

Importing text files

You can import text files into the Adobe Illustrator program from other applications. Use the Open command to import text into a new file, or use the Place command to import type into the current file. (See "Opening and placing artwork" on page 73.)

Most of the styles used in the original file are retained. If the original text is word wrapped and you import it as a point-type object, each paragraph appears on a single line. Font information is not retained for text-only (.txt) files.

If the imported text uses an outline font that is not available on your system, a message appears. If you choose to import the text, letterforms in the missing font are converted to compound paths. (See "Modifying letterforms as graphic objects" on page 303.) You can modify these paths as graphic objects, but you can't edit them as text.

Note: You can paste text cut from another application that is now on the Clipboard. However, the styles and fonts are not retained.

To import text using the Place command:

1 Select any type tool and define the point or area in which you want the imported text to appear. If no point is defined, Illustrator places the imported text into a box in the center of the window.

2 Choose File > Place.

3 Select the text file you want to open, and click Place. The text from the file you select flows into the type container.

Exporting text files

The Export command exports text from point type, type paths, and type containers to a new text file in one of many file formats supported by Illustrator (for example, Microsoft Word or Rich Text Format).

To export text:

1 Using a type tool, select the text to export.

2 Choose File > Export.

3 Select the desired file format in the Export File pop-up menu.

4 Enter the name of the new text file in the name box, and click Save.

Displaying overflow text

If a type container is too small, you cannot see all of the text within it. You can adjust the type container so that all of the text is visible.

To display all text:

Do one of the following:

• Adjust the size of the type container.

• Link the type container to another type container so that the overflow text flows into the second type container. Create one or more copies of the type container, if necessary.

Linking type containers

You can link type containers created with the type tool or the area-type tool. When you link type containers, the text flows from one type container to another to fill in blank areas in one type container. Thus, the text can fill several different objects, such as several columns or several irregular shapes.

Type flows from one object to another based on the type container's stacking order. Type flows first into the backmost object in the stacking order and continues to the next object in the stacking order. The most recently created object is frontmost. (See "Stacking objects" on page 131.)

The following options are available when working with linked type containers:

• You can change the order in which type flows by changing the stacking order of type containers using the Send to Front and Send to Back commands. You can adjust the stacking order before or after linking type.

• If you are working with type containers and you run out of room in a container, you can create a copy of the container for overflow type.

• You can also unlink type containers to change their stacking order without affecting the flow of type. Unlinking does not return the type to its original object and does not reflow the text. To return it to its original object, you must cut and paste the type. If you want to delete a single or unlinked type container without deleting the type within it, copy and paste the text elsewhere, and then delete the container.

To create a linked copy of a type container:

1 If you are not already in Outline view, choose View > Outline.

2 Select the group-selection tool (▶︎⁺) and position the pointer on the type container. Make sure the baselines aren't selected.

3 Alt-drag (Windows) or Option-drag (Mac OS) the copy of the container to its new position. Shift-drag to constrain the tool to multiples of 45 degrees.

4 When the new type container is in position, release the mouse button, and then Shift+Alt (Windows) or Shift+Option (Mac OS). You must release the mouse button *before* you release the keys.

The type flows from the first type container to the second, and the two type containers are linked.

You can choose Object > Transform > Transform Again to create additional columns.

To link or unlink type containers:

1 Select the selection tool (▶︎).

2 Drag a marquee through the type containers to be linked, or Shift-click with the selection tool. The baselines should be selected.

3 Choose either Type > Blocks > Link or Type > Blocks > Unlink.

To remove or replace a linked type container without deleting the type:

1 Select the group-selection tool (▶︎⁺).

2 Click the edge of the type container you want to remove.

3 Click Delete. The type container you selected disappears, and the type that it contained flows into the next grouped or linked object in the stacking order.

4 To add a new type container, create or select a type container, select the group-selection tool, and Shift-click the type container to which you want to link the new type container. Then choose Type > Blocks > Link. The type flows into the new type container.

Creating rows and columns

By using the Rows & Columns dialog box, you can divide rectangles and text blocks into blocks of rows and columns and precisely change the height, width, and gutter size between rows and columns. The Rows & Columns dialog box can also be used to change the way in which text flows (from left-to-right or right-to-left for both vertical and horizontal text) by clicking the Text Flow buttons.

It is also possible to create rows and columns of linked type containers. (See "Linking type containers" on page 306.)

Because the rows and columns created are simply graphic objects unless they contain type, you can also use the Rows & Columns dialog box to create rectangles. Select an existing rectangle and divide it into multiple rectangles using the dialog box.

In addition, using the Rows & Columns dialog box is a fast way to create guides for laying out artwork. (See "Using guides" on page 118.)

To divide a rectangular graphic object or type container into rows and columns:

1 Using the selection tool ( ), select a rectangle or type container. If the selected object is not rectangular, it is converted into rows and columns based on the object's rectangular bounding box.

2 Choose Type > Rows & Columns.

3 Enter the number of columns you want in the Number (Columns) text box, and the number of rows you want in the Number (Rows) text box. You can either enter the number in the text boxes or use the buttons on the sides of the text boxes to increase or decrease the values. The dialog box adjusts the column-width and row-height values to fill the selected text box.

4 Change the dimensions of the column width, row height, column gutter, row gutter, or overall width and height by entering a new value in the corresponding text box or by using the buttons to increase or decrease the values.

5 Do any of the following:

• To change the direction of vertical or horizontal text flow from left-to-right or right-to-left, click the Text Flow buttons.

• To preview the effect, select Preview.

• To add path guides along the row and column edges, select Add Guides.

6 Click OK.

Wrapping type around a graphic object

You can make type wrap around a graphic object (except a brush object), including type paths and compound paths, by using the Make Wrap command. You must use area type when wrapping type around a path; point type and path type do not wrap around an object. You can make one or several type containers wrap around any number of objects.

To wrap type around a graphic object:

1 Make sure that the object or objects around which you want to wrap type are in front of the type. If necessary, use either the Bring to Front or Paste in Front command to position the objects in front.

2 If desired, use any of the drawing tools to outline a graphic boundary for the area around which the type wraps. (This is necessary if you want to wrap text around a placed EPS file or bitmap image.) If the boundary is stroked or filled, it must be behind the graphic element but in front of the type.

You can use an unpainted graphic boundary to control how closely type wraps around an object. A boundary is useful to wrap type around a large type container consisting of a single piece of type, such as a large initial capital letter. You can then adjust and resize the unpainted boundary using a selection tool to achieve the exact kind of text wrap you want.

3 Using the selection tool (▶), select the type containers that you want to wrap and the graphic object around which to wrap them.

4 Choose Type > Wrap > Make. The type wraps around the graphic object.

To separate a wrapped type container from a graphic object:

1 Select the type container or graphic object.

2 Choose Type > Wrap > Release.

Greeking type below a specified font size

Adobe Illustrator *greeks*—displays as a dimmed bar—type below a specified type size, as set in the Greeking Limit text box in the Type & Auto Tracing Preferences dialog box. Any type at or below the specified type size is replaced on-screen with non-letterforms that act as placeholders in the artwork. Greeking type affects only artwork displayed on-screen, not the printed image.

In addition, if you reduce the document view so that type on-screen falls below the greek type limit, the type appears greeked. For example, if the greek type limit is set at 6 points, 12-point type viewed at a 50% zoom level appears greeked.

To set the greek type limit:

1 Choose Edit > Preferences > Type & Auto Tracing.

2 Enter a value in points in the Greeking text box, and click OK.

Formatting columns and paragraphs

The Paragraph palette includes a number of features especially useful for working with larger groups of type, such as type laid out within columns. These functions enable you to set the paragraph indentation and text alignment, change the amount of space between paragraphs, set tab marks, and fit type to fill a set width. You can even specify where words break in paragraphs, using the hyphenation feature.

To open the Paragraph palette:

Choose Type > Paragraph. If the paragraph options are not visible, choose Show Options from the Paragraph palette menu.

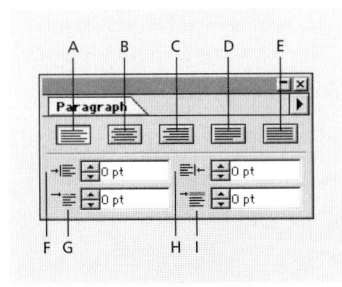

A. Align left B. Align center C. Align right D. Justify full lines E. Justify all lines F. Left indent G. First line left indent H. Right indent I. Space before paragraph

Specifying paragraph indentation

Indentation specifies the amount of space between the ends of each line of type and the path that contains that type. You can indent from the left or the right side of the path, and you can choose additional indentation for the first line of a paragraph. Negative indentation moves the type outside the margin.

Note: The First line left indent and the Left indent on the Paragraph palette also appear on the Tab Ruler palette as small triangles. (See "Using the Tab Ruler palette" on page 315.)

Indentation is measured in the units specified in the Type pop-up menu in the Units & Undo Preferences dialog box and is selected using the Paragraph palette.

Indentation affects only the selected paragraph or paragraphs, so you can easily set different indentations for paragraphs.

To specify paragraph indentation:

1 Select any type container or type path using a selection tool, or set an insertion point, or select a block of type using the type tools.

2 Choose Type > Paragraph.

3 Select the indentation text box you want to change: Left indent, Right indent, or First line left indent.

4 Enter an indentation value.

To create a first line hanging indentation, type a negative value in the First line left indent text box.

5 Press Enter, Return, or Tab.

Specifying alignment options

Alignment controls how lines of type are arranged in paragraphs. Each paragraph (or line in point type) can be aligned left, right, centered, or justified.

Justify All Lines justifies all the type and forces the last line in a paragraph to be justified to both margins. By default, the last line of a justified paragraph is left aligned with a ragged right margin.

To change alignment options from the Paragraph palette:

1 Do one of the following:

• Select any type container or type path using a selection tool.

• Set an insertion point or select a block of type using the type tools.

2 Choose Type > Paragraph.

3 Click the alignment style you want.

Specifying hanging punctuation

Hanging punctuation controls whether punctuation marks fall inside or outside the margins. Hanging punctuation is controlled by the Hang Punctuation option in the Paragraph palette. If hanging punctuation is turned on, the following characters appear outside the margins: periods, commas, single-quotation marks, double-quotation marks, apostrophes, hyphens, em dashes, en dashes, colons, and semicolons.

Punctuation hangs when text is aligned right, aligned left, centered, or justified. When a punctuation character is followed by an end quotation mark, both characters hang.

If you select Hang Punctuation on 2-byte text, punctuation hangs only when there is no room to adjust spacing and prevent hanging; otherwise, punctuation does not hang. You can ensure that punctuation always hangs by also deselecting the Punctuation Hangs Only If Space Unavailable option in the Paragraph palette menu. (See "Using the Kinsoku Shori (line breaking) option" on page 312.)

To select hanging punctuation:

1 Select any type container or type path using a selection tool, or set an insertion point, or select a block of type using the type tools.

2 Choose Type > Paragraph. If the paragraph options are not visible, choose Show Options from the Paragraph palette menu.

3 Select the Hang Punctuation option.

Specifying spacing options

Spacing options control the word spacing and letterspacing in lines of justified or unjustified type. In unjustified type, you can adjust the word spacing without affecting the letterspacing. The Word Spacing and Letter Spacing options apply primarily to justified type, although you can also apply spacing to unjustified type.

Spacing options are always applied to an entire paragraph. To adjust the spacing in a few characters but not an entire paragraph, use the Tracking option.

To change spacing in type:

1 Select any type container or type path using a selection tool, or set an insertion point.

2 Choose Type > Paragraph. If the Word Spacing and the Letter Spacing options are not visible, choose Show Options from the Paragraph palette menu.

3 Do one of the following:

• To change the amount of space between words in a line of type, enter minimum, desired, and maximum values in the Word Spacing text boxes. (If the text is not justified, only the Desired text box is available.) For justified type, the default values for word spacing are 100% minimum, 100% desired, and 200% maximum. At 100%, no additional space is added between words.

• To change the amount of space between letters in a line of type, enter minimum, desired, and maximum values in the Letter Spacing text boxes. (If the text is not justified, only the Desired text box is available.) The default values for letter-spacing are 0% minimum, 0% desired, and 5% maximum. At 0%, no space is added between letters.

Word spacing and letterspacing are both measured as percentages of the width of a space in the selected type size.

Using the Tsume (proportional spacing) option

Most CJK characters are traditionally monospaced; that is, each character is the same horizontal width (and height when using vertical text) as all other characters. Some fonts, however, use built-in proportional spacing to account for differing widths among characters.

You can change the default monospacing to proportional width (and height) spacing for text by using the Tsume option in the Character palette.

You can change monospaced text into proportionally spaced text with the following fonts:

• Type 1 CID fonts (Mac OS), which contain the proportional width data.

• Japanese TrueType fonts shipped with KanjiTalk 7.5 and later (Mac OS).

To use proportional spacing between CJK characters:

1 Select the text to which you want to apply proportional spacing.

2 Choose Type > Character. If the multilingual options are not visible, choose Show Multilingual from the Character palette menu.

3 Select the Tsume option.

Using the Moji Gumi (Japanese layout rules) option

The Moji Gumi option in the Character palette lets you specify the amount of spacing placed between CJK characters and punctuation, or between Roman characters and CJK characters. By changing the percentage of space between different types of characters, the Moji Gumi option eliminates spacing problems that can arise when using a mixture of these characters in a single file.

When the Moji Gumi option is used with the Tsume option, proportional spacing is applied first, followed by the Japanese layout rules.

To specify Japanese layout rules:

1 Select the text to which you want to apply layout rules.

2 Choose Type > Character. If the multilingual options aren't visible, choose Show Multilingual from the Character palette menu.

3 Select the Moji Gumi option.

4 To change the spacing between CJK characters and punctuation marks (such as parentheses) in the text, enter a spacing percentage, from 0% to 200%, in the CJK/CJK text box.

A value of 100% is standard spacing, a value of 0% eliminates the extra space between characters, and a value of 200% doubles the standard spacing.

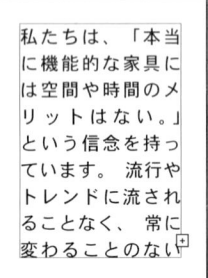

CJK/CJK text setting of 0% and 200%

5 To change the spacing between CJK characters and Roman characters, enter a spacing percentage, from 0% to 200%, in the CJK/Roman text box.

CJK/Roman value of 0% and 200%

Using the Kinsoku Shori (line breaking) option

Where a line breaks in CJK text is generally determined by the boundaries of the text bounding box, the size of the characters, and the amount of spacing between the characters. In general, a line breaks when there is no more room for the next character.

Illustrator allows for control of characters that must not end a line, begin a line, or be divided over two lines. Selecting the Kinsoku Shori option and by using the options in the Kinsoku Shori dialog box, you can control how these characters are handled during line breaking, and you can choose which sets of characters to include. For example, you can have a line of text compressed to accommodate a punctuation mark (such as an end quotation mark), which must remain on the same line as the text it encloses.

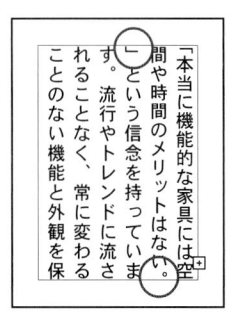

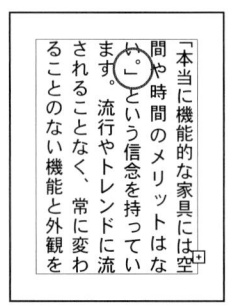

Kinsoku Shori option unselected and selected

To specify a character set for breaking lines:

1 Choose Type > Paragraph. If the paragraph options aren't visible, choose Show Options from the Paragraph palette menu.

2 Select the Kinsoku Shori option.

3 In the Kinsoku Shori pop-up menu, choose a character set to which to apply line breaking rules.

• Hard includes all characters that should not begin or end a line.

• Soft includes a subset of the hard characters. This option is selected by default.

Hard Set
2-byte characters
、。，．・：；？！ー")〕］｝〉》」』】 ヽヾゝゞ々 ぁぃぅぇぉっゃゅょゎ ァィゥェォッャュョワカケ ' " （ 〔 ［ ｛ 〈 《 「 『 【
1-byte characters
,.:;?!-"')]}([{

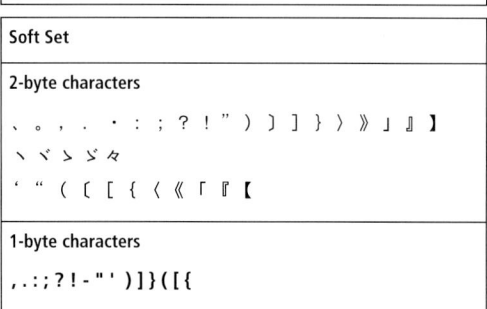

Soft Set
2-byte characters
、。，．・：；？！")〕］｝〉》」』】 ヽヾゝゞ々 ' " （ 〔 ［ ｛ 〈 《 「 『 【
1-byte characters
,.:;?!-"')]}([{

Characters included in Hard set and Soft set

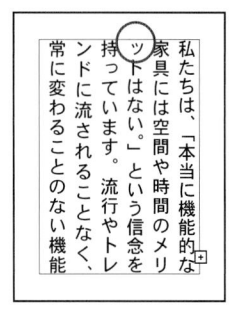

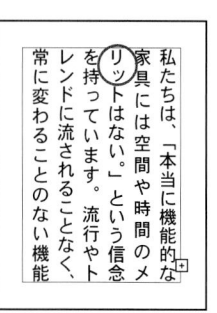

Soft option selected and Hard option selected

Note: With the addition of single-byte characters, the Soft set is consistent with the set included in the Kinsoku Shori option of Adobe Illustrator 5.5J; the Hard set is consistent with the set of Adobe Illustrator 7.x.

To set line breaking options:

1 Choose Type > Paragraph. If the paragraph options aren't visible, choose Show Options from the Paragraph palette menu.

2 Choose Kinsoku Shori from the Paragraph palette menu.

3 Select options to apply to the character set selected in the Kinsoku Shori option in the Paragraph palette:

• Oikomi Maximum Spacing includes the character on the same line and condenses all characters evenly to fit on the line (when text is justified). In the text box, enter a maximum value by which to condense text. When the option is unselected, the character is moved to the next line and characters on the original line are evenly spaced to fill the width (or height) of the line. This option is selected by default.

• Don't Condense Space After Punctuation keeps spacing after a two-byte period uncondensed. This option is unselected by default.

• Bunri Kinshi Moji Shori includes the .. , … , and — characters in the set of characters (Soft or Hard) to which line breaking rules are applied. This option is unselected by default.

• Delete Space Between Bunri Kinshi Moji closes up space between the .. , … , and -- characters. This option is unselected by default.

• Hang Punctuation Only If Space Unavailable ensures that text always hangs. This option is selected by default.

4 Click OK.

About the Punctuation Hangs Only If Space Unavailable option

When the Hang Punctuation option is selected in the Paragraph palette, the Punctuation Hangs Only If Space Unavailable option is available and selected in the Kinsoku Shori dialog box. When this option is unselected, text hangs under any circumstance. If you want punctuation to hang only when there is no room to adjust spacing and prevent hanging, select the Hang Punctuation Only If Space Unavailable option.

Note: When you open a file created or saved in Illustrator 7.0 and the Punctuation Hangs Only If Space Unavailable option is unselected, text in the file is reformatted.

Working with repeated characters

You can control how repeated characters in Japanese text are handled using the Kurikaeshi Moji Shori option in the Paragraph palette. By default, a repeat character mark is substituted for the second character when two identical characters follow one after the other in a body of text. When this option is selected, both characters are displayed if they are separated by a line break.

Kurikaeshi Moji Shori option turned off and on

To use repeated character processing:

1 Using any type tool, select a paragraph of text to which you want to apply repeated character processing. If no text exists, the setting applies to new text typed.

2 Choose Type > Paragraph. If the paragraph options aren't visible, choose Show Options from the Paragraph palette menu.

3 Select the Kurikaeshi Moji Shori option.

Using the Tab Ruler palette

The Tab Ruler palette lets you quickly set left, right, center, and decimal-point tabs in horizontal type, and top, bottom, center, and decimal-point tabs in vertical type (up to 15 tab stops). When you set tabs, a visual tab guide appears in the selected type to help you set them, even when the type path is rotated or wrapped. The units of measure for the tab ruler are defined by the General units specified in the Units & Undo Preferences dialog box (for all files) or by the units specified in the Document Setup dialog box (for the current file).

When using the Tab Ruler for vertical type, the Tab Ruler appears in a vertical format. When used for horizontal type, the Tab Ruler appears in a horizontal format.

To set tabs in text:

1 Do one of the following:

• Select any type container or type path using a selection tool.

• Set an insertion point or select a range of text using type tools.

2 Choose Type > Tab Ruler.

3 Do one of the following:

• Click the Alignment box (Windows only) at the upper right of the palette to align the Tab Ruler with the left margin of the selected text for horizontal type, or with the top margin for vertical type.

• Drag the Extend Tab Ruler button at the lower right of the palette to extend the ruler.

• Select Snap to snap tabs to ruler units as you drag them. You can also Ctrl-drag (Windows) or Command-drag (Mac OS) tabs to turn Snap on or off temporarily.

4 Click the Tab Ruler where you want the tab to appear. The tab position (relative to the left margin of the selected horizontal text or the top margin of the vertical text) appears in the top center of the palette.

5 Select a type tool, and click to set an insertion point in the text. Then press Tab to move the text to the next tab.

To change an existing tab setting:

1 With the Tab Ruler palette open, click a tab mark to highlight it. Click a Tab Style button to change the tab style:

• Left-Justified Tab aligns horizontal text to the left, keeping the right margin ragged.

• Center-Justified Tab centers text on the tab mark.

• Right-Justified Tab aligns horizontal text to the right, keeping the left margin ragged.

• Bottom-Justified Tab aligns vertical text to the bottom margin, keeping the top margin ragged.

• Decimal-Justified Tab places text in alignment with a decimal point (useful for creating columns of numbers).

2 Do any of the following:

• To move a tab, drag it to a new position. As you drag, a line indicates where the tab is moving in the text.

• To remove default tabs, drag to the right (horizontal text) or toward the bottom (vertical text).

• To replace default tabs, drag to the left (horizontal text) or to the top (vertical text).

• To move all tab stops simultaneously to the right/bottom of the selected tab, Shift-drag the tab stop.

• To remove a tab, drag it off the top right or left side of the ruler.

Fitting headline type

Illustrator lets you fit type across the full width of a type path in an object by using the Fit Headline command. The Fit Headline command was designed to work with Adobe Multiple Master fonts by adjusting the weight of the font and the tracking value when distributing type along a path. However, the Fit Headline command also works with other fonts by adjusting only the tracking value. (See "Specifying kerning and tracking" on page 297.)

If you change the tracking value or the type, be sure to reapply the Fit Headline command.

To fit headline type across a specified area:

1 Enter type in a type container using a type tool (T) or an area-type tool ( ).

2 Select the type using any type tool.

3 Choose Type > Fit Headline.

Hyphenating words

The autohyphenation feature automatically hyphenates words where appropriate at the ends of lines. You can set the hyphenation parameters in the Paragraph palette. When you select the autohyphenation option, you can specify the minimum number of letters allowed at the beginning or end of a hyphenated word. You can also limit the number of consecutive hyphenated lines.

You can enter a *discretionary hyphen* to hyphenate a word manually. Illustrator always breaks a word at a discretionary hyphen, regardless of the autohyphenation setting.

You can also specify the hyphenation for a specific word or exclude a word from being hyphenated by using the Hyphenation Options command. In addition, you can select the language in which the hyphenation exception takes place.

To enter a discretionary hyphen:

1 Select a type tool, and click where you want to enter the hyphen.

2 Press Shift+Ctrl+hyphen (Windows) or Shift+Command+hyphen (Mac OS).

To set the autohyphenation feature:

1 Choose Type > Paragraph.

2 Click Auto Hyphenate. If the option is not visible, choose Show Options from the Paragraph palette menu.

3 Choose Hyphenation from the Paragraph palette menu.

4 In the Hyphenate text boxes, enter the minimum number of letters allowed from the beginning and end of a hyphenated word.

5 If desired, enter the maximum number of consecutive hyphenated lines in the Limit Consecutive Hyphens To text box.

6 Click OK.

To specify how a word is hyphenated in Illustrator:

1 Choose Edit > Preferences > Hyphenation Options.

2 If desired, choose the language in which the hyphenation rules apply (to new text typed) from the Languages pop-up menu. When you select a different language, the rules for hyphenating words change to match that language's rules.

You can also change the hyphenation language for just the selected text by using the Languages pop-up menu in the Character palette. (If the pop-up menu isn't visible, choose Show Multilingual from the Character palette menu.) Doing so is useful for hyphenating multilingual projects easily, such as a brochure with instructions in several languages.

3 Enter the word for which you want to specify hyphenation characteristics. If you enter the word with no hyphens inserted, Illustrator never hyphenates the word. If you enter the word with one or more hyphens inserted, Illustrator hyphenates the word only at those places.

4 Click Add.

5 To remove a word from the hyphenation list, click the word to select it, and press Backspace or Del (Windows) or Delete (Mac OS).

Note: Hyphenation information is saved with the application, and not with the file. For example, if you use the file on a different computer that has different hyphenation exceptions, your text may hyphenate differently.

Editing text

Once you have selected type, you can use any standard word-processing method to edit the text.

You can use the Cut, Copy, Paste, Clear, and Select All commands in the Edit menu to copy type from Illustrator to other applications, to bring type from another application into an Illustrator file, or to edit type within an Illustrator file. When you use the Copy command to copy type to and from other applications, you copy only the characters, not the styles.

Illustrator also includes commands designed specifically for editing blocks of type. These tools enable you to check your spelling, find and replace text, modify capitalization, and add typographically correct punctuation marks in your text.

Checking spelling

The Check Spelling command compiles a list of misspelled words in a file and offers a list of alternative spellings. If Illustrator has incorrectly identified a word as misspelled, you can either skip the word without changing it in the file or add the word to the dictionary list. These new words are then added to the custom file AI User Dictionary in the Text Filters folder in the Plug-ins folder. You can edit this list of words as well.

Note: The Check Spelling command can be used only with Roman fonts; CJK fonts cannot be spell checked with the Check Spelling command.

To check the spelling in a file:

1 Choose Type > Check Spelling.

The Check Spelling dialog box displays a list of words not found in the current Adobe Illustrator dictionary.

2 To list separately words that are misspelled in the same way but that are in different cases (such as *Mispell* and *mispell*), select the Case Sensitive option.

3 To see a list of alternative spellings for a misspelled word, click the word in the Misspelled Words list. The first instance of that word is highlighted in your file, and any alternative spellings appear in the Suggested Corrections list.

4 Do one of the following:

• To enter a new spelling for a misspelled word, either click the correct spelling in the Suggested Corrections text box or type the corrected spelling in the text box. To change the first instance of the misspelled word in the file, click Change or double-click the correct word. To change every instance of the selected misspelled word in the file, select the correct word, and click Change All.

• To skip a word without changing it, click Skip. To skip every instance of the word in the file, click Skip All. This option removes the word from the Misspelled Words list, but the word reappears the next time the file is checked.

• To add the word to your dictionary, click Add to List. To add several words at once, hold down Ctrl (Windows) or Shift+Command (Mac OS) while clicking or dragging the mouse to select the words.

5 To edit your current dictionary list, click Edit List and do one of the following:

• To change a word in the dictionary list, select a word in the list, retype it in the text box, and click Change.

• To add a new word, type it in the text box, and click Add.

• To remove a word, select the word, and click Remove.

6 Click Done.

To change language dictionaries in the Spell Checking filter:

1 Choose Type > Check Spelling.

2 Click Language. Locate the language dictionary in the Text Filters folder in the Plug-ins folder inside the Adobe Illustrator folder.

3 Select the language dictionary you want to use, and click Open.

Finding and replacing text

The Find command finds and replaces text strings on paths and within type containers while retaining the type style, color, kerning, and other type attributes of the text.

To find and replace text:

1 Choose Type > Find/Change.

2 Enter the text string you want to find and, if desired, the text string with which to replace it.

3 Select one of the following options:

• Whole Word searches only for entire words that match the text in the Find text box.

• Case Sensitive searches only for text strings that exactly match the uppercase and lowercase text in the Find text box.

• Search Backward searches the file in reverse order from the insertion point to the beginning of the file.

• Wrap Around searches the entire file, starting from the text selection point to the end of the file and then from the beginning of the file to the text selection point.

4 Select one of the following options:

• Find Next searches for the next instance of the text string, without replacing it.

- Change/Find replaces the text string and then searches for the next instance of it.

- Change replaces just the currently found instance of the text string in the file.

- Change All replaces all occurrences of the text string in the file.

5 Click Done.

Changing capitalization

The Change Case command enables you to change text from the current case setting to all uppercase, all lowercase, or mixed case (that is, each word beginning with an uppercase letter).

Note: The Change Case command only works with 1-byte Roman text. CJK Roman (2-byte) text is not affected.

To change the capitalization of selected text:

1 Select a type tool, and select the text to be changed.

2 Choose Type > Change Case.

3 Select Uppercase, Lowercase, or Mixed Case, and click OK.

Using smart punctuation

The Smart Punctuation dialog box searches for keyboard text symbols and replaces them with publishing text symbols. It can also report the number of symbols replaced.

Note: Smart punctuation works with OpenType fonts only in Mac OS.

To replace standard keyboard characters with publishing characters:

1 Choose Type > Smart Punctuation.

2 Select one or more of the following options:

- V, W, Y Ligatures changes any occurrence of the ff, fi, or letter combinations into *ligatures* (that is, a text symbol that combines two or more letters into a single, special character). To change to the V and Y ligatures, you must have the appropriate Adobe Expert font installed on your system.

- V, X, Z Ligatures changes any occurrence of the ff, fl, or ffl letter combinations into ligatures. To change to the V and Z ligatures, you must have the appropriate Adobe Expert font installed on your system.

- Smart Quotes (" ") changes straight keyboard quotation marks (" " and ' ') into printer's quotation marks (" " and ' ').

- Smart Spaces (.) replaces multiple spaces after a period with a single space.

- En, Em Dashes (--) replaces a double keyboard dash (--) with an en dash (–) and to replace a triple keyboard dash (---) with an em dash (—).

- Ellipses (. . .) replaces three keyboard periods (...) with ellipsis points (. . .).

- Expert Fractions replaces separate characters used to represent fractions with their single-character equivalents. To change to expert fractions, you must have the appropriate Adobe Expert font installed on your system.

3 Select one of the following options:

- Entire Document searches and replaces text symbols in the entire file.

- Selected Text Only replaces symbols only in selected text.

4 Select Report Results to see a list of the number of symbols replaced.

5 Click OK to search for and replace selected characters.

Using the Glyph Options command (Mac OS only)

Some Japanese fonts contain information on alternative or historical variants for certain characters. You can specify an alternative glyph for an existing kanji using the Glyph Options command. When you use Type 1 CID fonts (Mac OS), you can substitute a standard character with a variant character belonging to the JIS 78, Expert, and Traditional character sets.

To print files containing alternative characters, the corresponding CID font containing the glyphs must be installed on the printer.

Note: Alternative glyphs revert to standard characters when an Illustrator file is imported to Adobe Photoshop, Adobe Premiere, or Adobe After Effects®. To save alternative glyph information, save the Illustrator file in EPS format (be sure to select Include Document Fonts in the EPS Format dialog box), and then import it.

To specify an alternative glyph for the current character set:

1 Using any type tool, select the character to be replaced. To select more than one character, Option-click the characters.

2 Choose Type > Glyph Options.

3 Select the character set from the scrolling menu in the Glyph Options dialog box, and click OK.

13

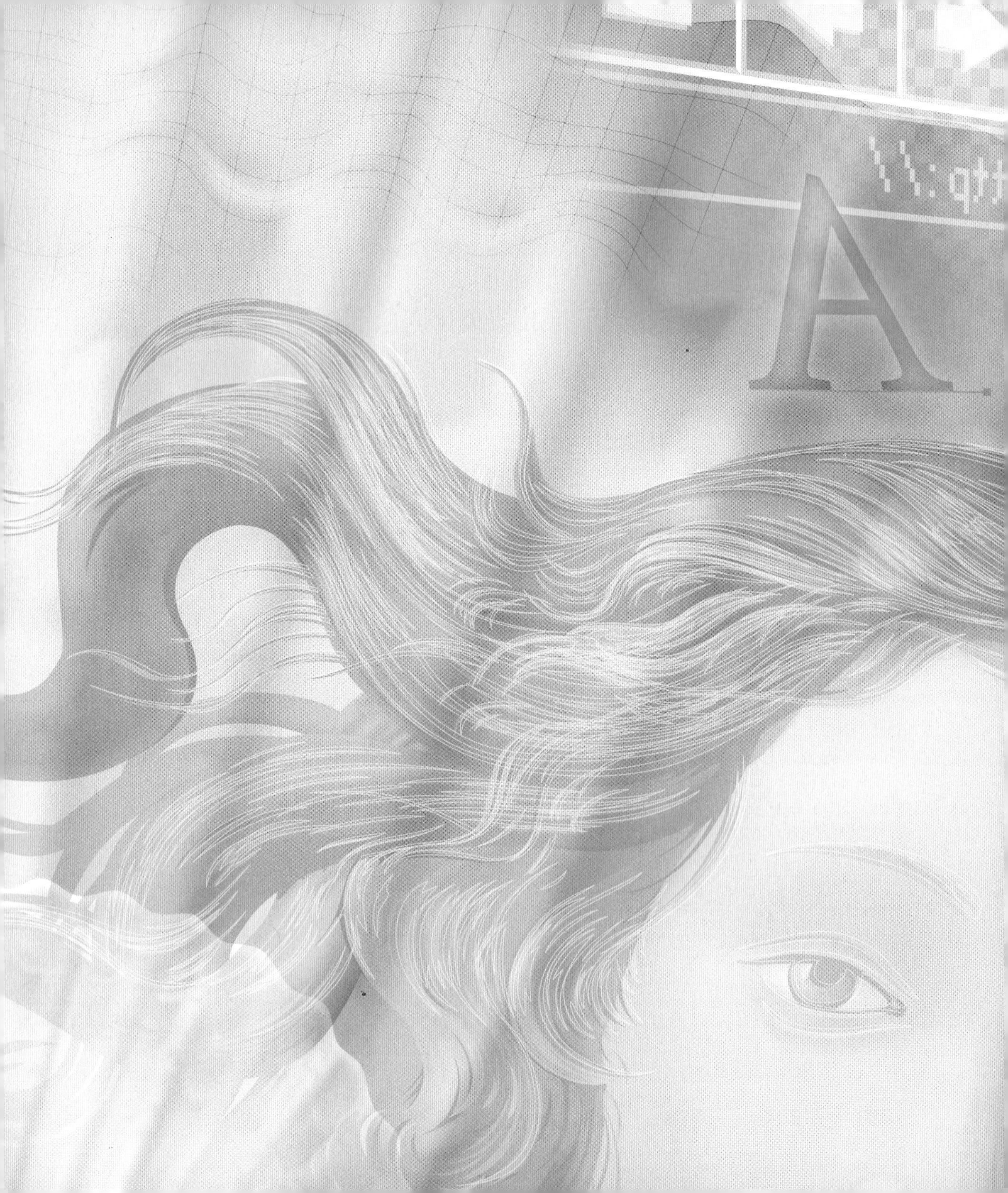
A

Chapter 13: Preparing Graphics for the Web

Creating small graphics files is key to distributing images on the World Wide Web. With smaller files, Web servers can store and transmit images more efficiently, and viewers can download images more quickly. Illustrator provides a variety of tools for creating and viewing Web graphics, as well as optimizing and exporting graphics for use on the Web.

Preparing Web graphics in Illustrator

You can make use of a variety of Illustrator tools to ensure that graphics you create for the Web display correctly in a Web browser. You should keep the following in mind as you prepare graphics for use on the Web:

• When you first start the Illustrator application, you can choose between the RGB and CMYK color modes for your file; if you are creating Web-based graphics, you should choose the RGB color mode. See "Color modes and models" on page 173 and "Creating a custom startup file" on page 190.

• To preview the artwork as it would display if rasterized for use on the Web, use the Pixel View mode. While you are working in Pixel View mode, artwork that you create will snap to a pixel grid. See "Viewing artwork as pixels" on page 326.

• To create a link from an object in your artwork to a Uniform Resource Locator (URL), you can use the imagemap option in the Attribute palette. See "Linking objects to URLs for Internet Web pages" on page 326.

• To apply Web-safe colors to artwork, you can use the Web-safe color options in the Color palette or the Color Picker. See "Using the Color palette" on page 180 and "Using the Color Picker" on page 191.

• To load an entire Web-safe library of colors, you can load the Web-Safe RGB color library using the Swatch Libraries command. See "Loading colors from other color systems" on page 188.

• To export images in specialized Web formats such as Scalable Vector Graphics (SVG) format or Macromedia Flash (SWF) format, as well as other formats for the Web, use the Export command. See "About exporting artwork" on page 349.

• To optimize images in several graphic file formats used on the Web, such as Graphics Interchange Format (GIF), Joint Photographic Experts Group (JPEG), and Portable Network Graphics (PNG-8 or PNG-24), use the Save for Web command. See "Optimizing in Illustrator" on page 327.

Viewing artwork as pixels

You can display your artwork as pixels, so that you can preview how graphics will display when rasterized and viewed in a Web browser. Using the Pixel Preview command, you can view the artwork as if it had already been rasterized, preview anti-aliased edges, and adjust the edges as needed before you save the artwork in a raster format.

When you are in Pixel Preview mode, any objects that you create or transform will by default snap to a pixel grid so that their edges are not anti-aliased. If you do not want the artwork to snap to the pixel grid—for example, if you want to shift your artwork in sub-pixel increments for precise placement—you can turn off the Snap to Pixel command.

Note: If you are working in Pixel Preview mode and want an object to snap to pixels when you drag it, turn off Use Preview Bounds in the General panel of the Preferences dialog box.

To view artwork as pixels:

Choose View > Pixel Preview.

To snap artwork to a pixel grid:

1 If you are not already in Pixel Preview, choose View > Pixel Preview.

2 Choose View > Snap to Pixel. To turn off snap to pixel, deselect the View > Snap to Pixel command.

Linking objects to URLs for Internet Web pages

Any object you create in Adobe Illustrator can be linked to a Uniform Resource Locator (URL) string, transforming the object into a button that links the user to an Internet Web site. This feature is useful when creating artwork for Web pages, allowing you to preattach Web links to individual objects before importing the artwork into a Web page design application.

After assigning a URL to an object in an illustration, you can verify that the URL is valid by using the Launch Browser button in the Attributes palette. If your computer has an Internet browser (such as Netscape™ Navigator™ or Microsoft Explorer), clicking the Launch Browser button automatically connects to the URL you have defined as the object's link.

To activate URL links to objects, you must designate the object as an imagemap using the Attributes palette. The imagemap defines the shape of the button that links to the assigned URL.

You can assign the imagemap shape as a rectangle, or as a free-form polygon that follows the outline of the selected object.

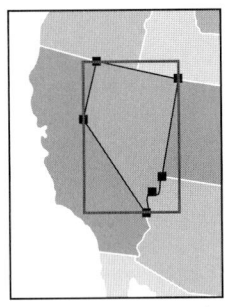

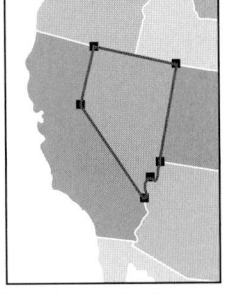

Imagemap set to Rectangle and to Polygon in Attributes palette

Important: *The prefix* http:// *must precede the URL address to ensure that the link works correctly.*

To designate an object as an imagemap and link the imagemap to a URL:

1 Select the object to which you want to link a URL.

2 Choose Window > Show Attributes.

3 Enter a URL in the URL text box, or choose one from the list of available URLs.

4 If you have a Web browser on your system, you can verify the URL location by clicking Launch Browser.

5 Choose from the following imagemap menu options:

• None to not designate an imagemap.

• Rectangular to create a rectangular imagemap around the object. The imagemap boundaries are similar to those of the selected object's bounding box.

• Polygon to create an imagemap that closely follows the outline of the selected object.

To increase the number of visible entries in the URL menu:

1 Choose Window > Show Attributes.

2 Choose Palette Options from the Attributes palette.

3 Enter a value from 1 to 30 to define how many URL entries you want displayed in the URL list.

4 Click OK.

Optimizing in Illustrator

For basic image optimization tasks, you can export an image in Illustrator as a GIF, JPEG, or PNG file. You can use the special optimization features in Illustrator to preview optimized images in different Web graphics file formats and with different file attributes. You can view multiple versions of an image simultaneously and modify optimization settings as you preview the image, to select the best combination of settings for your needs.

To apply a set of commonly used Web optimization settings, you can choose from a range of predefined settings in Illustrator. When working with GIF or PNG-8 files, you can view the color table and manipulate colors in an image.

For information on saving and exporting in other file formats for the Web, including SVG and Flash formats, see "About exporting artwork" on page 349.

Viewing images during optimization

The View options in the Save for Web dialog box enable you to switch easily between optimized and original (non-optimized) versions of an image and view up to four versions of an optimized image simultaneously.

In 2-Up and 4-Up view an annotation area appears by default below each optimized image, showing its optimization settings.

To select a view when optimizing images:

1 Choose File > Save for Web.

2 In the Save for Web dialog box, click a tab at the top of the image display to select a view:

• Original to view the image with no optimization.

• Optimized to view the image with the current optimization settings applied. See "Optimizing files and choosing options" on page 331.

• 2-Up to view two versions of the image side by side.

• 4-Up to view four versions of the image side by side.

Note: When you choose 2-Up or 4-Up view, Illustrator determines a layout for the images, depending on the aspect ratio (width/height ratio) of the image, and whether annotations or rules are shown. Images can appear in vertical layout, horizontal layout, or 2 X 2 layout (two rows and two columns). 2 X 2 layout is available for 4-Up view only.

By default, 2-Up view displays the original image and the optimized image with current optimization settings, and 4-Up view displays the original image, the optimized image with current settings, and two smaller, lower-quality versions of the image based on modifications of the current optimization settings.

You can select a version of the image in 2-Up or 4-Up view to apply new optimization settings. You can automatically *repopulate* 2-Up and 4-Up views—generate new optimized versions of the image based on the selected version. You can also revert an optimized version to the original version of the image.

To repopulate optimized versions of an image in 2-Up or 4-Up view:

1 Select an optimized version of the image in the 2-Up or 4-Up view.

2 In the Settings panel of the Save for Web dialog box, select Repopulate Views from the menu.

Illustrator generates smaller optimized versions of the image based on the optimization settings of the selected version. The selected version and the original version, if present, are not altered during repopulation. For this reason, the Repopulate Views option works with 2-Up view only if the original version of the image is not present.

To restore an optimized version of an image to the original version:

1 Select an optimized version of the image in the 2-Up or 4-Up view.

2 In the Save for Web dialog box, choose Original from the Settings pop-up menu.

Choosing a file format for optimization

The file format you choose for an optimized image is determined by the color, tonal, and graphic characteristics of the original image. In general, continuous-tone images should be compressed as JPEG files. Illustrations with flat color or sharp edges and crisp detail, such as type, should be compressed as GIF or PNG-8 files.

PNG-24 file format is suitable for continuous-tone images. However, PNG-24 files are often much larger than JPEG files of the same image. PNG-24 format is recommended only when working with a continuous-tone image that includes multilevel transparency. (Multilevel transparency is supported by the PNG-24 format but not the JPEG format. See "Preserving multilevel transparency in PNG-24 images" on page 341.)

Depending on the format, you can specify image quality, background transparency or matting, color display, and downloading method.

The appearance of an image on the Web also depends on the computer platform, color display system, operating system, and browser used to display the image. Preview images in different browsers on different platforms and with different color bit depths to see how the images will appear on the Web.

About JPEG format

The JPEG format supports 24-bit color and preserves the broad range and subtle variations in brightness and hue found in photographs and other continuous-tone images. JPEG is supported by most browsers.

JPEG compresses file size by selectively discarding data. Because it discards data, JPEG compression is referred to as *lossy*. A higher quality setting results in less data being discarded, but the JPEG compression method can degrade sharp detail in an image, particularly in images containing type or vector art.

Note: *Artifacts, such as wave-like patterns or blocky areas of banding, are added to a file each time you save the file as a JPEG. You should always save JPEG files from the original image, not from a previously saved JPEG.*

You can create a *progressive* JPEG file, in which a low-resolution version of the image appears in a browser while the full image is downloading.

The JPEG format does not support transparency. When you save an image as a JPEG, transparent pixels are filled with the Matte color. (See "Making transparent and matted images" on page 339.) If you know the background color of the Web page where you will place the image, you can match the Matte color to the Web page background color to simulate the effect of background transparency. If your image contains transparency and you do not know the Web page background color, or if the background will be a pattern, you should use a format that supports transparency (GIF, PNG-8, or PNG-24).

About GIF format

The GIF format uses 8-bit color and efficiently compresses solid areas of color while preserving sharp detail, such as that in line art, logos, or illustrations with type. GIF is supported by most browsers.

The GIF format traditionally uses a *lossless* compression method, in which no data is discarded during compression. You can save a GIF file multiple times without discarding data. However, because GIF files are 8-bit color, optimizing an original 24-bit image as an 8-bit GIF will generally degrade image quality.

In addition, Illustrator allow you to create a lossy version of a GIF file. The lossy GIF format includes small compression artifacts (similar to those in JPEG files) but yields significantly smaller files.

You can reduce the number of colors in a GIF and choose options to control the way colors dither in the application or in a browser. GIF supports background transparency and background matting, in which you blend the edges of the image with a Web page background color.

About PNG-8 format

The PNG-8 format uses 8-bit color. Like the GIF format, PNG-8 efficiently compresses solid areas of color while preserving sharp detail, such as that in line art, logos, or illustrations with type.

Because PNG-8 is not supported by all browsers, it may be advisable to avoid this format for situations in which your image must be accessible to the widest possible Web viewing audience. For more information on browser support for PNG, see your browser's documentation.

The PNG-8 format uses a *lossless* compression method, in which no data is discarded during compression. However, because PNG-8 files are 8-bit color, optimizing an original 24-bit image as a PNG-8 can degrade image quality. PNG-8 files use more advanced compression schemes than GIF, and can be 10–30% smaller than GIF files of the same image, depending on the image's color patterns.

Note: With certain images, especially those with very few colors and very simple patterns, GIF compression may create a smaller file than PNG-8 compression. View optimized images in GIF and PNG-8 format to compare file size.

As with the GIF format, you can reduce the number of colors in the image and choose options to control the way colors dither in the application or in the browser. The PNG-8 format supports background transparency and background matting, in which you blend the edges of the image with a Web page background color.

About PNG-24 format

The PNG-24 format supports 24-bit color. Like the JPEG format, PNG-24 preserves the broad range and subtle variations in brightness and hue found in photographs. Like the GIF and PNG-8 formats, PNG-24 preserves sharp detail, such as that in line art, logos, or illustrations with type.

The PNG-24 format uses the same lossless compression method as the PNG-8 format, in which no data is discarded. For that reason, PNG-24 files are usually larger than JPEG files of the same image. PNG-24 browser support is similar to that for PNG-8.

Like the PNG-8 format, the PNG-24 format supports background transparency and background matting, in which you blend the edges of the image with a Web page background color. In addition, the PNG-24 format supports multilevel transparency, in which you can preserve up to 256 levels of transparency to blend the edges of an image smoothly with any background color. However, multilevel transparency is not supported by all browsers.

Optimizing files and choosing options

You use the Settings panel of the Save for Web dialog box to select the compression file format and other optimization settings for an image. You can also optimize an image to a specified file size, using current optimization settings or automatically generating a GIF or JPEG file.

To view the Save for Web dialog box:

Choose File > Save for Web.

Controlling optimization

By default, Illustrator automatically regenerates the optimized image when you click the Optimized, 2-Up, or 4-Up tab at the top of the document (if you have modified the image since the last optimization), when you change optimization settings with the optimized image displayed, or when you edit the original image.

Using named optimization settings

You can save optimization settings as a named set and apply the settings when working with other images. Settings that you save appear in the Settings pop-up menu of the Save for Web dialog box. Illustrator also include several predefined named settings.

When you adjust optimization settings so that they no longer match a named set, the Settings menu displays the term "Unnamed."

To save optimization settings:

1 With desired settings selected in the Settings panel of the Save for Web dialog box, choose Save Settings from the Settings panel menu.

2 Name the settings and choose a location where they will be saved. By default, named settings are saved in the Optimize folder inside the Settings folder within the Adobe Illustrator application folder.

3 Click OK.

To apply named optimization settings to an image:

With an optimized image displayed, select a named set of optimization settings from the Settings pop-up menu.

To edit a named set of optimization settings:

1 Select the named set from the Settings pop-up menu.

2 Adjust settings in the Settings panel of the Save for Web dialog box.

(The Settings menu displays the term "Unnamed," since the settings no longer match a named set.)

3 Choose Save Settings from the Settings panel menu, and save the settings with the name of the original set.

4 Click OK, and then click Replace.

To delete named optimization settings:

1 In the Save for Web dialog box, select a named set of optimization settings from the Settings pop-up menu.

2 Choose Delete Settings from the Settings panel menu.

Applying optimization settings

To optimize a file for the Web, you open the original file and choose a format and options for the format. You can also optimize an image to match a specified file size. This feature enables you to quickly achieve a desired file size without having to test different optimization settings.

To optimize an image as a JPEG:

1 Open the original file, and then choose JPEG from the Settings pop-up menu of the Save for Web dialog box.

2 Choose an option for specifying image quality:

- Drag the Quality pop-up slider.
- Enter a value in the Quality box.

A higher quality setting preserves more color information but results in larger file sizes. View the JPEG at several quality settings to determine the best balance of quality and file size.

3 To create an enhanced JPEG with a slightly smaller file size, click Optimize.

Note: The Optimize option is recommended for maximum file compression when using the JPEG format. However, some older browsers do not support this feature.

4 Select Progressive to create an image that displays progressively in a Web browser. The image will display as a series of overlays, enabling viewers to see a low-resolution version of the image before it downloads completely.

Progressive JPEGs require more RAM for viewing, and are not supported by some browsers.

5 To apply a blur to the image to smooth rough edges, enter a value for Blur or drag the pop-up slider.

This option blurs pattern artifacts created along sharp edges in the image and creates a smaller file size, but may also reduce image detail. A setting of 0.1 to 0.5 is recommended.

The Blur option applies an effect identical to that of the Gaussian Blur filter.

6 To preserve the ICC profile of the image with the file, select ICC Profile.

ICC profiles are used by some browsers for color correction. The ICC profile option preserves ICC profiles embedded by Illustrator. The option is only available with images created in Illustrator, in Illustrator file format. For information on ICC profiles, see Illustrator online Help.

7 If the original image contains transparency, select a Matte color to simulate the appearance of background transparency. See "Making transparent and matted images" on page 339.

8 Click OK and save the file with the .jpg extension.

To optimize an image as a GIF or PNG-8:

1 Open the original file, and then choose GIF or PNG-8 from the Settings pop-up menu of the Save for Web dialog box.

2 For GIF format only: Drag the Lossy slider or enter a value to allow the compression process to remove pixels from the image (and reduce file size).

You can often apply a Lossy value of 5%–10%, and sometimes up to 50%, without degrading the image. File size can often be reduced 5%–40% using the Lossy option. See "Previewing browser dither" on page 341.

Note: You cannot use the Lossy option with the Interlaced option, or with Noise or Pattern Dither algorithms.

3 Select a color palette, as described in "Selecting a color table option" on page 335.

4 To choose a specific number of colors, select a number from the Colors pop-up menu, enter a value in the number field, or use the arrows to change the number of colors.

This option specifies the maximum number of colors. If the image contains fewer colors than the number specified, the color palette will contain only the number of colors in the image.

5 Select Interlaced to create an image that displays as low-resolution versions in a browser while the full image file is downloading. Interlacing can make downloading time seem shorter and assures viewers that downloading is in progress. However, interlacing also increases file size.

6 Select a Dither option and amount. For information on dither, see "Previewing browser dither" on page 341.

7 If the image contains transparency, choose an option for preserving or filling transparent pixels:

• Select Transparency (the default setting) to preserve fully transparent pixels as transparent. (Partially transparent pixels are filled with the Matte color or converted to fully transparent or fully opaque pixels, depending on the Matte option you choose.)

• Deselect Transparency to fill fully and partially transparent pixels with the Matte color.

For more information on setting transparency and Matte color, see "Making transparent and matted images" on page 339.

8 To automatically shift colors to the closest Web palette equivalents (and prevent the colors from dithering in a browser), drag the Web Snap slider or enter a value to specify a tolerance level for colors to be shifted. A higher value shifts more colors. See "Minimizing browser dither" on page 341.

9 Click OK and save the file with the .gif or .png extension.

To optimize an image as a PNG-24:

1 Open the original file, and then choose PNG-24 from the Settings pop-up menu of the Save for Web dialog box.

2 Select Interlaced to create an image that displays low-resolution versions in a browser while the full image file is downloading. Interlacing can make downloading time seem shorter, and assures viewers that downloading is in progress.

3 If the image contains transparency, choose an option for preserving or filling transparent pixels:

• Select Transparency (the default setting) to preserve transparent pixels as transparent.

• Deselect Transparency to fill transparent pixels with the Matte color.

4 Click OK and save the file with the .png extension.

To optimize a file according to a specified file size:

1 In the Save for Web dialog box, select Optimize to File Size from the Settings panel menu.

2 Specify a Start With option:

• Current Settings to use current optimization settings.

• Auto Select GIF/JPEG to automatically generate a GIF or JPEG. (Illustrator selects GIF or JPEG format, depending on an analysis of colors in the image.)

3 Enter a value for file size.

4 Click OK.

Resizing the image

You can resize the image to specified pixel dimensions or to a percentage of the original size.

Changing the pixel dimensions (and therefore display size) of an image is referred to as *resampling*. When you *downsample* (or decrease the number of pixels), information is deleted from the image. When you *resample up* (or increase the number of pixels), new pixel information is added based on color values of existing pixels. You specify an *interpolation* method to determine how pixels are added or deleted. Keep in mind that changing pixel dimensions affects not only the size of an image on-screen, but also its image quality.

To change the pixel dimensions of an image:

1 Choose File > Save for Web.

2 In the Save for Web dialog box, click the Image Size tab.

3 To maintain the current proportions of pixel width to pixel height, select Constrain Proportions.

4 Specify any one of the following variables (if the Constrain Proportions option is selected, the other variables automatically change to maintain the artwork's proportions):

- Width to change the artwork's width.
- Height to change the artwork's height.
- Percent to resize the image by a percent value.

5 To clip the artwork size to match the document's Artboard boundary, select the Clip to Artboard option.

Note: Any artwork outside the Artboard boundary will be clipped out of the image if you select the Clip to Artboard option.

6 Click Apply.

Selecting a color table option

Both the GIF and PNG-8 formats allow you to determine the color table for the image. This color table then appears in the Color Table panel when that image is selected, and you can make changes to these colors. The color table for an 8-bit image has a maximum of 256 colors.

When you select either GIF or PNG formats, you can select different types of color table formats from a pop-up menu in the Settings panel. The color table formats are as follows:

Perceptual Creates a custom color table by giving priority to colors for which the human eye has greater sensitivity.

Selective Creates a color table similar to the Perceptual color table, but favoring broad areas of color and the preservation of Web colors. This color table usually produces images with the greatest color integrity. Selective is the default option.

Adaptive Creates a custom color table by sampling colors from the spectrum appearing most commonly in the image. For example, an image with only the colors green and blue produces a color table made primarily of greens and blues. Most images concentrate colors in particular areas of the spectrum.

Web Uses the standard 216-color color table common to the Windows and Mac OS 8-bit (256-color) palettes. This option ensures that no browser dither is applied to colors when the image is displayed using 8-bit color. (This palette is also called the Web-safe palette.)

Using the Web palette can create larger files, and is recommended only when avoiding browser dither is a high priority. See "Minimizing browser dither" on page 341.

Custom Preserves the current perceptual, selective, or adaptive color table as a fixed palette that does not update with changes to the image.

Other color tables appear in the menu if you have saved them previously. See "Loading and saving color tables" on page 338.

Working with the color table

The color table displays all colors in a GIF or PNG-8 image. You use the Color Table panel in the Save for Web dialog box to work with the color table.

You can add and delete colors in the color table, shift selected colors to Web-safe colors, and lock selected colors to prevent them from being dropped from the palette.

Note: If your image has fewer colors than the total number specified in the color palette, unused colors are removed from the color table to reduce file size.

Sorting the color table

You can sort colors in the color table by hue, luminance, or popularity, making it easier to see an image's color range and locate particular colors.

To sort a color table:

Choose a sorting order in the Color Table panel menu:

- Sort by Hue. Neutral colors are assigned a hue of 0, and located with the reds.

- Sort by Luminance, or by the lightness or brightness of a color.

- Sort by Popularity, or by the colors' frequency of occurrence in the image.

- Unsorted. Restores the original sorting order.

Adding new colors

You can add colors that were left out in building the color table. If the color table already contains the maximum number of colors (256, or 255 with transparency), you cannot add a new color.

To add a new color:

1 Select the eyedropper tool ( ) in the Save for Web dialog box.

2 Click in the image to select a color.

The color appears in the eyedropper color sample box in the Save for Web dialog box.

3 Add the new color:

• Click the Add Eyedropper Color to Palette button ( ) in the Color Table panel.

• Select New Color from the Color Table panel menu. To view the menu, click the triangle in the upper right corner of the Color Table panel.

The new color appears in the Color Table panel. A small white square with a red center appears in the lower right corner, indicating that the color is locked. See "Locking colors" on page 337.

Selecting colors

You select colors directly in the image or in the Color Table panel to make changes to the colors.

To select a color from the original or optimized image:

1 Select the eyedropper tool ( ) in the Save for Web dialog box.

2 Click a color in the image. A white border appears around that color in the Color Table panel.

To select a color directly in the Color Table panel:

Click the color in the Color Table panel.

To select a contiguous group of colors, press Shift and click another color. All colors in the rows between the first and second selected colors are selected.

To select a discontiguous group of colors, press Ctrl (Windows) or Command (Mac OS) and click each color that you want to select.

To select all colors:

Choose Select All Colors from the Color Table panel menu.

To select all non-Web-safe colors in the image:

Choose Select All Non-Web Safe Colors from the Color Table panel menu.

Note: The optimized image must contain at least one non-Web-safe color in order to select non-Web-safe colors.

To deselect all colors:

Choose Deselect All Colors from the Color Table panel menu.

Editing colors

You can change a selected color in the Color Table panel to any other RGB color value. When you regenerate the optimized image, the selected color will be changed to the new color wherever it appears in the image.

To edit a color:

1 Double-click the color in the Color Table panel to display the default color picker.

2 Select a color.

A small black diamond appears in the center of each edited color.

Locking colors

You can lock selected colors in the Color Table panel to prevent them from being dropped when the number of colors is reduced and to prevent them from dithering in the application. For information on protecting colors from browser dithering, see "Previewing browser dither" on page 341.

Note: Locking colors does not prevent them from dithering in a browser.

To lock a color:

1 With a GIF or PNG-8 image displayed, select one or more colors in the Color Table panel, as described in "Selecting colors" on page 336.

2 Lock the color:

• Click the Lock button ( ).

• Choose Lock/Unlock Selected Colors from the Color Table panel menu.

A white square with a red center appears in the lower right corner of each locked color.

Note: *If the selected colors include both locked and unlocked colors, all colors will be locked.*

To unlock a color:

1 Click the locked color to select it.

2 Unlock the color:

• Click the Lock button (🔒).

• Choose Lock/Unlock Selected Colors from the Color Table panel menu.

The white square disappears from the color swatch.

Deleting colors from the color table

You can delete selected colors from the color table to decrease the image file size. When you delete a color, areas of the optimized image that previously included that color are rerendered using the closest color remaining in the palette.

When you delete a color, the color palette type is automatically changed to Custom. This is because the Adaptive, Perceptual, and Selective palettes would automatically add the deleted color back into the palette when you reoptimize the image. (The Custom palette does not change when you reoptimize the image.)

To delete selected colors:

1 With a GIF or PNG-8 image displayed, select one or more colors from the Color Table panel, as described in "Selecting colors" on page 336.

2 Delete the color:

• Click on the Trash button.

• Choose Delete Color from the Color Table panel menu.

Deleting a color changes the color palette type to Custom to prevent the color from being added back to the palette if you reoptimize the image. To return to an Adaptive, Perceptual, or Selective palette, select the palette from the color palette menu. (See "Selecting a color table option" on page 335.)

Loading and saving color tables

You can save color tables from optimized images to use with other images and load color tables created in other applications. Once you load a new color table into an image, the colors in the optimized image are changed to reflect the colors in the new color table.

To save a color table:

1 With a GIF or PNG-8 image displayed, select Save Color Table from the Color Table panel menu.

2 Name the color table and choose a location where it will be saved. By default, the color table file is given the extension .act (for Adobe Color Table).

If you want to access the color table when selecting Optimization options for a GIF or PNG image, save the color table in the Adobe Illustrator/Settings/Optimize folder.

3 Click Save.

To load a color table:

1 With a GIF or PNG-8 image displayed, select Load Color Table in the Color Table panel menu.

2 Navigate to a file containing the color table you want to load–either an Adobe Color Table (.act) file, or a GIF file (to load the file's embedded color table).

3 Click Open.

Making transparent and matted images

Transparency makes it possible to place a non-rectangular graphic object against the background of a Web page. Background transparency, supported by GIF and PNG formats, preserves transparent pixels in the image. These pixels blend with the Web page background in a browser.

Background matting, supported by GIF, PNG, and JPEG formats, simulates transparency by filling or blending transparent pixels with a matte color which you choose to match the Web page background on which the image will be placed. Background matting works only if the Web page background will be a solid color, and if you know what that color will be.

The original image must contain transparent pixels in order for you to create background transparency or background matting in the optimized image. You can create transparency when you create a new layer.

To create background transparency in a GIF or PNG image:

In the Settings panel in the Save for Web dialog box, select Transparency. The option is selected by default.

Fully transparent pixels in the image are preserved as transparent. If the image is anti-aliased, you can matte partially transparent pixels to blend with a Web page background color. If the image contains alpha transparency, you can create multi-level transparency to preserve up to 256 levels of transparency (in PNG-24 format only).

Creating background matting in GIF and PNG images

When you know the Web page background color on which an image will be displayed, you can use the matting feature to fill or blend transparent pixels with a matte color that matches the Web page background. The Web page background must be a solid color, not a pattern.

You can matte GIF and PNG images in two ways. You can choose to preserve fully transparent pixels as transparent, and matte only the partially transparent pixels, such as those at the edge of an anti-aliased image. When the image is placed on a Web page, the Web background shows through the transparent pixels, and the edges of the image blend with the background. This feature prevents the halo effect that results when an anti-aliased image is placed on a background color that differs from the image's original background. This feature also prevents the jagged edges that result with GIF hard-edged transparency.

You can also deselect Transparency to fill all transparent pixels with the matte color. Fully transparent pixels are filled with the matte color, and partially transparent pixels are blended with the matte color.

To create a matted GIF or PNG image:

1 Open or create an image that contains transparency.

2 In the Settings panel in the Save for Web dialog box, select GIF, PNG-8, or PNG-24 from the format menu.

3 Choose whether to preserve transparency:

• Select Transparency to preserve fully transparent pixels as transparent.

• Deselect Transparency to fill fully transparent pixels with the matte color.

4 Select a color from the Matte pop-up menu; you can select None, Eyedropper (to use the color in the eyedropper sample box), White, Black, or Other (using the color picker).

Creating hard-edged transparency in GIF and PNG-8 images

When you apply background matting to images that include anti-aliasing, a halo effect can result when the matte color is different from the original background color of the image. Anti-aliasing creates partially transparent pixels around the edges of the image to blend the image with the original background color.

When working with GIF or PNG-8 files, you can create hard-edged transparency, in which all pixels that are more than 50% transparent in the original image are fully transparent in the optimized image, and all pixels that are more than 50% opaque in the original image are fully opaque in the optimized image. Hard-edged transparency prevents the halo effect. However, hard-edged transparency can cause jagged edges in the image. To prevent jagged edges, apply background matting to the image. See "Creating background matting in GIF and PNG images" on page 339.

To create hard-edged transparency in a GIF or PNG-8:

1 Open or create an image that contains transparency.

2 In the Settings panel in the Save for Web dialog box, select GIF or PNG-8 from the file format menu.

3 Select Transparency.

4 Select None from the Matte pop-up menu to make all pixels with greater than 50% transparency into fully transparent pixels, and all pixels with 50% or less transparency into fully opaque pixels.

ADOBE ILLUSTRATOR 9.0 **341**
User Guide

Creating background matting in JPEG images

When creating a JPEG from an original image that contains layer transparency, you must matte the image against a matte color. Since the JPEG format does not support transparency, blending with a matte color is the only way to create the appearance of background transparency in a JPEG. Fully transparent pixels are filled with the matte color, and partially transparent pixels are blended with the matte color. When the JPEG is placed on a Web page with a background that matches the matte color, the image appears to blend with the Web page background.

To create a matted JPEG image:

1 Open or create an image that contains transparency.

2 In the Settings panel in the Save for Web dialog box, select JPEG from the format menu.

3 Select a color from the Matte pop-up menu. You can elect None, Eyedropper (to use the color in the eyedropper sample box), White, Black, or Other (using the color picker).

Preserving multilevel transparency in PNG-24 images

When you create a PNG-24 image, you can preserve variable transparency, such as that in an anti-aliased image on a transparent layer, using a feature called *alpha transparency*. Alpha transparency preserves up to 256 levels of transparency in a PNG image. When the PNG is displayed in a browser using a plug-in that supports alpha transparency, the PNG displays multilevel transparency, and the image's edges will blend with any Web background.

To create variable transparency in a PNG-24 image:

1 Open or create an image that contains transparency.

2 In the Settings panel in the Save for Web dialog box, select PNG-24 from the format menu.

3 Select Transparency.

4 Select None from the Matte menu.

Previewing browser dither

You can preview browser dither in a browser that uses an 8-bit color display (256-color mode).

Minimizing browser dither

To protect colors from dithering in a browser, you can shift the colors to their closest equivalents in the Web palette. This ensures that the colors won't dither when displayed in browsers on either Windows or Macintosh operating systems capable of displaying at least 256 colors.

To shift a single color to its closest Web palette equivalent:

1 With an optimized image displayed, click a color in the Color Table panel. Alternatively, you can use the eyedropper tool ( ) in the Save for Web dialog box to select a single color.

2 In the Color Table panel, click the Web Shift button (⬚) to shift the color.

A small white diamond appears in the center of a Web-shifted color and in all Web-safe colors.

To shift a group of selected colors to the closest Web palette equivalents:

1 With an optimized image displayed, select colors in the Color Table panel, as described in "Selecting colors" on page 336.

2 Click the Web Shift button or choose Web Shift/Unshift Selected Colors from the Color Table panel menu.

A small white diamond appears in the center of selected colors that have been Web-shifted (and in all Web-safe colors). If the selection includes both shifted and unshifted colors, all colors in the selection become shifted colors.

To revert Web-shifted colors to their original colors:

Do one of the following:

• In the Color Table panel, select a Web-shifted color and click the Web Shift button or choose Web Shift/Unshift Selected Colors from the palette menu.

• In the Color Table panel, choose Unshift All Colors from the palette menu.

To specify tolerance for shifting colors automatically to the closest Web palette equivalents:

In the Settings panel, enter a value for Web Snap or drag the pop-up slider. A higher value shifts more colors.

Saving optimized images

You can save an optimized image in Illustrator in its current state, and save the HTML file for the image along with the image file. Any URLs that you have assigned to the artwork are saved in the HTML file. The HTML file also includes the image name, the image dimensions, and other code necessary to specify the image for display on a Web site.

To save an optimized file:

1 Click OK in the Save for Web dialog box.

2 In the Save Optimized As dialog box, type a filename, and choose a location for the file. The file is saved in the format specified in the Settings panel of the Save for Web dialog box.

3 Select Save HTML File to save the HTML file with the image file, and click Save. If you have linked a URL to an imagemap in the artwork, the imagemap and URL link will be saved in the HTML file as well. (See "Linking objects to URLs for Internet Web pages" on page 326.)

14

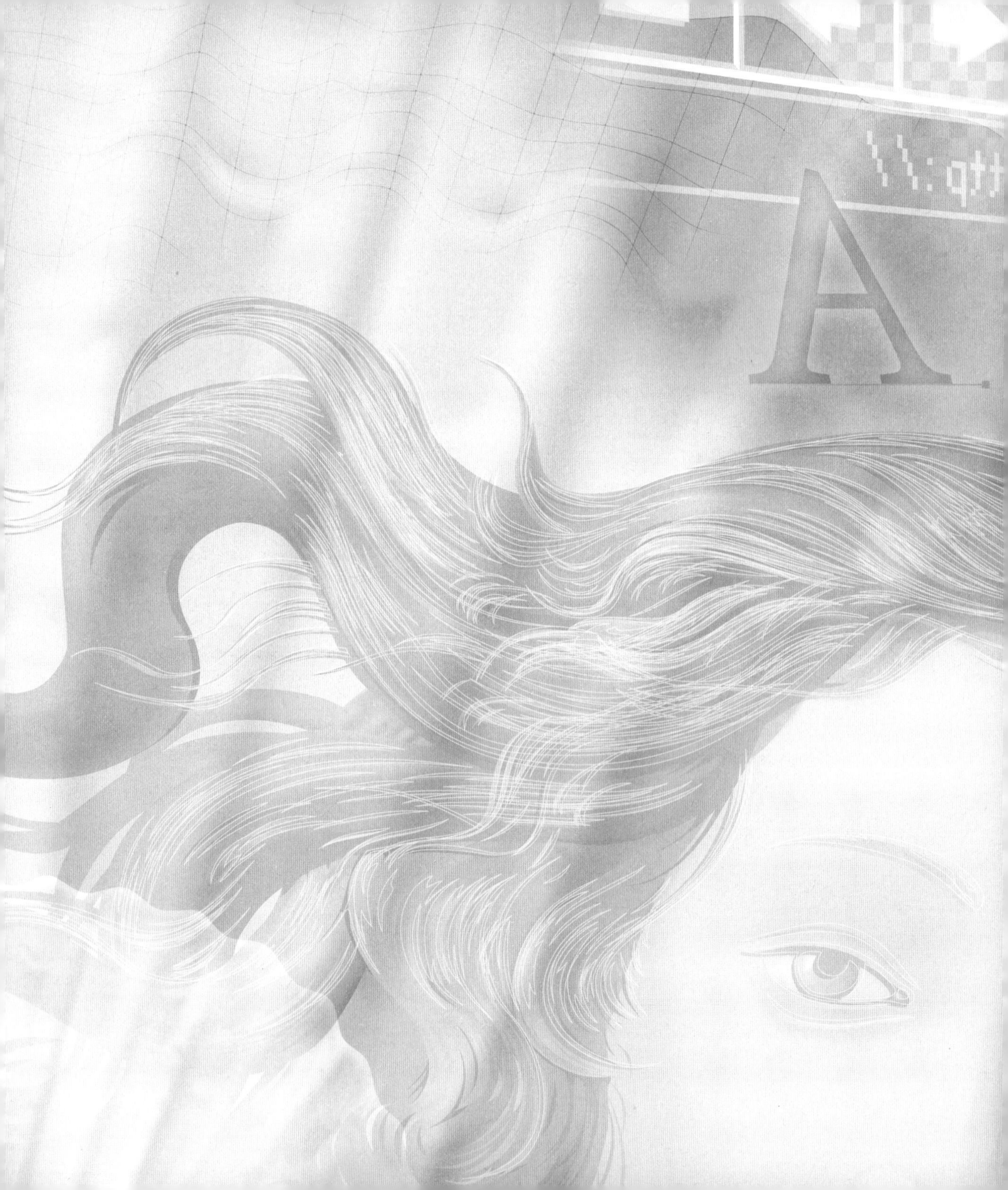

Chapter 14: Saving and Exporting Artwork

Illustrator can save artwork in a variety of formats. You can save in Portable Document Format (PDF) and Encapsulated Postscript format (EPS) using the Save commands, and you can export in a variety of other common graphic file formats. You can also save artwork in optimized Web formats using the Save for Web dialog box, or in the Flash (SWF) or Scalable Vector Graphics (SVG) formats using the Export dialog box.

Saving files

Adobe Illustrator provides several ways to save files:

• The Save command saves the file with its current name, location, and file format.

• The Save As command lets you save an alternative version of the file with a different name, location, or file format.

• The Save a Copy command saves an identical copy of the file, with the word *Copy* added to the filename. This command leaves the original file as the active file.

Saving a file as a previous version of Adobe Illustrator

Many applications can import Illustrator file formats without requiring that the files first be saved in a different format. However, there are some applications that may not be able to import the current version of the Illustrator file format.

Note that many features new to a given version of Illustrator are not preserved when you save the file as a previous version. For example, when saving an Illustrator 9 file as an Illustrator 4 format, gradient fills and layers are not preserved. Text features such as hanging punctuation may not be preserved, causing text breaks and text flows to change. Also, all transparency effects are flattened when saving to all versions previous to Illustrator 9.

To save a file in an earlier version of Illustrator:

1 Choose File > Save As.

2 Select Illustrator in the Save as Type (Windows) or Format (Mac OS) pop-up menu.

3 In the Illustrator Native Format Options dialog box, select the desired version from the Compatibility pop-up menu; then click OK.

A warning appears, indicating that some features may be disabled when the file is opened.

Important: *When saving a Japanese format file to an earlier version than Illustrator 5.5, you must select the Use Japanese File Format option to preserve formats in the file.*

Saving files in EPS format

One common way of sharing Illustrator artwork is to save the artwork as an EPS file. Saving an Illustrator file in EPS format provides the following features:

• Virtually all page layout, word-processing, and graphic applications accept imported or placed EPS files.

• Unlike many other graphic file formats, EPS files preserve many of the graphic elements you can create with Adobe Illustrator.

• Illustrator files saved as EPS files can be reopened and edited as Illustrator files.

• Although most applications cannot display EPS artwork directly, they can display a preview image saved as part of the EPS file. When working with other applications, you can use the preview image to locate and size the EPS artwork. (See "About graphic file formats" on page 356.)

• Artwork that has had transparency features applied with the Transparency palette is flattened according to the preferences set in the Transparency panel of the Document Setup dialog box. (See "Setting transparency preferences" on page 221.) Transparent artwork is flattened if you have chosen the Preserve Paths option in the EPS Options dialog box. Transparency features are discarded if you have selected the Preserve Appearance option in the EPS Options dialog box.

Note: When saving with an EPS compatibility of version 8.0 or less, transparent artwork is flattened. When saving with an EPS compatibility of 9.0, transparency is preserved and therefore transparency features are available when reopening the file in Illustrator.

To save a file as an EPS file:

1 Choose File > Save.

2 Select the folder where you want to save the EPS file and enter a name for the file.

3 Choose Illustrator EPS from the Save as Type (Windows) or Format (Mac OS) pop-up menu.

4 If desired, select the Adobe Illustrator version with which you want your file to be compatible. Keep in mind that certain features, such as gradients and layers, may not be supported by earlier versions of the Illustrator file format.

5 Set the export parameters:

• Select an EPS preview format for the file. You can select between a black-and-white TIFF or an 8-bit color TIFF preview. In Mac OS, you can also choose from a Macintosh black-and-white or Macintosh 8-bit color preview.

- Select either the Transparent or the Opaque background preview option (these options are only available if you have selected a 8-bit color TIFF preview format). Selecting transparent produces a transparent background for the preview image; selecting Opaque produces a solid (opaque) background for the preview image. Users should use the Opaque background preview format if the EPS document will be used in a Microsoft Office application.

- Select the Preserve Paths option to save the file without transparency features such as opacity masks, blending modes, and other transparency options. All objects are reset to 100 percent opacity.

- Select the Preserve Appearance option to flatten the artwork while maintaining the appearance of transparency.

- Select the Include Linked Files option if the Illustrator document contains linked files that you want embedded in the saved EPS document.

- Select the Include Document Thumbnails option to display a thumbnail image of the EPS artwork in the Illustrator Open or Place dialog boxes.

- Select the Use Japanese File Format option to save the file as a Japanese language file compatible with Illustrator versions 3, 4, or 5. The option is not available for later Illustrator versions.

- Select the Include Document Fonts option to force any fonts used in the file to be saved with the file. Protected Japanese fonts cannot be embedded in the file.

- Select the CMYK PostScript option to allow RGB color documents to be printed from applications that do not support RGB output. When the EPS file is reopened in Illustrator, the RGB colors are preserved.

- Select a PostScript format for the file. You can select PostScript Level 2 or PostScript LanguageLevel 3. (For versions of Illustrator earlier than 9.0, you can also select PostScript Level 1.) If gradient mesh objects are included in the file and you expect to print the file to a PostScript® 3™ printer, you should select PostScript 3 to eliminate slow print times or error messages.

Note: *When placing an EPS image containing a gradient mesh object as an embedded file (that is, the Link option is deselected in the Place dialog box), the file should be saved as an EPS Level 1 file.*

6 Click OK.

Saving files as PDF

You can save an Illustrator file as an Adobe PDF file, and also link and embed PDF files within the Illustrator file. (See "Importing EPS and PDF files into Illustrator" on page 75.) In addition, you can use the Preserve Illustrator Editing Capabilities option to format the PDF file so that you can later open the file as an Illustrator file, without losing features such as fonts, color characteristics, patterns, or vertical type blocks.

To save in PDF:

1 Choose File > Save.

2 Select the folder where you want to save the file and enter a name for the file.

3 Select Adobe PDF from the Save as Type (Windows) or Format (Mac OS) pop-up menu.

4 In the Adobe PDF Format Options dialog box, select from the following options in the Options Set menu:

• Select the Default option to use the default PDF general settings and compression settings.

• Select Screen-Optimized to use default settings appropriate for use on the Web. When selecting Screen-Optimized, the file is automatically converted to the RGB color mode.

• Select Custom to create your own customized general settings and compression settings.

To change the general settings when saving a PDF file:

1 In the Adobe PDF Format Options dialog box, select General from the menu below the Option Set box and then select from the following options:

• Select either Acrobat 5.0 or 4.0 in the File Compatibility panel. Transparent artwork will be preserved only when saving in the Acrobat 5.0 format.

• Select Preserve Illustrator Editing Capabilities to export the file in a Acrobat PDF format that allows you to reopen and edit the file in Adobe Illustrator.

• Select the Embed All Fonts option to save the fonts used in the file with the saved file. Protected Japanese fonts cannot be embedded in the file.

• Select the Subset Fonts When Less Than _ % of the Characters are Used option to minimize the PDF file size by embedding only those characters of the font that are used in the document—that is, a subset of the font. This option is available when you select Embed All Fonts. Type the character threshold that determines when a font subset is created. If the percentage of characters used in the document exceeds this setting, then the entire font is embedded in the file rather than a subset of the font.

• Select the Embed ICC profile option to embed a color profile into the saved file. The color profile is determined in the Color Settings dialog box. (See "Producing Consistent Color" on page 199.) This embedded color profile is then applied to the file when the file is reopened in Adobe Illustrator.

• Select the Generate Thumbnails option to save a thumbnail image of the artwork with the saved file.

To change the compression settings when saving a PDF file:

In the Adobe PDF Format Options dialog box, select Compression from the menu below the Options Set menu. Then select from the following options:

1 Select the Average Downsampling at __dpi option in any of the compression panels if you want to set downsampling for the PDF file. Downsampling is a technique whereby information represented by several pixels in a bitmap are combined to make a larger pixel. Downsam-

pling reduces the resolution of the image to the specified dpi setting by choosing a pixel in the center of the sample area and replacing the area with a pixel of the averaged color.

2 Select a compression method for the PDF file:

Automatic 3 The Automatic option automatically lets Illustrator set the best possible compression and quality for the artwork contained in the file. For most files, this option produces satisfactory results.

ZIP ZIP is a compression method that works well on images with large areas of single colors or repeating patterns and for black-and-white images that contain repeating patterns. Illustrator provides 4-bit and 8-bit ZIP compression options. If you use 4-bit ZIP compression with 4-bit images, or 8-bit ZIP compression with 4-bit or 8-bit images, the ZIP method is lossless; that is, data is not removed to reduce file size and so image quality is not affected. Using 4-bit ZIP compression with 8-bit data can affect the quality, however, because data is lost.

JPEG The JPEG compression method is suitable for grayscale or color images. JPEG is lossy, which means that it removes image data and may reduce image quality; however, it attempts to reduce file size with a minimum loss of information. Because JPEG eliminates data, it can achieve much smaller files sizes than ZIP.

CCITT The Consultative Committee on International Telegraphy and Telephony (CCITT) compression method (only available when compressing as a monochrome bitmap image) is appropriate for black-and-white images and any images scanned with an image depth of 1 bit. CCITT is a lossless method. Illustrator provides CCITT Group 3 and Group 4 compression options. Group 4 is a general-purpose method that produces good compression for most monochromatic images. Group 3, used by most fax machines, compresses monochromatic bitmaps one row at a time.

Note: *The Consultative Committee on International Telegraphy and Telephony (CCITT) was renamed as the International Telecommunications Union, Telecommunications Standard Sector (ITU-T); however the compression standard is still referred to as CCITT Group 3 and Group 4.*

Run Length The Run Length option is a lossless encoding option that produces the best results for images that contain large areas of solid black or white.

4 Select the Compress Text and Line Art option to apply the ZIP compression method (a lossless compression method) to all text and line art in the file.

About exporting artwork

To use an Adobe Illustrator file in another application, you must save or export the file in a graphics file format that the other application can use.

To save a file as an Illustrator file (AI), an Illustrator EPS file, or a PDF file, use the Save, Save As or Save a Copy command. To save files in an optimized Web format (JPEG, GIF, or PNG), use the Save for Web command. All other file formats are exported using the Export command. If a file format does not appear, install the format's plug-in module as described in "Using plug-in modules" on page 61.

In addition to being able to save complete Illustrator files in various graphic formats, you can also export selected portions of Illustrator files using the Clipboard and the drag-and-drop feature. (See "Using the Clipboard to copy artwork" on page 127, and "Using the drag-and-drop feature to copy artwork" on page 128.)

File Format	Export Methods	Considerations
AI	Save, Save As, Save a copy	Files may be saved as Illustrator version 3.0 and later.
EPS	Save, Save As, Save a copy	When saving as EPS, selecting the "CMYK PostScript" option prints all RGB colors as their CMYK equivalents.
PDF	Save, Save As, Save a copy	
Photoshop (PSD)	Export	Layers are preserved when exporting to Photoshop format. Use to preserve transparency effects when exporting transparent objects. Drag-and-drop artwork directly into Photoshop (flattens layers).
PICT	Export	

File Format	Export Methods	Considerations
Meta-File formats	Export	Enhanced Meta-File (EMF); Windows Meta-File (WMF); Computer Graphics Meta-File (CGM)
All raster formats supported by Photoshop-compatible filters	Export	Supports the following formats: Amiga IFF, BMP, PCX, Pixar, and Targa.
Flash (SWF)	Export	The exported SWF file may go directly to the Web or may be imported into Flash for further editing.
Optimized Web formats (JPEG, GIF, and PNG)	Save for Web; Export	Save for Web supports JPEG, GIF, and PNG. For CMYK files, use JPEG in the Export dialog box.
Scalable Vector Graphics (SVG)	Export	The SVG plug-in is normally installed with Illustrator. If you need to find the plug-in separately, go to the SVG page on www.adobe.com to download it.
Text Format	Export	Supports .txt format.
CAD formats	Export	Supports AutoCAD Drawing (DWG) and AutoCAD Interchange File (DXF) formats.

To export an Illustrator file to another file format:

1 Choose File > Export.

2 Select the folder where you want to save the file, and type a name for the file in the Name text box.

3 Choose a file format from the Save as Type (Windows) or Format (Mac OS) pop-up menu.

4 Click Save (Windows) or Export (Mac OS). If you are exporting the file to a bitmap format, you may be asked to choose a resolution and bit depth for the bitmap. (See "About resolution in bitmap images" on page 68 for more information.)

Exporting Illustrator files containing transparent artwork

The best method of preserving transparency effects is to export the file to the Photoshop (PSD) file format. Exporting to the Photoshop file format retains the transparency masks and links that were created in the Transparency palette, and also retains layers as they were created in Illustrator. However, only top-level layers are preserved; if you have created nested layers in Illustrator, the nested layers are flattened into the top-level layer.

If you export to file formats other than Photoshop, transparent artwork will be flattened according to the options set in the Transparency section of the Document Setup dialog box.

For information about using the Transparency palette to create transparent objects, see "Specifying transparency" on page 221.

Exporting Illustrator files to Photoshop format

You can export Illustrator files to the Photoshop (PSD) file format using the Export command. When exporting to Photoshop, you can choose to maintain layers as Photoshop layers, or to export hidden layers as hidden Photoshop layers. If you have any text-only layers in the Illustrator file, each text layer is exported as an editable Photoshop text layer.

The same color mode that you have selected for the Illustrator file—either CMYK or RGB—is maintained when you export to Photoshop. Spot colors are converted to the closest equivalent color in the color mode you have selected.

You can also import or place Photoshop files in Illustrator; see "Opening files" on page 73 or "Placing files" on page 74.

To export from Illustrator to Photoshop file format:

1 Choose File > Export.

2 Select the folder where you want to save the file, and type in a name for the file in the Name text box.

3 In the Export dialog box, choose Photoshop from the Save as Type (Windows) or Format (Mac OS) pop-up menu.

4 In the Photoshop Options dialog box, set the export parameters:

• Select a color model (CMYK, RGB, or Grayscale) from the Color Model pop-up menu. The exported file will be in the color model that you select. For a description of color models, see "Color modes and models" on page 173.

• Select a resolution setting for the exported file: 72 dpi, 150 dpi, 300 dpi, or a custom setting that you may enter in the Other box.

- Select the Anti-alias option to remove jagged edges in the artwork. Deselecting this option helps maintain the hard edges of line art when it is rasterized.

- Select the Write Layers option to export each Illustrator top-level layer as a separate Photoshop layer. If there are any nested layers, the nested layers are flattened into the top-level layer during export, unless the Nested Layers option is also selected. If Write Layers is deselected, all layers are flattened into a single Photoshop layer.

- Select the Write Nested Layers option (only available if the Write Layers option is also selected) to write each individual nested layer to a separate Photoshop layer. If this option would result in more than 100 Photoshop layers, only the first 100 layers are exported. If you have applied effects or transparency to any nested layers, choosing the Write Nested Layers option may result in a modified appearance.

- Select the Hidden Layers option to export all hidden layers in the Illustrator file to hidden Photoshop layers.

- Select the Embed ICC profile option to embed a color profile into the saved file. The color profile is determined in the Color Settings dialog box. (See "Producing Consistent Color" on page 199.)

5 Click OK to accept the selected options and export the file.

Creating Web-based graphics using the SVG format

The Scalable Vector Graphics (SVG) format is an open-standard vector graphics language that lets you design Web pages with high-resolution graphics that can contain sophisticated elements, such as gradients, animation, and filter effects. Since SVG exports artwork as vector paths, it helps bring a new level of precision to Web graphics and design.

You can create graphics using standard Illustrator tools and then add event-based JavaScript interactivity using the SVG Interactivity palette. When the artwork is finished, you can export the final design to SVG format using the Export dialog box. The artwork can be viewed using a browser that contains the SVG plug-in.

You should keep the following in mind when you export files to the SVG format:

- You can compress the export file by selecting the SVGZ format in the Export dialog box.

- When you export in SVG format, gradient meshes are rasterized.

- Images in the artwork that have no alpha channel are converted to the JPEG format. Images with an alpha channel are converted to the PNG format.

Using the SVG Interactivity palette

You use the SVG Interactivity palette to add interactivity to your artwork when it is exported for viewing in a Web browser. For example, by creating an event that triggers a JavaScript command, you can quickly create movement on a Web page when the user performs an action such as moving a mouse cursor over an object.

The SVG Interactivity palette also lets you see all the events and JavaScript files associated with the current file.

To add SVG interactivity features to your artwork, you select an object using a selection tool, and then add the event and corresponding JavaScript to that object in the SVG Interactivity palette. For example, you could select an object in your artwork and specify that the object will move on a Web page when a user clicks on the object in a Web browser.

To add a JavaScript event to an object:

1 Select an object using a selection tool.

2 Choose Window > Show SVG Interactivity.

3 In the SVG Interactivity palette, choose an event in the Event pop-up menu to trigger an action. For example, selecting an "**onmousedown**" event will trigger an action only when the user clicks down on the mouse button when the mouse pointer is over the object.

4 In the JavaScript text window, write a JavaScript command that will be triggered by the event you selected in step 3.

5 Click the Add Event & Function button ( ) or press Enter to add the entry to the event list.

To delete a JavaScript event from the SVG Interactivity palette:

1 In the SVG Interactivity palette, click on a JavaScript event to highlight it.

2 Click the Remove Selected Entry button ( ), or choose Delete Event from the SVG Interactivity palette menu.

To list, add, or remove JavaScript events linked to the file:

1 In the SVG Interactivity palette, click the JavaScript Files button ( ), or choose JavaScript Files from the SVG Interactivity palette menu.

2 In the JavaScript Files dialog box, select a JavaScript entry. Click Add to browse for additional JavaScript files; click Remove to remove the selected JavaScript entry.

Exporting in SVG or SVGZ formats

You use the Export command to export an Illustrator file in either SVG or SVGZ formats. (The SVGZ format is a compressed version of the SVG format.)

To export in SVG or SVGZ format:

1 Choose File > Export.

2 Select the folder where you want to save the file, and type in a name for the file in the Name text box.

3 In the Export dialog box, choose SVG or SVG Compressed from the Save as Type (Windows) or Format (Mac OS) pop-up menu.

4 In the SVG Options dialog box, set the export parameters:

- The Font Subsetting option lets you embed only those characters of the font that are used in the document—that is, a subset of the font. Select All Glyphs to subset every font character that occurs in the file (including non-Roman fonts such as Japanese characters). Select the Common English or Common Roman options to subset only English or Roman-letter font characters that occur in the document.

- The Embedded Font Location option lets you either embed the subset fonts directly in the document (which increases file size but ensures that the fonts will always be included with the file), or link the file to the exported subset of fonts from the original Illustrator file.

- The Embedded Font Formats option lets you assign what source font formats are converted to the CEF embedded font format: either Adobe Type 1 fonts, TrueType fonts, or both font types.

- The Raster Image Location option allows you to either embed rasterized images in the export file (which increases file size but ensures that the rasterized image is always included with the file), or link the file to the JPEG images exported from the original Illustrator file.

- The Decimal Places option lets you specify the precision of the vectors in the exported artwork. You can set a value of 1 to 7 decimal places. A high value results in a larger file size and increased image quality.

- The Encoding options let you choose between ASCII characters or characters encoded using the Unicode Transformation Format (UTF). UTF-8 is an 8-bit format; UTF-16 is a 16-bit format.

- The Cascading Style Sheet (CSS) Property Location option lets you choose between three methods of saving style attributes in SVG code. The default method, Style Attributes <Entity Reference>, results in faster rendering times and reduced SVG file size. The Style Attributes method is used if the SVG code will be used in transformations—for example, transformations using Extensible Stylesheet Language Transformation (XSLT)—but results in slightly larger file size. The Style Element method is used when sharing files with HTML documents. By selecting Style Element, you can then modify the SVG file to move a style element into an external stylesheet file that is also referenced by the HTML file—however, the Style Element option also results in slower rendering speeds.

Creating Web-based graphics using the Flash format

The Macromedia Flash (SWF) file format is a vector-based graphics file format for the creation of scalable, compact graphics for the Web. Since the file format is vector-based, the artwork maintains its image quality at different resolutions and is ideal for the creation of animation frames. In Illustrator, you can create individual animation frames on layers and then export the image layers into individual Flash frames for use on a Web site.

You should keep the following in mind when preparing artwork to be exported to the Flash file format:

- Transparency effects such as blending modes and opacity masks are not exported into the Flash format. If you wish to maintain the appearance of a transparency effect, flatten the transparency of the art before exporting to Flash. See "Setting transparency preferences" on page 221.

- Gradient meshes and gradients with more than eight stops are rasterized and will appear as bitmap-filled shapes. Gradients with fewer than eight stops are exported as gradients.

- Patterns are rasterized into small images the size of the pattern art and tiled to fill the art.

- Only rounded caps or joins are supported in Flash. Beveled or square caps and joins are converted to rounded when exported to Flash.

- Pattern-filled text and pattern-filled strokes are converted to paths and filled with the pattern.

- Although text retains many of its features when exported to Flash, some information is lost. When importing the SWF file into Flash, leading, kerning, and tracking are not maintained. Instead, the text is broken up into separate records to *simulate* the look of leading. When the SWF file is then played in a Flash player, the appearance of the leading, kerning, and tracking in the file is maintained. If you wish to export text as paths, convert the text to outlines before exporting to Flash, using the Create Outlines command.

To export artwork in Flash format:

1 Choose File > Export.

2 Select the folder where you want to save the file, and name the file in the Name text box.

3 In the Export dialog box, choose Flash from the Save as Type (Windows) or Format (Mac OS) pop-up menu.

4 In the Flash (SWF) Format Options dialog box, select from the following options in the Export As pop-up menu:

AI File to SWF File This option exports the Illustrator file in its entirety to a single Flash frame.

AI Layers to SWF Frames This option exports each layer in the Illustrator file into its own Flash frame, creating an animated SWF.

AI Layers to SWF Files This option exports the artwork on each layer of the Illustrator file into its own Flash file. Flash automatically puts each file on a Flash layer, thereby placing each Illustrator layer to its corresponding Flash layer. The result is multiple Flash files, each containing a single frame with the artwork from a single layer.

5 Select other options in the Flash dialog box as follows:

- Frame Rate is only available when the AI Layers to SWF Frames option is selected. Enter a frame rate at which the SWF file will be played in a Flash viewer. The default frame rate is 12 frames per second (fps).

- Auto-Create Symbols creates a symbol for each object in the artwork. Each symbol then shows up in the Symbol Library in the Flash application. This option may be used if you intend to edit the SWF file in Flash, since it is necessary to create a corresponding symbol for each object that will be edited in the Flash application.

- Note: When creating symbols with the Auto-Create Symbol option, a duplicate frame is created for every frame in the file to hold the symbol generation hook. You should remove the duplicate frames in the file before your final export from Flash.

- Read Only prohibits users from modifying the exported Flash file.

- Clip to Artboard Size exports the entire artboard (and any artwork within the artboard borders) to the export file. Any artwork outside the artboard borders will be clipped off.

- The Curve Quality slider adjusts the accuracy of the bezier curves. A low number decreases the exported file size with a slight loss of curve quality. A higher number increases the accuracy of the bezier curve reproduction, but results in a larger file size.

- Image Format lets you choose between Lossless and Lossy (JPEG) compression formats. The Lossy option is used primarily for bitmapped images. The Lossless option is used for images containing large solid colors or black-and-white patterns. Users who intend to continue to work on artwork in Flash should choose the Lossless option, so that image quality isn't compromised at the intermediate stage.

- JPEG Quality let you adjust the amount of detail in the exported bitmap images. The higher the quality, the larger the file size.

- Method lets you choose between a standard baseline or optimized baseline.

- Resolution lets you adjust the screen resolution for bitmap images. Resolution for exported Flash files can be 72 to 2400 pixels per inch (ppi). The default value is 72 ppi. Higher resolution values result in better image quality but larger file sizes.

About graphic file formats

Adobe Illustrator can import and export many common file formats. Graphic file formats are distinguished by the way they represent graphic information. Graphic information can be represented as either vector drawings or bitmap images. Some graphic file formats contain only vector drawings or only bitmap images, but many can include both in the same file.

Amiga (IFF) format The Amiga™ Interchange File Format is used for working with Video Toaster and transferring files to and from the Commodore Amiga system. In addition, this format is supported by a number of paint programs on IBM-compatible computers, including Deluxe-Paint from Electronic Arts; IFF is the best export format to use with that program.

AutoCAD Drawing (DWG) and AutoCAD Interchange File (DXF) formats DWG is the standard file format for saving vector graphics created in AutoCAD®. DXF is a drawing interchange format for exporting AutoCAD drawings to or importing drawings from other applications. The DXF format is a tagged data representation of all the information contained in an AutoCAD drawing file.

Note: By default, white strokes or fills in Illustrator artwork exports to the DWG and DXF formats as black strokes or fills.

Bitmap (BMP) format BMP is the standard Windows bitmap image format on DOS and Windows-compatible computers. When saving an image in this format, you can specify either Microsoft Windows or OS/2® format, but your choice is limited to 24-bit depth for the image.

Computer Graphics Metafile (CGM) format CGM is a vector-based file format for the exchange of two-dimensional graphical data. The metafile format is primarily for the exchange of graphical images, including complex engineering or architectural images and complex illustrations. CGM is not the primary choice for text-based artwork.

Encapsulated PostScript (EPS) format The EPS file format is used to transfer PostScript language artwork between applications and is supported by most illustration and page-layout programs. Typically, EPS files represent single illustrations or tables that are placed onto a host page, but an EPS file can also represent a complete page.

Because EPS files are based on the PostScript language, they can contain both vector and bitmap graphics. Like PostScript language files, early versions of EPS files contain only grayscale vector bitmap graphics, whereas later versions support color graphics and compressed bitmap images.

In addition to the PostScript language representation of the graphics to be placed, many EPS files contain a bitmap preview of the graphic that the application can display. EPS files intended to be used by Macintosh applications, for example, can contain PICT or TIFF images for screen preview; those intended for use by Windows applications contain either TIFF or Windows Metafile bitmap images.

Not all applications that create EPS files create preview images, however. When you place an EPS file without a preview image, Illustrator displays a box with an "*X*" to represent the EPS artwork. For more information on importing and exporting EPS files in Illustrator, see "Opening and placing artwork" on page 73 and "Managing linked and embedded images" on page 76.

Filmstrip (FLM) format The Filmstrip (FLM) format is an image-editing format used primarily by the Adobe Premier and Adobe Photoshop applications. FLM organizes images into a long vertical strip containing numbered frames as well as the Society of Motion Picture and Television Engineers (SMPTE) time code.

Flash (SWF) format   The Flash format is a version of the Macromedia Flash Player vector-based graphics format for interactive, animated Web graphics. You can export artwork to the Flash format for use in Web design, and view the artwork in any browser equipped with the Macromedia Flash Player.

PCX format   PCX format, established by Z-Soft® for its PC Paintbrush® software, is commonly used by IBM PC-compatible computers. Most PC software supports version 5 of the PCX format. Version 3 files do not support a custom color palette. For this reason, when you open a version 3 PCX file in Illustrator, the palette is ignored and a standard VGA color palette is used instead.

Portable Document Format (PDF)   The PDF format is used by Adobe Acrobat, Adobe's electronic publishing software for Macintosh, Windows, UNIX, and DOS. You can view PDF files using the Acrobat Reader software included on your Adobe Illustrator CD.

PDF can represent both vector and bitmap graphics. PDF pages are identical to PostScript pages, but PDF files can also contain electronic document search and navigation features. PDF files, for example, can contain hypertext links and an electronic table of contents.

Because Illustrator can open a PDF file, you can use the vector artwork or bitmap images from any PDF file in an Illustrator file.

You can also use Illustrator to make changes to individual PDF pages. To modify a page within a PDF file, open the PDF file, select the page to modify, make changes, and save the modified PDF file. The modified page is restored to its original position in the PDF file.

Macintosh PICT format (PIC)   The PICT format is widely used among Macintosh graphics and page-layout applications as an intermediary file format for transferring files between applications. The PICT format is especially effective at compressing images that contain large areas of solid color.

PIXAR format (PXR)   The PIXAR format is designed specifically for exchanging files with PIXAR image computers. PIXAR workstations are designed for high-end graphics applications, such as those used for rendering three-dimensional images and animation.

PostScript file format (PS)   PostScript is a page description language that is built into many desktop printers and virtually all high-end printing systems. Because it is built into so many printers, most Macintosh, Windows, and UNIX applications can create PostScript files for printing.

The first version of the PostScript file format, PostScript Level 1, represents both grayscale vector graphics and grayscale bitmap images. The second version, PostScript Level 2, represents color as well as grayscale vector and bitmap images, and supports RGB, CYMK, and CIE-based color models for both vector and bitmap graphics. (Some PostScript Level 1 files also represent color with extensions to the PostScript language that were generalized in PostScript Level 2.) PostScript Language Level 3 provides additional functionality to Level 2, including the ability to print gradient mesh objects when printing to a PostScript® 3™ printer. Since printing to PostScript Level 1 and Level 2 devices converts gradient mesh objects to bitmap images, it is preferable to print artwork that contains gradient mesh objects to a PostScript 3 printer.

Note: PostScript Level 1 is not supported for export to EPS in Illustrator 9.0, and is not supported for printing Illustrator 9.0 documents. However, Level 1 export is supported for Illustrator 8.0 and lower EPS formats.

PostScript Level 2 supports a number of compression techniques for bitmap images, including the LZW, CCITT (ITU-T), and JPEG methods.

Illustrator does not save PostScript files directly (though it does open PostScript files), but if you are using a PostScript printer, you can use the Print-to-File option in the Print dialog box to create a PostScript file.

Note: For best results, Adobe recommends that you create PostScript files with the Apple LaserWriter 8 or Adobe PostScript printer driver.

Scalable Vector Graphics (SVG) and Scalable Vector Graphics Compressed (SVGZ) formats The Scalable Vector Graphics formats are a World Wide Web Consortium (W3C) specification for a standard, two-dimensional vector graphics language for the Web. SVG works well with HTML and JavaScript, giving Web designers creative control in designing an interactive and dynamic Web experience.

Targa (TGA) format The TGA format is designed for use on systems that use the Truevision® video board and is commonly supported by MS-DOS color applications. If you are saving artwork in this format, you have the option of choosing the resolution and color depth you want.

Tagged-Image File Format (TIFF) TIFF is used to exchange files between applications and computer platforms. TIFF is a flexible bitmap image format that is supported by virtually all paint, image-editing, and page-layout applications. Also, virtually all desktop scanners can produce TIFF images.

TIFF supports RGB, CMYK, and grayscale color models. It also supports LZW compression, a lossless compression method that does not discard detail from the image.

When you export Illustrator artwork in TIFF, you can choose an RGB, CMYK, or grayscale color model and define the image resolution. To compress the file to a smaller size automatically, click the LZW Compression option.

15

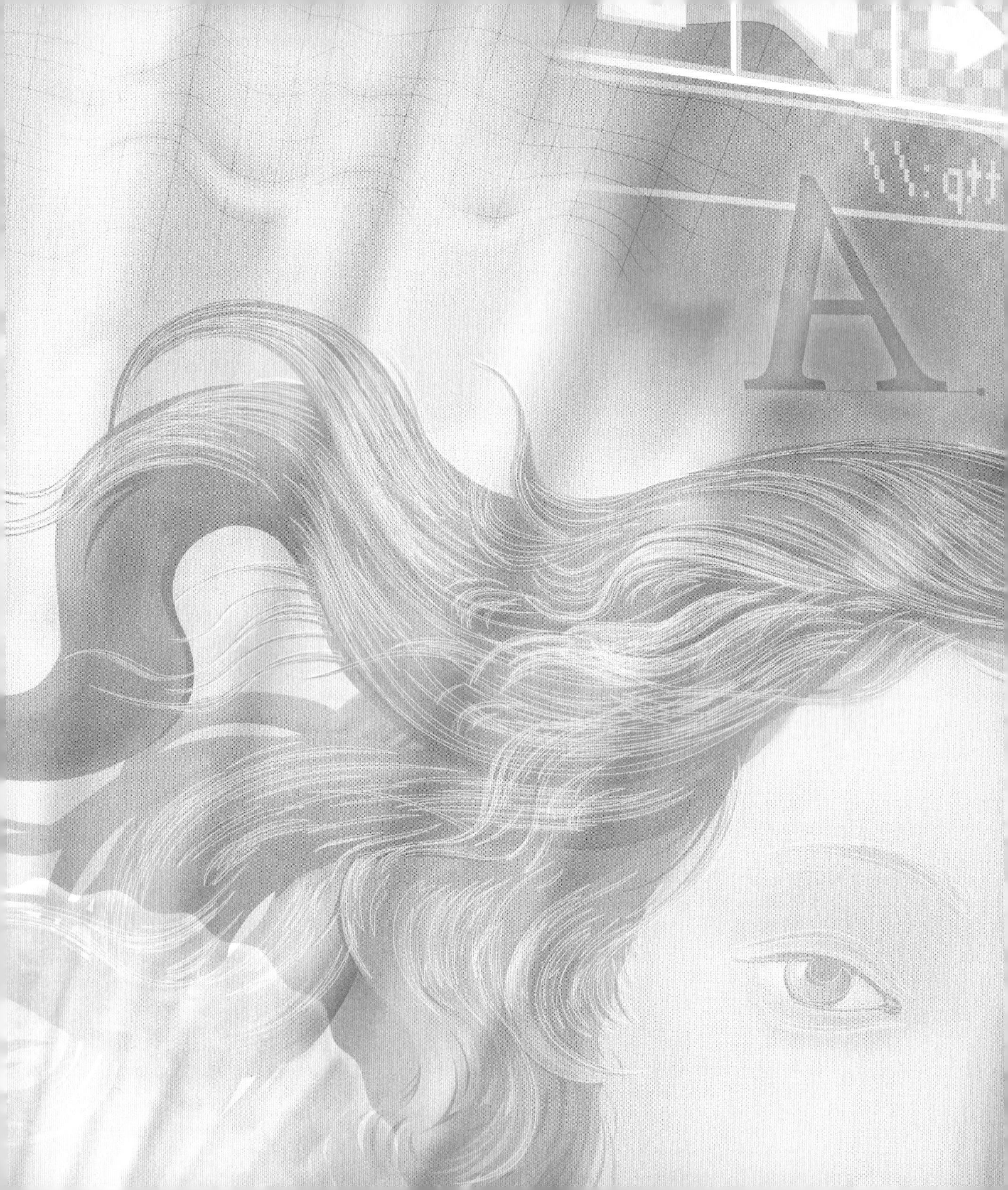

Chapter 15: Printing

You will probably want to print intermediate copies of your artwork as you design it, before you print the final version. To make optimum decisions about printing, you should understand basic printing principles, including how the resolution of your printer or the calibration and resolution of your monitor can affect the way your artwork appears when printed.

About printing

Whether you are providing multicolored artwork to an outside service bureau or just sending a quick draft of a drawing to an inkjet or laser printer, knowing a few basics about printing will make the print job go more smoothly and help ensure that the finished artwork appears as intended.

Types of printing When you print a file, the Adobe Illustrator program sends it to a printing device, either to be printed directly onto paper, to a digital printing press, or to be converted to a positive or negative image on film. In the latter case, the film can then be used to create a master plate for printing by a mechanical press.

Types of images The simplest types of images, such as a page of text, use only one color in one level of gray. A more complex image is one whose color tones vary within the image. This type of image is known as a *continuous-tone image*. A scanned photograph is an example of a continuous-tone image.

Halftoning To create the illusion of continuous tone when printed, images are broken down into a series of dots. This process is called *halftoning*. Varying the sizes and densities of the dots in a halftone screen creates the optical illusion of variations of gray or continuous color in the image.

Color separation Artwork that will be commercially reproduced and that contains more than a single color must be printed on separate master plates, one for each color. This process is called *color separation.*

Getting detail The detail in a printed image results from a combination of resolution and screen frequency. The higher an output device's resolution, the finer (higher) a screen ruling you can use. (See "Specifying the halftone screen ruling" on page 392.)

Transparencies If the artwork contains objects that have transparency features added with the Transparency palette, the transparent artwork will be flattened according to settings in the Document Setup dialog box. Using the Quality/Speed slider, you can affect the ratio of rasterized versus vector images in the printed artwork. (See "Specifying rasterization settings with the Quality/Speed slider" on page 368.)

Printing artwork and composites

You can choose from a set of standard printing options in Adobe Illustrator for any type of artwork you print. These printing options appear in the Print Setup > Properties dialog box (Windows) or Page Setup (Mac OS) dialog box. You can then print the artwork using the Print dialog box.

If you are making color separations, you can print a color or grayscale composite proof to check your work. A composite image can help you to design and proof your artwork before printing final (and costly) separations.

When Illustrator prints a composite, it prints all of the colors used in the file on one plate, regardless of whether any individual colors are selected.

Any overprinting options that you have selected in the document will print correctly on a composite, unless you have chosen the Ignore Overprinting in Composite Output option in the Print dialog box. You should also remember that, as with color monitors, color printers vary greatly in color reproduction quality; thus, composites from a color printer never substitute for proofs made by the print shop.

To select printing options:

1 Choose File > Print Setup (Windows) or File > Page Setup (Mac OS).

2 Do one of the following:

• In Windows, click Properties.

• In Mac OS, select Page Attributes or PostScript Options from the pop-up menu.

3 Do one of the following:

• In Windows, select the options you want in the Properties dialog box, and click OK.

• In Mac OS, select the options you want from the selected pop-up menu, and click OK.

To print a file:

1 Choose File > Print.

The number of pages that Illustrator prints is determined by the View options selected in the Artboard panel of the Document Setup dialog box. If the Single Full Page option in the Document Setup dialog box is selected, a single page prints. If any other View option is selected, for example, the Tile Full Pages option, you can specify a page or a range of pages to print by entering beginning and ending page numbers in the From and To text boxes.

2 Indicate which pages you want printed.

3 Choose from the following options in the Print dialog box (Windows) or choose Adobe Illustrator 9.0 from the pop-up menu (Mac OS) and set the advanced printing options:

• PostScript. If your printer driver and printer support PostScript Level 2 or LanguageLevel 3, you can select one of these options. These options enable you to optimize printing of gradient mesh objects or other complex artwork. (See "Printing with gradient mesh objects" on page 373 and "Additional tips for efficient printing" on page 375.)

- Output. Select Composite to print a single composite color image or Separate to print a four-color separation. The Separate option only becomes available after you have set the separation options in the File > Separation Setup dialog box.

- Data. This option for printing bitmap images to PostScript printers is available only in Mac OS. Select Binary to decrease the amount of data and therefore to speed up the printing of bitmap images, or ASCII to make the data usable on a wider variety of printers and networks.

- Bitmap Printing. This option for non-PostScript printers is available only in Windows. Select Bitmap Printing when printing documents that contain complex objects (such as objects with smooth shading or gradients) on a low-resolution printer. The image is sent to the printer as a bitmap image; although the print speed may be diminished, the possibility of error messages is reduced.

- Ignore Overprinting in Composite Output. This option specifies that any Overprint Fill or Overprint Stroke settings you have set in the Attribute palette do not appear on the composite. With this option selected, overprinting in composites occurs as in Adobe Illustrator 8 or earlier.

- Force Fonts to Download. This option temporarily downloads fonts from the computer to the printer.

Note: If double-byte fonts print diagonally and do not show the correct typeface, the fonts are not stored on your printer. Forcing the fonts to download allows you to print them (with reduced print quality). For better print quality, install the fonts on the printer.

4 Click OK (Windows) or Print (Mac OS).

By default, Adobe Illustrator prints all visible layers. To print an individual layer, see "Making selected layers, groups, or objects nonprintable" on page 250.

Important: Adobe Illustrator does not support PDF Writer format; if you attempt to print to PDF Writer you may experience delays or errors in printing.

Using color management when printing

When you print a color-managed RGB or CMYK document, you can specify additional color management options to keep color consistent in the printer output. For example, suppose that your document currently contains a profile tailored for prepress output, but you want to proof the document colors on a desktop printer. In the Print dialog box, you can convert the document's colors to the color space of the desktop printer; the printer profile will be used instead of the current document profile when printing. Because various RGB profiles are available in the Print dialog box, you can send color data as RGB values to printers.

When printing to a PostScript printer, you also have the option of using PostScript color management. In this workflow, Illustrator sends the document's color data along with the document profile directly to the PostScript printer and lets the printer convert the document to the printer color space. The exact results of the color conversion can vary among printers. To use PostScript color management, you must have a printer that uses PostScript Level 2 or later; it is not necessary to install an ICC profile for the printer on your system.

For information on profiles and color-managed workflows, see "About color management" on page 199.

To color-manage a document while printing:

1 Choose File > Print.

2 Under Print Space, choose an option for Profile:

• To print using the document's current color profile, choose Same As Source. No conversions will be performed on the colors of the document when it is printed.

• To print using a different destination profile, choose that profile from the list.

• To print to a PostScript printer and have colors managed at the level of the printer, choose PostScript Color Management.

3 For Intent, choose the rendering intent to use when converting colors to the destination profile space. For more information, see "Specifying a rendering intent" on page 209.

Printing with Adobe PressReady

If it is installed on your system, Adobe PressReady™ simplifies the color management of documents printed on inkjet printers by automatically converting the colors of documents to the correct printer color space.

To set up PressReady for use with Illustrator:

1 Open the Adobe Print Color control panel installed with PressReady.

2 Set the CMYK setting in the control panel to the same profile specified for your CMYK working space in Illustrator 9.0.

3 Set the RGB setting in the control panel to the same profile specified for your RGB working space in Illustrator 9.0.

To print a color-managed document with PressReady:

1 Choose File > Print.

2 Under Print Space, for Profile, choose Same As Source.

PressReady automatically converts the document's colors to the correct printer color space.

Note: Selecting a printer profile under the Print Space in the Print dialog box when printing with PressReady may result in colors that are not what you intend or see on your monitor.

Setting crop marks and trim marks

Crop marks define where the artwork is trimmed after it is printed. You can place crop marks directly into your artwork using the Object > Crop Marks > Make command. If you select Japanese Crop Marks in the General Preferences dialog box, any crop marks you create in your file will appear as Japanese-style crop marks.

Like crop marks, *trim marks* also define where a printed image should be trimmed; however, you use trim marks to create multiple marks inside your artwork. The Trim Marks filter creates trim marks based on an imaginary rectangle drawn around the imageable area of the object.

Illustrator does not recognize trim marks created with the Trim Marks filter as special objects when creating color separations. As a result, trim marks do not affect the printing bounding box around the artwork. Trim marks are useful, therefore, when you want to create several sets of marks around objects on a page—for example, when you are creating a sheet of business cards to be printed.

To set crop marks directly in the artwork:

1 Draw a rectangle to define the boundaries of where you want the crop marks to appear. (It doesn't matter if the rectangle is filled or stroked.)

2 Select the rectangle.

3 Choose Object > Crop Marks > Make. If you have selected a rectangle as the border, the crop marks replace the selected rectangle. If no rectangle has been selected, crop marks are placed at the corners of the artboard.

Once you've set crop marks, you cannot directly select or edit them. To indirectly edit crop marks, you can choose Object > Crop Marks > Release, edit the rectangle that defines the crop marks boundary, and then remake them using the Object > Crop Marks > Make command. If you want to delete the existing crop marks, you can use the Object > Crop Marks > Release command.

You can use the Make Crop Marks command without first creating and selecting a rectangle to define the boundaries of the crop marks. The crop marks are set at the outer corners of the document.

If you plan to separate a color Illustrator file, you should first set crop marks in the artwork. If you don't set crop marks, by default Illustrator sets them around the bounding box of all objects in the artwork.

For more information on setting crop marks in color separations, see "Step 4: Set the printing bounding box and place crop marks around the image to be separated" on page 388.

To eliminate crop marks:

Choose Object > Crop Marks > Release. The original rectangle reappears to define the bounding area of your artwork. The rectangle may then be deleted or moved.

To specify Japanese crop marks:

1 Choose Edit > Preferences > General.

2 Select Japanese Crop Marks, and then click OK.

To create trim marks around an object:

Select the object, and choose Filter > Create > Trim Marks.

Trim marks created with the Trim Marks filter do not replace crop marks created with the Color Separation Setup dialog box or with the Object > Crop Marks > Make command.

Changing resolution and rasterization settings for complex or transparent artwork

When exporting or printing artwork that contains transparent effects it is often necessary to change resolution and rasterization settings to obtain the best output results. Using settings in the Document Setup dialog box, you can vary the percentage of vector artwork to rasterized artwork when flattening transparent artwork, or you can change the output resolution for rasterized artwork.

Specifying rasterization settings with the Quality/Speed slider

You can specify the degree of rasterization of flattened artwork using the Quality/Speed slider in the Document Setup dialog box. By selecting one of five slider settings, you can determine the percentage of rasterized artwork to vector artwork.

To specify rasterization settings:

1 Choose File > Document Setup.

2 Select Transparency from the pop-up menu in the Document Setup dialog box.

3 Drag the Quality/Speed slider to determine the percentage of rasterization. The settings from left to right are as follows:

• Position 1 rasterizes all objects in the artwork. This setting should be used when printing or exporting very complex artwork with many transparent objects.

• Position 2 maintains simple vector objects but rasterizes most complex areas. This setting is ideal for objects containing only a few transparent objects.

• Position 3 (the default setting) maintains most objects as vectors but rasterizes the most complex transparent areas. This setting provides the best results for most artwork.

• Position 4 maintains most of the artwork in vector form and rasterizes very complex artwork. This setting can increase processing time when the artwork contains much transparent artwork.

• Position 5 maintains as much as the artwork as possible in vector form. However, very complex artwork may still be rasterized. This setting is both time and memory intensive, but usually produces the highest-quality resolution.

4 Click OK.

Note: When the Quality/Speed slider is set to positions 2, 3, or 4, rough transitions may be created between areas that are vectors and areas that will be rasterized on some printers. If you observe rough transitions on flattened artwork, you can deselect the color optimization settings for your printer or print driver. If you still see rough transitions, change the Quality/Speed setting to 1 or 5 before printing to eliminate the problem.

Setting the resolution of rasterized objects

When artwork is rasterized during printing or exporting, the resolution for most objects (except for gradient mesh objects) is determined by the Rasterization Resolution setting in the Document Setup dialog box. To set the resolution of gradient mesh objects, use the Mesh option in the Document Setup dialog box.

Note: Live effects such as drop shadows, bevels and some filters are rasterized using settings in the Rasterize Effects Settings command.

To change the output resolution of rasterized objects:

1 Choose File > Document Setup.

2 Choose Printing & Exporting from the pop-up menu.

3 Set the rasterization resolution of all objects or gradient mesh objects as follows:

• Enter a value in the Rasterization Resolution text box, to set an output resolution in dots per inch (dpi) for all objects to be rasterized (except for gradient mesh objects). The default is 150 dpi.

• Enter a value in the Mesh text box to set an output resolution for gradient mesh objects.

4 Click OK.

Changing the path output resolution

Curves in artwork are defined by the PostScript interpreter as small line segments; and the smaller the line segments, the more accurate the curve. However, when small line segments are used to draw a curve, the total number of line segments increases, thereby increasing the complexity of the curve. If a curve is too complex for a PostScript interpreter to rasterize, a PostScript error can result, and the curve won't print.

The output resolution determines the flatness of the curve: A lower output resolution results in greater flatness, and thus longer and fewer line segments. Using a lower output resolution creates a less accurate curve, but improves printing performance.

Adobe Illustrator prints fastest and best by using a default output resolution setting of 800 dots per inch (dpi). However, in some cases, you might want to decrease the output resolution—for example, if you draw a very long curved path that won't print due to a limit-check error, if printing is slow, or if objects are not being printed at an adequate resolution.

To avoid or correct the limit-check error, you can split long paths, as described in "Splitting paths to print large, complex shapes" on page 374, or you can set the output resolution for that object to a lower value. If objects are not being printed at an adequate resolution, you can increase the output resolution for the object.

Output resolution for all new objects is set at the value in the Output Resolution text box in the Printing & Export panel of the Document Setup dialog box.

Note: You can also change the output resolution of future objects you create with the Document Setup dialog box. Changing the Output Resolution value in the Document Setup dialog box does not affect existing objects.

To change the output resolution of an existing object, use the Output text box in the Attributes palette. When you change output resolution for the object, you set *flatness* for that object. Flatness determines the number of straight-line segments that are used to define a given curve and is based on the resolution of the printing device and the output resolution set for the object in Adobe Illustrator. (See "Creating a printer override (EPSF Riders) file" on page 377.)

$$\text{Flatness} = \frac{\text{Printing device resolution}}{\text{Output resolution setting}}$$

The flatness value is greater than 1 if the printer resolution is greater than the output resolution set for the artwork. For example, if the printer resolution is 2400 dpi and the output resolution for an object is set at 800 dpi, the flatness value equals 3. If the calculated flatness value is smaller than 1.0, a flatness value of 1.0 is used.

To change the output resolution for an object:

1 Select the object for which you want to adjust the output resolution.

2 Choose Window > Show Attributes.

3 Enter the output resolution for the object. (Recommended values are between 100 dpi and 300 dpi for printing at 300 dpi, and between 800 and 2400 dpi for printing at 2400 dpi. The limits are 100 and 9600 dpi.)

Printing gradients, gradient mesh objects, color blends, and transparencies

Files with gradients, gradient mesh objects, or color blends can be difficult for some printers to print smoothly (without discrete bands of color) or at all. There are ways to improve the printed results of gradients, gradient meshes, and color blends on such printers. You can also improve the way that transparencies are printed.

Follow these general guidelines:

• Use a blend that changes at least 50% between two or more process color components.

- Use shorter blends. The optimum length depends on the colors in your blend, but try to keep blends shorter than 7.5 inches. (See "Calculating the maximum blend length based on the color change" on page 371.)

- Use lighter colors or make dark blends short. Banding is most likely to occur between very dark colors and white.

- Use an appropriate line screen that retains 256 levels of gray.

- When the document contains complex artwork, transparencies, gradients, gradient meshes, or blends, make sure that you have selected the right resolution and Quality/Speed settings in the Document Setup dialog box. For information, see "Changing resolution and rasterization settings for complex or transparent artwork" on page 368.

Ensuring your resolution/line screen produces 256 grays

In printing your file, you may find that the resolution of your printer, when combined with the chosen line screen, allows fewer than 256 levels of gray. A higher screen frequency decreases the levels of gray available to the printer. (For example, if you are printing at a resolution of 2400 dpi, using a line screen higher than 150 results in fewer than 256 levels of gray.)

The following table lists the maximum line screens you can use with printers to maintain all 256 levels of gray.

Final Imagesetter Resolution	Maximum Line Screen to Use
300	19
400	25
600	38
900	56
1000	63
1270	79
1446	90
1524	95
1693	106
2000	125
2400	150
2540	159
3000	188
3252	203
3600	225
4000	250

Calculating the maximum blend length based on the color change

Adobe Illustrator calculates the number of steps in a gradient based on the percentage of change between the colors in the gradient. The number of steps, in turn, determines the maximum length of the blend before banding occurs.

The gradient's number of steps and maximum length assume that you are printing the file with a line screen and resolution that produce 256 levels of gray.

To determine the maximum blend length based on the color change:

1 Select the measure tool (✎), and click the beginning point and the endpoint of the gradient.

2 Note the distance displayed in the Info palette on a piece of paper. This distance represents the length of the gradient or color blend.

3 Calculate the number of steps in the blend using this formula:

Number of steps = 256 (number of grays) ✕ *Percentage change in color*

To figure out the percentage change in color, subtract the lower color value from the higher color value. For example, a blend between 20% black and 100% black is an 80%—or 0.8—change in color.

When blending process colors, use the largest change between the colors. For instance, a blend from 20% cyan, 30% magenta, 80% yellow, and 60% black to 20% cyan, 90% magenta, 70% yellow, and 40% black indicates a 60% change, because the greatest change occurs in magenta, from 30% to 90%.

4 Using the number of steps calculated in step 3, see if the length of the gradient is larger than that indicated in the chart. If it is, reduce the length of the gradient or change the colors.

Number of Steps Adobe Illustrator Recommends	Maximum Blend Length Points	Inches	Cms
10	21.6	.3	.762
20	43.2	.6	1.524
30	64.8	.9	2.286
40	86.4	1.2	3.048
50	108.0	1.5	3.810
60	129.6	1.8	4.572
70	151.2	2.1	5.334
80	172.8	2.4	6.096
90	194.4	2.7	6.858
100	216.0	3.0	7.620
110	237.6	3.3	8.382
120	259.2	3.6	9.144
130	280.8	3.9	9.906
140	302.4	4.2	10.668
150	324.0	4.5	11.430
160	345.6	4.8	12.192
170	367.2	5.1	12.954
180	388.8	5.4	13.716
190	410.4	5.7	14.478
200	432.0	6.0	15.240
210	453.6	6.3	16.002
220	475.2	6.6	16.764
230	496.8	6.9	17.526
240	518.4	7.2	18.288
250	540.0	7.5	19.050
256	553.0	7.7	19.507

Using the Compatible Gradient and Gradient Mesh Printing option

Some printers have difficulty printing gradients and gradient mesh objects. For example, gradients may print with a banding effect on older PostScript Level 2 devices. In addition, gradient mesh objects may print incorrectly to some PostScript 3 devices. The Compatible Gradient and Gradient Mesh Printing option enables such printers to print your files by converting the objects to JPEG format.

Important: *Use this option only with files that contain gradients and gradient mesh objects that will be printed on devices that have difficulty printing such files. This option can slow printing on printers that don't have problems with gradients.*

To improve gradient printing:

1 Choose File > Document Setup. Then choose Printing & Export from the pop-up menu at the top left of the Document Setup dialog box.

2 Select the Compatible Gradient and Gradient Mesh Printing option. Click OK.

Printing with gradient mesh objects

Adobe Illustrator 7.0 and earlier cannot read gradient mesh objects created with later versions of Adobe Illustrator. If you want to use files with gradient mesh objects in Adobe Illustrator 6.0 or 7.0, save the file in the earlier format.

Since all but the most complex gradient mesh objects are printed as vector objects when printing to a PostScript Level 3 printer, you can usually optimize printing results by printing to a Level 3 printer. When printing to a Level 2 printer, the gradient mesh objects are written both as a vector object as well as a JPEG image. The resolution of the JPEG image is determined by the Mesh setting in the Document Setup dialog box. See "Setting the resolution of rasterized objects" on page 369.

Note: *Even if you are printing to a Level 3 printer, printing may be delayed if the PostScript field in the Print dialog box is set to Level 2. Therefore, when printing to a Level 3 printer only, you can optimize the speed by setting the PostScript field to Level 3.*

Improving gradient printing on low-resolution printers

When a gradient fill is applied to an object, Illustrator uses the printer's default screen. If you turn off the printer's default screen in the Printing & Export panel of the Document Setup dialog box, Illustrator uses Adobe screens to enhance the output of gradients when printing to low-resolution printers (600 dpi and less) that support fewer than 256 gray levels. On some low-resolution printers, turning off the Use Printer's Default Screen option may improve the output quality of gradients, gradient meshes, and raster images.

Note: *Do not turn off Use Printer's Default Screen if you want to use a printer override (EPSF Riders) file.*

To turn off the printer's default screen, with low-resolution printers:

1 Choose File > Document Setup. Then choose Printing & Export from the pop-up menu at the top left of the Document Setup dialog box.

2 Deselect Use Printer's Default Screen, and click OK.

Improving printer performance

Objects that contain overly complex paths are a main cause of printing problems. A path's complexity is determined by the number of line segments and anchor points it contains. The more complex the path, the longer it takes to print. Before printing, make sure that paths contain only the necessary anchor points.

Here are some suggestions for simplifying paths:

• Use the pen tool instead of the pencil tool, when possible. Drawings made with the pen tool typically contain fewer points than those created with the pencil tool.

• Use the Object > Path > Simplify command to simplify the path. (See "Simplifying paths" on page 95.)

• Remove unnecessary points. (See "Adding, deleting, and converting anchor points" on page 92.)

• Delete stray points. (See "Simplifying paths" on page 95.)

• Change the output resolution. (See "Changing the path output resolution" on page 369.)

• Increase the flatness of curves. (See "Creating a printer override (EPSF Riders) file" on page 377.)

• Split overly complex paths.

Splitting paths to print large, complex shapes

If you are printing Adobe Illustrator files containing overly long or complicated paths, the file may not print and you may receive limit-check error messages from your printer. To simplify paths, you can split long, complex paths into two or more separate paths using Split Long Paths in the Printing & Export panel of the Document Setup dialog box.

When Split Long Paths is selected, the Adobe Illustrator program checks whether a closed path is too long to print whenever you save or print an image. If the path length exceeds what the printer's memory can handle, Illustrator breaks the closed path into pieces represented on-screen by lines through the path. These lines appear only in Outline view; they do not preview or print. The image previews and prints as if the paths were joined.

Keep the following in mind when using Split Long Paths:

• It's a good idea to save a copy of your original artwork before splitting paths. That way, you still have the original, unsplit file to work with if needed.

- Illustrator treats split paths in the artwork as separate objects. To change your artwork once paths are split, you must either work with the separate shapes or rejoin the paths to work with the image as a single shape.

- Split Long Paths has no effect on stroked paths or compound paths. When you use Split Long Paths on an object that is both filled and stroked, the object is split into two objects.

To split long paths:

1 Choose File > Document Setup. Then choose Printing & Export from the pop-up menu at the top left of the Document Setup dialog box.

2 Select Split Long Paths, and click OK. Illustrator splits paths as needed when you print or save the file.

To split a stroked path:

Split the path with the scissors tool.

To split a compound path:

1 Choose Object > Compound Paths > Release to remove the compound path.

2 Break the path into pieces using the scissors tool.

3 Redefine the pieces as compound paths.

To split a mask:

1 Choose Object > Mask > Release to remove the mask.

2 Break the path into pieces using the scissors tool.

3 Redefine the pieces as masks.

To rejoin a split path:

1 Delete any extra lines created with Split Long Paths by selecting the lines and pressing Delete.

2 Select all of the split paths that made up the original object.

3 Choose Window > Pathfinder and click the Unite button in the Pathfinder palette. The path is rejoined, with an anchor point placed at each intersection where a split path was reconnected.

Additional tips for efficient printing

You may not be able to print your artwork, your artwork may take a long time to print, or your printer may simply quit with or without issuing an error message. Error messages include a range-check error and VM error (virtual memory error). Many of these errors are caused by overly complex paths in your artwork.

If your artwork takes a long time to print, consider simplifying its shape. Other tips to help you print more efficiently include the following:

- Limit the complexity of patterns, masks, and compound paths you use in the artwork file. Delete unused patterns from the Swatches palette.

When painting objects with patterns, note that patterns can significantly slow performance. Painting compound paths with patterns or using several patterns in your artwork may slow printing or cause your file not to print at all.

- If the artwork contains ink pen effects, gradients, or patterns that are too complex to print on the current printer, you can print it on a PostScript Level 2 or PostScript 3 imagesetter instead. You can also copy the file and rasterize the nonprinting artwork as described in "Changing vector graphics into bitmap images" on page 275.

- The same version of Adobe Illustrator that was used to create the files must be used to print them.

Newer versions of Illustrator contain various printing enhancements and new text features. Using earlier versions of Illustrator to open or print an Illustrator file strips many of these enhancements from the file and reflows any tabbed text. Make sure that you or your service bureau uses the same version of Adobe Illustrator to print files as was used to create the artwork.

To retain Illustrator 9.0 printing and text enhancements when your service bureau does not have version 9.0, use Adobe Illustrator 9.0 to save a copy of the 9.0 file in EPS format so that it can be placed into an earlier version of Adobe Illustrator or into another desktop publishing program. When you save a file in EPS format, you do not lose any of the printing enhancements or tabs in the file. (See "Using the Tab Ruler palette" on page 315.)

- Limit the number of downloadable typefaces you use in the artwork file.

About the EPSF Riders file

The EPSF Riders file sets the screen frequency, angle, spot function, and flatness for all files, or adds an annotation or an error handler message to all files. The settings you specify in the EPSF Riders file override any settings you specified using the Separation Setup dialog box. Before you can create an EPSF Riders file, you must move the EPSF Riders plug-in into the Plug-ins folder.

To use the EPSF Riders plug-in:

1 Move the Riders plug-in into the Plug-ins folder. The Riders plug-in is located in the Riders Folder, within the Utilities folder.

2 Once you have moved the Riders plug-in to the Plug-ins folder, quit Illustrator and then restart the program. Restarting the program acknowledges the presence of the Riders plug-in the Plug-ins folder.

Once the Riders plug-in is in your directory or Plug-ins folder and you have created an EPSF Riders file, all files saved or printed from Illustrator are affected. To remove the EPSF Riders information from your files, you can either delete the Adobe Illustrator EPSF Riders file or move it out of the Plug-ins folder, and then resave all the files that contain the embedded Riders information.

Creating a printer override (EPSF Riders) file

The Make Riders filter creates an Adobe Illustrator EPSF Riders file. The EPSF Riders file contains PostScript code that, when added to an Adobe Illustrator file, overrides how a file prints. The Delete Riders filter removes the EPSF Riders file from your system. Only one file, named EPSF Riders, is created when you choose the Make Riders filter. You cannot create multiple Riders files, and you must not change the name of the EPSF Riders file.

To create an EPSF Riders file:

1 Choose Filter > Other > Make Riders.

Note: If you haven't moved the Riders plug-in into the Plug-ins folder, the Other category does not appear in the Filter menu. If necessary, follow the steps in the previous section to move the Riders plug-in into the correct location.

2 Do any of the following:

• Choose a screen frequency, or *line screen*, to designate the number of rows of halftone dots per inch when printing. The screen frequency value must be between 1 and 999.

• Choose a screen angle to determine the angle at which the rows of halftone dots print. (The default setting for black-and-white printing, 45 degrees, is intended to make the dot rows less conspicuous to the eye.) The screen angle value must be between 0 and 360.

• Choose a spot function to determine the halftone dot's shape. Choose Import from the Spot Function pop-up menu to select and import a spot function.

Important: An imported spot function must be in PostScript language, correctly formatted. Importing an incorrectly formatted spot function can make a file unprintable. See the Spot Function Template file, located in the Utilities/Riders folder.

• Choose a flatness setting to simplify complex paths. The Riders flatness setting must be between 0.2 and 200 and is applied to all curves in an Illustrator file.

Note: The Riders flatness setting overrides the output resolution setting and is not recommended in most cases. (See "Changing the path output resolution" on page 369.)

• Choose Setup from the Annotation pop-up menu, and enter an annotation of up to 254 characters. The annotation appears at the bottom left corner of the printed page.

• Choose Error Handler to print error information on the page if a PostScript error occurs. If you are using the Adobe PSPrinter™ or the LaserWriter 8.0 or later printer driver, turn on the printer driver's error handling instead of the Riders' error handler.

3 When you have selected the options you want, click Make.

Important: Do not rename the EPSF Riders file. (The name Adobe Illustrator EPSF Riders *is selected by default.) If you change the name, Illustrator ignores the file.*

4 Save the EPSF Riders file in the Plug-ins folder.

To delete the Riders file:

1 Choose Filter > Other > Delete Rider.

2 Select the Adobe Illustrator EPSF Riders file.

3 Click Delete.

To move a Riders file:

1 Locate the EPSF Riders file in the Plug-ins folder.

2 Move the EPSF Riders file out of the Plug-ins folder. You can move it anywhere, but you may want to move it into the Illustrator folder.

3 Quit Adobe Illustrator, then restart the program, and resave all the files that contain embedded Riders information.

File data and annotating objects

The Document Info command lists general file information and object characteristics, as well as the number and names of styles, custom colors, patterns, gradients, fonts, and placed art.

You can use the Note text box in the Attributes dialog box to annotate an object so that it can easily be located in the PostScript file with a text editor. This feature can help service bureaus or other professionals trying to troubleshoot printing problems.

To view file information using the Document Info command:

1 If you want information on a particular set of objects, select the objects.

2 Choose File > Document Info. To view information on only the selected object, select Selection Only in the pop-up menu of the palette.

3 Choose from the information screens listed in the Show Info For pop-up menu: Document, Objects, Styles, Brushes, Spot Color Objects, Pattern Objects, Gradient Objects, Fonts, Linked Images, Embedded Images, and Font Details.

4 To save a copy of the file information as a text file, click Save.

To annotate an object:

1 Select the object you want to annotate.

2 Choose Window > Show Attributes.

3 Choose Show Note from the Attributes menu; then type the annotation.

You can enter up to 240 characters in the Note text box. For example, you can enter a short description of the object, the creation date, and the name of the creator of the artwork.

When you save the artwork, the object is annotated in the PostScript language program with your annotation preceded by the text string *%AI3_Note*.

16

Chapter 16: Producing Color Separations

The most common way to print color artwork is to produce a positive or negative image of the artwork on paper or film and then transfer the image to a printing plate to be run on a press. To prepare artwork for this process, called *color separation*, you first separate the composite art into its component colors used in the printing process—cyan, magenta, yellow, black, and any spot colors needed to print the artwork.

About separations

To produce high-quality separations, it helps to be familiar with the basics of printing, including line screens, resolution, process colors, and spot colors.

It is also recommended that you work closely with the print shop that will produce your separations, consulting its experts before beginning each job and during the process.

To reproduce color and continuous-tone images, printers usually separate artwork into four plates—one plate for each of the cyan, magenta, yellow, and black portions of the image. When inked with the appropriate color and printed in register with one another, these colors combine to reproduce the original artwork. The process of dividing the image into two or more colors is called *color separating,* and the films from which the plates are created are called the *separations*.

Outputting to CMYK

Artwork is separated into CMYK output when you're preparing an image to be printed using the process colors cyan (C), magenta (M), yellow (Y), and black (K). (The letter *K* is used for black to avoid confusion, because *B* might also stand for blue.)

Outputting spot colors

You can use custom inks, called *spot colors*, in addition to or in place of process colors. Because a spot color is printed on its own plate, spot colors can often reduce the complexity and cost of printing artwork.

For example, instead of using the four process colors to reproduce artwork consisting of black text and bluish-green line drawings, you could use two spot colors—one of black and one representing that exact shade of green. In addition, you can use spot color inks to produce colors not reproducible by CMYK inks, such as fluorescent and metallic colors.

You can use the Color palette to display the CMYK equivalent of a spot color.

To view the process color equivalent of a spot color:

1 In the Swatches palette, double-click the spot color whose process color equivalent you want to view.

2 In the Swatch Options dialog box, choose Process Color from the Color Type menu and click OK.

The CMYK equivalent values for the spot color are displayed in the Color palette.

Outputting registration colors

If you want to print a color on all plates in the printing process, including spot color plates, you can convert it into a *registration color*. Registration color is typically used for crop marks and trim marks. (See "Setting crop marks and trim marks" on page 367.)

To output registration color:

1 Select the object on which you want to apply registration color.

2 Choose Window > Show Swatches.

3 In the Swatches palette, click the Registration color swatch (⊕), located in the first row of swatches. The selected objects are converted into registration color objects.

4 To change the color from the default black registration color, use the Color palette:

• To change the registration color to a tint of black, use the Tint slider in the Color palette.

• To change the registration color to a CMYK or Grayscale color, select the color model from the pop-up menu in the Color palette and use the sliders to adjust the color.

Note: The color you specify will be used for representing registration-colored objects on the screen. These objects will always print as gray on composites and as an equal tint of all inks in separations.

Step 1: Calibrate your monitor and check colors in your artwork

Printed colors may not match the colors that were displayed on your monitor. For example, an object that looked red on-screen before may now look orange. At this point, you need to correct any color problems in your artwork. You also should verify that your monitor has been color-calibrated, as described in "Producing Consistent Color" on page 199.

If your artwork is color managed, you can preview how the color will appear when reproduced on a particular output device. (See "Soft-proofing colors" on page 210.)

Types of colors you can use, and how they are separated

You can paint artwork with process colors, spot colors, or a combination of both. For information on your color choices, see "Adding, duplicating, and deleting swatches" on page 184 and "Loading colors from other color systems" on page 188.

When printing separations, you can convert spot colors to their process color equivalents so that they will be printed on the CMYK plates. (See "Separating spot colors as process colors" on page 392.)

Printing gradients as separations

A gradient that contains process colors will be separated onto the process plates. A gradient that contains two tints of the same spot color will be separated on a single spot color plate. To create a gradient that separates on one piece of film between a spot color and white, create a gradient fill between the spot color and a 0% tint of the color.

Note: If you create a gradient between two spot colors, you should assign different screen angles to those spot colors in the Separation Setup dialog box. This is because if two spot colors have the same screen angle, they will overprint each other. If you're not sure what the angles should be, consult your print shop. (See "Specifying the halftone screen ruling" on page 392.)

You cannot separate gradients as a combination of custom (spot) and process color plates, because the spot color is automatically converted to its process color equivalents.

Printing gradient mesh objects as separations

Gradient mesh objects that are composed of different tints of the same spot color will print on a single spot color plate. However, if the mesh object contains different colors, it will be separated on the process color plates.

Step 2: Select overprint options for overlapping colors

If you have not changed the transparency of your artwork with the Transparency palette, the fills and strokes in the artwork will appear opaque because the top color *knocks out,* or cuts out, the area underneath. You can prevent knockout by using the Overprint option in the Attributes palette to make the topmost overlapping printing ink appear transparent in relation to the underlying ink.

Note: The degree of transparency in printing depends on the ink, paper, and printing method used. Consult your print shop to determine how these variables will affect your final artwork.

You can see the effects of overprinting by using the Overprint Preview command. When the Overprint Preview mode is on, you can see an approximation of how overlapping colors will print. (See "Viewing how colors will overprint" on page 59.)

You can also set overprinting features using the Multiply blending mode in the Transparency palette (see "Selecting blending modes" on page 223), or by using the Hard Mix command (see "Using the Hard Mix and Soft Mix commands" on page 194). You can also use the Overprint Fill or Overprint Stroke options in the Attributes palette, as described below.

After you have set your overprinting options, you should use the Overprint Preview mode to see an approximation of how the overprinting colors will print. However, it is important that you carefully check overprinted colors on separated artwork using integral or overlay proofs.

The Filter > Color > Overprint Black command allows you to set black fill or black stroked lines to overprint (or, alternatively, to remove overprinting commands from black fill or black stroked lines).

You may want to overprint in the following situations:

• Overprint 100% black lines against a color background when the illustration style allows.

• Overprint when the artwork does not share common ink colors and you want to create a trap or overlaid ink effects. When overprinting process color mixes or custom colors that do not share common ink colors, the overprint color is added to the background color. For example, if you print a fill of 100% magenta over a fill of 100% cyan, the overlapping fills appear violet, not magenta.

To set overprinting on objects:

1 Select the object or objects that you want to overprint.

2 Choose Window > Show Attributes.

3 Select Overprint Fill.

If you use the Overprint option on a 100% black stroke or fill, the black ink may not be opaque enough to prevent the underlying ink colors from showing through. To eliminate the show-through problem, use a four-color (rich) black instead of a 100% black. Consult with your print shop about the exact percentages of color to add to the black.

To set or remove overprinting from black lines:

1 Select the objects to have overprinting added or removed. You can set overprinting for custom colors whose process equivalents contain specific percentages of black or for process colors that include black.

2 Choose Filter > Colors > Overprint Black.

3 In the dialog box, choose Add Black to add overprinting or Remove Black to remove overprinting commands.

4 Enter the percentage of black to indicate which objects have overprinting added or removed. For example, enter 80% to select only objects containing at least 80% black.

5 Choose any of the following options:

• Fill, Stroke, or both options to apply overprinting to filled paths, stroked paths, or both types of paths.

• Include Blacks with CMY to apply overprinting to paths painted with cyan, magenta, or yellow if the path also contains black at the specified percentage.

• Include Spot Blacks to apply overprinting to custom colors whose process equivalents include black at the specified percentage.

Note: If you are overprinting a spot color that also contains black at the specified percentage, it is necessary to choose both *the Include Blacks with CMY option and the Include Spot Blacks option.*

6 Click OK.

Step 3: Create a trap to compensate for misregistration on press

Misregistration can cause gaps between colors on the final output when colors printed from separate plates overlap or adjoin one another. To compensate for potential gaps between colors in artwork, print shops use a technique called *trapping* to create a small area of overlap (called a *trap*) between two adjoining colors.

You can use a separate, dedicated trapping program to create traps automatically, or you can use Illustrator to create traps manually.

About traps

When overlapping painted objects share a common color, trapping may be unnecessary if the color that is common to both objects creates an automatic trap. For example, if two overlapping objects contain cyan as part of their CMYK values, any gap between them is covered by the cyan content of the object underneath.

Note: When artwork does contain common ink colors, overprinting does not occur on the shared plate.

There are two types of trap: a *spread*, in which a lighter object overlaps a darker background and seems to expand into the background; and a *choke*, in which a lighter background overlaps a darker object that falls within the background and seems to squeeze or reduce the object.

You can create both spreads and chokes in the Adobe Illustrator program.

It is generally best to scale your graphic to its final size before adding a trap. Once you create a trap for an object, the amount of trapping increases or decreases if you scale the object (unless you deselect the Scale line weight option in the Scale dialog box). For example, if you create a graphic that has a 0.5-point trap and scale it to five times its original size, the result is a 2.5-point trap for the enlarged graphic.

Trapping with tints

When trapping two light-colored objects, the trap line may show through the darker of the two colors, resulting in an unsightly dark border. For example, if you trap a light yellow object into a light blue object, a bright green border is visible where the trap is created.

To prevent the trap line from showing through, you can specify a tint of the trapping color (in this example, the yellow color) to create a more pleasing effect. Check with your print shop to find out what percentage of tint is most appropriate given the type of press, inks, paper stock, and so on being used.

Trapping type

Trapping type can present special problems. Avoid applying mixed process colors or tints of process colors to type at small point sizes, because any misregistration can make the text difficult to read. Likewise, trapping type at small point sizes can result in hard-to-read type. As with tint reduction, check with your print shop before trapping such type. For example, if you are printing black type on a colored background, simply overprinting the type onto the background may be enough.

To trap type, you can add the stroke below the fill in the Appearance palette, and set the stroke to overprint (or set it to Multiply blending mode).

Using the Trap command

The Trap command creates traps for simple objects by identifying the lighter artwork—whether it's the object or the background—and overprinting (trapping) it into the darker artwork.

Note: The Trap command is only available when you are working on CMYK documents.

You can apply the Trap command as a Pathfinder command or as an effect. For more information on effects, see "Using effects" on page 271. For instructions on using the Stroke palette to create a trap with strokes on individual objects, see "Trapping by overprinting" on page 387.

In some cases, the top and bottom objects may have similar color densities so that one color is not obviously darker than the other. In this case, the Trap command determines the trap based on slight differences in color; if the trap specified by the Trap dialog box is not satisfactory, you can use the Reverse Trap option to switch the way in which the Trap command traps the two objects.

To create a trap using the Trap command:

1 Do one of the following:

- To apply the command as a Pathfinder command, select two or more objects, and choose Window > Show Pathfinder. (In the Pathfinder palette, if the Trap icon is not displayed, choose Show Options from the pop-up menu.) Then click the Trap button at the lower right of the Pathfinder dialog box.

- To apply the command as an effect, select an object or group in the artwork, or target a level in the Layers palette. (For more information on targeting, see "Targeting layers, groups, and objects to apply appearance attributes" on page 252.) Then choose Effect > Pathfinder > Trap.

2 In the Thickness text box, enter a stroke width of between 0.01 and 5000 points. Check with your print shop to determine what value to use.

3 Enter a value in the Height/Width% text box to specify the trap on horizontal lines as a percentage of the trap on vertical lines.

Specifying different horizontal and vertical trap values lets you compensate for on-press irregularities, such as paper stretch. Contact your print shop for help in determining this value. The default value of 100% results in the same trap width on horizontal lines and on vertical lines.

To increase the trap thickness on horizontal lines without changing the vertical trap, set the Height/Width value to greater than 100%. To decrease the trap thickness on horizontal lines without changing the vertical trap, set the Height/Width value to less than 100%.

4 Enter a Tint Reduction value to change the tint of the trap. The default value is 40%.

The Tint Reduction value reduces the values of the lighter color being trapped; the darker color values remain at 100%. The Tint Reduction value also affects the values of custom colors.

5 Select additional trapping options as required:

• Traps with Process Color if you want to convert spot color traps to equivalent process colors. This option creates an object of the lighter of the spot colors and overprints it.

• Reverse Traps to trap darker colors into lighter colors. This option does not work with rich black—that is, black that contains additional CMY inks.

6 Click OK to create a trap on the selected objects. Click Defaults to return to the default trapping values.

Trapping by overprinting

For more precise control of trapping and for trapping complex objects, you can create the effect of a trap by stroking an object and setting the stroke to overprint.

To create a spread or choke by overprinting:

1 Select the topmost object of the two objects that must trap into each other.

2 In the Stroke box in the toolbox or the Color palette, do one of the following:

• Create a spread by entering the same color values for the Stroke as appear in the Fill option. You can change the stroke's color values by selecting the stroke and then adjusting its color values in the Color palette. This method enlarges the object by stroking its boundaries with the same color as the object's fill.

• Create a choke by entering the same color values for the Stroke as appear in the lighter background (again, using the Color palette); the Stroke and Fill values will differ. This method reduces the darker object by stroking its boundaries with the lighter background color.

3 Choose Window > Show Stroke.

4 In the Stroke palette, in the Weight text box enter a stroke width of between 0.6 and 2.0 points.

A stroke weight of 0.6 point creates a trap of 0.3 point. A stroke weight of 2.0 points creates a trap of 1.0 point. Check with your print shop to determine what value to use.

5 Choose Window > Show Attributes.

6 Select Overprint Stroke.

In a spread, the lighter object traps into (overprints) the darker background. In a choke, overprinting the stroke causes the lighter background to trap into the darker object.

To trap a line:

1 Select the line to be trapped.

2 In the Stroke box in the toolbox or the Color palette, assign the stroke a color of white.

3 In the Stroke palette, select the desired line weight.

4 Copy the line, and choose Edit > Paste in Front. The copy is used to create a trap.

5 In the Stroke box in the toolbox or the Color palette, stroke the copy with the desired color.

6 In the Stroke palette, choose a line weight that is wider than the bottom line.

7 Choose Window > Show Attributes.

8 Select Overprint Stroke for the top line.

To trap a portion of an object:

1 Draw a line along the edge or edges that you want to trap. If the object is complex, use the direct-selection tool ( ) to select the edges, copy it, and choose Edit > Paste in Front to paste the copy directly on top of the original.

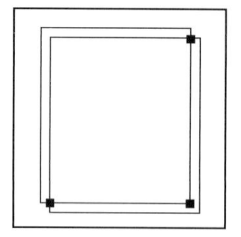

Drop shadow with a trap. The line drawn at the intersection of two shapes creates a trap.

2 In the Stroke box in the toolbox or the Color palette, select a color value for the Stroke to create either a spread or a choke.

If you are uncertain about what type of trap is appropriate, see "About traps" on page 385.

3 Choose Window > Show Attributes.

4 Select Overprint Stroke.

Step 4: Set the printing bounding box and place crop marks around the image to be separated

You can place crop marks around the image to be separated, either directly on the artwork or in the separations. Crop marks indicate the image area.

Keep these points in mind when creating crop marks for color separations:

• If you are setting crop marks in the original artwork and want the artwork to contain a *bleed* (a margin added to the image so that it can be trimmed after printing), make sure that you extend the artwork past the crop marks to accommodate the bleed. (See "Specifying the bleed area" on page 396.)

• If you plan to separate several small pieces of artwork in the same file, you can create a set of trim marks for each piece of artwork. You might want more than one set, for example, if the file contains several business cards that you plan to separate. To create more than one set of crop marks, draw them in the artwork or use the Trim Marks filter. See "Setting crop marks and trim marks" on page 367.

Specifying the printing bounding box in the separation

The printing bounding box is represented as a gray rectangle surrounding the artwork in the Separation Setup preview window. The bounding box sets the position of the crop marks on your separations and defines the printable boundaries of the artwork, as well as nonprintable boundaries such as direction lines.

You can define the printing bounding box either by using the Object > Crop Marks > Make command, or by using the Separations Setup dialog box to set the bounding box at the artwork boundaries. You can also modify the current bounding box dimensions in the Separations Setup dialog box.

The numbers in the Margins text boxes show where the image lies within the page. These numbers measure the distance from the 0,0 point in the imageable area to the edges of the bounding box. The 0,0 point is in its default position at the bottom left corner of the page boundary.

If you select a different page size, the margin numbers change as Illustrator calculates the distance of the bounding box from the edge of a new page size.

Note: The Margins numbers for a given page size (such as Letter) may vary by PPD file. This is because printers and imagesetters may differ in how they define the size of an imageable area.

To specify the printing bounding box using crop marks:

1 Do one of the following:

• Draw a rectangle to define a customized printing bounding box, and then select the rectangle.

• Choose Edit > Deselect All to set the printing bounding box around the artboard.

2 Choose Object > Crop Marks > Make.

To define the printing bounding box boundary using the Separation Setup dialog box:

1 Do not set any crop marks in the document, or remove existing crop marks by choosing Objects > Crop Marks > Release. If the existing crop marks were created using a rectangle, delete that rectangle.

2 Choose File > Separation Setup. The printing bounding box is placed by default as tightly as possible around all the artwork.

To modify the existing printing bounding box:

1 In the Separation Setup dialog box, do one of the following:

• Enter values in the Left, Right, Top, and Bottom margin text boxes. Press Tab to go to the next text box.

• Drag any of the size handles in the preview.

• Select Revert to cancel any changes and revert to the previous bounding box settings.

2 Specify another separation option, or click OK.

Specifying printer's marks

When you prepare artwork for printing, a number of marks are needed for the printer to register the artwork elements precisely and verify correct color. These marks include elements such as crop marks, registration marks, star targets, calibration bars, and labels. The Separation Setup dialog box enables you to add these marks to your separations.

In Illustrator, the printer's marks are either turned on or turned off. You cannot choose individual marks to be placed around the artwork. The Use Printer's Marks option adds the following marks to the separations:

Registration marks and star targets Illustrator places around your artwork two types of marks that the print shop uses to align the separations: *registration marks* and *star targets*. Registration marks are the most commonly used marks in printing, because they are easy to line up accurately. Star targets are harder than registration marks to align, but they are extremely accurate.

Labels Illustrator labels the film with the name of the file, the line screen used, the screen angle for the separation, and the color of each particular plate. These labels appear at the tops of the images.

Crop marks Illustrator places crop marks at the edges of the printing bounding box. If the Japanese Crop Marks option is selected in the General Preferences dialog box, a double set of crop marks is displayed.

To include printer's marks on the separations:

1 In the Separation Setup dialog box, select Use Printer's Marks.

2 Specify another separation option, or click OK.

Step 5: Set separation options

Setting up a separation involves choosing the separation options and then printing or saving the file.

Preparing a file for separation includes specifying which printer settings and halftone screen ruling to use and whether the separation should be a positive or negative image. In addition, you can specify a bleed around the artwork.

The separation settings you choose for a file are saved with the separated file. If you open a file that has never been separated in Illustrator, the program returns to the default settings.

To choose separation options:

1 Choose one of the following options:

• File > Separation Setup.

• File > Print, and then click Separation Setup in the Print dialog box.

2 Select the PPD file that corresponds to your printer or imagesetter, as described in "Selecting a PPD file." Choose options as described in the rest of that section.

3 Click OK or Print.

Selecting a PPD file

To define the output device for the separation, you select the PostScript Printer Descriptions (PPD) file that corresponds to your PostScript printer or imagesetter. (You cannot separate to a non-PostScript device.) To obtain PPD files not included with the program, see the Read Me file in the Utilities/PPDs folder in the Adobe Illustrator folder.

A PPD file contains information about your output device, including its resolution, available page sizes, line screen rulings, and screen angles. Loading the file displays the different settings for the output device, in the Separation Setup dialog box.

To select a PPD file:

1 Choose File > Separation Setup. In the Separation Setup dialog box, click Open PPD.

2 Locate the System folder in the Windows folder (Windows) or the Printer Descriptions folder in the Extensions folder within the System Folder (Mac OS).

3 Select a PPD file that corresponds to the output device you use to print your separations. The filenames correspond to the printer or imagesetter name and model and have a *.ppd* file extension (Windows).

4 Click Open. The name of the PPD file you selected appears in the dialog box. The name of the currently selected printer appears in the title of the dialog box.

5 Choose other separation options as described in the following sections, or click OK.

Specifying which layers to separate

The Layer pop-up menu lets you specify which layers to include in the separation.

To specify which layers to separate:

1 In the Separation Setup dialog box under Options, choose one of the following options from the Separate menu:

• Printable, Visible Layers to separate only layers that are both printable and visible. These correspond to the layers that print when creating a composite proof.

• Visible Layers to separate only the visible layers.

• All Layers to separate all layers.

2 Specify another separation option, or click OK.

Specifying which colors to create separations for

In the Separation Setup dialog box, each separation is labeled with the color name that Illustrator assigned it. If an icon of a printer ( ) appears next to the color name, Illustrator creates a separation for the color.

To specify whether to create a separation for a color:

1 Do one of the following:

• By default, Illustrator creates a separation for each CMYK color in the art. To create a separation, make sure the printer icon is displayed next to the color name in the Separation Setup dialog box.

• To choose not to create a separation, click the printer icon next to the color's name. The printer icon disappears, and no separation is created.

Separating spot colors as process colors

You can separate spot colors or named colors as equivalent CMYK process colors in the Separation Setup dialog box. When spot colors or named CMYK colors are converted to their process color equivalents, they are printed as separations rather than on a single plate.

To separate all spot colors as process colors:

In the Separation Setup dialog box, click Convert to Process. (This option is on by default.)

A four-color process icon (■) appears next to all the spot colors in the artwork.

To separate individual spot colors as process colors:

1 In the Separation Setup dialog box, deselect Convert to Process.

2 Click the printer icon next to the spot color in the list of colors. A four-color process icon appears.

3 For each spot color you want to convert to a process color, click the printer icon next to its name in the list of colors.

4 Specify another separation option, or click OK.

Specifying the halftone screen ruling

The Halftone menu displays one or more sets of line screens (lines per inch, or *lpi*) and resolutions (dots per inch, or *dpi*) available on the printer or imagesetter that prints the color separations.

A high line-screen ruling (for example, 150 lpi) spaces the dots used to create an image closely together to create a finely rendered image on the press; a low screen ruling (60 lpi to 85 lpi) spaces the dots farther apart to create a coarser image. The size of the dots is also determined by the line screen. A high line-screen ruling uses small dots; a low screen ruling uses large dots. The most important factor in choosing a line-screen ruling is the type of printing press your job uses. Ask your print shop how fine a line screen its press can hold, and make your choices accordingly.

The PPD files for high-resolution imagesetters offer a wide range of possible line-screen rulings paired with various imagesetter resolutions. The PPD files for lower-resolution printers typically have only a few choices for line screens, and they are coarser screens of between 53 lpi and 85 lpi. The coarser screens, however, give optimum results on lower-resolution printers. Using a finer screen of 100 lpi, for example, actually decreases the quality of your image when a low-resolution printer is used for final output.

To specify a halftone screen ruling and resolution:

1 In the Separation Setup dialog box, choose one of the following options:

• To select one of the preset halftone screen ruling and printer resolution combinations, choose an option from the Halftone pop-up menu.

- To specify a custom halftone screen ruling, select the plate to be customized and then enter the lpi value in the Frequency text box and a screen angle value in the Angle text box.

Note: *The default angles and frequencies are determined by the selected PPD file. Be sure to check with your print shop for the preferred frequency and angle before creating your own halftone screens.*

2 Specify another separation option, or click OK.

Specifying the page size and orientation

Adobe Illustrator normally uses the page size default in the PPD file for the selected printer. However, you can change the page size to any of the sizes listed in the PPD file as well as specify portrait (vertical) or landscape (horizontal) orientation. Page sizes are listed by familiar names (such as *Letter*) and by dimensions in points. The dimensions shown in parentheses after the page size are the limits of the *imageable area*. The imageable area is the total page size less any unprintable border used by the printer or imagesetter. Most laser printers cannot print to the exact edge of a page.

If you select a different page size (for example, change from letter to legal), the artwork is rescaled in the preview window. This is because the preview window displays the entire imageable area of the selected page; when the page size is changed, the preview window automatically rescales to include the imageable area.

Note: *The imageable area may vary by PPD file, even for the same page size (for example, Letter), because different printers and imagesetters define the sizes of their imageable areas differently.*

Make sure that your page size is large enough to contain your artwork as well as crop marks, registration marks, and other necessary printing information. To conserve imagesetter film or paper, however, select the smallest page size that accommodates your artwork and necessary printing information.

To specify a page size:

1 In the Separation Setup dialog box, choose an option from the Page Size pop-up menu.

2 Specify another separation option, or click OK.

To specify the orientation of the page:

1 In the Separation Setup dialog box, choose Portrait or Landscape from the Orientation pop-up menu.

2 Specify another separation option, or click OK.

Specifying a custom page size

You can specify a custom page size using the Custom Page Size option in the Page Size pop-up menu. This option is available only if you are using a printer that accommodates various page sizes, such as a high-resolution imagesetter. The PPD file for a laser printer, for example, does not provide this option.

The largest custom page size you can specify depends on the maximum imageable area of your imagesetter. Consult the documentation on your specific printer for more information.

To specify a custom page size:

1 In the Separation Setup dialog box, choose Custom from the Page Size pop-up menu.

2 Do one of the following:

• To specify the smallest page size needed for your artwork and printer's marks, click OK to accept the default values.

• To specify a page size larger than the default, enter a new width and height in the Width and Height fields. Be sure to increase the values; decreasing the default values may clip your artwork.

• If desired, change the placement of the page by entering a value in the Offset field.

In the first illustration, the page placement is off; in the second illustration, Offset shifts the pages to the left.

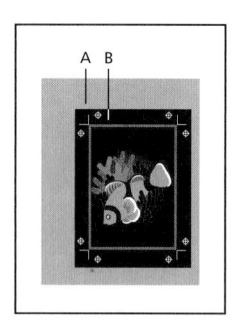

A. Film B. Page C. Offset

The Offset value specifies the amount of space along the right side of the imageable area. For example, entering a value of 30 points in the Offset option moves your page 30 points to the left.

• To rotate your page 90 degrees, select Transverse and click OK.

If your imagesetter can accommodate the longest side of your imageable area, you can conserve a considerable amount of film or paper by using Transverse in conjunction with Offset. Compare the following examples of an image printed by Adobe Illustrator with Transverse on and off.

Transverse off and film saved with Transverse on:
A. Offset value B. Film saved

When both Offset and Transverse are selected, Offset controls the amount of space between the separations.

Specifying the emulsion

Emulsion refers to the photosensitive layer on a piece of film or paper. *Up (Right Reading)* means that type in the image is readable (that is, "right reading") when the photosensitive layer is facing you. *Down (Right Reading)* means that type is readable when the photosensitive layer is facing away from you. Normally, images printed on paper are printed Up (Right Reading), whereas images printed on film are often printed Down (Right Reading). Check with your print shop to determine which emulsion direction it prefers.

To tell whether you are looking at the emulsion side or the nonemulsion side (also referred to as the *base*), examine the final film under bright light. One side appears shinier than the other. The dull side is the emulsion side; the shiny side is the base.

To specify the emulsion:

1 In the Separation Setup dialog box, choose Up (Right Reading) or Down (Right Reading) from the Emulsion pop-up menu. The image flips.

2 Specify another separation option, or click OK.

Specifying the image type

The image options determine the image exposure: negative or positive. Typically, print shops require negative film in the United States and positive film in Europe and Japan. If you are unsure about which image type to use, consult your print shop.

To specify the image type:

1 In the Separation Setup dialog box, choose Positive or Negative from the Image pop-up menu.

2 Specify another separation option, or click OK.

Overprinting black in the separation

It can be cheaper and easier to have the print shop overprint black on the press. You can choose whether to overprint black when printing or saving selected separations.

See "Step 2: Select overprint options for overlapping colors" on page 383.

To overprint black in the separation:

1 Under Options in the Separation Setup dialog box, select Overprint Black.

Note: The Overprint Black option works only for objects that have the color black applied through values in the K channel. It does not work for objects that appear black because of their transparency settings or styles.

2 Specify another separation option, or click OK.

Specifying the bleed area

Bleed is the amount of artwork that falls outside of the printing bounding box, or outside the crop marks and trim marks. You can include bleed in your artwork as a margin of error—to ensure that the ink is still printed to the edge of the page after the page is trimmed or to ensure that an image can be stripped into a keyline in a document. Once you create the artwork that extends into the bleed, you can use Illustrator to specify the extent of the bleed.

Changing the bleed moves the crop marks farther from or closer to the image; the crop marks still define the same size printing bounding box, however.

To specify bleed:

1 Under Options in the Separation Setup dialog box, enter an amount in the Bleed text box.

By default, Illustrator applies a bleed of 18 points. This means that the artwork extends 18 points beyond the crop marks on your film. The maximum bleed you can set is 72 points; the minimum bleed is 0 points.

The size of the bleed you use depends on its purpose. A *press bleed* (that is, an image that bleeds off the edge of the printed sheet) should be at least 18 points. If the bleed is to ensure that an image fits a keyline, it needs to be no more than 2 or 3 points. Your print shop can advise you on the size of the bleed necessary for your particular job.

2 Specify another separation option, or click OK.

Step 6: Print and save separations

When you have completed setting up the separations, you are ready to print or save your separations.

Note: The printer or imagesetter you plan to use to print separations must match the PPD file you specified when setting up the separations. If the output device and PPD file don't match, you will receive a warning message.

Saving the file saves the separation setup, the PPD information, and any color conversions you have specified in the Separation Setup dialog box.

To print the separations you selected:

1 Select the separations you want to print, as described in "Specifying which layers to separate" on page 391. (For information about placing crop marks with the Separation Setup dialog box, see "Setting crop marks and trim marks" on page 367 and "Specifying printer's marks" on page 390.)

2 Choose File > Print, or return to the Print dialog box if it is still open.

3 Choose any print options.

4 Choose a method for selecting the Separate output option:

• On Windows, choose Separate from the Output pop-up menu.

- On Mac OS, choose Adobe Illustrator 9.0 from the Options pop-up menu. Then choose Separate from the Output pop-up menu.

5 Make sure Print to File is deselected, and click OK (Windows) or select Printer from the Destination pop-up menu and click Print (Mac OS).

To save the separations you selected as a PostScript file:

1 Select the separations you want to save, as described in "Specifying which layers to separate" on page 391.

2 Choose File > Print, or return to the Print dialog box if it is still open.

3 Choose any print options.

4 Choose a method for selecting the Separate output option:

- Choose Separate from the Output pop-up menu (Windows).

- Choose Adobe Illustrator 9.0 from the Options pop-up menu. Then choose Separate from the Output pop-up menu (Mac OS).

5 Select the Print to File option (Windows) or choose File from the Destination pop-up menu (Mac OS).

6 Do one of the following:

- Click OK and enter a filename in the Print to File dialog box. Then click OK again (Windows).

- Accept the default filename or enter another name for the separation and click Print (Mac OS).

17

Chapter 17: Automating Tasks

Adobe Illustrator makes it easy to record a series of commands and then replay the commands as needed.

About actions

You can automate tasks by grouping a series of commands into a single *action*. For example, you can create an action that applies a series of commands to reproduce a favorite effect or combine commands to prepare artwork for online publishing. Actions can be grouped into sets to help you better organize your actions.

Illustrator also provides prerecorded actions to create special effects on graphic objects and type. These prerecorded actions are installed as a default set in the Actions palette when you install the Illustrator application. More action sets can also be found in the Illustrator Extras folder on the Adobe Illustrator CD.

Using the Actions palette

You use the Actions palette to record, play, edit, and delete actions. It also lets you save, load, and replace action sets.

To display the Actions palette:

Choose Window > Show Actions.

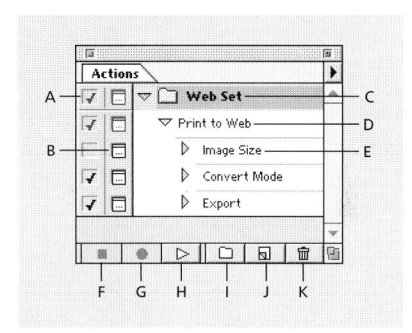

A. Toggles item on or off B. Toggles modal control on or off C. Set D. Action E. Recorded command F. Stop playing/recording G. Begin recording H. Play current selection I. Create new set J. Create new action K. Delete selection

You can display actions in the Actions palette in either list view or button view. In list view, sets can be expanded to display actions, which in turn can be expanded to display individual commands. Commands can then be expanded to display recorded values.

To display actions as buttons:

Choose Button Mode from the Actions palette menu. Choose Button Mode again to return to list view.

To expand and collapse sets and commands:

Click the triangle to the left of the set or command in the Actions palette.

Creating and recording actions

When you create an action, Illustrator records the commands (including any specified values), palettes, and tools you use, in the order you use them.

The following guidelines can help you in designing actions:

• Most, but not all, commands can be recorded. However, you can allow for commands that cannot be recorded. (See "Inserting nonrecordable commands" on page 403.)

• Nonrecordable commands include those that change your view of the screen (including most commands in the View menu), commands that display or hide palettes, commands in the Effect menu, and gradient mesh commands. Also, tools such as the gradient and gradient mesh tools, eyedropper, paint bucket, and scissors are not recordable.

• When recording an action, keep in mind that playback results depend on such variables as the current fill and stroke colors, and on file and program settings.

Because Illustrator executes the commands as you record them, it's a good idea to record a complicated action using a copy of a file, and then play the action on the original.

• Until you specifically save a set of actions with the Save Actions command, actions are automatically saved in the preferences file. For information on this file, see "Setting preferences" on page 63.

To create and record an action:

1 Open a file.

2 In the Actions palette, click the Create New Set button to create a new actions set if desired, or click on an existing set to add the new action to that set.

3 In the Actions palette, click the Create New Action button ( ) or choose New Action from the pop-up menu on the palette.

4 Name the action, assign it to any combination of the Ctrl key (Windows) or Command key (Mac OS), the Shift key, and the Function keys (for example, Ctrl+Shift+F3), and choose a color for its display in the Actions palette.

Note: *If you assign an action the same shortcut that is used for a command, the shortcut will apply the action rather than the command.*

5 Click Record. The Begin Recording button in the Actions palette turns red.

Pressing Alt (Windows) or Option (Mac OS) and clicking the Create New Action button creates an action and begins recording.

6 To guard against mistakes, record the File > Save a Copy command at the beginning of the action.

7 Choose commands as you want them recorded.

If the command you choose opens a dialog box, clicking OK records the command and clicking Cancel does not record it. If a chosen command is not recorded, it must be inserted in the action. (See "Inserting nonrecordable commands" on page 403.)

8 Stop recording by clicking the Stop Playing/Recording button.

9 If you want to keep the action for use in future work sessions, save the action. (See "Organizing sets of actions" on page 409.)

Recording paths

The Insert Selected Path command lets you record a path as part of an action. When played back, the entire path is reproduced as part of the action.

To record a path:

1 Start recording an action.

2 Select a path.

3 Choose Insert Select Path from the Actions palette menu.

Selecting an object during an action

The Select Object command lets you select a particular object during the course of an action. You identify the object to be selected using the Note text box in the Attributes palette. The Select Object function is useful for choosing a particular object during an action on which to perform commands, use palettes, or make selections in dialog boxes. For example, you could pick a specific ellipse in the artwork on which to perform transformation effects such as scale or rotate, change stroke characteristics using the Stroke palette, or apply colors with the Color palette.

To name an object for use during an action:

1 Select the object to be used in the action.

2 Choose Window > Show Attributes.

3 Choose Show Note from the pop-up menu in the Attributes palette.

4 Type a name for the object in the Note text box. The object now can be used in an action sequence.

To select an object during an action:

1 Record an action, as described in "Creating and recording actions" on page 402, up to the point where the object is to be selected.

2 Choose Select Object from the pop-up menu in the Actions palette.

3 Enter the object name in the Set Selection dialog box. (The name should match the object name entered in the Note text box of the Attributes dialog box.)

4 Set the following options in the Set Selection dialog box:

• Select Case Sensitive to select only objects that exactly match the uppercase or lowercase words in their Note text.

• Select Whole Word to select only objects whose names match every word listed in the Note text box associated with the object.

5 Click OK and continue recording the actions.

Inserting nonrecordable commands

The painting tools, tool options, effects, view commands, and preferences cannot be recorded. However, many commands that cannot be recorded can be inserted into an action using the Insert Menu Item command.

An inserted command is not executed until the action is played. No values for the command are recorded in the action, so the file remains unchanged when the command is inserted. If the command has a dialog box, the dialog box appears during playback, and the action pauses until you click OK or Cancel. You can insert a command when recording an action or after it has been recorded.

To insert a menu item in an action:

1 Choose where to insert the menu item in the Actions palette:

• Select an action's name to insert the item at the end of the action.

• Select a command to insert the item after the command.

2 Choose Insert Menu Item from the Actions palette menu.

3 Do one of the following:

• Choose a command from its menu.

• Enter a command in the Insert Menu Item dialog box. If you don't know the full name of the command, enter part of it and click Find. You can also use the Tab key to find the command.

4 Click OK.

Inserting stops

You may want to include a stop in your action so that you can perform a task that cannot be recorded. Once you've performed the task, you can then continue by clicking the Play Current Selection button in the Actions palette.

You can also display a short message when the action reaches the stop. For example, you can remind yourself what you need to do before continuing with the action. A Continue button can be included in the message box. This way you can check for a certain condition in the file (for example, a selection) and continue if nothing needs to be done. You can insert a stop when recording an action or after it has been recorded.

To insert a stop:

1 Choose where to insert the stop in the Actions palette:

• Select an action's name to insert the stop at the end of the action.

• Select a command to insert the stop after the command.

2 Choose Insert Stop from the Actions palette menu.

3 Type the message you want to appear.

4 If you want the option to continue the action without stopping, select Allow Continue.

5 Click OK.

Setting modal controls and excluding commands

After recording an action, you can insert a *modal control*. This lets you pause a command to display its dialog box and specify different values, and to manipulate a modal tool to apply new settings. (A modal tool requires pressing Enter or Return to apply its effect.)

If you do not use a modal control, Illustrator runs the command using the values specified when you first recorded the action (and the dialog box does not appear).

You can also exclude commands that you don't want to include as part of a recorded action or that you don't want to play when running the action.

To set a modal control:

1 Make sure that the Actions palette is in list view. (If necessary, deselect Button Mode in the Actions palette menu.)

2 Do one of the following:

• Click the column to the left of the command name to display the dialog box icon. Click again to remove the modal control.

• To turn on or disable modal controls for all commands in an action or set, click the column to the left of the action or set name.

To exclude or include a command:

Do one of the following:

• Click to clear the check mark to the left of the command name. Click again to include the command.

• To exclude or include all commands in an action or set, click the check box to the left of the action or set name.

• To exclude or include all commands *except* the selected command, Alt-click (Windows) or Option-click (Mac OS) the command.

Playing actions

When you play an action, Illustrator executes the series of commands as you recorded them. But you can begin with any command, exclude commands, or play a single command in an action. If you have inserted a modal control in your action, you can specify values in a dialog box or reapply a modal tool (any tool that requires you to press Enter or Return to apply it) when the action pauses. (See "Setting modal controls and excluding commands" on page 404.)

In button view, clicking a button executes the entire action—though commands previously excluded are not executed.

To play an action or set on a single file:

1 Open the file.

2 Specify what to play:

• To play a set of actions, select the set name.

• To play a single action, select the action name.

• To play only part of an action, select the command from which you want the action to start.

3 To exclude or include a command within an action from playing, click the check box to the left of the action name.

4 Click the Play Current Selection button in the Actions palette or choose Play from the pop-up menu.

To play a single command in an action:

1 Select the command you want to play.

2 Do one of the following:

- Ctrl-click (Windows) or Command-click (Mac OS) the Play Current Selection button in the Actions palette.
- Hold down Ctrl (Windows) or Command (Mac OS), and double-click the command.

Slowing actions during playback

Sometimes a long, complicated action does not play properly, but it is difficult to tell where the problem occurs. The Playback Options command gives you three speeds at which to play actions, so that you can watch each command as it is carried out.

To specify how fast actions should play:

1 Choose Playback Options from the Actions palette pop-up menu.

2 Specify a speed:

- Accelerated to play the action at normal speed (the default).
- Step by Step to complete each command and redraw the image before going on to the next command in the action.
- Pause and enter the amount of time Illustrator should pause between carrying out each command in the action.

3 Click OK.

Batch processing

The Batch command lets you play an action on a folder of files and subfolders.

When batch processing files, you can leave all the files open, close and save the changes to the original files, or save modified versions of the files to a new location (leaving the originals unchanged). If you are saving the processed files to a new location, you may want to create a new folder for the processed files before starting the batch.

To batch process files:

1 Choose Batch from the Actions palette menu.

2 For Set, choose the desired set.

3 For Action, choose the desired action.

4 For Source, click Choose to specify a folder and play an action on files (including subfolders) already stored on your computer.

5 To open the files from the specified folder, select Override Action "Open" Commands. Any Open commands recorded as part of the original action are ignored.

6 To process all files and folders within the specified folder, select Include All Subdirectories.

7 For Destination, choose an option:

- None to leave the files open without saving changes (unless the action included a Save command).
- Save and Close to save the files in their current location.
- Folder to save the altered files to another location. Click Choose to specify the destination folder.

- If you chose Folder, select Override Action "Save" Commands to save the processed files to the specified destination folder and not to a location recorded with the Save As or Save a Copy commands.

- Select Override Action "Export" Commands to export the processed files to the specified destination folder rather than to a location recorded with the Export commands. Click Choose to specify the destination folder.

Saving files using the Batch command options always saves the files in the same format as the original files. To create a batch process that saves files in a new format, record the Save As or Save a Copy command, followed by the Close command, as part of your original action. Then choose None for the Destination when setting up the batch process.

8 For Errors, choose an option:

- Stop for Errors to suspend the batch process until you confirm the error message.

- Log Errors to File to record each error in the file without stopping the batch process. If errors are logged to this file, a message appears after files are processed, alerting you to review the error file. If you select this option, click Save As, and name the error file.

To batch process using multiple actions, create a new action, and record the Batch command for each action you want to use. This technique also lets you process multiple folders in a single batch. To batch process multiple folders, create aliases within a folder to the other folders you want to process.

Editing actions

You can edit actions in the following ways:

- Rearrange actions, or rearrange commands within an action and their order of execution.

- Add commands to an action.

- Record new commands or new values for actions with dialog boxes.

- Change action options such as the action name, button color, and shortcut key.

- Duplicate actions and commands. This helps you experiment with changing an action without losing the original version, and for creating an action based on an existing one.

- Delete actions and commands.

- Reset the actions to the default list.

To move an action to a different set:

In the Actions palette, drag the action to a different set. When the highlighted line appears in the desired position, release the mouse button.

To rearrange commands within an action:

In the Actions palette, drag the command to its new location within the same action. When the highlighted line appears in the desired position, release the mouse button.

To record additional commands:

1 Do one of the following:

- Select the action name to insert the new command at the end of the action.

• Select a command in the action to insert the command after it.

2 Click the Begin Recording button on the Actions palette.

3 Record the additional commands.

4 Click the Stop Playing/Recording button to stop recording.

Note: *You can also insert nonrecordable commands or drag commands from other actions. (See "Inserting nonrecordable commands" on page 403.)*

To record an action again:

1 Select an action and choose Record Again from the Actions palette menu.

2 If a modal tool appears, do one of the following:

• Use the tool differently, and press Enter or Return to change the tool's effect.

• Press Enter or Return to retain the same settings.

3 If a dialog box appears, do one of the following:

• Change the values and click OK to record them.

• Click Cancel to retain the same values.

To record a single command again:

1 Select an object of the same type for which you want to rerecord the action. For example, if a command is only available for vector objects, then you must have a vector object selected when you rerecord.

2 In the Actions palette, double-click the command.

3 Enter the new values, and click OK.

To change action options:

1 Do one of the following:

• Double-click the action name.

• Select the action, and choose Action Options from the Actions palette menu.

2 If desired, type a new name for the action, choose a color for the action button, assign a Function key and select the Shift or Ctrl key (Windows) or the Command key (Mac OS) to combine with the function key for an action shortcut.

3 Click OK.

To duplicate a set, action, or command:

Do one of the following:

• Select a single set, action, or command. You can Shift-click or Ctrl-click (Windows) or Command-click (Mac OS) to select multiple items. Then choose Duplicate from the Actions palette menu. The copied sets appear at the bottom of the Actions palette. The copied commands or actions appear after the original command or action.

• Drag an action or command to the Create New Action button at the bottom of the Actions palette, or drag a set to the Create New Set button at the bottom of the Actions palette. The copied action appears at the bottom of the Actions palette. The copied command appears after the original command. The copied set appears after the original set.

To delete a set, action, or command:

1 In the Actions palette, select the set, action, or command you want to delete. You can Shift-click, or Ctrl-click (Windows) or Command-click (Mac OS) to select multiple commands within an action.

2 Do one of the following:

• Click the Delete Selection button on the Actions palette. Click OK to delete the action or command.

• Drag the selection to the Delete Selection button on the Actions palette.

• Choose Delete from the Actions palette menu.

To delete all actions:

Choose Clear Actions from the Actions palette menu. Click OK to delete all the actions.

To delete a selected action or command automatically, Alt-click (Windows) or Option-click (Mac OS) the Delete Selection button.

To reset actions to the default set:

1 Choose Reset Actions from the Actions palette menu.

2 Click Append to add the set of default actions to the current actions in the Actions palette, or OK to replace the current actions in the Actions palette with the default set.

Organizing sets of actions

To help you organize your actions, you can create sets in which to place them and save the sets to disk. You can organize sets of actions for different types of work—for example, print publishing and online publishing—and transfer sets to other computers. You can save only the entire contents of the selected set in the Actions palette, not individual actions.

Note: Unsaved actions are automatically saved to the preferences file. If this preferences file is lost or removed, any unsaved actions you may have created will be lost. Be sure to use the Save Actions command in the Actions palette to save your actions to a separate actions file so you can load them later, and to keep them safe.

Replacing a saved set of actions replaces all existing actions. Loading a saved set adds to existing actions, with new ones appearing at the bottom of the Actions palette.

To create a new set for actions:

1 In the Actions palette, do one of the following:

• Choose New Set from the pop-up menu.

• Click the Create New Set button at the bottom of the Actions palette.

2 Enter the name of the set and click OK.

To rename a set of actions:

1 In the Actions palette, do one of the following:

• Double-click the name of the set in the Actions palette.

- Select the name of the set and choose Set Options from the pop-up menu.

2 Enter the name of the set, and click OK.

To save a set of actions:

1 Select a set.

2 Choose Save Actions from the Actions palette menu.

3 Type a name for the set, choose a location, and click Save. The default actions set is saved in the Actions Sets folder within the Adobe Illustrator application folder.

To replace all actions in the Actions palette with a new set of actions:

1 Choose Replace Actions from the Actions palette menu.

2 Locate and select an actions file.

3 Click Open.

Important: *Using the Replace Actions command will replace all sets of actions in the current document. Before using the Replace Actions command, you should make sure that you have already saved a copy of your current set of actions using the Save Actions command.*

To load a set of actions:

1 Choose Load Actions from the Actions palette menu.

2 Locate and select the actions file.

3 Click Open (Windows) or Select (Mac OS).

Index

A

About Plug-ins command 277
Absolute Colorimetric rendering intent 209
Accelerated option 406
Acrobat 358
actions
 default set 409
 deleting 409
 editing 407–409
 excluding and including commands 405
 inserting modal controls 404
 inserting stops 404
 nonrecordable 402
 playing 402, 405–407
 recording 402–404
 recording paths 403
 resetting 409
 saving 402–403
 sets of 409
 setting button or list view 401
Actions palette 30, 401–403
active layer 242
Actual Size command 60
Adaptive color table 335
Adaptive palette
 using with GIF 335
Add Anchor Points command 93
Add Around Object option 276
Add Arrowheads filter 154
Add Guides option 307
add-anchor-point tool 92

Adjust Colors filter 195
adjusting
 axis of reflection 144
 compound paths 167
 corners of rounded rectangles 98
 horizontal and vertical scale 299
 paths 85, 92, 95, 102
Adobe Acrobat Reader 1
Adobe Certification program 6
Adobe Dimensions 127
Adobe Expert font, creating ligatures 320
Adobe Gamma command 216
Adobe Gamma utility 214
Adobe Gamma wizard 216
Adobe Online 3, 4
Adobe Photoshop. *See* Photoshop
Adobe Premiere 127
Adobe Streamline
Adobe Web site 3, 62
AI File to SWF File option 355
AI Layers to SWF Files option 355
AI Layers to SWF Frames option 355
aligning objects 129
 See also Transform palette
 options 129
 using guides and grids 118
 using Smart Guides 120
aligning type
 along a path 291
 in paragraphs 310
Alignment option 310

alignment point. *See* center point of objects
alpha transparency
 in PNG images 341
alternative glyphs (characters), choosing and importing 321
Amiga Interchange File Format (IFF) 356
anchor points 83
 adding 87, 92, 93
 adjusting 94
 averaging 96
 changing type 93
 corner 83
 deleting 92
 drawing and 87–92
 removing extra 95
 selected 122
 smooth 83, 94
 unselected 122
Angle menu 120
angle of constraint 130
angle of rotation 56, 130
Angle option, for gradients 228
angles
 for rotating objects 140
 for shearing 146
 Smart Guide 120
annotating
 files 377
 objects 378
ANPA colors 190
Anti-Alias option 256, 276, 352

INDEX

appearance attributes 259, 260
   adding fills and strokes 263
   applying by dragging 261
   duplicating 263
   editing 262
   moving, copying, and deleting with the Layers palette 253
   removing 264
   reordering 262
   targeting objects, groups, and layers 260
   targeting with the Layers palette 260
Appearance palette 28, 260, 261
area type, entering on open path 290
area-type tool 29, 290
Arrange command 132
Arrange Icons command 58
arrowheads, adding to lines 154
Art brushes 101
   setting options 106
artboard 12, 70, 71, 72
   showing and hiding 71
Artistic filters and effects 280
artwork
   masking 167
   tracing 111
ASCII option 365
Ask When Modified option 77
Assign Profile command 211
attaching to path. *See* path-type tool
attributes
   stroke 181
   type 293
Attributes palette 37, 370
Auto Hyphenate option 317

auto trace tool 111
AutoCAD Drawing format 357
AutoCAD Interchange format 357
Auto-Create Symbols option 355
Auto-Kerning option 298
Auto-Leading option 296
Automatically option 77
Average command 96
axes, rotation of 131
axis of reflection 144

B

background color
   preview options 347
background matting 339–341
   and anti-aliased images 339
   in GIF or PNG format 339
   in JPEG format 341
background transparency 339–341
   hard-edged, in GIF or PNG-8 format 340
   in GIF and PNG images 340
   variable-level in PNG-24 format 341
banding in blends and gradients 371
base (non-emulsion side) 395
base color 223
baseline
   leading 297
   selecting type from 288
   setting preferences 288
baseline shift 299
Batch command 406
batch processing 406
bending. *See* Scribble and Tweak filter *and* Distort filters
bevel join 181

Binary option 365
bitmap images 67–70, 275
   See also raster images
   applying filters 277, 281, 282
   colorizing 276
   converting from vector objects 275
   defined 68, 128
   in Illustrator 275
   loading 278
   rasterizing 275
   resolution 276
   setting resolution for 368–369
   speeding printing of 365
   texturizing 279
Bitmap Printing option 365
bleed 390, 396
blend color 223
Blend Front to Back command 159
Blend Horizontally command 159
Blend Vertically command 159
blending
   length, maximum 371–372
   printing issues 370
   shapes 155–157
Blending Mode command 125
blending modes 41, 223–226
   Isolate Blending option 41
   isolating within group 41
blends, banding in 371
Blur filters and effects 280
Blur option (JPEG) 332
BMP format 357
bounding box
   in patterns 234
   in separations 389
   moving objects with 123

preferences 123
resetting angle after transformation 147
resizing and 94
rotating objects with 140
scaling objects with 142
showing or hiding 123
transforming objects with 123
Break Link to Style command 270
breaking lines. *See* Kinsoku Shori (line breaking) options
breaking. *See* Release command
brightness 173
Bring Forward command 132
Bring to Front command 132
browser dithering 341, 342
Brush Libraries
   creating 111
   displaying names 110
   importing brushes from 110
Brush Libraries command 110
brush strokes
   selecting 125
Brush Strokes command 111, 125
Brush Strokes filters and effects 280
brushes 101
   adding to Brushes palette 104
   Art 106
   Calligraphic 101
   changing key color 109
   changing options 110
   changing preferences for all 101
   colorizing 108
   converting brushes to masked objects 102
   deleting from palette 103
   displaying by name 103
   displaying by type 103
   displaying pattern names 56
   duplicating 103
   importing from Brush Libraries 110
   moving 103
   Pattern 107
   previewing effects 104
   removing from path 103
   Scatter 105
   selecting unused 103
   tips for using 111
Brushes palette 24, 110
Button Mode command 401
button view 401, 405

C

Calligraphic brushes 101
Calligraphic pen. *See* Calligraphic brushes
capitalization, changing 320
Cascade command 58
center point of objects 97
   displaying and hiding 98
centered alignment 310
centered ellipses and rectangles, drawing 98
CGM format 357
Change Case command 320
characters
   auto-kerning 298
   changing direction 302
   changing type size 295
   changing type size units 295
   changing type style 294
   changing type units 300
   displaying hidden 293
   displaying options in Character palette 293
   kerning and tracking 297
   selecting a font from 294
characters (type)
   setting font 294
charts. *See* graphs
Check Spelling command 318
choke 385
chroma 173
circles, drawing 97, 98
   See also ellipses, drawing
CJK text
   checking spelling 318
   displaying options in Character palette 294
   displaying options in Paragraph palette 309
   divided note option 303
   hanging punctuation in 314
   Japanese layout rules option 312
   line breaking options 312
   proportional spacing option 311
Classroom in a Book 5
Cleanup command 292
Clear Guides command 119
Clip to Artboard option
   in Web-optimized images 335
Clipboard, importing and exporting artwork with 127
Clipping Mask command 167, 168
clipping masks 42, 167, 253
clipping sets 253
cloning. *See* Copy command *and* Paste in Front command
Close command 58
closed paths, drawing and splitting 85, 87, 90, 96, 102
CMM. *See* color management engine

CMYK 175
   PostScript option 347
   output 381
   color model 174
   converting to 276
   icon 182
CMYK mode
   selecting color in 192
   selecting for new documents 70
CMYK Startup file 183, 190–191
Collect in New Layer command 249, 250
color blends, printing 370–374
Color Burn mode 224
Color button 179
Color Dodge mode 224
Color folder for Windows profiles 213
color gamuts 175
Color Halftone command 280
color management
   black point compensation 210
   calibrating monitors 214
   characterizing monitors 214
   color spaces in 199
   loading settings 210
   policies 203–205, 207–208
   predefined settings 202
   printing options 365
   profiles. *See* profiles
   rendering intents 209
   saving settings 210
   setting up 201–203
   soft-proofing 210
   viewing environment 200
   working spaces 203, 205
color management engine 200, 208

color management system. *See* color management
color matching module 200
Color mode option 225
Color Model menu 255
color models 11, 173–175
color modes
   selecting color in 191–192
   selecting for new documents 70
Color option 119
Color palette 26, 35, 180
color palette
   selecting for GIF 333
   selecting for PNG-8 333
color picker 35, 191–192
Color Picker dialog box. *See* color picker
Color Picker option 191
color profiles
   See profiles
color separations. *See* separations
Color Settings command 202, 205
color slider 191–192
color spaces 175, 199
color table format
   Adaptive palette for GIF 335
   Perceptual palette for GIF 335
Color Table panel 336
color tables
   adding colors in 336
   deleting colors from 338
   editing colors in 337
   loading 338, 339
   locking colors in 337
   saving 338
   selecting 335
   selecting colors in 336

sorting 336
   unlocking colors in 338
color transitions, quality of 69
color values 56
   specifying 192
color wheel 173
colors
   adding swatches from other documents 187
   adding to 1-bit images 276
   adding to gradient fills 229
   adding to gradient mesh 233
   adjusting 195
   changing for brushes 108
   changing globally 185
   choosing 26
   choosing for layers 244
   complementary 174
   deleting 338
   desaturating 196
   deselecting in the color table 337
   device-independent 200
   editing 337
   global process 185
   importing from desktop 193
   inverting 196
   loading color table 339
   loading from other color matching systems 189
   locking 337
   measuring RGB 174
   merging swatches 187
   mixing 194, 194
   non-global process 185
   nonprintable 192
   nonprinting 176
   non-Web-safe 192

number for GIF 333
number for PNG-8 333
painting with 178
PANTONE 189
printing color composites 365
saturating 196
selecting by color system numbers 189
selecting objects filled with 186
selecting Web-safe colors 191
shifting to Web palette equivalents 341
soft-proofing 210
spot 176, 185
subtractive 174
unlocking 338
Web-shifting 342
Colors option 333
colors, base 223
columns text. *See* text columns
combining. *See* compound paths
commands
   in actions 405
   keyboard shortcuts 62–63
Compatible Gradient and Gradient Mesh Printing option 373
complementary colors 174
Composite option 365
compound paths 163, 167
   converting to type 303
   converting type into 303
   creating and adjusting 167
   defined 163
   releasing 167
   reversing 167
Compound Paths command 166, 375

Compress Text and Line Art option 349
compressing files
   using LZW 359
   using TIFF format 359
compressing images 332, 333, 334
compression 329, 330
   lossless and GIF format 330
   lossless and PNG-8 format 330
   lossy and JPEG format 329
compression format 329
Computer Graphics Metafile format 357
conserving paper, film 393, 394
Constant option (ink pen) 161
Constrain Angle option 125, 131
Construction Guides option 120
context-sensitive menus 57, 139
Continue button 404
continuous-tone images 363
Convert filters 195
Convert Photoshop Layers to Objects option 74
Convert to Process option 228
Convert to Shape commands 149
convert-anchor-point tool 93
converting
   strokes to filled objects 165
   type to compound paths 303
converting to curves. *See* Create Outlines command
converting to paths. *See* Create Outlines command
Copy command 126
copying
   and placing precisely 127
   between applications 125, 128
   by dragging 126

   by pasting 126
   in a circular pattern. *See* Transform Again command
   objects 20
   paint attributes 193
   type attributes 300, 301
CorelDRAW
   importing from 72
corner points 83, 94
corner radius value 98
corners, rounding 149
correcting mistakes 115
Create Clipping Mask option 276
Create Gradient Mesh command 231
Create New Action button 402
Create Outlines command 303
creating files 11
Crop command 164
crop marks 367, 388, 390
   eliminating 367
   Japanese 367
   setting 367, 396
Crop Marks command 367
cropping artwork. *See* masks
cross hair 84
crosshatch photo images 282–283
current tool, displaying 61
Cursor Key option 126
cursors
   locked layers 250
   precision 55, 84
curve handles. *See* direction points
Curve Quality option 356
curves
   See also drawing
   adjusting 95

drawing 88, 90
smoothing 86
curves, drawing 18
custom color tables 335
custom colors 189–190
   converting to process colors 392
   in gradients 228, 229
custom startup files 190
Cut command 126
cutting
   with knife tool 166
   with scissors tool 96, 111
   with Slice command 166
cutting contents. *See* Clipping Mask command

D

Darken mode 224
dashed lines, creating 181
Dashes and Stripes dialog box. *See* Stroke palette
dashes, replacing in text 320
default actions 409
De-Interlace command 280
De-Interlace filter 280
Delete (layers) command 251
Delete Brush command 103
Delete Color command 338
Delete Empty Text Paths option 292
Delete Riders filter 377
Delete Style command 270
delete-anchor-point tool 92
deleting
   actions 409
   brush attributes 102
   brushes 103
   brushes from paths 103

colors 338
layers 251
objects 130
DeluxePaint 356
Density option (ink pen) 161
Density Photo Crosshatch option 283
Deselect All Colors command 337
Deselect All command 87, 124, 125
deselecting
   colors 337
   objects 19, 124, 125
device-independent color 200
dictionaries, changing 319
Difference mode 225
Dim Images To option 245, 247
direction lines 87
   adjusting 90, 92, 94
direction points 87, 88, 122
direct-lasso tool 20, 122, 133
direct-selection tool 19, 121, 133
   activating temporarily 94
   adjusting paths with 92, 94, 95
Disable Auto Add/Delete option 93
discretionary hyphens, in type 317
Dispersion Noise option 283
Dispersion option (ink pen) 161
Display Preview Bounds option 148
Display Stroke Weight option 148
displaying
   See also showing
   character options 293
   documents 70–72
   layers 243
   multilingual options 294
   paragraph options 309

distance, measuring 56, 117
Distort filters and effects 148, 280
distorting images 280
distorting objects 146, 148
Distribute Objects option 129
Distribute Spacing option 129
distributing objects 129
   See also transforming objects
   space between objects 129
Dither option 333
   for GIF or PNG-8 333
dithering, browser 341, 342
Divide & Outline Will Remove Unpainted Artwork option 165
Divide command 164
divided note. *See* Wari-Chu option
Document Info command 168, 378
Document Setup command 12, 61, 71, 364
documentation overview 2
dots per inch (dpi) 69, 392
Downloadables command 4
downsampling 334
drag and drop 128, 180
drawing
   adjusting segments 92, 94
   changing point types 93
   circles 97, 98
   curved segments 89
   ellipses 97, 98
   mixing straight and curved segments 90
   open and closed paths 84
   polygons 99
   rectangles 97, 98
   rounded rectangles 97, 98
   shapes 97

spirals 99
squares 97, 98
stars 100
with cross hair 84
with pen tool 87
with pencil tool 84
Drop Shadow command 152
Duplicate Brush command 103
Duplicate Layer command 250
Duplicate Swatch command 184
duplicating
   brushes 103
   layers 249
   objects 123
   See also eyedropper tool *and* Transform Again command
   type 300
duplicating objects 20
DWG format 357
DXF format 72, 357

E

edges, feathering and softening 153
Edit Column button 250
Edit Original option 79
Edit Selected Paths option 86
Edit Views command 58
Effect menu 260, 271
effects 36, 45, 271–272
   applying to text 271, 303
   Artistic 280
   Blur 280
   Brush Strokes 280
   changing objects and paths 148
   Color Halftone 280
   defined 260
   Distort 280

editing 272
Fresco 279
Glass 278, 279
Grain 279
Outline Type 303
Pixelate 280
removing 272
Rough Pastels 278, 279
Sharpen 280
Sketch 280
Stylize 280
Texture 280
Video 280
Ellipse command 149
ellipse tool 97
ellipses, drawing 97, 98
ellipsis (symbol), in text 320
em space 297
Embed ICC profile option 348, 352
Embed Image command 78
embedded objects 76–79
emulsion 395
en and em dashes, in text 320
Encapsulated PostScript (EPS). *See* EPS format
endpoints 83
   joining 96
endpoints, joining 96
engraved effects. *See* Pen and Ink filter
EPS format 346
   placing files 75–76
   printing embedded 77
   problems with spot colors and transparent artwork 177
   saving in 357
   setting transparent or opaque backgrounds 347

EPSF Riders file 377
erase tool 86
Error Handler option 377
Exclude command 164
Exclusion mode 225
Exit command 71
Expand Appearance command 102
Expand command
   converting fills and strokes to objects 237–238
   converting gradients and patterns 237–238
   creating mesh object from gradients 231
   expanding complex objects 238
Expand Stroke. *See* Outline Stroke command
Expert Fractions option 320
Export command 255
exporting
   files 349–359
   layers to Photoshop 255, 256
   text files 305
   to Clipboard 127
   to Photoshop format 351
   transparencies 351
eye icon 244
eyedropper tool 193
   changing paint attributes 193
   copying type 300
   importing color with 193
   painting with 193

F

Feather command 43, 153
feathering edges 153
feathering objects 43
file formats

compression 329
importing into Illustrator 72
Photoshop 5 255
saving in different 356
See also individual formats
files, batch-processing 406–407
fill 178–179
See also patterns
attributes 260
for masks 169
Fill box 25
Fill button 179
Fill Color command 124
filled objects, selecting 123
filling objects 25, 28
film
base 395
conserving 393, 394
Filmstrip format 357
filters
See also individual filter names
applying to bitmap images 277, 280, 281, 282
Artistic 280
Blur 280
Brush Strokes 280
changing objects and paths 148
Color Halftone 280
De-Interlace 280
Distort 280
Fresco 279
Gaussian Blur 280
Glass 278, 279
Grain 279
improving performance 279
installing 277
last used 277

NTSC Colors 280
Object Mosaic 281
Pen and Ink 282
Photo Crosshatch 282
Pixelate 280
plug-ins 277
previewing effects 277
Rough Pastels 278, 279
Sharpen 280
shortcuts 277
Sketch 280
special purpose 280
Stylize 280
Texture 280
Video 280
Find Font command 296
finding and replacing
fonts 296
text 319
Fit Headline command 316
Fit In Window command 60
Flash animation 248
Flash format 38, 358
exporting in 354–356
Flash frames 248
flat-color image
compression format for 329
flatness 370, 377
Flatten Artwork command 252
Flatten Photoshop Layers to a Single Image option 74
flattening layers 251, 256
Flip Horizontal command 148
Flip Vertical command 148
FLM format 357
FOCOLTONE colors 189
Font command 295

font family 294
fonts
Adobe Expert 320
changing 294
changing monospaced to proportional 311
choosing 294
creating ligatures 320
finding and replacing 296
multiple master 292
OpenType 304
proportional 311
single master 292
Type 1 292
Type 1 CID 311
Force Fonts to Download option 365
four-color process printing 175
Four-Up view. *See* Two-Up and Four-Up view 328
fractions. *See* Expert Fractions option
Frame Rate option 355
Free Distort command 148
Free Distort filter. *See* free transform tool
free memory (RAM) 61
free transform tool 146
defined 139
distorting objects 146
reflecting objects 144
rotating objects 140
scaling objects 142
shearing objects 145
freeform paths
See also pencil tool
changing 85
drawing 84

FreeHand
    importing from 72
freehand tool. *See* pencil tool
Fresco filter 279
full screen mode 58

G

Gamma utility 215
gamuts 175
Gaussian Blur filter 280
General preferences 2
geometric patterns 236–237
GIF
    and Adaptive palette 335
    and lossless compression 330
    and Perceptual palette 335
    background matting in 339
    background transparency in 339
    custom color table 335
    file format 330
    formatting as 333
    hard-edged transparency 340
    selecting a color palette 333
    selecting a color table 335
    specifying number of colors 333
    Web Snap slider 334, 342
    Web-safe color table 335
GIF format 37
Glass filter 278, 279
global colors 185
global process color 185
Glyph Options command 321
Glyph options command 321
glyphs (characters), alternative 321
Go to Link command 78
gradient bar 229
Gradient button 28, 179, 228

gradient fill. *See* gradients
gradient mesh 230–233
    adding color 233
    optimizing printing 373
    printing 383
    setting resolution when printing 369
    transforming and editing 232
gradient mesh tool 231
Gradient palette 28, 228
gradient tool 229
gradients 228
    adding color to 229
    applying across multiple objects 229
    applying with Transparency palette 227
    colors 228
    converting into objects 237
    creating 228
    customizing 28
    displaying names 56
    importing 188
    in masked objects 237
    linear 228
    modifying 229
    printing 370–374, 376
    printing as a spot color 228
    printing as separations 383
    radial 228
    stop 229
Grain filter 279
graphic file formats 72
Graphic Style command 124
graphic styles 45
graphs 100
gray levels for printing 371

grayscale 175
    converting to 276
greeking 308
Gridline Every option 119
grids 13, 119
Grids in Back option 120
Group command 22, 133
grouped objects
    hiding and showing 135
    in layers 242
    locking and unlocking 135
    moving 132
    nesting 133
    selecting 133
    stacking 134
grouping objects 22
groups, creating 22
group-selection tool 23, 122
guide objects
    converting objects to 119
    See also guides
guides 13, 118
    hiding and showing 119
    preferences 119
    Smart Guides 120
Guides & Grid command 119
gutters, changing 307

H

halftone screens 392
    See also screen frequency 69
halftoning 363
hand tool 13, 58
Hang Punctuation option 314
hanging indentation 309
hanging punctuation 310, 314
Hard light mode 224

INDEX

Hard Mix command 194
hard-edged transparency 340
Hatch Layers option 282
hatch style 162
headline type, fitting 316
Help 2
hidden characters 293
Hidden Layers option 352
Hide Artboard command 71
Hide Bounding Box command 123
Hide Center Point option 98
Hide command 55, 134
Hide Guides command 119
Hide Others command 244
Hide Rulers command 115
Hide Selection command 135
Hide Tools command 55
hiding
    center point of object 98
    layers 243, 250
    objects 134
horizontal scale, adjusting 299
horizontal type 291
    aligning along path 291
    entering 287
    entering along path 290
    entering in objects 290
HSB color model 173
HSB mode
    selecting color in 192
HTML files, saving 342
hue 173
Hue mode 225
hyphenation 317
    preferences 317

Hyphenation Options command 317
hyphens, discretionary 317

I

I-beam pointer 287
IBM PC formats 357
ICC Profile option 333
    for JPEG 333
ICC profiles 200
    monitor 214
IFF. *See* Amiga Interchange File Format
Ignore Overprinting in Composite Output option 365
Illustrator
    Check Spelling command 318
    importing images from 72–76
    online Help 2
    preferences file 64
    vector graphics 67, 68
Image Format option 356
image maps 37
imageable area 70, 393
imagemap, assigning to an object 326–327
images
    adding color to 1-bit 276
    importing 72–76
    negative or positive 395
    optimization format 331
    optimizing 329, 330, 332, 333
    previewing 61
    resizing 334
    resolution 68–70
    saving optimized 342
    See also bitmap images

imagesetters 71, 276
importing
    alternative glyphs (characters) 321
    artwork 72–76
    brushes 110
    colors 188
    Illustrator files 72–76
    layers 255
    paths 127
    text files 127, 305
Include All Subdirectories option 406
Include Document Fonts option 347
Include Document Thumbnails option 347
Include Linked Files option 347
indentation, hanging 309
indenting paragraphs 309
    hanging 309
Info palette 56, 117
    measuring with 56
ink tool. *See* Pen and Ink command
Inner Glow command 152
Insert Menu Item command 403
Insert Select Path command 403
installation 1
integration with other Adobe products 47–49
Intent option
    destination color space 366
Interactive drop shadow tool 152
Interlace option 333, 334
Internet, linking artwork to 326
interpolation methods 334
Intersect command 164

Inverse command 124
Invert Colors command 196
Invert Mask option 223
Isolate Blending command 225

J

Japanese crop marks 367
Japanese file format 347
Japanese fonts, alternative characters in 321
Japanese layout rules (Moji Gumi option) 312
Join command 96
joining
   brush paths 111
   endpoints and paths 96
JPEG 329
   and lossy compression 329
   background matting in 341
   compression 349
   compression artifacts in 329
   formatting as 332
JPEG format 37
justifying lines 310

K

kerning
   auto 298
   changing 297
key color, changing 109
keyboard shortcuts 62–63
Keyboard Shortcuts command 62
Kinsoku Shori (line breaking) options 312, 314
knife tool 166
knockouts 226–227
Kumi Moji option 302
Kurikaeshi Moji Shori option 315

L

labels
   separations 390
landscape (horizontal) orientation 393
language dictionaries, changing 319
laser printer output 276
lasso tool 20, 122, 133
Layer/Group Overrides Color command 265
layers 241–256
   applying appearance attributes to 252
   choosing colors for 244
   clipping masks 42
   creating 246–247
   current 242
   deleting 251
   dimming images in 245
   displaying in Outline view 245
   duplicating 249
   expanding levels 243
   flattening 251, 256
   grouped objects in 242
   hiding and showing 243
   hierarchy 241
   locking and unlocking 250
   merging 249
   moving objects between 248–249
   nesting 241
   nonprinting 251
   preserving on export 256
   printable and nonprintable 250
   Release to Layers command 36
   remembering order when pasting 133
   reversing order of 248
   selecting 242
   separating 391
   stacking order 241
   targeting 252
   template 254
   viewing 243, 245
Layers palette 30, 44, 242, 243, 246
leading
   auto 296
   changing 296, 297
   setting as font size 297
letterforms, changing 303
levels of gray 371
Library Open command 163
Library Save As command 163
ligatures, creating 320
Lighten mode 224
limit-check error 369, 374
line attributes. *See* stroke attributes
line breaking options. *See* Kinsoku Shori (line breaking) options
line screen 377
   maximum 371
   printer 392
line trap, creating 387
line weight. *See* stroke weight
linear gradient 228
Linear option (ink pen) 161
lines
   See also paths
   adding arrowheads 154
   dashed 181
   drawing 84, 87, 90
   selecting 122
   trapping 387
   wavy and Zig Zag 154

lines per inch (lpi) 69
Link Blocks command 306
linking 77
   EPS or PDF files 75
   images 76–79
   objects 76–79
   type blocks 306
   type containers 306
Links palette 77–79
list view 401
live effects 36, 45
live shapes 36
Load Texture command 279
loading
   bitmap images and textures 278
   color tables 338, 339
Locate Layer command 244
Locate Object command 244
Lock command 134, 135
Lock Guides command 119
Lock option 247, 250
Lock/Unlock Selected Colors command 337
locking
   colors 337
   layers 250
   masks 169
   objects 134
Log Errors to File option 407
lossless compression 330, 331
lossy compression 329
Lossy option 333
lowercase and uppercase, changing 320
Luminosity mode 225

M
Macintosh Drag Manager 128
magnifying and reducing views 13, 59–61
magnifying. *See* zoom tool
Make Clipping Mask command 254
Make command (clipping mask) 168
Make Guides command 119
Make Riders command 377
Make Wrap command 308
Manually option 77
marquee 60, 122
masks 160
   adding fill and stroke 169
   creating 168
   locking and unlocking 169
   opacity 222–223
   selecting 125, 168
   splitting 375
   using outlined type as 304
Masks command 125
mathematical operations in text boxes 116
Matte menu 340, 341
Matte option 333
   for JPEG 333
matted background 339
Max. Line Length option 283
measure tool 117
measuring
   Info palette 56
memory and printing 374
Merge command 164
Merge Selected command 250
Merge Styles command 269
Merge Swatches option 187

merged objects. *See* Pathfinder commands
merged paths. *See* compound paths
merging layers 249
mesh lines 230
mesh patches 230
mesh points 230
Mesh resolution setting 369
mesh tool. *See* gradient mesh tool
meshes
   improving printing of 373
   setting resolution when printing 369
Microsoft Explorer 326
Microsoft Office
   setting preview image options 347
Minus Back command 164
Minus Front command 164
misregistration 385
missing fonts 304
mistakes, correcting 115
miter join 181
MM Design palette 293
   CMS. *See* color management 199
modal controls, using with actions 404
models. *See* color models
modes. *See* color models
Moji Gumi (Japanese layout rules) option 312
monitor profiles 214
monitors
   calibrating 214
   characterizing 214
   output 276
   resolution 68–69

size 68–69
monospaced fonts, changing to proportional 311
Move command 127
Move option 129
moving
   brushes 103
   direction lines and points 87
   type along path 291
moving objects 20, 126
   between Illustrator and Photoshop 126
   between layers 132
   by dragging 126
   grouped 129, 132
   pasting 126
   specified distance and direction 127
   to front or back 132
   while drawing 97
   with arrow keys 126
   with bounding box 123
   with free transform tool 126
   with Smart Guides 121
multilingual options, displaying 294
multiple master fonts 292
Multiply mode 224

N

named optimization settings 331, 332
National Television Standards Committee (NTSC) 280
Navigator palette 60
negative and positive film 395
nesting 241
Netscape Navigator 326
New Brush command 104, 107
New Color button 336
New Color command 336
New command 11, 70
New Layer button 246
New Layer command 246, 255
New Style command 269
New Sublayer button 246
New Sublayer command 246
New View command 58
New Window command 58
None button 179
None option
   in GIF hard-edged transparency 340
   in PNG background transparency 341
None swatch 182
Non-Global option 185
nonimageable area 70
nonprintable colors 192
nonrecordable actions 402
Non-Uniform Scaling option 143
non-Web-safe colors 192
   selecting 337
Normal mode 223
NTSC Colors command 280
NTSC Colors filter 280
numeric values
   for specifying colors 192

O

Object Highlighting option 120
Object Mosaic filter 281
object, merged. *See* Pathfinder commands
objects
   aligning and distributing 129
   changing with filters and effects 148
   converting to guide objects 119
   converting to rectangles and ellipses 149
   copying between Illustrator and Photoshop 125
   deleting 130
   deselecting 124, 125
   displaying and hiding center point 97, 98
   distorting with free transform tool 146
   dragging between Illustrator and Photoshop 126
   drawing 97
   duplicating 123
   entering type in 290
   grouping and ungrouping 133
   hiding and showing 134
   locking and unlocking 135
   masking 167
   moving 123, 125, 126
   moving between layers 248, 249
   moving while drawing 97
   moving with bounding box 123
   offsetting 130
   overlapping 167
   pasting to Photoshop 126
   reflecting 144
   reflecting tool 144
   removing brush attributes from 102
   reordering 132
   resetting bounding box 147
   reshaping 95
   rotating 140, 141
   scaling 123, 142, 143
   selecting 121, 124

shearing 145, 146
Smart Guides 121
smoothing 95
stacking order 131
transforming 139
twirling 151
wrapping type around 308
objects, overlapping. *See* Exclude command
Official Adobe Print Publishing Guide 5
Offset option 394
Offset Path command 130
OLE 128
online display pixel dimensions 68
online Help 2
online publishing
   colors and 177
Online Settings preference 4
Only Web Colors option 191
Opacity and Mask Define Knockout Shape option 226
Opacity command 125
opacity masks 42, 222–223
   applying gradients or patterns 227
   inverting 223
Open command 11, 71, 73, 74, 75
open paths
   joining brush 111
   joining endpoints and paths 96
Open Recent Files command 74
opening
   files 73
   Illustrator files 72–76
   palettes 55
opening files 11
OpenType fonts 304

Optimize Colors palette 338
Optimize to File Size option 334
Optimized option 332
   for JPEG 332
optimizing
   2-Up and 4-Up view 328
   auto-regeneration 331
   choosing a format 331
   choosing a view for 328
   controlling 331
   GIF format 330
   images 332, 333, 334
   JPEG format 329
   named settings 331
   PNG-24 format 330
   PNG-8 format 330
   Save for Web dialog box 331
   settings 332
   to file size 334
optimizing files for the Web 37
Options for command 244, 246, 251
Options of Selected Object command 110
order. *See* Arrange command
OS/2 format 357
Other Library command 110, 188, 270
Outer Glow command 152
Outline command 59, 164, 245
Outline Stroke command 165
Outline Type effect 303
Outline view 59, 245, 247
outlining objects. *See* strokes
out-of-gamut colors 175, 180
   displaying in color picker 192
output options. *See* Document Setup command 71

output resolution 369
Output Resolution option 370
output, for raster images 276
ovals, drawing. *See* ellipses, drawing
overlapping objects. *See* Pathfinder commands
overlapping paths. *See* compound paths
Overlay mode 224
Overprint Black command 384
Overprint Black option 395
Overprint Fill option 384
Overprint Preview command 59, 383
overprinting 383–384, 387–388
   black 395
   on composite proofs 364
   previewing 383
   printing on composites 365
   to create spread trap 387
Override Action "Open" Commands option 406
Override Action "Save In" Commands option 407

P

page boundaries 72
Page Setup dialog box 364
page size 71, 393
   See also artboard
paint
   copying attributes of 193
   setting attributes 178–179
paint bucket tool 193
   copying type with 301
   using with gradient mesh 233
Paint Style command 124

paintbrush tool 25, 101
   adjusting path with 102
   setting preferences 101
painting
   brush strokes 25
   with a fill 25
   with a gradient 27
   with a pattern 27
   with a stroke 26
   with multiple fills and strokes 28
painting order. *See* stacking order
painting type 300
palettes 10, 55–56
   docking 56
   showing 55
   sizing 56
PANTONE color 189
paper stretch 386
Paragraph palette 293, 309
paragraphs
   aligning type in 310
   indenting 309
   indenting first line 309
Paste command 126, 248
Paste in Back
   command 126, 132, 249
Paste in Front
   command 126, 132, 248
Paste Remembers Layers
   option 133, 248
path guides for text, adding 307
Path Simplify command 95
Pathfinder commands 163
   RAM requirements 163
   repeating last 164
   setting options 165
Pathfinder palette 163
paths

See also compound paths
adjusting 92, 94
adjusting with pencil tool 84
adjusting with reshape tool 95
anchor points 83
blending 157
changing with filters and
   effects 148
connecting 93
converting type to 303
drawing 87, 89, 90
drawing curved 18
drawing with pencil tool 84
endpoints 83
entering type on 291
erasing 86
extending 93
fitting headline type across 316
in Photoshop 128
joining brushed 111
joining endpoints 96
masking 167
overview 83
recording 403
rejoining 375
removing brushes from 103
reversing 167
segments in 83
simplifying 35, 95
smoothing 85
splitting 96, 374–375
type 290, 292
paths, closed 87, 90
   drawing with paintbrush
      tool 102
   drawing with pencil tool 85
paths, drawing straight 17

paths, empty
   deleting 292
paths, freeform
   drawing 84
paths, reshaping 22
path-type tool 29, 291
pattern bounding box 234
Pattern brushes 101, 107
pattern tile 234
patterns 233–235, 235–237
   converting into objects 237
   creating brushes with 101
   importing 188
   masked objects 237
   modifying 236
   moving 236
   printing 376
   tiling 236
   transforming 236
Pause option 406
PC Paintbrush 358
PCX format 358
PDF
   viewing with Acrobat Reader 1
PDF files 358
   opening in Illustrator 73
   placing 75–76
   saving in 347
PDF format 48
PDF Writer 365
Pen and Ink command 282
Pen and Ink filter 160–163
pen tool 17–18, 87
   See also curves
   adjusting paths with 92
   measuring coordinates with 57
pencil tool 15–16, 84

See also freeform paths
  adjusting paths with 85
  setting preferences 86
Perceptual color table 335
Perceptual palette
  using with GIF 335
Perceptual rendering intent 209
performance, improving 279
Persistent command 189
Photo CD 72
Photo Crosshatch command 282
Photo Crosshatch filter 282–283
Photoshop
  compatible file formats 72
  copying objects into
    Illustrator 125
  dragging Illustrator files into 128
  dragging objects into
    Illustrator 128
  exporting from Illustrator to 351
  exporting transparency
    features 220
  importing and exporting
    from 255
  importing and exporting
    layers 255, 256
  integration with
    Illustrator 47–48
  Photoshop 5 file format 255
PICT format 358
picture clipping 128
PIXAR file format 72, 358
pixel dimensions 68
  changing 334
Pixel Preview
  command 34, 59, 326
Pixelate filters and effects 280
pixelation 69
pixels 68

resolution and 68–69
using as measurement unit 34
pixels per inch (ppi) 69
Place command 73, 75, 255
placing
  EPS or PDF files 75–76
  images 61
  text 305
Playback Options command 406
plug-ins 61, 277
  filters 276, 277
  making aliases 61
Plug-ins Preferences command 61
PNG format 37, 358
  background matting in 339
  background transparency in 339
PNG-24
  format 330
  lossless compression and 331
  saving image as 334
  variable-level background
    transparency 341
PNG-8
  Colors menu 333
  Custom color table 335
  format 330
  formatting file as 333
  hard-edged transparency 340
  lossless compression and 330
  selecting a color palette 333
  selecting a color table 335
  specifying number of colors 333
  Transparency option 333
  Web Snap slider 334, 342
  Web-safe color table 335
point of origin 139
  for scaling objects 142

pointer
  changing to cross hair 84
  changing to precision pointer 55
points
  See also anchor points
  changing 93
  for ruler 116
  for type size 300
polygon tool 99
Portable Document Format. *See*
  PDF files
portrait (vertical) orientation 393
positive and negative film 395
positive image 395
PostScript
  file format 358
  Level 1 and Level 2 359
  saving as EPS 347
PostScript Color Management
  option 366
PostScript Printer description files.
  See PPD files
PPD files 391, 392
  and page size 393
  selecting 391
preferences
  angle of constraint 131
  constrain angle 125, 131
  Corner Radius 98
  Disable Auto Add/Delete 93
  Display Stroke Weight 148
  general 2
  grids and guides 119
  hyphenation 317
  Japanese crop mark 367
  Keyboard Increment 126
  paintbrush tool 101

Paste Remembers
   Layers 133, 248
pencil and smooth tools 86
Plug-ins 61
ruler units 116
Scale Strokes and Effects 143
scaling objects 143
Smart Guides 120
Transform Pattern Tiles 125
transparency 221
type 288
Type Area Select 288
type units 300
undo levels 115
units of measure 116
Use Area Select 123
Use Precise Cursors 84
Preferences command 64
Preserve Appearance option 347
Preserve Illustrator Editing
   Capabilities option 348
Preserve Path option 347
PressReady and printing 366
Preview All Layers command 245
Preview command 59, 245
Preview option 247
preview options
   setting background color 347
Preview view 247
Preview view command 245
previewing 59
   brush effects 104
   filter effects 277
Print command 364
Print option 247, 251
printable area. *See* tiling pages
printable colors 192

printer resolution 69
printer's marks 390
printer's quote marks 320
printing
   color blends 370–374
   color management options 365
   embedded EPS images 77
   error information 377
   file information 378
   four-color 175
   gradients 370–374, 376
   gradients as separations 383
   layers 250
   memory and path splitting 374
   methods 363
   options in Page Setup dialog
      box 364–365
   patterns 376
   PDF Writer support 365
   separations 396
   tips for efficient 374
   transparencies 370
   with Adobe PressReady 366
   with grayscale printers 279
process color icon 182
process colors 175, 177, 178
   editing 185
   printing 175
profiles 200
   adding or updating 213
   displaying in status bar 61
   embedding in output 212
   for printing 365
   guidelines for monitors 215
   obtaining 212
   reassigning 211
   storage location 213

   updating 213
program installation 1
Progressive option 332
Progressive option, for JPEG 332
Proof Colors command 211
Proof Setup commands 211
proportional spacing (Tsume) 311
publishing text symbols 320
punctuation
   hanging 310, 314
   smart 320
Punctuation Hangs Only If Space
   Unavailable option 314
Punk & Bloat filter 149

Q

Quality option 332
Quality option, for JPEG 332
Quality/Speed slider
   settings for 368–369
Quick Reference Card 2
Quit command 71
quotation marks
   changing 320
   Smart Quotes 320

R

radial gradient 228
RAM
   increasing for Pathfinder
      commands 163
Random option 129
Random option (ink pen) 161
rangecheck error 375
raster images 68
   See also bitmap images
   applying filters 280

converting to crosshatched drawing 282
creating from bitmap images 275
Rasterization Resolution setting 369
Rasterize command 275, 276
rasterizing 128, 275
Rectangle command 149
rectangle tool 97
rectangles, drawing 97
 See also squares, drawing
 centered 98
 squares 97, 98
rectangles, text 289
 dividing into rows and columns 307
Redo command 115
reference card 2
Reflect command 145
Reflect option (ink pen) 161
reflecting objects 144
 by specifying axis 144
 with free transform tool 144
 with reflect tool 144
reflection tool 22
registering 1
Registration color 182
registration marks 390
Relative Colorimetric rendering intent 209
Release Clipping Mask button 254
Release command 167
Release command (clipping mask) 168
Release Guides command 119
Release to Layers command 247
releasing compound paths 167

Remove Brush Strokes command 103
removing overlap. *See* Unite command
rendering intents 200, 209
Repeated Character Processing option 315
repeating last command 147, 164
Replace "(style name)" command 269
Replace Link command 78
Replace Spine option 159
Repopulate Views command 328
repositioning objects 20
resampling 334
Reset Actions command 409
reshape tool 95
reshaping objects and paths 95
resizing
 images 334
 objects 21
 palettes 56
 See also scaling objects
resolution 68
 changing output 369–370
 setting for rasterized objects 368–370
 specifying in separations 392
 specifying when rasterizing 276
Resolution option 351
restoring files 115
resulting color, in blending modes 223
Reverse Front to Back command 159
Reverse Order command 248, 249
Reverse Spine command 159
Reverse Trap option 386
Reverse Traps option 387

reversing
 compound paths 167
 paths 167
Revert command 115
RGB color model 174, 191
RGB command 35
RGB icon 182
RGB images
 converting to 276
 specifying colors numerically 192
RGB mode 70
 selecting color in 192
RGB startup file 183, 190–191
Riders file 377
right alignment 310
right reading 395
Rotate command 141
rotate tool 22, 140
rotating objects 140
 by specifying angle 140
 individually in a group 141
 with bounding box 140
 with free transform tool 140
 with rotate tool 140
 x and y axes 130
Rotation Noise option 283
Rotation option (ink pen) 161
Rotation Variance option 283
rotation, angle of 56, 130
Rough Pastels filter 278, 279
Roughen filter 150
Round Corners filter 149
round joins, setting 181
Rounded Rectangle command 149
rounded rectangles, drawing 97
 adjusting corners 98

centered 98
rounded-rectangle tool 97
rounding corners 149
roundtripping between file formats 348
Rows & Columns command 307
rows in text
    changing gutter size 307
    changing height 307
ruler guides 118
ruler origin, 117
rulers 13, 115–117
    changing units 116
    showing and hiding 115
Run Length option 349
running around selection. *See* Wrap command

S

Same Appearance command 124
Same As Source option 366
Same Blending Mode command 125
Same Fill & Stroke command 124
Same Fill Color command 124, 186
Same Opacity command 125
Same Paint Style command 186
Same Stroke Color command 124, 186
Same Stroke Weight command 124, 186
sampling. *See* eyedropper tool
Saturate command 196
saturation 173
Saturation mode 225
Saturation rendering intent 209
Save a Copy command 345, 348, 407

Save As command 345, 348, 407
Save command 345
Save for Web command 37
Save for Web dialog box 331
saving
    batch-processed files 407
    color tables 338
    HTML files 342
    in other file formats 345–348
    optimized images 342
Scale command 142
Scale option (ink pen) 161
Scale Stroke Weight option 148
Scale Strokes and Effects option 143
Scale Strokes and Effects preference 143
scale tool 142
scaling objects 21, 123, 142
    individually in a group 143
    setting preferences 143
    specifying scale factors 142
    with bounding box 142
    with free transform tool 142
    with scale tool 142
Scatter brushes 101
    resetting Random options 106
scissors tool 96, 111
scratch area 12, 70
screen angle 281, 377
screen frequency 377
    image resolution and 70
Screen mode 224
Scribble and Tweak filter 150
segments 89
    defined 83
    drawing 90

editing 94
selecting 122
Select Again command 124, 186
Select All Colors command 337
Select All command 124
Select All Unused command 183
Select Inverse command 124
Select Masks command 168
selecting
    all objects 124
    all unselected objects 124
    anchor points 121
    anchor points and segments 122
    brush strokes 125
    filled objects 123
    grouped objects 122, 133
    layers, groups, and objects 242
    lines 122
    masks 125
    multiple objects 124
    objects 19–20, 121
    objects with same attributes 124, 125
    paths 121
    paths by dragging 122
    segments 122
    stray points 125
    type 288
    type blocks 288
selection marquee 122
selection tool 19, 121, 133
    activating 94
selection tools 121
selections
    adding and removing 122
    copying between applications 128

Selective color table 335
Send Backward command 132
Send to Back command 132
Separation Setup option 390
separations 381
   color 363
   controlling space between 394
   converting spot colors to process colors 392
   printing 396
   problems with spot colors and transparent artwork 177
   saving 396
   setting options 390
settings
   online 4
Settings menu 331
shade stepping 152
shadows. *See* drop shadows
shapes
   changing with Pathfinder palette 163
   circles 16
   converting to rectangles and ellipses 149
   drawing circles 97
   drawing ellipses 97
   drawing polygons 99
   drawing rectangles 97
   drawing reshaping 95
   drawing rounded rectangles 97
   drawing spirals 99
   drawing squares 97
   drawing stars 100
   ellipses 16
   polygons 16
   rectangles 16
   rounded rectangles 16
   spirals 16
   squares 16
   stars 16
Sharpen filter and effect 280
shear tool 22, 145
shearing objects 145
   by specifying angle and axis 146
   with free transform tool 145
   with shear tool 145
shortcuts
   keyboard 62–63
Show Align command 129
Show All command 135
Show All Layer command 244
Show Appearance command 261
Show Artboard command 71
Show Bounding Box command 123
Show Center Point option 98
Show Color command 178
Show command 55
Show Gradient command 228
Show Grid command 13, 119
Show Guides command 119
Show Hidden Characters command 293
Show Images in Outline option 61, 76, 246
Show Info command 56
Show Layers command 242, 255
Show Links command 77
Show Multilingual command 294
Show option 247
Show Options command 129
   Character palette 293
   Paragraph palette 309
Show Rulers command 13, 115, 118
Show Stroke command 181
Show Styles command 268
Show Tool Tips option 2
Show Tools command 55
Show Transform command 147
showing
   center point of objects 98
   hidden characters 293
   layers 243
   pointer or cross hair 84
Simplify command 35
Simulate Colored Paper option 221
Single Full Page option 72, 117
single master fonts 292
size
   changing row gutter 307
   changing type 295
   measuring 56
Size command 295
Sketch filters and effects 280
skewing. *See* shearing objects
Slice command 166
Smart Guides 120
   choosing a point 120
   creating, moving, and transforming objects 121
   preferences 120
   turning on and off 120
   working with 121
Smart Guides command 120
Smart Punctuation command 320
Smart Punctuation dialog box 320
Smart Quotes 320
Smart Spaces 320
Smooth Color option, in blends 158
smooth points 83, 94

smooth tool 86
smoothing paths 95
smoothing paths or strokes 85
Snap to Grid command 119
Snap to Pixel command 326
Snap to Point command 126
Snapping Tolerance option 120
Soft light mode 224
Soft Mix command 194–195
softening edges 153
soft-proofing colors 210
Sort by Hue command 336
Sort by Kind command 79
Sort by Luminance command 336
Sort by Names command 79
Sort by Popularity command 336
Sort by Status command 79
spacing options
    for type 310
    proportional 311
Specified Distance option 158
Specified Steps option 158
Spell Checking filter 319
spelling, checking 318
    changing language dictionaries for 319
    for CJK fonts 318
spiral tool 99
Split Long Paths option 374
splitting paths
    to print complex shapes 374–375
    with filled and stroked objects 375
    with scissors tool 96, 111
splitting. *See* Release command
spot color icon 182
spot colors 176, 178
    and blended objects 156
    editing swatches 185
    problems exporting with overlapping transparent artwork 177
    See also custom colors 190
Spot Function Template file 377
spread trap 385
squares, drawing 97, 98
    See also rectangles, drawing
stacked objects
    grouping 134
    moving forward or backward 132
stacking order 131
    layers 241
standard screen mode 58
star targets 390
star tool 100
startup files 183, 190–191
    creating customized 190
status bar 14, 61
Step by Step option 406
Stop for Errors option 407
straight lines, drawing 17, 87
Stray Points command 125
stroke attributes 260
    See also Stroke palette
    Bevel Join 181
    Dashed Lines 181
    Miter Join 181
    Round Join 181
    setting 181
    Stroke Weight 181
Stroke box 25
Stroke button 179
Stroke Color command 124
Stroke palette 27
    See also stroke attributes
    displaying 181
    using 181–182
stroke weight
    preserving while scaling objects 143
    setting 181
Stroke Weight command 124
strokes
    adding to masks 169
    adjusting with paintbrush tool 102
    adjusting with pencil tool 85
    converting to filled objects 165
    erasing 86
    setting attributes for 181
    smoothing 85
stroking objects 26, 28
style libraries 270
Style Libraries command 270
Style option 119
styles 45, 259, 265–270
    applying 267, 268
    applying by dragging 268
    applying to text 266
    applying to type 303
    changing order of 269
    choosing a view for 268
    creating 268
    creating style libraries 270
    deleting 270
    disassociating from selection 270
    dragging from the Appearance palette 269
    duplicating 269
    importing from a library 270
    merging 269

modifying 265, 268
renaming and replacing 265, 269
unlinking from selection 270
Styles palette 30, 45, 259, 268
Stylize filters and effects 280
Subdivisions option 120
subscripts and superscripts 298
subtractive colors 174
surface controls 279
SVG format 38, 39
advanced options 353–354
exporting in 352–354
SVG Interactivity palette 39, 353
swatch libraries
creating persistent palettes 189
loading colors from other files 188
moving swatches to Swatches palette 188
selecting by color system number 189
swatches 178
displaying 183
loading into Illustrator 189
merging 187
modifying 184–185
sorting 183
Swatches palette 26, 30, 182, 182–185
Swatches palette, updating 187
SWF format 38, 358
exporting in 354–356
Symmetric option (ink pen) 161

T
Tab Ruler command 315
Tab Ruler palette 315
tabs, setting 315

Targa. *See* TGA format
television, filters and effects for 280
template layer 254
creating 254
Template option 247
text
See also type
changing column width 307
changing orientation 302
changing row height 307
creating rectangles 289
editing 318
exporting 305
finding and replacing 319
importing 305
overflow 305
placing 305
replacing symbols 320
replacing text symbols 320
selecting 288
text boxes 116
using for masking 304
working with columns 304
text boxes
mathematical operations in 116
text columns
changing width 288, 307
working with 304
Text Label Hints option 120
Text Orientation command 302
text symbols, publishing 320
Texture filters and effects 279, 280
TGA format 359
Thickness option (ink pen) 161
Thickness Photo Crosshatch option 283
third-party developers 62

TIFF format 359
Tile command 58
Tile Full Pages option 72, 117
Tile Imageable Areas option 72
tiles, for Object Mosaic filter 281
tiling pages 72
time and date, displaying current 61
Tint Reduction value 387
tints
creating and changing globally 185–186
displaying names 56
tips
for colorizing brushes 109
for using brushes 111
tolerances, for tools 86
toolbox 10, 55
tools
See individual tool names
changing pointer to cross hair 84
hidden 10
keyboard shortcuts 62–63
selecting 10, 55
setting preferences for 86, 101
Top Angle option 283
Toyo colors 189
tracing artwork 111
tracking, changing 297
Transform Again command 21, 147
Transform Both command 148
Transform Each command 129, 141, 143
Transform Object Only command 148
Transform palette 147
See also aligning objects

displaying menu 148
Transform Pattern Only
  command 148
Transform Pattern Tiles
  option 125, 237
Transform Tools option 120, 121
transformation tools 139
transforming objects 22, 123, 139
  distorting 146
  reflecting 144
  repeating transformations 147
  resetting bounding box 147
  rotating 140
  scaling 142
  shearing 145
transforming type 301
transparency 40
  applying gradients or
    patterns 227
  background matting for GIF or
    PNG 340
  background transparency in
    PNG 341
  creating knockouts 226–227
  exporting files containing 351
  exporting in Flash format 355
  exporting in Photoshop
    format 220
  for GIF or PNG-8 333
  for PNG-24 334
  hard-edged 340
  hard-edged for GIF 340
  inverting opacity
    masks 222–223
  Knockout Group option 41
  printing 370
  setting preferences 221
  targeting layers 220, 221–222
  tips for using 219

using grouped objects 220
transparency grid 40
  displaying or hiding 220
Transparency option 333
Transparency palette 40, 220–221
Transparent option 276, 347
Transverse option 394
Trap command 386
trapping
  by overprinting 387–388
  compensating for paper
    stretch 386
  with similar color densities 386
  with tints 385
Trapping type 385
traps 385
  creating 385–388
  horizontal and vertical
    values 386
  reverse 387
Traps with Process Color
  option 387
Trash button 251
Trim command 164
Trim Marks filter 367–368, 388
TrueType fonts 304
TRUMATCH colors 189
Tsume (proportional spacing)
  option 311
Twirl command 151
twirl tool 151
twirling objects 151
Two-Up and Four-Up view 328
  repopulating 328
  restoring optimized version to
    original version 328
type
  See also text
  adding path guides 307

aligning along paths 291
aligning paragraphs 310
alternative glyphs in CID
  fonts 321
applying styles and effects 303
area type 287
area type on open path 290
as a graphic object 303
as a mask 304
autohyphenation 317
auto-kerning 298
auto-leading 296
changing attributes 301
changing capitalization 320
changing character
  direction 302
changing kerning 297
changing leading 296
changing letterforms 303
changing orientation 302
changing shape of 303
changing size 295
changing spacing 310
changing style 294
changing tracking 297
changing type size 295
changing type units 300
choosing a font 294
copying attributes with
  eyedropper tool 300
copying attributes with paint
  bucket tool 301
creating ligatures 320
creating paths 291
creating rows and columns 307
deleting empty paths 292
displaying and hiding hidden
  characters 293

displaying character options 293
displaying Character palette 293
displaying MM Design palette 293
displaying multilingual options 294
displaying paragraph options 309
dividing containers into rows and columns 307
duplicating 300
entering along horizontal or vertical path 290
entering at specific point 287
entering in file 287
entering in objects 290
entering on path 291
Expert Fractions option 320
finding and replacing a font 296
greeking 308
headline fitting 316
hinting 304
hyphenating 317
indenting first line 309
indenting paragraphs 309
justifying 310
linking and unlinking blocks 306
linking and unlinking containers 304, 306
moving along path 291
painting 300
path type 287
point type 287
replacing text symbols 320
selecting 288
selecting blocks 288
selecting containers 301

selecting from baseline 288
setting attributes 293
setting baseline shift 299
setting leading as font size 297
setting preferences 288
setting tabs 315
tools 287, 292
transforming 301
trapping 385
typing text in file 287
using alternative characters 321
using discretionary hyphens 317
using ellipses 320
using em spaces 297
using en and em dashes 320
using hanging punctuation 310
using in columns 288, 304
using in objects 290
using multiple master fonts 292
using smart punctuation 320
using Smart Quotes 320
using Smart Spaces 320
using subscripts and superscripts 298
using Tab Ruler palette 315
using vertical 287
vector graphics and 67
wrapping around graphic objects 308
Type & Auto Tracing command 299
Type 1 fonts 304
Type Area Select option 288
type attributes 293
type paths, deleting 292
type tool 29, 287

U
Undo command 115
undo levels 115
Ungroup command 133
ungrouping objects 133
Uniform Resource Locator. *See* URL format
unit of measure 116
　allowed 116
　converting 116
unit values, converting in text boxes 12
Unite button 375
units of measure
　specifying 12
Units option 116
units, type 300
units, type size 295
Unlink Blocks command 306
Unlock All command 135
Unlock All Layers command 250
unlocking
　layers 250
　masks 169
　objects 135
unlocking colors 338
unnamed colors 178
Unshift All Colors command 342
Unsorted command 336
Update Link command 78
updating links 77
uppercase and lowercase, changing 320
URL format 325, 326
　linking to an object 326–327
Use Area Select option 123, 125

Use Japanese File Format option 346
Use Page Setup option 71
Use Precise Cursors option 55, 84
Use Print Setup option 71

V

variable pen. *See* Calligraphic brushes
vector graphics 67
   changing to bitmap images 275
vectors 67
vertical scale, adjusting 299
vertical type
   entering along path 290
   entering at specific point 287
   entering in objects 290
vertical type tool 287
Video filters and effects 280
view
   actual size 60
   enlarging 59
   moving 58
   reducing 59
   setting up 58
view box 61
viewing 57–60
artwork in color or as paths 59
entire document 60
layers 243
magnified 13
overprinting of colors 59
placed images 61
reduced 13
VM error (virtual memory error) 375

W

Wari-Chu (divided note) option 303
wavy lines, creating 154
Web Shift button 342
Web Shift/Unshift Selected Colors command 342
Web site for Adobe 4
Web Snap slider 342
   for GIF or PNG-8 334
Web-safe colors 35, 37
   recognizing non-Web-safe colors 192
   table 335
Web-safe RGB 180
Web-shifted colors 342
White option 276
windows
   arranging multiple 58
   opening new 58
   setting up 58
working spaces
   defined 203
   specifying 205
World Wide Web
   linking artwork to 326
Wrap command 308
wrapping paragraph text. *See* Wrap command
Write Layers option 256, 352
Write Nested Layers option 352

X

x and y axes, rotating and constraining 130
x and y coordinates, measuring 56

Z

zero origin, specifying 117
Zig Zag filter 154
ZIP compression options 349
Zoom commands 59
zoom tool 13, 59
Z-Soft 358